T0366205

Transnational Communities

Transnational communities are social groups that emerge from mutual interaction across national boundaries, oriented around a common project or "imagined" identity which is constructed and sustained through the active engagement and involvement of at least some of its members. Such communities can overlap in different ways with formal organizations but, in principle, they do not need formal organization to be sustained. This book explores the role of transnational communities in relation to the governance of business and economic activity. It does so by focusing on a wide range of empirical terrains, including discussions of the Laleli market in Istanbul, the institutionalization of private equity in Japan, the transnational movement for open content licenses, and the mobilization around environmental certification. These studies show that transnational communities can align the cognitive and normative orientations of their members over time and thereby influence emergent transnational governance arrangements.

Marie-Laure Djelic is Professor of Management at ESSEC Business School, France. She is the author of *Exporting the American Model* (1998), which obtained the 2000 Max Weber Award for the Best Book in Organizational Sociology from the American Sociological Association.

Sigrid Quack is Head of the "Institution Building across Borders" research group at the Max Planck Institute for the Study of Societies, Cologne, and Associate Professor in the Faculty for Management, Economics, and Social Sciences at the University of Cologne.

Transnational Communities

Shaping Global Economic Governance

Marie-Laure Djelic

Sigrid Quack

CAMBRIDGE
UNIVERSITY PRESS

CAMBRIDGE
UNIVERSITY PRESS

University Printing House, Cambridge CB2 8BS, United Kingdom

Cambridge University Press is part of the University of Cambridge.

It furthers the University's mission by disseminating knowledge in the pursuit of education, learning and research at the highest international levels of excellence.

www.cambridge.org
Information on this title: www.cambridge.org/9780521518789

© Cambridge University Press 2010

First published 2010

A catalogue record for this publication is available from the British Library

Library of Congress Cataloguing in Publication data
Transnational communities : shaping global economic governance / [edited by] Marie-Laure Djelic, Sigrid Quack.
    p.   cm.
ISBN 978-0-521-51878-9
1. International business enterprises.   2. Communities.   3. International economic relations.   I. Djelic, Marie-Laure.   II. Quack, Sigrid.   III. Title.
HD2755.5.T6877   2010
338.8′8–dc22

                                                                    2010004175

ISBN 978-0-521-51878-9 Hardback
ISBN 978-1-107-40616-2 Paperback

Contents

Figures

Tables

Appendices

Contributors

Tim Bartley is Associate Professor of Sociology at Indiana University–Bloomington. He received a Ph.D. in sociology from the University of Arizona. Much of his work has focused on transnational private regulation of labor and environmental conditions in global supply chains – with particular attention to certification systems for sustainable forestry and decent labor conditions. He has published articles in the *American Journal of Sociology, Annual Review of Law & Social Science, Politics and Society, Social Problems, Research in Political Sociology*, and elsewhere. His current projects include analyses of the interactions between social movements and firms and of the uses and abuses of "corporate social responsibility" in developing countries.

Heidi Dahles is Full Professor of Organizational Anthropology in the Department of Culture, Organization and Management of the Vrije Universiteit Amsterdam. She holds a Ph.D. in cultural and social anthropology from Radboud University Nijmegen (Netherlands). Her research interest is in transnational networks and processes of identity formation among ethnic Chinese entrepreneurs in Southeast Asia and beyond. She has published articles in peer-reviewed journals such as the *Asian Journal of Social Sciences, Culture & Organization, East Asia – An International Quarterly, Asian Ethnicity*, and *Journal of Developmental Entrepreneurship*. Among her recent books are *Capital and Knowledge: Changing Power Relations in Asia* (2003, co-edited with Otto van den Muijzenberg) and *Multicultural Organizations in Asia* (2006, co-edited with Loh Wei Leng).

Marie-Laure Djelic is Professor of Management at ESSEC Business School in France. She holds a Ph.D. in sociology from Harvard University. She has worked on capitalism and its transformation, institutional change, and the diffusion of practices, ideas, and organizational forms across institutional contexts. More recently her research interests have moved to transnational rule-making, globalization and its governance, and the ethical foundations of contemporary capitalism. She is the author of *Exporting the American Model* (1998) for which she received the 2000 Max Weber Award for the Best Book in Organizational Sociology from the American Sociological Association. She has co-edited *Globalization and Institutions* with Sigrid Quack (2003), *Transnational Governance* with Kerstin Sahlin-Andersson

(Cambridge University Press, 2006), and *Moral Foundations of Management Knowledge* with Radu Vranceanu (2007). Her work has also appeared in journals such as *Organization Science*, *Theory and Society*, *Organization Studies*, and *Socio-Economic Review*.

Leonhard Dobusch is Research Fellow in the Department of Management at Freie Universität Berlin. Prior to Berlin, he was a postdoctoral fellow at the Max Planck Institute for the Study of Societies in Cologne and visiting researcher at Stanford Law School's Center for Internet and Society. He holds a Ph.D. in business administration from Freie Universität Berlin and is currently working on innovation and the development of transnational market institutions in the field of copyright. His recent publications include the book *Windows versus Linux* (2008) and the article "Why Is Economics Not an Evolutionary Science? – New Answers to Veblen's Old Question" (co-authored with Jakob Kapeller, 2009 in the *Journal of Economic Issues* **43** (4): 867–98).

Mine Eder is Full Professor in the Department of Political Science and International Relations at Boğaziçi University in Turkey, where she teaches courses on the political economy of development, the political economy of Turkey, international relations theory, and international political economy. She holds a Ph.D. from the University of Virginia. She is the co-author of *Political Economy of Regional Cooperation in the Middle East* (1998) and has written extensively on various aspects of Turkey's political economy. She is currently working on Turkey's informal markets and migrant workers and recently spent her sabbatical at Yale University.

Thomas Fetzer is Assistant Professor in European Studies at Central European University (Budapest). He holds a Ph.D. from the European University Institute Florence, and he was a Marie Curie postdoctoral fellow at the London School of Economics in 2007/08. He has worked on the history and contemporary development of industrial relations and trade unionism from a comparative and transnational perspective. His book *Paradoxes of Internationalisation: British and German Trade Unions at Ford and General Motors* is due to be published in 2010. His work has appeared in such journals as the *European Journal of Industrial Relations*, *Contemporary European History*, and *Labour History Review*.

Charles Harvey is Professor of Business History and Management at Newcastle University, where he serves as Pro-Vice-Chancellor. His main interests are in corporate leadership, strategy, and the exercise of power and authority in business, government, and society. He is twice winner of the Wadsworth Prize for business history for his books *The Rio Tinto Company* (1981) and *William Morris* (1991). He jointly edited *Business History* between 1988 and 2007. In recent years his research has focused on longitudinal comparative studies of business elites, corporate governance, and strategic change, co-authoring *Business Elites and Corporate Governance in France and the UK* (2006) with Mairi Maclean and Jon Press and

Breakout Strategy (2007) with Sydney Finkelstein and Thomas Lawton. He is author of numerous articles in the fields of business history and management, including contributions to the *Economic History Review, Business History Review, Business History, Journal of Management Studies, Human Relations*, and *Organization Studies*.

Asma A. Hussain is a D.Phil student at Saïd Business School, University of Oxford. She received an MSc in management research while she was a Rhodes Scholar at the University of Oxford. Presently she has taken some time off from her D.Phil to work with a major consultancy in London. Working in the financial services sector, she is experiencing the impact of the current financial crisis first hand. She has worked on institutional change and the diffusion of practices, ideas, and organizational forms across institutional contexts. Recent interests include the study of globalization and the historical development of finance.

Izumi Kubo is a fund manager at Plaza Asset Management Co. Ltd. in Tokyo and a chartered member of the Securities Analysts Association of Japan. Prior to Plaza Asset Management, she worked at BNP Paribas Asset Management and Tokyo-Mitsubishi Asset Management. She has worked in the financial industry for twenty years. She holds a Ph.D. from Warwick Business School and continues her research on changes in Japanese financial institutions in a personal capacity through the University of Warwick.

Mairi Maclean is Professor of International Business in the Department of Strategy at Bristol Business School, where she is Director of Research Degrees. She was previously a Reader in International Business at Royal Holloway, University of London, and before that a lecturer at the University of Aston, Birmingham. She holds an MA and a Ph.D. from the University of St. Andrews, Scotland, and an MBA from the University of Bath. Her research interests include business elites, business history, business transformation, corporate governance, and comparative organization studies. Recent books include *Business Elites and Corporate Governance in France and the UK* (2006), written jointly with Charles Harvey and Jon Press. She is the author of four books, and editor of a further four. Recent publications include contributions to *Human Relations, Business History*, and the *Sociological Review*.

Åge Mariussen is Senior Researcher at the NIFU STEP Institute in Oslo, with affiliated positions in Åbo Academy, Vasa, Finland and Nordland Research Institute, Bodø, Norway. Mariussen is a sociologist specializing in studies on innovation, globalization, and regional development. He has worked at Nordregio, Stockholm. Mariussen has published articles and books on industrial restructuring in the Nordic countries, and he co-edited *Household, Work and Economic Change* (1997), with Jane Wheelock, University of Newcastle.

Renate Mayntz is Emeritus Director of the Max Planck Institute for the Study of Societies. She held chairs at the University of Cologne, the Hochschule für Verwaltungswissenschaften in Speyer and the Freie Universität Berlin and was a visiting professor at Stanford University and Columbia University, FLACSO (Chile), and the University of Edinburgh. She is the author, co-author, or editor of forty-five books and more than a hundred scholarly articles on topics ranging from social stratification, organization theory, network analysis, technological and scientific development to issues of national and global governance.

Anca Metiu is Professor at ESSEC Business School in France. She holds a Ph.D. from the University of Pennsylvania. Her research focuses on collaboration dynamics in distributed work. Some of her current projects examine the creation of group engagement in teams, the dynamics of professional identity formation for women in the free/open source software communities, and the role of writing in creating and sustaining dispersed communities. Her work has been published in journals such as *Administrative Science Quarterly*, *Organization Science*, and *Organization Studies*.

Glenn Morgan is Professor of Organizational Behaviour at Warwick Business School. He is one of the editors in chief of the journal *Organization: The Critical Journal of Organization, Theory and Society*. Recent publications include *Images of the Multinational Firm* (2009, co-edited with Simon Collinson) and *Changing Capitalisms?* (2005, co-edited with Richard Whitley and Eli Moen) as well as articles in various journals including *Organization Studies*, *Journal of Management Studies*, *Human Relations*, and *Socio-Economic Review*. He is a visiting professor at the International Center for Business and Politics at Copenhagen Business School as well as an associate of the Centre for the Study of Globalization and Regionalization at the University of Warwick. His current research focuses on the governance of global financial markets.

Özlem Öz is Associate Professor in the Department of Management at Boğaziçi University in Turkey, where she teaches courses on organization theory. She holds a Ph.D. from the London School of Economics and Political Science. She has authored several articles and two books, *The Competitive Advantage of Nations: The Case of Turkey* (1999) and *Clusters and Competitive Advantage: The Turkish Experience* (2004). She is currently working on local networks, geographic clusters, and economic geography in Turkey.

Dieter Plehwe is Senior Fellow in the Department of Internationalization and Organization at the Social Science Research Center Berlin. He holds a Ph.D. from Philipps-Universität Marburg and has conducted research in the fields of international political economy, regional integration in North America and Western Europe, and the history and globalization of neoliberalism. His current research focuses on global knowledge networks and the history of development economics and politics. His publications in English include *The Road from Mont Pèlerin* (2009, co-edited with Phil Mirowski) and *Neoliberal Hegemony: A Global Critique* (2006, co-edited with Bernhard Walpen and Gisela Neunhöffer).

Sigrid Quack is Head of the research group "Institution Building across Borders" at the Max Planck Institute for the Study of Societies and Associate Professor in the Faculty of Management, Economics, and Social Sciences at the University of Cologne. She holds a Ph.D. in sociology from Freie Universität Berlin and has conducted research in the fields of institutional change, comparative organization analysis, and the internationalization of professions and professional service firms and their role in transnational rule-setting. Her current research interests focus on how the dynamics of transnational governance affect standards in the fields of copyright, accounting, the environment, and labor. Her publications in English include *Globalization and Institutions* (2003, co-edited with Marie-Laure Djelic) and articles in the journals *Organization, Organization Studies, Theory and Society*, and *Socio-Economic* Review.

Carlos Ramirez is Associate Professor at the HEC Graduate School of Management in Paris. He received his Ph.D. in sociology in 2005 from the Ecole des Hautes Études en Sciences Sociales and also holds an *agrégation de sciences sociales*. Before joining the Graduate School's faculty he was a research officer for four years in the Department of Accounting and Finance of the London School of Economics and Political Science. His research, which is mainly concerned with the sociology and history of professional groups, has been published in journals such as *Actes de la Recherche en Sciences Sociales* and *Accounting Organizations and Society*. The topics he is currently investigating include the constitution of a transnational market for accounting and auditing services and its consequences for the national accountancy professions, with special reference to the role of big multinational firms; the organization of big multinational audit firms after the Enron scandal; and the relevance of Bourdieu's theory of domination for the study of organizational fields.

Mark Lawrence Schrad is Visiting Assistant Professor in the Department of Political Science at the University of Illinois at Urbana-Champaign, where he teaches courses in international relations and comparative politics. He holds a Ph.D. in political science from the University of Wisconsin–Madison, and has conducted research in the fields of historical institutionalism, transnational activism, organizational sociology, and the interface of ideas and institutions in policy-making. His work has appeared in scholarly journals including *Policy Studies Journal, Journal of Policy History*, and *Nationalities Papers*. He is the author of *The Political Power of Bad Ideas: Networks, Institutions, and the Global Prohibition Wave* (2010) and is currently writing a book about the history of alcohol-control politics in Russia and prospects for addressing the post-Soviet demographic catastrophe.

Shawna N. Smith is currently a doctoral candidate in sociology at Indiana University–Bloomington. Prior to Indiana, she received her M.Phil in sociology from the University of Oxford. Her research interests are in political, economic, and legal sociology, with a specific focus on cross-national work. She is currently working on her dissertation, a study of equal employment legislation in the USA, the UK, and Canada.

Marc J. Ventresca is University Lecturer in Management Studies at Saïd Business School, Fellow of Wolfson College, and University Fellow at the James Martin Institute for Science and Civilization, all at the University of Oxford. He is an associate fellow of the Institute for Science, Innovation and Society, and on the Academic Programme Committee of the Rothmere American Institute. He earned his Ph.D. in sociology at Stanford University, after master's degrees in policy analysis and education and in sociology. He served on the faculty at the Kellogg School of Management at Northwestern University and has held visiting faculty positions at the University of Illinois, the Copenhagen Business School, the Center for Work, Technology, and Organizations at Stanford University, and the Stanford Institute for Research on Higher Education. His research and teaching interests focus on institutions, organizations, and industry entrepreneurship; organizational learning; organization design and managing change; environmental management; power and leadership in organizations; and economic sociology of strategy. He is author of over twenty scholarly articles, chapters, and books.

Preface

This volume explores the role of transnational communities in economic governance. Transnational communities are social groups emerging from mutual interaction across national boundaries, oriented around a common project and/or "imagined" identity which is constructed and sustained through the active engagement and involvement of at least some of its members. Transnational communities can overlap in different ways with formal organizations but, in principle, they do not need formal organization to be sustained. Transnational communities imply transnational networks, but they are more than that since the notion of community connotes a sense of belonging to a common "culture" in the broadest sense. The sociological literature has had a tendency to attach positive civic values to the concept and reality of "communities." In contrast, we take, in this volume, a more agnostic stance. As social formations, transnational communities can pursue benevolent and collectively useful goals as well as more particularistic and self-serving ones. They can engage in legal but also in illegal or "gray" activities. As a result, the functions they perform will be judged as desirable in some cases and from certain perspectives but will appear as radically undesirable in other cases or from other perspectives.

The various contributions to this volume explore transnational communities in different empirical terrains – from the Laleli market in Istanbul to private equity in Japan; from the transnational movement for open content licenses to the mobilization in favor of environmental certification or against global warming. Throughout, these diverse studies show that processes of transnational community-building can be closely connected to and interact with the dynamics of transnational economic governance. Transnational governance involves an expansive set of dynamic processes and a complex array of activities crossing many boundaries. The contributions to this volume show that transnational communities, which often cut across formal organizations, networks, and national boundaries, can align the cognitive and normative orientations of their members over time and thereby influence emergent transnational governance arrangements. In addition to highlighting the role of community-like social formations in transnational economic governance, the authors in this volume shed new light on the general nature and workings of transnational communities.

The idea for this book arose when we were collaborating on an earlier edited volume, *Globalization and Institutions* (Edward Elgar 2003). Taking stock in the book's conclusion, we identified what we then called "self-disciplining transnational communities" as one of three main scenarios for institution-building in a transnational context. The insight that there was something like "transnational communities" playing a role in processes of transnational governance was strongly reinforced as we drew the lessons from a second collaborative project that culminated in the publication of *Transnational Governance*, which Marie-Laure Djelic co-edited with Kerstin Sahlin-Andersson (Cambridge University Press 2006). We were convinced by then that there was a need for a much more systematic exploration and understanding of the role of community in transnational governance processes, particularly as they impact upon business and economic activity.

We launched the new project when we convened a conference subtheme on the subject at the annual Colloquium of the European Group of Organization Studies (EGOS) in Vienna in July 2007. The quality of the contributions and the intensity of the discussions quickly convinced us that there was indeed rich material for a joint publication. We were adamant from the start, however, that we wanted to construct a tight and closely integrated volume. So we planned a second meeting that took place in April 2008 in Cologne with the generous support of the Max Planck Institute for the Study of Societies (MPIfG). Working toward this volume has involved several rounds of comments and revisions. We are grateful to all the authors for their patience, diligence, and good spirits throughout this process. The MPIfG has been a tremendously supportive environment for the production of this book. We are very grateful for the substantive encouragement and infrastructural support we received from Jens Beckert and Wolfgang Streeck as the directors of this institution. At an early stage, Christina Glasmacher was very helpful in organizing the workshop at the MPIfG and following up on the correspondence with the contributors. As for the later stage of preparing the volume for publication, we do not really know what we would have done without the insistent but flexible support of Cynthia Lehmann, who held all the strands together while adapting flexibly when the editors missed self-determined deadlines. James Patterson and Dona Geyer did a terrific job of language editing all the chapters. Thomas Pott gave the figures a consistently professional, high-quality look. At Cambridge University Press, we are deeply indebted to the support of Paula Parish, who always believed in this project and generously led it through its various phases from birth to adolescence and, finally, maturity.

As always, along the way, we benefited from stimulating discussions with many members of our intellectual community – or rather of our multiple, overlapping intellectual communities. John Meyer, as always, has been a profound source of insight, which we deeply appreciate. We would also like to thank Lars Engwall, Kerstin Sahlin, and the Uppsala team to whom we presented early versions of the introduction. In alphabetical order, our thanks also extend to Laszlo Bruszt, Barbara Czarniawska, Jürgen Feick, Royston Greenwood, Peer Hull Kristensen, James March, Marc Schneiberg, Dick Scott, Arndt Sorge, David Stark, Richard Whitley, and Jonathan Zeitlin.

Like its predecessors, this project has stolen time from our respective families. We thank Alma, Milena, Nepheli, and Philippe for their patience and understanding. When we dedicated our last joint book, *Globalization and Institutions*, to our daughters, they were too young to read it. It might still be a bit early this time, too! Nevertheless, we dedicate this volume to Alma, Milena and Nepheli in the hope that it will spur their appetite for social inquiry and lure them – and others of their generation – to develop an interest in deconstructing the complexities of the transnational world we live in.

Part I

Introduction

1 Transnational communities and governance

Marie-Laure Djelic and Sigrid Quack

The dichotomy of *Gemeinschaft* and *Gesellschaft*, as coined originally by Ferdinand Tönnies, has profoundly shaped the use of the concept of "community" in the social sciences (Tönnies 2002 [1897]). As shown by Renate Mayntz in this volume, the term "community," when used alone and not qualified, still tends to suggest close-knit if not primary groups with rich emotional ties. It also conjures up geography and bounded space, local connectedness and physical proximity.

As such, the concept of community often stands in an awkward position in the study of contemporary, differentiated, and individualist societies. It has been mobilized descriptively to suggest the resilience of certain traditional ties, even in the context of rapid individualization and differentiation (Park and Burgess 1921; Park 1952). It has also been used normatively to argue for the need to preserve such forms of close-knit social organization in the face of progressive social *anomie* and disintegration (Bellah *et al.* 1985; Putnam 2000). On the whole, however, the decline of community (*Gemeinschaft*) has tended to be contrasted with the progress of *Gesellschaft* – understood as an association of individual and differentiated members coming together more or less permanently, mostly to serve their own interests. In contemporary literature, an urge to reconcile the term "community" with the evolution of our world – including the progress of *Gesellschaft* as a dominant form of social organization more or less everywhere – is palpable. This urge often manifests itself in the use of the term in a qualified fashion – as in "communities of limited liability" (Janowitz 1952), "communities of interest," "epistemic communities," or "communities of practice" (Wenger 1998; Haas 1992a, 1992b; see also Mayntz in this volume).

Exploring the notion of community

We propose that there may be a need to go one step further and to question altogether the stark dichotomy and evolutionary polarity theorized by

Tönnies. In fact, we already find support for this proposition in the work of some of Tönnies's best known contemporaries.

Moving beyond dichotomies . . .

In a review of Tönnies' book *Gemeinschaft und Gesellschaft* (Tönnies 2002 [1897]), Emile Durkheim made it clear that he did not follow the logic advocated by the author to its conclusion. He stopped short, in particular, of systematically opposing modern society and a sense of community. Durkheim's argument was as follows:

I believe that the life of large social aggregates is entirely as natural as that of small aggregates . . . Beyond purely individual movements, there is in our contemporary societies a genuinely collective activity that is as natural as that of smaller societies of former times. It is different, to be sure; it is of a different sort but between these two species of the same kind, as different as they might be, there is no difference in nature. (Durkheim 1889: 8)[1]

In his own work, Durkheim contrasted societies regulated by "mechanical solidarity" on the one hand and those characterized by what he called "organic solidarity" on the other (Durkheim 1984 [1893]). The latter type of societies reflected the progress of differentiation and individualization, as well as organic complementarities symbolized by an intense division of labor. Still, according to Durkheim, even in the most modern of our societies the social link normally should not disappear. That is, it could, but in that case we would be on the way towards social pathology – characterized in particular by *anomie* and revealed by increasing rates of suicide (Durkheim 1997 [1897]). The social link, the collective consciousness, the totem that brought group or society members together was naturally bound to change its form in those societies. Its profound nature and function, however, essentially remained unchanged. As Durkheim argued:

no society can exist that does not feel the need at regular intervals to sustain and reaffirm the collective feelings and ideas that constitute its unity and personality. (Durkheim 2001 [1912]: 322)

A complete reading of the work of Durkheim thus suggests the persistence of community in the midst of society, not as an archaic remnant but as a reinvented and adapted form of social connection.

If we look closely, we find that Max Weber reached similar conclusions, also taking his distance, as it were, from Tönnies's strong dichotomy. Weber

contrasted communal social relations and associative ones. A social relationship he called "communal" (*Vergemeinschaftung*) "if and so far as the orientation of social action is based on a subjective feeling of the parties, whether
affectual or traditional, that they belong together." In contrast, he labeled
"associative" (*Vergesellschaftung*) those relationships where "the orientation
of social action rests on a rationally motivated adjustment of interests or a
similarly motivated agreement, whether the basis of rational judgment be
absolute values or reasons of expediency" (Weber 1978: 40). Weber's level of
analysis was the relationship and not society as a whole. This allowed him to
bypass the evolutionary polarity proposed by Tönnies. This level of analysis
made it possible to acknowledge and allow for the permanent coexistence – to
different degrees and in different forms, naturally – of a sense of community
and associative differentiation. According to Weber,

> [t]he great majority of social relationships has this characteristic [communal] to some
> degree, while being at the same time to some degree determined by associative
> factors. . . . Every social relationship that goes beyond the pursuit of immediate
> common ends, which hence lasts for long periods, involves relatively permanent
> social relationships between the same persons and these cannot be exclusively con-
> fined to the technically necessary activities. (Weber 1978: 41)

What we can draw from this is that any social aggregate coming together around
a common end, objective, or project for a certain period of time could eventually
come to exhibit a sense of community. This would naturally vary in degree,
intensity, and forms of expression. Weber provides us with further tools to
recognize community when we see it. The simple existence, he tells us, of a
common situation, common modes of behavior, or a common feeling is not
enough to allow us to talk of community. A communal relationship implies, first
of all, a relationship. This means that individuals in a similar situation or
predicament should come to do more than simply coexist. They should engage
with each other and reciprocally around that situation or predicament. The social
relationship that emerges in the process can become "communal" if this reciprocal engagement generates "feelings of belonging together" (Weber 1978: 42).

Georg Simmel proposed a slightly different but compatible approach to the
issue, also distancing himself somewhat from the strong dichotomy suggested
by Tönnies. Simmel saw the progress of individualization as coming together
with a transformation (and not the disappearance) of social bonds. Individual
differentiation came together, in fact, with an opening up of narrow social
circles and with the emergence of new forms of social belonging. In reality,
individualization opened up the possibility of and created the need for

belonging to a multiplicity of more or less interconnected social groups or communities. In the words of Simmel,

differentiation and individualization loosen the bond of the individual with those who are most near in order to weave in its place a new one – both real and ideal – with those who are more distant. (Simmel 1971: 256)

The use of a counterexample allows him to clarify this argument further:

The insularity of the caste [in India] – maintained by an internal uniformity no less strict than its exclusion of outsiders – seems to inhibit the development of what one has to call a more universal humanity, which is what makes relationships between racial aliens possible. (Simmel 1971: 256)

In other words, social links, group belonging, and community feeling do not disappear with the progress of differentiation and individualization – far from it. The meaning and form associated with these notions is certainly bound to change in the process. But, in the event, we might even witness an intensification of the possibilities for social belonging and hence a multiplication of community forms.

   Norbert Elias makes a different and quite interesting contribution to this discussion (Elias 1974). He also moves away from the stark dichotomy theorized by Tönnies, while calling for a recontextualization of the study of communities. The development and transformation of communities, he argues, cannot be understood in isolation from the development of society as a whole, particularly in relation to state formation. Communities exist, Elias tells us, in less or more differentiated societies alike but their features and structures vary markedly, depending on the degree of differentiation of the society. In more differentiated societies, communities tend to be less differentiated. The process is the following. As societies become more complex and differentiated, many of the prerogatives and decision-making powers traditionally exercised at the community level move upwards and are taken up at higher levels of integration (that is, at the level of the region or of the nation-state). In Elias's own words: "The scope and differentiation of functions at the community level decreases as those at other levels of integration [national in particular, *authors' comment*] increase" (Elias 1974: xxxi–xxxii).

... to a focus on process

These types of contingency perspectives on communities turn our attention to dynamics and processes. Seen from this angle, communities are no longer static, essentialist structures. They are fluid, relational constructs, constantly on the move and in process. We should consider, rather than communities, processes of community formation, maintenance, decline, and even disintegration.

Weber has underscored the importance of "time" in community-building – a "time" that could be reduced to more or less "long periods," but did not suggest eternity. According to Weber, social aggregates coming together around common ends, objectives, projects, or identity-building can potentially become communities – and one of the conditions for this is their inscription in time (Weber 1978: 40–43). Community-building and maintenance are very much processes set in time. Weber did not take the next step, but one can easily extend the argument to consider community decline or disintegration. A community that has been built up and sustained over time could certainly become threatened, weakened, or even destroyed, too, under certain conditions and pressures. Hence, any kind of community should be understood as a time-bound entity and construction, and not as a necessary, permanent, timeless, or essential collective.

Simmel provides a slightly different perspective on this question of temporality. In less differentiated societies, community-belonging has a tendency to be quite stable and limited to a small number of proximate groups that the individual, on the whole, does not "choose." In a differentiated and individualized society, every single one of us enjoys much greater freedom to associate with or, on the contrary, to leave or dissociate from different social circles or communities. Hence, individual involvement in particular communities could turn out to be only temporary – naturally with a great deal of variation. Morris Janowitz (1952) comes up with a vivid image of what this implies. He coins the term "community of limited liability" to describe the temporal inscription of community involvement and belonging. The notion of "community of liability"

emphasizes that in a highly mobile society, people may participate extensively in local institutions and develop community attachments, yet be prepared to leave those communities if local conditions fail to satisfy immediate needs or aspirations. (Suttles 1972: 48)

Janowitz originally coined this term to describe the partial and temporally bound involvement of individuals in local communities. However, the notion can apply more broadly to communities in general, even when they are not associated with local territory or physical proximity. According to Janowitz, the notion of "community of limited liability" also suggested the possibility that members were differentially involved and invested at any point in time.

A community did not imply, nor did it require, the same type of intense involvement on the part of all its members. In fact, a community could even survive with only a small minority of "active custodians." The rest of the membership could be connected in a more passive manner (Janowitz 1952; Suttles 1972: 9).

The contingency perspective can be taken one step further. We can think of communities as being actively constructed and shaped over time by members or individuals involved in one way or another. The web of multiple group affiliations, as described by Simmel (1955 [1908]), suggests a multiplicity of latent identities that can all generate community mobilization. Out of their situated interactions with many different "others," people select and give priority to certain relations and connections. Over time, naturally, we should not forget that orders of priority may change. Hence, a particular individual may give priority through time to different relations and connections. If reciprocated, the orientation to particular relations can become the foundation of community construction. Processes of community construction imply, in turn, the stabilization of collective identities. These collective identities, at any point in time, unite but also differentiate a given member set. The construction of communities hence also implies in parallel the setting up and structuration of social boundaries. Exclusion and separation are the other face of community inclusion and belonging.

The notion of social boundaries is an old one in sociology, at the core of the classical contributions of Durkheim, Weber, and Marx. Social boundaries are "called into being by the exigencies of social interaction" and become established as "communities interact in some ways or others with entities from which they are, or wish to be distinguished" (Cohen 1985: 12). The collective identity of a community thus becomes constituted through the dialectical interplay of processes of internal but also external definition (Jenkins 1996; Lamont and Molnár 2002). Simmel went a step further in the exploration of the notion of social boundaries when he placed the individual at the center of multiple group affiliations. Boundary-making and boundary-spanning activities should be conceived, then, as happening in parallel, across and between a multiplicity of communities. This obviously generates significant complexity and fluidity, and calls for a focus on dynamics and processes.

The symbolic construction of community

Simmel's argument that differentiation and individualization mean both a weakening of local links and a greater likelihood of community bonds at a distance points us towards the symbolic dimension of communities. This symbolic construction is attributable both to the members of those communities and to those standing outside, all the more as they exchange and interact. Clifford Geertz defined man as "an animal suspended in the webs of significance he himself has spun" (1975: 5). For a number of contemporary social anthropologists and sociologists, communities are best understood as being progressively turned or woven into symbolic constructs. As such, a community becomes for individual members "a resource and repository of meaning, and a referent of their identity" (Cohen 1985: 118).

The notion of symbolic construction makes communities conceivable even in the absence of direct and regular contact or interaction. Benedict Anderson argued as much when he explored the emergence of nations as "imagined communities" (Anderson 2006). In his words:

A community is imagined if its members will never know most of their fellow-members, meet them or even hear of them, yet in the mind of each lives the image of their communion. (Anderson 2006: 6)

Anderson describes the emergence of nation-states as reflecting the symbolic construction of a unique type of political community. Towards the end of the eighteenth century, the nation as a community developed out of the confluence and convergence of different historical forces. The nation-state emerged progressively as an imagined community bounded by well-defined borders and acting as a sovereign entity in – at least theoretical – independence of others. The development of capitalism combined with the emergence of publishing to allow for the emergence of those imagined communities. Nation-states as imagined communities were then shaped in distinctive ways by social groups in different parts of the world. Local languages often played an important if not determinant role in the mobilization of a perceived common identity in those young nations. Once it had been established, the nation as an imagined community attained the character of a model. It was then diffused, applied, merged, and fused, across the world, with different political and ideological frames.

While the nation as an imagined community has in many respects unique features, it nevertheless shares its symbolic character with many other types of communities. Benedict Anderson acknowledges as much when he proposes that "all communities larger than primordial villages of face-to-face contact (and perhaps even these) are imagined" (Anderson 2006: 6). All communities thus could be envisioned and redefined as "imagined communities." What makes the nation unique and distinct as a community is that symbolic construction there largely transcends the social links connecting members. Furthermore, the success of the nation and associated nation-state as a model is quite unparalleled. This model has diffused and institutionalized success-fully across the world as a core imagined political and social community.

Imagined communities are collective attractors but they are also polarizing entities. The imagined community is constituted as much through shared belonging and meaning inside as through differentiation and separation from the outside. Social anthropologist Anthony Cohen summarizes this quite well when he claims that

[t]he quintessential referent of community is that its members make, or believe they make, a similar sense of things either generally or with respect to specific and significant interests, and, further, that they think that that sense may differ from one made elsewhere. (Cohen 1985: 16)

This should not be taken to mean that imagined communities are perfectly homogeneous and tightly bounded spheres, however. In fact, imagined com-munities do not necessarily suggest the same things for all their members. Their very nature as "webs of significance" or "webs of meaning" leaves room for variation. Even though a sense of belonging can be broadly shared, the parti-cular meaning associated with the community, as well as the understanding of community boundaries, can vary between members. While communities are constituted by culture and function as culture, they also generate and define "tool kits" that members – or for that matter non-members – can use to strategize upon the further development and symbolic constitution of those communities (Swidler 1986). An understanding of communities as being at the same time relational, social, and symbolic constructs allows us to conceive of communities as being differentially homogeneous with respect to shared mean-ings. Some communities can be relatively uniform and exhibit "a common way of thinking, feeling and believing" (Kluckhohn 1962: 25). Differentiated socie-ties might be populated, on the other hand, by increasing numbers of internally more pluralist communities, consisting of a *mélange* or variety of ways of thinking, feeling, and believing that different members attach to the community.

Of course, there are limits to such aggregation. The community can be a container of diversities – but within bounds. At the same time as the com-munity can accommodate diversities it also keeps them within limits. In the words of Cohen:

The triumph of community is to so contain this variety that its inherent discordance does not subvert the apparent coherence which is expressed by its boundaries. If the members of a community come to feel that they have less in common with each other than they have with the members of some other community, clearly, the boundaries have become anomalous and the integrity of the "community" they enclose has been severely impugned. (Cohen 1985: 20)

Taking stock – what does it take to talk of "community"?

This exploration of classical and more current debates around the notion of community allows us to draw up a number of propositions. The progress of differentiation and individualization associated with modern and postmodern societies neither destroys nor threatens the possibility of community feeling. Traditional communities can survive even if they come to be transformed. But what is more interesting is the increasing possibility for different forms of community-building. In more differentiated and individualized societies, individuals have the possibility to enter into and belong to a multiplicity of more or less open, more or less interconnected, more or less distant communities. These communities reflect and build upon social interactions but they are also symbolic constructions. A rethinking of community along the lines proposed here makes it possible to think of community-building even in the absence of local territory and physical proximity (see also Mayntz in this volume). It shows, furthermore, that an imagined community, once established, is conceivable even in the absence of much direct and regular interaction or social interconnection.

Hence, we can propose here that territory and physical proximity, not to mention direct interaction, are neither necessary nor defining components of the concept of community. Territory, physical proximity, and direct interaction define one particular form – important, but only one amongst others – in which a sense of community has expressed itself and expresses itself in human history. We suggest moving away from rigid evolutionary frames and from a picture of social transformation that follows a linear sense of time – where, for example, tightly knit and localized communities would precede in time distant, loosely tied, and more differentiated communities. Only then can we understand and explain the existence, as early as the Middle Ages, of communities that had little to do with a traditional sense of *Gemeinschaft*. Anderson describes what he calls "classical" or "pre-national" communities, which existed and thrived in spite of physical distance, "virtuality," absence of common territory, and even lack of direct interaction, and this well before the kind of technologies we are familiar with today. The Roman Catholic Church, its associated "European" universities, and the transregional commercial guilds are amongst the examples that Anderson identifies and discusses (Anderson 2006: 15).

Moving from there, it is easy to understand that similarity and homogeneity – particularly those stemming from ascriptive characteristics – are not indispensable either. They can naturally serve as the basis of community-building, but community-building is also possible around a limited convergent object with an only partial sense of belonging between individuals that remain otherwise profoundly different. Community-building in an individualizing and differentiating society might increasingly be taking place through the relational and symbolic connection of individuals, who might be extremely different from each other in many respects. Community-building might be happening successfully in spite of these differences (Simmel 1971: 251ff.). Finally, a related reflection leads us to question also the absolute requirement of long-term, if not permanent, bonds as the measure of community, as often assumed in classical community studies (Bell and Newby 1974). The understanding of community as promoted in particular by Weber and Simmel, and later on by Janowitz, points to much more flexible configurations, in which individuals can be connected to communities for only a limited period of time and communities themselves are social forms changing significantly through time.

To bring together and summarize this discussion, we would therefore suggest that a number of attributes traditionally associated with the notion of community are possible but not necessary. They define and characterize certain types of community, but a community does not have to exhibit those features in order to be one. Below is a list of those possible but non-necessary attributes:

- Bounded territory;
- Physical proximity;
- Direct and regular interactions;
- Similarity and homogeneity;
- Ascriptive bond;
- Permanence and stability.

If these attributes are not necessary to the concept of community, the next question concerns which dimensions in fact structure and define that concept. What does it take to talk of "community"? Building upon the discussion we had above, at this point we can offer a proposition.

We can talk of community when a social aggregate is characterized by the mutual orientation of members. This mutual orientation is articulated around a common – constructed or imagined – identity and/or a common project.

This mutual orientation creates a form of dependence between members. The common identity or project, furthermore, is constructed, sustained, or defended through a form of active engagement and involvement on the part of at least a minority of members. All this activity translates into and sustains a sense of belonging. The bullets below are a summary presentation of those constitutive dimensions or necessary attributes.

- Mutual orientation of members;
- Articulated around a common identity and/or a common project;
- A sense of reciprocal dependence;
- A form of active engagement and involvement from at least a minority of members;
- All this translating into and sustaining a sense of belonging.

Bringing the notion of community into the study of transnational phenomena

In the notion of the nation as imagined community, the symbolic construct reaches well beyond direct social relations and physical networks. The nation as imagined community implies a sense of belonging to a social and political formation much larger than the local and face-to-face communities that the concept of *Gemeinschaft* traditionally summons up. The nation as a community carries with it a symbolic meaning with potentially significant scope and reach. Anderson provided a convincing description of how, in the process of nation-building, one particular social identity among others came to be carved out and shaped as a collectively shared mindset (Anderson 2006 [1983]). Anderson also underscored the important institutional work involved in the stabilization and diffusion of that mindset, in particular through the socialization and control of current members and future generations.

Our world, however, can no longer be understood – if it ever could – as expressing an international "concert of nations," where national sovereignty combines with a Westphalian "balance of power." Most spheres of economic and social life, in most corners of the world, are not only constrained by national communities and their associated institutions but also become enmeshed in transnational dynamics. We live in a world in which order-creating capacities are no longer reducible to nation-state power (Held 1995). Transnational governance has been a reality of our world for quite some time. The nation-state is not disappearing but it has to accept the significance of transnational governance and adapt to it (Jordana and Levi-Faur 2004; Djelic and Sahlin-Andersson 2006; Djelic and Quack 2008; Graz and Nölke 2008). The current financial and economic crisis will possibly only reinforce this trend, and calls for global governance with more bite are being heard in all policy-making circles (for example, *Daily Telegraph* 2008; Zeng 2008; G20 2009).[2] We need, as a consequence, to fit our conceptual tools to the multi-level nature of contemporary governance (Djelic and Quack 2008). We suggest in that context that bringing the notion of community into the study of transnational governance can be extremely useful.

Naturally, we do not have to start from scratch. First, we can draw inspiration and insights from various contributions that have brought the notion of community to the study of global processes – such as migration, social and political activism, or expertise. Second, we can build upon a budding attempt to consider transnational governance fields as social but also potentially symbolic arenas (Morgan 2001; Djelic and Sahlin-Andersson 2006). In the remainder of this section, we explore those different contributions to see what happens when we bring the notion of community into the study of transnational phenomena.

Transnational migration

A first important strand of literature points to the increasing geographical extension, across local and national borders, of "natural" communities, that is, communities based on ascriptive characteristics such as ethnicity or kinship (Wyman 1993; Soysal 1994; Portes 2000). In a seminal article, Alejandro Portes (2000: 254) states:

What common people have done, in response to the process of globalization, is to create communities that sit astride political borders and that, in a very real sense, are "neither here nor there" but in both places simultaneously.

Transnational communities, in that sense, are composed primarily of migrants and of relatives and friends of migrants. Those communities tend to be seen as emerging from the aggregation of multiple grassroots initiatives. They are cultural and social containers, reproducers and transformers. They facilitate local integration while at the same time maintaining real and symbolic connections with the original cradle of the community. They can articulate themselves around political projects both in the home and the host countries but also very much at the interconnection of the two. Communities constructed around processes of transnational migration often also have an economic dimension and reality. They embed and generally facilitate microeconomic initiatives. The latter tend to materialize around the exploitation of structural advantages stemming from the existence of national borders and/or from the capacity of members of the community to cross those borders. According to Portes, transnational economic activity of this kind has a cumulative and aggregative character, which means in the end

the transformation of the original pioneering economic ventures into transnational communities, characterized by dense networks across space and by an increasing number of people that lead dual lives. Members are at least bilingual; move easily between different cultures; frequently maintain homes in two countries; and pursue economic, political, and cultural interests that require a simultaneous presence in both. (Portes 2000: 264)

Not all migrants, naturally, can thus be labeled "transnational." Portes suggests instead that the term should be reserved for those activities that require the involvement of participants on a "regular basis as a major part of their occupation" (Portes 2000: 264). Nor does every migration network constitute a community. Instead, mutual orientation and a shared sense of identity and belonging may vary among the members of networks, and in some instances may be absent altogether.

Recent migration studies have increasingly pointed to everyday practices, artifacts, and ideas as making sense of the complexity of inter-related social relationships in migration networks (Vertovec 2001). This body of work suggests that migrant and diaspora communities are often "pluri-local" in the sense that their members maintain multiple and overlapping ties to their region or place of departure, as well as to their place of arrival. The malleability and changeability of migrant communities becomes particularly apparent in what Ludger Pries (2001: 67) identifies as "transmigrants".

Transmigrants are moving in new pluri-local transnational social spaces where individual and collective biographical life projects, everyday life as well as the real "objective" sequence of life stations span between different geographical-spatial extensions.

The notion of "transnational social spaces" has, as Thomas Faist (2000: 13) recognizes, broadened the scope of migration studies. Beyond the movement of people, migration studies should also consider the transnational circulation of ideas, symbols, and material culture. Faist goes on to propose a typology of transnational social spaces. His first type, "kinship groups," is predicated on ties of reciprocity. His second type, "transnational circuits," is structured by instrumental exchange-based connections. For his third type he uses the label "transnational community", in a way that is perfectly compatible with the propositions we offered in the previous section. According to Faist, "transnational communities" are based on diffuse solidarity with a collective identity (Faist 2000: 202–10).

The notion of transnational social spaces also raises questions about the often presumed social and cultural homogeneity of transnational migrant communities. The success of Chinese business networks, in particular, is often portrayed as a by-product of a closely knit and culturally homogenous diaspora community. Heidi Dahles (in this volume), in contrast, shows that this community is both "socially constructed and mediated through institutional and policy frames, and therefore better described as a loosely connected patchwork of partly converging and partly conflicting practices and principles." In other instances, transnational circuits of exchange between different ethnic groups might give rise to strategizing that leads to the formation of trans-ethnic business communities. The case of the shuttle traders in Laleli, Istanbul, studied by Mine Eder and Özlem Öz (in this volume) provides an example of such a newly formed trans-ethnic and translocal community which is nourished by its members partly for – but cannot be reduced entirely to – economic reasons. Overlaps of multiple group affiliation and entangled economic and social motivations can also be observed among Chinese- and Indian-born engineers who have worked in Silicon Valley and use their double-community affiliation to transfer technical and institutional know-how back to the economies of their or their parents' home country (Saxenian 2005, 2006).

In sum, the most interesting recent contribution of transnational migration studies is to make us go through the looking glass. Apparently homogeneous and closely knit ascriptive communities in fact turn out to be socially constructed, hence malleable and open to transformations over time as interactions of their members unfold across multiple group affiliations and locations.

Transnational activism

A second strand of literature considers the progress of transnational social formations that are activated by and around social or political issues, common goals or interests. Interestingly, this literature has, on the whole, not used or appropriated the term "community," preferring terms such as "networks" or "social movements" (Smith *et al.* 1997; Keck and Sikkink 1998; Katzenstein *et al.* 1999; Guidry *et al.* 2000; Smith and Johnston 2002; Tarrow 2005).

Margaret Keck and Kathryn Sikkink (1998) come close to the notion of transnational community, even though they do not use the word. Keck and Sikkink propose that

a transnational advocacy network includes those relevant actors working internationally on an issue, who are bound together by shared values, a common discourse, dense exchanges of information and services. (Keck and Sikkink 1998: 2)

The authors talk of "networks" rather than of "communities." Still, the description they propose of transnational advocacy networks as "communicative structures," as "political spaces, in which differently situated actors negotiate – formally and informally – the social, cultural, and political meanings of their joint enterprise" (Keck and Sikkink 1998: 3) suggests that they are, at least implicitly, talking about transnational networks that, in certain instances, come close to being communities. Keck and Sikkink focus primarily on how transnational advocacy networks are able to affect policy outcomes and implementation, in particular through the reformulation of issues and the reframing of debates. This is directly applicable to our preoccupation with transnational governance processes – including regulatory outcomes and their implementation. Still, Keck and Sikkink pay much less attention to the social interactions that might in time transform networks into communities with actor-like qualities. In contrast, Mark Schrad in this volume is interested in the process through which a budding transnational activist network with a focus on temperance could, in time and step-by-step, turn into what was effectively a transnational imagined community.

The work of Sidney Tarrow takes us in complementary and quite interesting directions. Tarrow explores the role and importance of transnational social formations that bring together around a common goal and/or common values a multiplicity of heterogeneous members (Tarrow 2005). According to Tarrow, transnational activists are

individuals and groups who mobilize domestic and international resources and opportunities to advance claims on behalf of external actors, against external opponents, or in favor of goals they hold in common with transnational allies. (Tarrow 2005: 43)

Tarrow focuses on the relational dimension of transnational activist groups as networks of heterogeneous members. Like Keck and Sikkink, he is much less explicit when it comes to symbolic interaction and to the development of shared understandings and meanings within those groups. Tarrow tends to understand cosmopolitan identities as mostly the products of social relations and he suggests, as a consequence, a focus on the relational roots of those identities. Åge Mariussen (in this volume) is also particularly interested in the reconciliation of diversities and heterogeneities through a common project or agenda with transnational reach. However, he proposes to explore, beyond mere social and relational dimensions, the ways in which activist networks come in time to exhibit community-like features in spite of great diversity. Similarly, Leonhard Dobusch and Sigrid Quack, and Anca Metiu (in this volume) focus their analyses on how locally rooted activists campaigning for open content copyright licenses and free/open software by means of virtual networking join like-minded groups from other locations in transnational social movements with shared orientations, mutual dependency, and common sets of norms and goals.

Tarrow's cosmopolitans are, interestingly, "rooted cosmopolitans," and undeniably this is one source of diversity or heterogeneity within transnational social formations (see also Cohen 1992). This insight and the associated qualification of "cosmopolitanism" are important, we suggest, for our argument. As we project the notion of community into transnational arenas, we should not forget that potential members of transnational communities remain at the very same time embedded and rooted in other, often national or more local communities. In particular, as actors move their activities, experiences, and cognitive references beyond and outside the boundaries of the nation-state(s) to which they belong, they remain linked and connected to those nation-states in various other ways. The degree, intensity, and nature of the links vary and are essentially matters for empirical investigation. In the end, however, we should not forget that transnational networks and communities have this dual character. The members of transnational networks and communities are simultaneously affiliated with (multiple) networks and communities of national, regional, or local scope. Out of those multi-level forms of affiliation and association, complementarities as well as conflicts in social roles and identities are likely to evolve. We suggest that a focus on the interaction between the local/national and the transnational is necessary to reach a better understanding of the nature and role of transnational communities. Only then can we identify and theorize the mechanisms turning transnational networks into transnational communities. Only then can we hope to understand and account for the specific features and functions of transnational communities as they broker across multiple boundaries. Most chapters in this volume provide clear evidence of rooted cosmopolitanism – although there is considerable variation as regards how deep the roots go. Most chapters also document the fact that this is not incompatible with processes of transnational community formation.

Transnational knowledge and expertise

A third interesting strand of literature points to the constitution of transnational networks or communities in the process of knowledge production and diffusion. Relevant concepts are professional and epistemic communities, as well as communities of practice.

Professional communities have typically been conceived as constituted within modern societies bounded by nation-states, or as a "community within a community" (Goode 1957). In this context, professions denote occupational groups that, based on their abstract knowledge and practical expertise, pursue what Margali Sarfatti Larson (1977) called a "common professional project": exclusive control over the exercise of particular knowledge and expertise in a specific jurisdiction based on educational credentials and recognition by the state (Abbott 1988). Professionalization in this sense inevitably involves the formation and development of a community where members share common professional norms and ethics, and orient their individual and group activities towards a shared collective goal and feeling of solidarity. While cross-border communication and exchange between professional communities has occurred for a long time through international conferences and associations, the contemporary period of globalization suggests the possibility of a more profound transformation of professional communities, in particular through transnationalization.

Research on the growth and internationalization of professional service firms in fields such as accounting, consulting, and law has pointed to the emergence of international networks of professionals (McKenna *et al.* 2003; Morgan and Quack 2005; Faulconbridge and Muzio 2007) and the increasing authority of expert knowledge in many transnational governance fields (Cutler 2008) and world society in general (Meyer *et al.* 1997). The spread of this transnational professionalism, however, is more often than not based on a diffuse public recognition of knowledge and expertise in dealing with highly specialized and complex matters rather than on the classical control over licenses to practice exercised by professional associations or the state (see Fourcade [2006] on the global profession of economists, and Kuhlmann and Saks [2008] on new forms of professional governance of health). In this volume, Glenn Morgan and Izumi Kubo, Asma Hussain and Marc Ventresca, and Carlos Ramirez, explore the degree to which transnational professionalism of this novel type gives rise to transnational communities of experts and practitioners and how they impact on previously insulated national professional communities.

While professional communities start from a national base, epistemic communities, as conceived by Peter Haas, are from the outset involved with "problems of global concern" (Haas 1992a: 1) and therefore are potentially transnational in reach. In an attempt to explain the formation of policy preferences of state actors in international politics, Haas has drawn attention to the notion of epistemic community as

a network of professionals with recognized expertise and competence in a particular domain and authoritative claim to policy-relevant knowledge within that domain or issue area. (Haas 1992a: 3)

Epistemic communities may consist of professionals from a variety of disciplines, but they usually have a shared set of principled beliefs, common causal beliefs, shared notions of validity, and a common policy enterprise. Empirical studies of epistemic communities point to their influence in shaping policy agendas at the international and national level (Drake and Nicolaïdis 1992; Haas 1992b; Verdun 1999). While most of the epistemic communities studied by Haas and his colleagues involved only a small number of members, transnational epistemic communities can be also "faceless" with members having direct interactions only with small subsets of the community (see, for example, the scientific epistemic communities discussed by Renate Mayntz in this volume). They are also characterized by the absence of ascriptive bonds and possibly even by a fair amount of diversity and heterogeneity within the membership.

Nevertheless, epistemic communities have all it takes, effectively to be communities. They are characterized by the mutual orientation of their members, one which is articulated around common cognitive and/or value frames and generally translates into some form of reciprocal dependence. They also exhibit a degree of engagement and involvement from at least a minority of members. This combines with socialization mechanisms that have a broader impact. In the process, this translates into and sustains a real sense of belonging and collective identity. While epistemic communities are increasingly transnational, their members are likely to retain some form of local or national presence, embeddedness, influence, and even authority. As the contributions by Dieter Plehwe, and Leonhard Dobusch and Sigrid Quack (in this volume) show, this combination can allow those communities to be powerful mechanisms at the interface between transnational and national spheres of governance. While Dobusch and Quack in their study of an epistemic community of copyright lawyers show how an originally US-based community of experts gradually extended across borders and was influential all along the rule-setting process, Plehwe points to the transnational discourse community of neoliberal intellectuals that has generated the principled beliefs underlying the activities and goals of many contemporary epistemic communities.

"Community of practice" is yet another concept that refers to transnational collectives occupied with the development of knowledge and expertise. Etienne Wenger (1998) used the term to describe like-minded groups of practitioners who are oriented towards a shared interest in learning and applying a common practice. Communities of practice operate within a knowledge domain that endows practitioners with a sense of a joint enterprise. People become a community of practice through relationships of mutual engagement that bind "members together into a social entity." Shared practices, in turn, are maintained by a repertoire of communal resources, such as routines and discursive patterns (Wenger 1998: 72–85). Communities of practice are in principle open to outsiders because their main purpose is to introduce newcomers to the practices of the field, as well as to further develop the knowledge and capabilities of their members. As knowledge accrues through interaction between members, communities of practice become social entities of collective learning.

More than through direct and regular contacts, the social "glue" in such communities is produced by a sharing of practices and discourse. Communities of practice can have highly dispersed memberships across a multiplicity of countries that are rarely in direct contact. Such communities of practice are likely to exist in many knowledge domains, including technology, management, finance, law and accounting, and education, but have rarely been studied in their transnational dimension. In this volume, Anca Metiu explores the potential of a virtual online community of free/open source developers for knowledge transfer between industrialized and developing countries. She finds positive spillover effects that go beyond the transfer of mere programming knowledge and foster social organization in regionalized subcommunities of practice. Tim Bartley and Shawna Smith (in this volume) show how originally localized small communities gave rise to transnational communities of certification practitioners and how initially separate certification communities in the fields of forest certification and labor are becoming increasingly interconnected.

A slightly different but related use of communities of practice can be found among scholars of international relations. Building on the work of Karl Deutsch and colleagues (1957) in *Political Community and the North Atlantic Area*, which highlighted the importance of communication between states and mutual responsiveness for the emergence of security communities, more recent work draws attention to the role of deliberation and learning in *transgovernmental* and *transnational* policy networks (Nye and Keohane 1971; Risse-Kappen 1994, 1995). Emanuel Adler, in particular, has investigated communities of practice in international politics (Adler 2005). In his work on the expansion of the NATO security community to states in Central and Eastern Europe during the 1990s, Adler (2008) shows how political practice among NATO officials fostered learning among old and new members, transformed goals and identities, and helped to institutionalize a norm of self-restraint.

While the above cited literature points to variations in the internal cohesion of communities in their norms, values, and practices, as well as to different degrees of openness to new members, studies on transnational elites, as presented below, depict communities that are more exclusive in nature.

Transnational elites

A number of interesting insights can be found in the literature on elites. The work of Ulf Hannerz on intellectual elites is particularly interesting. We can also profit from the literature on power elites, though it tends to restrict its scope to the national level and only rarely addresses the transnational.

Hannerz has studied a particular kind of transnational cosmopolitan. In his book *Cultural Complexity*, written in 1992, he provides a description of transnational intellectuals, insisting that they constitute a "community without boundaries." To make this more explicit, he cites George Konrad who portrays the transnational culture of intellectuals as follows:

We may describe as transnational those intellectuals who are at home in the cultures of other peoples as well as in their own. They keep track of what is happening in various places. ... They have friends all over the world ... They fly to visit one another as easily as their counterparts two hundred years ago rode to the next town to exchange ideas. (Konrad 1984: 208–9, cited in Hannerz 1992: 258)

The label "communities without boundaries" refers here to the relatively free flow of like-minded individuals engaged in intellectual production and recognizing each other as equals in this respect. The focus here is on "flows," the movements and interactions of a number of individuals across multiple borders and "boundaries." The focus is also on the mutual recognition of those individuals as belonging to similar social and cognitive strata (Hannerz 1992). According to Hannerz, culture, meaning, and, as a consequence, identities are all processual. In his words, he wanted to emphasize that only by being constantly in motion, forever being recreated, can meanings and meaningful forms become durable ... To keep culture going, people as actors and networks of actors have to invent culture, reflect on it, experiment with it, remember it (or store it in some other way), debate it and pass it on. (Hannerz 1997: 5)

This processual picture emphasizes the multiplicity of possible flows, the crossing of many boundaries. It also gives a sense of permanent fluidity. The sense of community that emerges is compatible with Simmel's take on the issue. Individuals are enmeshed in a web of group affiliations; they belong to multiple social circles or communities. The latter are fluid constructs. The collective sense of identity and belonging is in constant (re)construction. The very boundaries of those communities are fluid and under permanent renegotiation (Hannerz 1996).

In 1956, C. Wright Mill, in *The Power Elite*, described the role, impact, and power in the United States of a small group of individuals who controlled a disproportionate amount of wealth, privilege, and leverage over decision-making (Mills 1956; see also Domhoff 1967). Mills insisted that this elite brought together individuals from diverse and heterogeneous spheres – business, politics, the military, the media, and academia. In spite of this internal diversity, the American power elite shared an "uneasy" alliance based on a "community of interests" and even a common world view. Mills (1956: 283) described this as follows:

Within the higher circles of the power elite, factions do exist; there are conflicts of policy; individual ambitions do clash ... But more powerful than these divisions are the internal discipline and the community of interests that bind the power elite together.

This power elite appears to be situated immediately upwards of – and is in fact served by – professional, expert, and knowledge communities of different kinds, even if some of the most prominent professionals and experts belong to the core.

The power elite are not solitary rulers. Advisers and consultants, spokesmen and opinion-makers are often the captains of their higher thought and decision. (Mills 1956: 4)

The notion of power elite certainly does not apply only to the United States (in very different contexts, see Lannes 1940; Djilas 1957). Furthermore, this notion can be extended across national borders. In the 1980s, the "Amsterdam school" pointed to the importance of transnational power networks. Kees van der Pijl and his colleagues explored the sociology and political economy of a transnational ruling class formation (van der Pijl 1984). Transnational in this context denotes, as Leslie Sklair (2001: 2) states, "forces, processes, and institutions that cross borders but do not derive their power and authority from the state." Studies have identified transnational interlocks in which directors serve on the boards of two or more corporations from different countries (Carroll and Fennema 2002; Kentor and Jang 2004) and report an increase of the proportion of non-domestic directors on the boards of transnational companies in the period 1993–2005 (Staples 2006). Whether these networks give rise to a sense of belonging and shared identities, however, remains an open question. As Charles Harvey and Mairi Maclean (in this volume) show in their in-depth study of directors of the hundred largest British and French companies, mindsets, dispositions, and predilections of corporate elites in spite of strong national embeddedness, are opening up progressively to broader transnational communities in the making. Given their multiple membership in national and transnational communities, the impact of such power elites on the structuring and regulation of human activity in various spheres is a question of great relevance, particularly in the context of the current economic crisis (Overbeek *et al.* 2007; Rothkopf 2008). In respect of the principled beliefs underlying much of pre-crisis political economy, Plehwe (in this volume) considers the community dimensions of a neoliberal transnational intellectual elite, symbolized by the Mont Pèlerin Society, and the ways in which it turned itself into a transnational power elite.

The transnational governance of business and the elusive notion of community

Empirical and theoretical contributions on transnational governance all point to the great multiplicity and variety of the actors involved (Morgan 2001; Djelic and Quack 2003; Tamm Hallström 2004; Djelic and Sahlin-Andersson 2006; Graz and Nölke 2008). Transnational governance processes bridge different divides and, in particular, bring together actors from the business, public, and civil society spheres. On the business side, multinational companies, service intermediaries, professional networks, and associations or business-oriented non-governmental organizations (BINGOs) are more or less prominently involved. On the public side, international organizations, supranational bodies, national governments, departments, ministries or agencies, policy networks, public think tanks, and quasi non-governmental organizations (QUANGOs) can all be present. On the civil society side, finally, independent non-governmental organizations, advocacy networks, academic experts, or the media, to the extent that they can be detached from both the business and the public spheres, are also potentially important actors (Boli and Thomas 1999; Florini 2003). Hence, insofar as the analysis of transnational governance has been actor-centered, it has tended to focus on organizations as formal structures and physical nodes in relational networks.

As Renate Mayntz shows in her contribution to this volume, the community-like nature of social formations has rarely been a central focus in studies of transnational economic governance. There are, of course, a number of interesting exceptions that point the way towards useful explorations. In his pioneering contribution, Glenn Morgan proposed that the structuring of "transnational imagined communities" might be an important background process in relation to the construction and monitoring of common transnational rules for the economic game (Morgan 2001). Mayntz (in this volume) also points to the partial but growing use, in the literature on transnational economic governance, of concepts such as "epistemic communities" or "social movements" that suggest more than formal connections or network interactions. Discussion of the different strands of the literature presented above leads us to draw up a number of preliminary propositions on the nature of communities as they play out in the transnational context – and more specifically in transnational governance fields.

First, it appears that transnational communities can be seen as representing a special instance of the "de-naturalization" of community-belonging described by Simmel (Simmel 1971). Joining and becoming part of a transnational community qualifies the adherence and connection to an imagined national community but it does not fully displace or destroy it. Transnational communities are bound to make the web of group affiliations much denser, at least for a number of individuals (Simmel 1955). The multiple community affiliations stemming from the involvement in transnational communities "de-naturalize" perceptions of traditional community adherence and belonging.

Second, members of those transnational communities – and more particularly those that are actively engaged and involved – are "cosmopolitans," but of the "rooted" kind (Hannerz 1990, 1992; Cohen 1992; Ackerman 1994; Tarrow 2005). The active membership of transnational communities spends a varying amount of time in "horizontal" forms of involvement – pursuing the common object of that community across and beyond a multiplicity of boundaries. Their loyalty is strongly bound to that common object, project, cognitive or expert base, or value system. In that sense, active members of transnational communities are "strangers" (Simmel 1971: 143–49) or "cosmopolitans" (Merton 1948; Gouldner 1957; Vertovec and Cohen 2002). In the words of Jeremy Waldron, "cosmopolitans" are positively viewed as "individuals who do not take their cultural identities to be defined by any bounded subset of the cultural resources available in the world" (Waldron 1992: 108). At the same time, the relevance and impact of transnational communities as regards different forms of activities, debates, governance, or policy-making implies a certain form of "rootedness" in local and, in particular, national groups or communities (Cohen 1992; Hannerz 1992, 1996; Tarrow 2005). Simmel's "stranger" is also "an element of the group itself; his position as full-fledged member involves both being outside it and confronting it" (Simmel 1971: 144).

Third, transnational communities are social and symbolic constructions. While members of transnational communities may remain rooted, to different degrees, in local or national settings, transnational communities provide for a common sense of belonging that is still compatible with a variety of inter-pretations and the specificity of meanings stemming from this differentiated rootedness. In fact, the active carving out of a common identity in private and public discourse by both members and non-members is reminiscent of the process described by Anderson involving the invention and propagation of the nation as an imagined community. Exactly because transnational com-munities are to be seen as imagined communities in addition to and, in a sense, on top of a number of other group affiliations, members have the possibility to strategize upon their membership in the pursuit of their goals. This multiplicity of affiliations is likely to provide members with a richer repertoire of reflexive practices of sense-making and generate strategies that stand at the crossroads of diverse community affiliations (Stark *et al.* 2006).

Fourth, and as a consequence of the above propositions, transnational communities allow for a fair amount of within-group diversity. Here again, Simmel provides a powerful formulation:

[W]ith the stranger, one has only certain *more general* qualities in common ... individuals share those in addition to their individual differences ... As such, the stranger is near and far at the same time ... Between those two factors of nearness and distance, however, a peculiar tension arises since the consciousness of having only the absolutely general in common has exactly the effect of putting a special emphasis on that which is not common. (Simmel 1971: 146–48)

The various strands of literature discussed in the previous section all highlight the existence, emergence, structuration, and relevance of social formations that reach beyond national borders. In those transnational social formations, people bring together and collectively reflect upon experiences in various national or local societies or communities. They develop joint activities, define and pursue common goals and projects with a transnational scope and reach. This all happens, however, without the necessary presumption of intense homogenization. In fact, the literature tends to underscore that, within the bounds of transnational social formations – whether labeled networks, groups, or communities – there remains considerable heterogeneity between members. This heterogeneity may ultimately be unbridgeable but it can be kept within bounds through various forms of socialization mechanisms, through the development and stabilization of common practices, goals, or norms. Heterogeneity is not a problem. It might even be a strength as long as it does not prevent a common orientation and a common sense of belonging around particular projects or goals, or around certain shared cognitive frames.

Finally, we need to pay attention to the temporal dimension of community involvement (McAdam and Sewell 2001). Using Janowitz's (1952) term, transnational communities are in all likelihood "communities of limited liability" to a greater extent than traditional communities of the ascriptive kind, closer to Tönnies's understanding of *Gemeinschaft*. The notion of "communities of limited liability" in this context refers to the fact that members are more likely to come and go and to exhibit varying degrees of involvement and participation through time (Smith and Wiest 2005). It also reflects the possibility of limits in temporality. Transnational communities are time-bound entities and constructions and not necessary, permanent, timeless, or essential collectives.

With these five propositions in mind, the contributions to this volume aim to explore the role of transnational communities in the governance of business activity. In addition to highlighting the relevance of community-like social formations in the coordination and regulation of economic and business processes, those contributions also confront and move to address some unresolved issues related to the nature, workings, and impact of those transnational communities that are present in the economic and business sphere. Six such issues are encountered throughout the different chapters of this volume:

1. The formation, rise, change, and possible weakening or even demise of transnational communities over time.
2. The two-sided interaction between transnational communities and local/national communities.
3. The emergence of "rooted cosmopolitans" and the process through which transnational communities are socially and symbolically constructed and reconstructed through time.

4. The ways in which members and non-members use the symbolic material associated with transnational communities to pursue their own strategies, locally or transnationally.
5. The interplay between processes of transnational community-building and parallel processes of formal organization.
6. The regulatory impact of transnational communities, particularly with respect to economic and business activity.

In all likelihood, some of our findings, on a number of issues at least, are more broadly applicable to transnational communities in general and hence could also be of use in transdisciplinary debates on transnational communities, their role and impact.

Contents of the book

The different chapters in this volume all start out from the five propositions on the nature of transnational communities described above and summarized below:

- One among several community affiliations;
- Members are rooted cosmopolitans;
- Imagined communities – of a fluid and dynamic kind;
- Fair amount of within-community diversity;
- Time-bound, non-essential, and non-permanent collectives.

All the chapters in this volume explore the role and impact of transnational communities in relation to governance – usually focusing on business activity. In addition – although the empirical terrains are extremely diverse – the chapters all encounter one or several of the five remaining open issues presented above and summarized below:

- The temporal ebb and flow of transnational communities;
- Transnational communities and local/national interplay;
- Processes of symbolic construction and reconstruction of transnational communities;
- Strategic uses of the symbolic building blocks of transnational communities;
- Transnational communities and organization;
- Transnational regulatory impact.

Part I of the volume explores the concept of community and its articulation in terms of transnational issues and phenomena. After the present introductory chapter, Chapter 2 by Renate Mayntz pushes further the understanding of transnational communities as a distinct social formation as compared to markets, hierarchies, and networks, which dominate the literature on global governance. While the coordinating mechanism in markets is exchange, in hierarchies command, and in networks negotiation, in communities it is mutual observation and the conscious orientation of individual behavior towards shared values, knowledge, or skills. The author points to the ubiquitous interpenetration of transnational communities with other social forms. Since transnational communities are often embedded in or cross over with other types of collective, in particular formal organizations, they are often overlooked and underestimated as regards their relevance for the formation and operation of transnational governance.

Parts II to V take up the two first chapters' pursuit of a comprehensive comparative analysis of transnational communities, each of them focusing on one particular kind of community. In each Part, different cases and "stories" are presented in an effort to elicit the complex articulation of communities in transnational contexts.

Part II brings together two "stories" of apparently classical, ascriptive communities with a view to examining what happens when they extend transnationally. Dahles, in Chapter 3, critically explores the notion and reality of a transnational Chinese community and its role in transnational business activity. Instead of an homogeneous and closely knit ascriptive community, she presents the "transnational Chinese community" as a complex and fragmented imagined community. It is socially constructed and often mediated through national institutional and policy frames, resulting in a loosely connected patchwork of partly converging and partly conflicting practices and principles. The case of the shuttle traders in Laleli, Istanbul, studied by Eder and Öz in Chapter 4, shows the physical encounter, interaction, and – in time – partial integration of diverse ascriptive groups into an emergent transethnic and translocal community which is nourished by its members partly for – though it cannot be reduced entirely to – economic interests.

In Part III, four different professional communities are examined, in each case exploring the particular context of transnational extension. In Chapter 5, Harvey and Maclean look at elite corporate directors in Britain and France. They find evidence that those elite directors are attuned to the demands and requirements of competing across international boundaries. They also show a growing recognition of shared values, assumptions, and beliefs at the transnational level. That said, it is also clear that community affiliations remain primarily national, regional, or local. In Chapter 6, Morgan and Kubo show that professionals in the private equity sector in Japan are connected to a broader transnational community in the making, but remain deeply embedded nationally. The evidence suggests the progressive constitution of a transnational community of private equity professionals, with emerging common modes of acting and organizing. The evidence also shows considerable regional or national variation, however, and Japan in particular remains very much on the edge of this community. Hussain and Ventresca, in Chapter 7, explore the historical development of global finance associations and the emergence of an archipelago of communities of professional practitioners, increasingly sharing common ideas and even a common culture. Finally, in Chapter 8, Ramirez investigates how a transnational community of accountants that was initially structured on the basis of the world's largest accounting firms attempted to spread their version of professionalism to France, which hitherto had followed a very different path in the professionalization of accounting. The author shows how this transnational professional community effectively expanded its regulatory leverage across national borders by linking up with and gradually transforming the previously insulated French accounting elite.

Parts II and III started from communities that originally had a local base and then explored what happens when those communities extend transnationally in one way or another. In Part IV, we turn to an exploration of virtual communities – communities that are created by interaction via the Internet or are based to a large extent on online interaction. Many of these communities from very early on define themselves transnationally without paying too much attention to nationalities or borders. Nonetheless, virtual communities are, as revealed in the contributions to this Part, also locally and/or nationally rooted. In Chapter 9, Metiu examines the role of gift exchange in free/open source software communities and its potential as a mechanism for knowledge transfer from industrialized to developing countries. The results show that free/open source communities contribute effectively to increasing the skills of developers in the South, fostering solidarity in local virtual communities in developing countries, and making free/open source software available in remote parts of the world. In Chapter 10, Dobusch and Quack investigate the multifaceted transnational community for open content copyright licenses, crystallizing around the non-profit organization "Creative Commons." The chapter highlights the mobilizing capacity of different types of transnational online communities, in particular the interaction between an epistemic community, a social movement, and a non-profit organization, and their capacity for effective transnational standard-setting.

Part V extends the exploration to interest or issue-based communities. We have a mixture of cases here, ranging from the difficult projection of nationally based communities into a transnational arena to the construction of diverse and fluid communities around an issue defined from the start as global. In Chapter 11, Schrad analyses the historical case of the transnational temperance community. He examines the development, structuration, and temporal evolution of the transnational temperance movement in terms that are clearly generalizable to movements of more recent vintage. He also shows how the temperance cause stimulated one of the first truly transnational communities. Fetzer, in Chapter 12, follows the historical development of an issue – industrial democracy – with a focus on how trade unions reacted to that issue in the European context. He argues that, until the late 1980s, trade union responses to European Community initiatives were premised solely on minimizing the impact of regulation on the achievements of industrial democracy at the national level. Since then, this defensive pattern has come to be modified and trade unions are now making greater efforts to give workers' participation a European dimension.

In Chapter 13, Plehwe investigates the historical roots and evolution of the Mont Pèlerin Society of neoliberal intellectuals. The author argues that in order to understand the origins of neoliberal values and principled beliefs one has to explore the constitution and working of a transnational comprehensive discourse community of intellectuals and organizations that has forged a normative worldview informing the development of knowledge, expertise, and practices in many issue areas, discourse fields, and countries. In Chapter 14, Mariussen explores the emergence of a new global market for carbon capture and storage and shows that a transnational community is being built in parallel around this essentially global issue. Finally, an examination of social and environmental certification by Bartley and Smith in Chapter 15 shows how communities of practice can be both cause and consequence of transnational governance. The authors point to older communities of practice, organized around political and religious resistance to American Cold War foreign policy, which laid the ground for the emergence of novel transnational communities of certification practitioners. The latter are likely to shape the future of transnational governance insofar as they may provide new actors with access to defining the rules of the game while also carrying the certification model into other domains.

Having explored such a wide range of cases, in the concluding chapter we draw together the theoretical insights that emerge from the systematic comparison and confrontation of the diverse empirical stories with regard to their impact on transnational economic governance.

NOTES

1. Our translation. The French text reads: "Je crois que la vie des grandes agglomérations sociales est tout aussi naturelle que celle des petits aggrégats . . . En dehors des mouvements purement individuels, il y a dans nos sociétés contemporaines une activité proprement collective qui est tout aussi naturelle que celle des sociétés moins étendues d'autrefois. Elle est autre assurément; elle constitue un type différent, mais entre ces deux espèces d'un même genre, si diverses qu'elles soient, il n'y a pas une différence de nature."
2. Naturally, an alternative scenario could be that the current financial and economic crisis leads in time and at least for a while to a recentering inwards in many nations, with a powerful return of states and the temptation to engage in different kinds of isolationism and protectionism.

REFERENCES

Abbott, A. 1988. *The system of professions: An essay on the division of expert labor.* University of Chicago Press.

Ackerman, B. 1994. "Rooted cosmopolitanism," *Ethics* **104**: 516–35.

Adler, E. 2005. *Communitarian international relations.* London: Routledge.

Adler, E. 2008. "The spread of security communities: Communities of practice, self-restraint, and NATO's post Cold War transformation," *European Journal of International Relations* **14**: 195–230.

Anderson, B. 2006 [1983]. *Imagined communities.* London and New York: Verso.

Bell, C. and Newby, H. (eds.) 1974. *The sociology of community: A selection of readings.* London: Frank Cass.

Bellah, R., Madsen, R., Sullivan, W., Swidler, A. and Tipton, S. 1985. *Habits of the heart.* Berkeley: University of California Press.

Boli, J. and Thomas, G. (eds.) 1999. *Constructing world culture: International nongovernmental organizations since 1875.* Stanford University Press.

Carroll, W. K. and Fennema, M. 2002. "Is there a transnational business community?," *International Sociology* **17** (3): 393–419.

Cohen, A. P. 1985. *The symbolic construction of community.* London and New York: Routledge.

Cohen, M. 1992. "Rooted cosmopolitanism," *Dissent* **39** (4): 478–83.

Cutler, C. 2008. "The legitimacy of private transnational governance." Paper presented at the conference "Law and legitimacy in the governance of transnational economic relations," Villa Vigoni, June 22–24.

Daily Telegraph. 2008. "EU ministers back financial regulation," November 5. www.telegraph.co.uk/finance/3382933/EU-ministers-back-financial-regulation.html. Accessed November 8, 2008.

Deutsch, K. W., Burell, S. A. and Kann, R. A. 1957. *Political community and the North Atlantic area.* Princeton University Press.

Djelic, M.-L., and Quack, S. (eds.) 2003. *Globalization and institutions: Redefining the rules of the economic game.* Cheltenham: Edward Elgar.

Djelic, M.-L. and Quack, S. 2008. "Institutions and transnationalisation," in Greenwood, R., Oliver, C., Suddaby, R. and Sahlin-Andersson, K. (eds.), *Handbook of organisational institutionalism*. Los Angeles: Sage, pp. 299–323.

Djelic, M.-L., and Sahlin-Andersson, K. (eds.) 2006. *Transnational governance: Institutional dynamics of regulation*. Cambridge University Press.

Djilas, M. 1957. *The new class*. New York: Praeger.

Domhoff, G. W. 1967. *Who rules America?* Englewood Cliffs, NJ: Prentice Hall.

Drake, W. and Nicolaïdis, K. 1992. "Ideas, interests, and institutionalisation: 'Trade in service' and the Uruguay round," *International Organization* **46**: 38–101.

Durkheim, E. 1889. "Communauté et société selon Tönnies," *Revue Philosophique* **27**: 416–22.

Durkheim, E. 1984 [1893]. *The division of labor in society*. New York: Macmillan–The Free Press.

Durkheim, E. 1997 [1897]. *Suicide*. New York: Macmillan–The Free Press.

Durkheim, E. 2001 [1912]. *The elementary forms of religious life*. Oxford University Press.

Elias, N. 1974. "Towards a theory of communities," Foreword, in Bell, C. and Newby, H. (eds.), pp. ix–xli.

Faist, T. 2000. *The volume and dynamics of international migration and transnational social spaces*. Oxford University Press.

Faulconbridge, J. R. and Muzio, D. 2007. "Reinserting the professional into the study of global professional service firms: The case of law," *Global Networks* **7** (3): 249–70.

Florini, A. 2003. *The coming democracy: New rules for running a new world*. Washington, DC: Island Press.

Fourcade, M. 2006. "The construction of a global profession: The transnationalization of economics," *American Journal of Sociology* **122** (1): 145–94.

G20. 2009. "Leaders' statement: The global plan for recovery and reform," Communiqué of the G20 Meeting in London, April 2. www.g20.org/Documents/final-communique.pdf. Accessed April 8, 2009.

Geertz, C. 1975. "Thick description: Toward an interpretative theory of culture," in Geertz, C., *The interpretation of cultures*. London: Hutchinson, pp. 3–30.

Goode, W. J. 1957. "Community within a community: The professions," *American Sociological Review* **22** (2): 194–200.

Gouldner, A. 1957. "Cosmopolitans and locals: Toward an analysis of latent social roles," *Administrative Science Quarterly* **2** (3): 281–306.

Graz, J.-C., and Nölke, A. (eds.) 2008. *Transnational private governance and its limits*. London: Routledge.

Guidry, J., Kennedy, M. and Zald, M. (eds.) 2000. *Globalizations and social movements: Culture, power and the transnational public sphere*. Ann Arbor: University of Michigan Press.

Haas, P. 1992a. "Introduction: Epistemic communities and international policy coordination," *International Organization* **46** (1): 1–35.

Haas, P. 1992b. "Banning chlorofluorocarbons: Epistemic community efforts to protect stratospheric ozone," *International Organization* **46** (1): 187–224.

Hannerz, U. 1990. "Cosmopolitans and locals in world culture," *Theory, Culture and Society* **7**: 237–51.

Hannerz, U. 1992. *Cultural complexity. Studies in the social organization of meaning*. New York: Columbia University Press.

Hannerz, U. 1996. *Transnational connections*. London: Routledge.

Hannerz, U. 1997. "Flows, boundaries and hybrids: Keywords in transnational anthropology," Department of Anthropology Working Paper WPTC-2K-02. Stockholm University.

Held, D. 1995. *Democracy and the global order: From the modern state to cosmopolitan governance*. Cambridge: Polity Press.

Janowitz, M. 1952. *The community press in an urban setting*. Glencoe, IL: The Free Press.

Jenkins, R. 1996. *Social identity*. London: Routledge.

Jordana, J. and Levi-Faur, D. (eds.) 2004. *The politics of regulation: Institutions and regulatory reforms for the governance age*. Cheltenham: Edward Elgar.

Katzenstein, P., Keohane, R. and Krasner, S. (eds.) 1999. *Exploration and contestation in the study of world politics*. Cambridge, MA: MIT Press.

Keck, M. E. and Sikkink, K. 1998. *Activists beyond borders*. Ithaca, NY: Cornell University Press.

Kentor, J. and Jang, Y. S. 2004. "Yes, there is a (growing) transnational business community," *International Sociology* **19** (3): 355–68.

Kluckhohn, C. 1962. "The concept of culture," in Kluckhohn, R. (ed.), *Culture and behavior*. New York: Free Press, pp. 19–73.

Konrad, G. 1984. *Antipolitics*. New York: Harcourt Brace Jovanovich.

Kuhlmann, E. and Saks, M. (eds.) 2008. *Rethinking professional governance: International directions in health care*. Bristol: Policy Press.

Lamont, M. and Molnár, V. 2002. "The study of boundaries in the social sciences," *Annual Review of Sociology* **28**: 167–95.

Lannes, R. 1940. *Les deux cents familles ou les maîtres de la France*. Paris: Sorlot.

Larson, M. S. 1977. *The rise of professionalism: A sociological analysis*. Berkeley: University of California Press.

McAdam, D. and Sewell, W. Jr. 2001. "It's about time: Temporality in the study of social movements and revolutions," in Aminzade, R. *et al.* (eds.), *Silence and voice in the study of contentious politics*. Cambridge University Press, pp. 89–125.

McKenna, C., Djelic, M.-L. and Ainamo, A. 2003. "Message and medium: The role of consulting firms in globalization and its local interpretation," in Djelic, M.-L. and Quack, S. (eds.), pp. 83–107.

Merton, R. 1948. "Patterns of influence: A study of interpersonal influence and of communications behaviour in a local community," in Lazarsfeld, P. and Stanton, F. (eds.), *Man in the city of the future*. London: Collier-Macmillan, pp. 180–219.

Meyer, J., Boli, J., Thomas, G. M. and Ramirez, F. O. 1997. "World society and the nation-state," *American Journal of Sociology* **103** (1): 144–81.

Mills, C. Wright. 1956 [2000]. *The power elite*. Oxford University Press.

Morgan, G. 2001. "Transnational communities and business systems," *Global Networks: A Journal of Transnational Affairs* **1** (2): 113–30.

Morgan, G. and Quack, S. 2005. "Institutional legacies and firm dynamics: The internationalisation of British and German law firms," *Organization Studies* **26**: 1765–86.

Nye, J. S. and Keohane, R. O. 1971. "Transnational relations and world politics: A conclusion," *International Organization* **25** (3): 721–48.

Overbeek, H., van Apeldoorn, B. and Nölke, A. (eds.) 2007. *The transnational politics of corporate governance regulation*. London: Routledge.

Park, R. 1952. *Human communities: The city and human ecology*. Glencoe, IL: The Free Press.

Park, R. and Burgess, E. 1921. *Introduction to the science of sociology*. University of Chicago Press.

Portes, A. 2000. "Globalization from below: The rise of transnational communities," in Kalb, D., van der Land, M., Staring, R., van Steenbergen, B. and Wilterdink, N. (eds.), *The ends of globalization: Bringing society back in*. Lanham: Rowman & Littlefield, pp. 253–70.

Pries, L. (ed.) 2001. *New transnational social spaces*. London: Routledge.

Putnam, R. 2000. *Bowling alone*. New York: Simon & Schuster.

Risse-Kappen, T. 1994. "Ideas do not float freely: Transnational coalitions, domestic structures and the end of the Cold War," *International Organization* **48**: 185–214.

Risse-Kappen, T. (ed.) 1995. *Bringing transnational relations back in*. Cambridge University Press.

Rothkopf, D. 2008. *Superclass: The global power elite and the world they are making*. New York: Macmillan-Farrar, Straus and Giroux.

Saxenian, A. 2005. "From brain drain to brain circulation: Transnational communities and regional upgrading in India and China," *Studies in Comparative International Development*, **40** (2): 35–61.

Saxenian, A. 2006. *The new argonauts: Regional advantage in a global economy*. Cambridge, MA: Harvard University Press.

Simmel, G. 1955 [1908]. "The web of group affiliations," in Simmel, G., *Conflict and the web of group affiliations*. New York: Free Press, pp. 125–95.

Simmel, G. 1971. *On individuality and social forms*, edited by D. Levine. University of Chicago Press.

Sklair, L. 2001. *The transnational capitalist class*. Oxford: Basil Blackwell.

Smith, J. and Johnston, H. (eds.) 2002. *Globalization and resistance: Transnational dimensions of social movements*. Lanham, MD: Rowman and Littlefield.

Smith, J. and Wiest, D. 2005. "The uneven geography of global civil society: National and global influences on transnational association," *Social Forces* **84** (2): 621–52.

Smith, J., Chatfield, C. and Pagnucco, R. (eds.) 1997. *Transnational social movements and global politics*. Syracuse University Press.

Soysal, Y. 1994, *Limits of citizenship: migrants and postnational membership in Europe*. University of Chicago Press.

Staples, C. L. 2006. "Board interlocks and the study of the transnational capitalist class," *Journal of World-Systems Research* **12** (2): 309–19.

Stark, D., Vedres, B. and Bruszt, L. 2006. "Rooted transnational publics: Integrating foreign ties and civic activism," *Theory and Society* **35** (3): 323–49.

Suttles, G. 1972. *The social construction of communities*. University of Chicago Press.

Swidler, A. 1986. "Culture in action: Symbols and strategies." *American Sociological Review* **51** (2): 273–86.

Tamm Hallström, K. 2004. *Organizing international standardization*. Cheltenham: Edward Elgar.

Tarrow, S. 2005. *The new transnational activism*. Cambridge University Press.

Tönnies, F. 2002 [1897]. *Community and society*. Mineola, NY: Dover Publications.

van der Pijl, K. 1984. *The making of an Atlantic ruling class*. London: Verso.

Verdun, A. 1999. "The role of the Delors Committee in the creation of EMU: An epistemic community?," *Journal of European Public Policy* **6**: 308–28.

Vertovec, S. 2001. "Transnational social formations: Towards conceptual cross-fertilization." Paper (WPTC-01–16) presented at workshop on "Transnational migration: Comparative perspectives," June 30–July 1, Princeton University.

Vertovec, S. and Cohen, R. (eds.) 2002. *Conceiving cosmopolitanism: Theory, context and practice*. Oxford University Press.

Waldron, J. 1992. "Minority cultures and the cosmopolitan alternative," *University of Michigan Law Review* **25**: 5–14.

Weber, M. 1978. *Economy and society*. 2 vols., edited by G. Roth and C. Wittich. Berkeley: University of California Press.

Wenger, E. 1998. *Communities of practice: Learning, meaning, and identity*. Cambridge University Press.

Wyman, M. 1993. *Round-trip to America: The immigrants return to Europe, 1880–1930*. Ithaca, NY: Cornell University Press.

Zeng, M. 2008. "World Bank President: Need to reform financial regulation, supervision systems," Dow Jones Newswires (October 13). www.fxstreet.com/news/forex-news/article.aspx?StoryId=b4602d9f-de06-4014-a088-de85dc8c947e. Accessed November 8, 2008.

2   Global structures: markets, organizations, networks – and communities?

Renate Mayntz

Community and globalization: diverging perspectives

In discussions of globalization, in which the evolving structures that trans-cend the boundaries of nation-states are the focus, markets, organizations, and networks predominate. Economic globalization takes place through the (potentially) worldwide expansion of markets and the growth of trans-national corporations (TNC), facilitated by the international expansion of communication and transportation networks. Political globalization – that is, global governance – involves the multiplication of international governmental and non-governmental organizations. The existence of global production networks and global public policy networks completes the inventory of social forms with transnational territorial scope. Transnational communities do not play a significant role in the discussion on global structures. In the *International Encyclopedia of the Social and Behavioral Sciences*, the term "global community" does appear (for example, on page 2383), but there is no specific entry. It seems that the theoretical approaches that dominate the study of globalization direct attention selectively to markets, organizations, and networks, neglecting other kinds of social collectives extending beyond national boundaries, such as commu-nities. This does not mean that the phenomenon is not being observed, as the chapters in this book also demonstrate. The role of legal professionals in transnational law-making has been studied (Quack 2007), scientific com-munities of varying geographical expansion are studied in the sociology of science, transnational communities of discourse are a topic in cultural studies (see Plehwe in this volume), and relevant contributions can also be found in research on migration. However, there is no common theoretical framework joining these widely dispersed contributions together, and only rarely is the role of these collectives in the process of globalization and in global governance considered.

By and large, globalization is analyzed as an economic process, with a focus on international trade, foreign direct investment, and TNCs. The parallel process of political globalization is studied by scholars of international relations and international political economy, who emphasize the development of different forms of international cooperation and coordination, in the UN, international organizations, and international regimes. Governance theory, which serves as the basis of this discussion, has offered various typologies of governance forms. In its widest and most general sense, governance includes all forms of social coordination, where social coordination refers to "the ways in which disparate but interdependent agencies are coordinated and/or seek to coordinate themselves through different forms of self-organization to achieve specific common objectives in situations of complex reciprocal interdependence. Among the many techniques and mechanisms deployed here are exchange, command, networking, and solidarity" (Jessop and Ngai-Ling 2006: 255). Of the four mechanisms Jessop and Ngai-Ling mention, the first three refer to the governance types that dominate in the discussion on globalization: market, hierarchy, and network. Starting from the dichotomy between market and hierarchy developed in the context of transaction cost theory, the taxonomy of governance forms has subsequently been extended to include organizations and/or networks (see Mayntz 2003). This dominant typology of governance forms bears the traces of two major political debates of recent decades: anti-authoritarianism, which pitted networks against hierarchy, and the debate about economic liberalization, which pitted the market against hierarchy. In analyses of global governance, community, if dealt with at all, plays only a minor part.

An important reason for this neglect lies in the frequent association of "community" with the notion of *Gemeinschaft* as used by Ferdinand Tönnies. He used *Gemeinschaft* to designate the communal life forms of primitive tribes, the extended family, and the (rural) neighborhood with their rich emotional ties, which he opposed to *Gesellschaft*, the instrumental relations that characterize a functionally differentiated society. In English-speaking countries, the term "community" has similarly been used to designate primary groups such as the family and local neighborhoods. Even today, most entries in the *International Encyclopedia of the Social and Behavioral Sciences* that have the term "community" in their title deal with local communities, for example, community organization, community health, community economic development, and community power structure. At the time of Tönnies, Durkheim, and Max Weber, there was a general feeling that industrialization and urbanization would lead to a weakening of social cohesion. Though the consequences of industrialization were a typical concern of the nineteenth century, the community/society debate continued well into the twentieth (see, for instance, Geiger 1960). The concept of community in the traditional, emphatic sense also played an important role in political discourse, from the early socialist utopians such as Owen to the ideological use of the term in the Nazi ideal of *Volksgemeinschaft*. Today the concept can be found in the Third Way ideology of Britain's New Labour, as Buckler (2007) shows, and in critiques of economic liberalism by the new communitarian writers (for example, Etzioni 1993, 1995). "Conceptions of community have provided a reference point for rejections of what is taken to be the excessively thin conception of the self, falsely shorn of any intrinsic attachments, offered by liberals, and for criticism of the commensurately thin, procedural picture of the just society" (Buckler 2007: 42).

As suggested by Jessop and Ngai-Ling's enumeration of governance forms quoted above, "community" is interpreted in the more comprehensive typologies of governance forms in the traditional understanding of primary groups based on solidarity.[1] In modern society, communal life forms have not disappeared, but at the societal level, hierarchical organization and market determine the social dynamics. At the same time, new social forms distinct from market, hierarchy, and network have developed within modern society, forms not based on kinship or propinquity (residence, locality) but on more narrowly defined characteristics such as specific values, beliefs, or cognitions. In distinction from communities of descent or propinquity, such groups came to be called communities of interest (Hillery 1955: 27; see Gläser 2006: 44–48) – a term used also here for lack of a better alternative, even though "interest" must be understood in a very general sense to avoid misinterpretation. The best known communities of interest are scientific communities, epistemic communities, policy communities, and so-called communities of practice, which include professional communities. The use of the label "community" for these social collectives is justified by the fact that the relations among their members are characteristically neither instrumental (as in markets), nor hierarchically ordered or formally coordinated. If the traditional concept of community is to be extended to communities of interest, "community" must be defined in relatively abstract and minimal terms. A correspondingly general definition of community can be based on the following criteria:[2] communities are composed of individuals who share a specific characteristic (descent, locality, value, belief, knowledge, skill, interest). Group members are peers with respect to the shared characteristic, they are conscious of sharing it, which means that the shared characteristic constitutes the identity of the collective and of its members, and is of practical relevance for their behavior. Note that according to this definition, the fact that a given skill, knowledge, or value is "shared" in the sense of being diffused among a certain group of persons is not enough to constitute a community. A community is not a social category, but a group in the socio-logical sense of the term: the common property engenders a "we" feeling and is the basis of individual and group identity.[3] Nor does "shared" imply full consensus; in scientific communities there can be disagreement over the best questions to ask and over the meaning of experimental results, and in policy communities over the measures to adopt in the pursuit of a policy goal. Similarly, while community members are peers with respect to the shared characteristic, they are often different with respect to other properties, such as resources, or, in scientific communities, reputation.

As already suggested, different shared characteristics give rise to different types of community, the major types being communities based on kinship and propinquity, and communities of interest. Small primitive tribes, kinship groups, and rural neighborhoods are held together by multiple bonds, contacts are typically face-to-face, and group membership constitutes an encompassing identity and life form. In such communities, members can be families or households rather than isolated individuals. In contrast, a specific shared conviction, shared expertise, or policy value creates a narrow, one-dimensional bond, membership is individual, and interaction among members can be largely indirect. Community, however, is an analytical con-cept, and in reality its defining criteria can be met to different degrees; thus communities can also be ephemeral, short-lived, and of little consequence for behavior. In addition, the same shared characteristic can give rise to different forms of community. Thus religion, ethnicity, and nationality can be the basis of highly integrated, multi-bonded social groupings, but in other contexts their binding force may be very small, smaller even than other properties on which communities of interest are based.

Communities based on shared convictions, values, or expertise have prop-erties that distinguish them clearly from other modes of social coordination. Community members are typically individuals, while the components of markets, hierarchies, and networks can also be formal organizations. Communities of interest differ most markedly from hierarchies in terms of the fact that the relations among members are by definition relations among equals with respect to the shared characteristic. While the coordinating mechanism in markets is exchange, in hierarchies command, and in networks negotiation, in communities of interest it is the conscious orientation of individual behavior towards the shared value, knowledge, or skill. The shared (and typically achieved rather than ascribed) characteristic is reasserted in communication among members, produces their collective identity, and defines the boundary of the group. Communities of interest are not organized to fulfill a common task or purpose: that is what organizations, what hierarchies do. However, the characteristic that serves as the basis of community formation often implies a shared goal, whether it is the production of scientific knowledge, a healthy environment, or, as in the case of unorganized social movements, some social or political vision. But in contrast to hierarchies and to networks as negotiating systems, the effects collectively produced by communities are emergent. While this does not distinguish communities from markets, which also produce emergent effects,[4] markets are based on a different coordinating mechanism, namely economic exchange. Most difficult is the distinction between community and network. Networks are defined by the incidence of interactive relations among network members. For communities of interest, mutual observation is constitutive; their members are often linked by indirect rather than direct relations. Interpersonal networks thus can, but need not be the basis of a community of interest.

The prevalence of communities based on different shared characteristics differs between local, national, and international levels of action. Communities based on propinquity, that is, neighborhoods, are locally circumscribed social units. With functional differentiation, and with the increasing importance of science and technology in modern society, narrowly based communities of interest of national scope have multiplied. At the transnational level, communities of interest are prevalent. Though transnational communities such as the Temperance movement and certain epistemic and scientific communities have existed before (see, for example, Schrad in this volume), social interactions across boundaries have increased and expanded geographically with globalization. In particular the intensification of international communication, measured for instance in terms of international telephony and the cross-border movements of persons (Kessler 2007), should facilitate the formation of transnational communities based on shared convictions, values, or expertise. The binding power of other shared characteristics can vary between levels. Religious communities are mostly geographically circumscribed and multi-bonded, religious belief being often linked with ethnicity and/or socio-economic position. Geographically circumscribed religious communities can also be politically important within nation-states, as the cases of Northern Ireland and Iraq illustrate. In transnational interactions, religious belief constitutes in most cases only a weak bond, but we are currently experiencing a return of the eminent bonding and motivating power that religious belief had in the Spanish *Conquista* and in the Thirty Years War. With globalization, ethnicity has similarly lost its traditional geographic circumscription and is proving to be an important bond not only in business relations among ethnic Chinese (see Dahles in this volume), but also in international terrorism and crime. In a foreign environment even nationality can be the basis of community formation (for example, the "German colony" in Moscow).

In the next section I shall look more closely at the potential of different kinds of communities of interest to expand transnationally. It will become apparent that certain aspects of the process of globalization do indeed provide new opportunities for the formation of transnational communities, and that such communities play an important role in the evolving global order.

Forms of transnational communities of interest

Transnational communities of interest differ in their basis and, closely connected with this, their composition. Scientific, epistemic, professional, and policy communities are the most intensely researched types of this social form. The boundaries between these types of community are imprecise and fluid, a fact easily obscured by the fragmentation of research lines that typically concentrate on one type only.

Though not explicitly called inter- or transnational, most scientific communities are today no longer confined geographically. By definition, scientific communities are composed of scientists who define themselves as belonging to the same discipline or research field; who share the knowledge so far acquired about a specific segment of reality, as well as the rules guiding the acquisition and certification of such knowledge; who take cognizance of each other's research findings; and both generate, and define in communication with each other the current "state of the art" in their discipline or field (for a comprehensive review of the literature on scientific communities see Gläser 2006). Not all scientific communities are transnational to the same extent. Scientific knowledge is presumably universal, not local, but this refers more to its validity than its substantive content, which varies with the universality or (national) specificity of the segment of reality in question. While the scientific communities of particle physics and astronomy are international in character, legal scholars in the field of *Sozialrecht*, a special part of German law that has no exact counterpart in other countries, form a largely nationally confined scientific community (Mayntz 2001: 20–27). Though scientific research has become organized in labs and research institutes, scientific communities are still composed of individual scientists who exchange results and new research questions in the relevant journals, at conferences, and in personal contacts with colleagues. This process of monitoring, of mutual observation among scientists constitutes the community.

In a sense, scientific communities are epistemic communities, but the latter term is usually understood differently. Epistemic communities are composed of individuals who are experts in a given field (Haas 1992a). The experts may be scientists, but they may also serve as officials in a government agency or some other organization. Thus Haas (1992b: 189) describes the epistemic community framing the negotiations about ozone depletion as "composed of atmospheric scientists and of policy-makers who were sympathetic to the scientists' common set of values." The knowledge in question can belong to different disciplines, not only the natural sciences. The shared values, cognitions, and so on, of members in epistemic communities are directly relevant to policy. Epistemic communities exert influence by information, persuasion, and by using the media. Generally, epistemic communities are influential in policy areas in which complexity and technical uncertainty reign. Since policy research has traditionally concentrated on domestic policy-making within the framework of nation-states, epistemic communities are predominantly conceived of as national. But nationally circumscribed epistemic communities can expand transnationally as the geographical scope of policy problems is seen to transcend national boundaries. An example is given by Adler (1992), who has shown that an American epistemic community composed of scientists and "strategists" played a key role in creating the shared international understanding of the nuclear threat that finally led to an agreement on arms control. With the shift of policy-making competences to international organizations, more transnational epistemic communities have formed and continue to be formed.

While epistemic communities are based on shared expert knowledge, policy communities are based by definition on a shared policy interest. As in epistemic communities, the members of policy communities can be officials, scientists, and representatives of interest groups. According to Jordan (1990), the concept of policy community is an extension of an observation made by Heclo and Wildavsky as early as 1974: "Community refers to the personal relationships between major political and administrative actors – sometimes in conflict, often in agreement, but always in touch and operating within a shared framework. Community is the cohesive and orienting bond underlying any particular issue" (Heclo and Wildavsky, quoted by Jordan 1990: 325). However, the distinction between a community formed on the basis of a certain kind of policy-relevant knowledge, and a community composed of persons interested in a specific policy is obviously tenuous and difficult to establish empirically. Experts on a matter that is ultimately relevant to policy tend to have normative views on it; epistemic communities thus merge into policy communities. In the vast literature on the organization of scientific advice to policy it has been shown repeatedly that there is no hard and fast boundary between merely providing scientific information, and formulating recommendations for political action. Nor can policy communities be easily distinguished from policy networks. In fact, the difference appears to be analytical rather than substantial: the concept of policy community emphasizes interest and preferences – that is, ideal or cognitive factors – while the network concept refers to interactions and social relations. In practice, policy communities and policy networks are therefore often linked, the policy network generating a decision and the policy community serving as decision-making arena (Epstein 1997). Jordan (1990: 327) even defines policy communities as a special type of stable network, and for Rhodes (1990), highly integrated policy communities similarly represent one pole on a continuum of networks extending to loosely integrated issue networks at the other end. As already implied in the quotation from Heclo and Wildavsky, the members of a given policy community need not have the same preferences with respect to a given policy decision, but they are all interested in the same policy issue.

The related concepts of policy community and policy network have been developed in the study of inter-governmental (that is, local/central and interdepartmental) relations, and of industry–government relations within nation-states (see Jordan 1990; Rhodes 1990). Interest in policy communities grew with the recognition of substantial differences in the political dynamics of different policy sectors. Unsurprisingly, a literature search therefore shows that research has concentrated on sectoral policy communities such as banking policy, farm, or health service. In such studies, reference is typically to national policies, but with the shift of policy-making competences to international institutions and with expanding efforts at global governance, transnational policy communities develop. An example is the global warming community discussed by Mariussen (in this volume).

In epistemic and policy communities, discourse plays a focal role. The concept of "community of discourse" cross-cuts these analytical categories, highlighting the process of social construction involved in the emergence of epistemic and policy communities. Communities of discourse develop together with a new value, vision, ideology, or policy issue: the discourse revolving about them may solidify into a new epistemic or policy community, but in many cases communities of discourse remain ephemeral, as when union members discuss industrial democracy when they happen to meet. Most people are intermittently involved in several different discourse communities without making that part of their identity. Discourse communities can therefore be fluid, even ephemeral; this underlines the fact that "community" should be understood as an analytical dimension, rather than a substance.

The useful, though less diffused concept of community of practice (Wenger 1998) is the practical counterpart of scientific communities, whose members are bent on the advance of knowledge rather than its application. The members in a community of practice share certain skills in some domain of human endeavor, and engage in a process of collective learning by communicating with each other. Wenger (2001: 2339) applies the term not only to professionals, but also to a group of engineers working on similar problems, students of a given discipline at a university, and the Impressionist painters in Paris. Communities of practice are ubiquitous within large formal organizations, and can also connect people across organizational boundaries – "and potentially across the globe" (Wenger 2001: 2341). Professional communities based on shared skills and shared rules for their use are undoubtedly the most important subtype of communities of practice. However, professionals are often organized formally in a professional association that controls market entry and compliance with the professional code of ethics.

As Wenger (2001: 2341) maintains, the concept of community of practice has been readily adopted by people in business. In the business world, persons holding different positions and possibly belonging to different firms often share, and communicate on the basis of, some specific body of knowledge "with substantial tacit components" (Wenger 2001: 2341). But the concept of community is rarely used in the analysis of business and the economy.[5] Social scientists are interested in business organizations, in the institutional framework of economies, and in the relations between business and politics. The concept of business community, while occasionally applied to a collective of firms with a shared economic interest, is not familiarly used even in economic sociology; the new economic sociology studies mainly how markets are embedded in social institutions. Nor is "transnational business community" a familiar concept in international political economy; in analyses of the power of business in global governance, the activities of corporate actors, and particularly TNCs, play the dominant role (Fuchs 2005). Nevertheless, transnational business communities do exist. Visible manifestations are the European Round Table of Industrialists, and the annual meeting of business leaders in Davos, at which CEOs interested in economic development exchange information about the economic situation. Less visible, but not less important are certain kinds of communities *underlying* market exchange. A prominent example is presented by Knorr Cetina (2005) in her study of the global currency market. It is undoubtedly a market, characterized by the selling and buying of currencies. Traders in trading centers all over the world have in common not only certain learned skills and rules for the exchanges they enter into, but they also have a shared perception of the currency market at any given moment. Without such shared elements, global financial markets could not function. The transnational business community which underlies and sustains the global currency market evolves together with market exchanges out of the actions of the market actors themselves. While different kinds of market actors have formed communities as long as there have been markets, incumbents of similar positions in different firms increasingly form transnational communities as corporations and markets become international.

An important point in Knorr Cetina's analysis of the global currency market is her emphasis on what she calls the "scopic system," the technical infrastructure that permits the traders to observe each others' actions at any moment in time. "Social scientists tend to think in terms of mechanisms of coordination ... Cooperations, strategic alliances, exchange, emotional bonds, kinship ties, 'personal relations' ... can all be seen to work through ties and to instantiate sociality in networks of relationships. But we should also think in terms of reflexive mechanisms of observation and projection" (Knorr Cetina 2005: 40). In the case of financial markets, the collected information is projected onto computer screens. Mutual observation also takes place in other kinds of transnational communities, and in scientific communities, too, it is supported by an increasingly sophisticated technology. When a "scopic system," a mechanism that facilitates the collection and integration of observations, is in place, a reality is constructed towards which the participating actors orient their behavior.

While the traders in the global currency market have similar positions in formal organizations and most of their interaction is mediated by the computer screen, other transnational communities are created by interaction via the Internet. The minimum basis of such "online communities," which have been transnational from the beginning, is the shared interest in a specific topic about which the members of the community communicate with each other.[6]

Since there is no personal contact between members, these groups are also called virtual communities. The best studied online community is the community producing open source software (see Kogut and Metiu 2001; Gläser 2006: 264–77; Metiu in this volume). The persons collectively producing open source software act independently and without coordination. As Kogut and Metiu (2001: 248) put it, open source software development is a production model that exploits the distributed intelligence of participants in Internet communities; the same can be said for scientific communities. Online communities may well be the fastest growing, though not necessarily the most important segment of transnational communities in terms of their effects.

Formation and functions of transnational communities of interest

Transnational communities have remained the object of different and unconnected research lines. The role that transnational networks based on religious belief and ethnicity play in business, organized crime, and terrorism is recognized, and there are case studies of transnational communities of interest, but transnational communities are largely neglected in research on the emerging global structure. As indicated in the preceding section, we may expect transnational communities of interest to expand and multiply. Efforts at the level of the European Union may strengthen some regional scientific communities, while the development of science in countries such as India and China may extend the geographical scope of others. Transnational epistemic and policy communities will develop further if there is a further shift of policy-making competences to international institutions of governance, and as international non-governmental organizations acquire growing expertise, some of their members will become implicated in such communities. The transnational expansion of markets and the growth of corporations with subsidiaries spread over several countries are leading to the multiplication of transnational communities of skill and practice as specific types of expertise are needed. Multinational auditing firms (see Ramirez in this volume) provide a good example, while there is also the possible emergence of a transnational community of board members and top management (see Harvey and Maclean in this volume). Another undisputed growth sector is likely to be transnational online communities of discourse.

While there is already a plethora of transnational communities of interest, there is practically no comparative analysis of their formation, linkages with other social forms, and functions. There are several reasons for such neglect, which have to do with the dominant perspective in the study of globalization, as well as with the character of transnational communities themselves. The discipline of economics dominates the study of globalization, since this is considered to be mainly an economic process. Social scientists studying globalization, unless they perceive international relations as a power game in a realist perspective, focus on institutions of global governance, using one of the prevalent varieties of institutionalist analysis. The concept of governance that emphasizes forms of coordination other than hierarchy fits well with the nature of the evolving international political order, where inter-organizational networks and negotiation involving both private and public actors dominate. The notion of "community" emphasizes a different aspect of social reality, one subsumed under "culture" rather than "institution." It is no accident that Karin Knorr Cetina, to whom we owe the case study of the transnational community of currency market traders, previously studied the epistemic cultures of physicists and molecular biologists (Knorr Cetina 1999). As Buckler notes, the notion of community "is consonant with what is thought of as an 'interpretive' approach in social theory, which seeks an account deriving from the exploration of constitutive, intersubjective rules and beliefs that form the conditions of meaningful conduct" (Buckler 2007: 41). To date, however, an interpretive approach in International Relations is largely used in the analysis of international decision-making, and not in the search for a (new) social form such as transnational communities.

Because of their very nature, transnational communities are also difficult to discern, for methodological as well as substantive reasons. Again this holds particularly for communities of interest. To establish the existence of a community empirically is made difficult by the fact that in communities of interest, the prevalent mode of interaction is indirect. Not being formally organized, communities of interest are also weakly bounded; though having a certain property (for example, being a scientist, a lawyer, an advocate of forest preservation) may be an objective precondition, membership depends basically on subjective identification. It is therefore often difficult to distinguish communities empirically from mere social categories. While in simple natural systems phase transitions have clear cutting-points, subjective criteria such as "we" feeling and behavioral orientation can be met to varying degrees, blurring the boundaries between a social category and a community. Whether or not a set of persons sharing a given skill, value, and so on, constitutes a community is a matter of degree.[7]

Transnational communities of interest are also difficult to observe because they are transient, unstable social forms, tending either to dissolve or to evolve into a different social form. Professional as well as scientific communities give rise to associations, epistemic communities evolve into policy communities, which in turn crystallize in a policy network or give rise to an organization; an excellent example of such transitions is the case of "Creative Commons" (see Dobusch and Quack in this volume). An epistemic community may also become a social movement, and there are many cases of a social movement leading to the formation of a non-governmental organization or of a new political party. In the case of such transformations, the community does not simply disappear; it persists as an ideal basis of a transformed relationship and in this sense has been stabilized. In fact, because of their weak internal bonds and uncertain external boundaries, transnational communities of interest mostly do not exist as separate collectives, but are embedded in other types of collectives, not least in formal organizations – whether a community has given rise to an organization, or whether it has arisen among organization members with a similar skill or policy interest.

We can observe in everyday life that there is a special type of relationship among people belonging to different organizations who share something that is not of the given organization, such as being a professional of a certain kind. The expert knowledge, skills, or values which members of scientific, epistemic, and policy communities and communities of practice share are often connected with their holding certain positions within scientific, economic, and political organizations.[8] Here two different social forms – community and formal organization – interpenetrate; both develop with increasing specialization in the course of social, scientific, and technological development. The ubiquitous interpenetration of different social forms is easily overlooked where social forms in general and governance forms in particular are thought of as substances, as natural kinds, instead of as principles or mechanisms of coordination. Actually existing formal organizations, voluntary associations as well as hierarchically structured firms and government departments, do not represent "pure types" of social coordination or governance. In the context of governance theory, there has been a tendency to think in terms of market *or* hierarchy, hierarchy *or* network. Colin Crouch in particular has insisted that real social entities, whether single organizations, complex institutions, or a whole (capitalist) society, always manifest a mixture of governance forms (see Crouch 2005).[9] But hybrid forms, the combination of different modes of coordination, have generally not been popular topics in organization research. It is true that in discussions of the principal–agent relationship within and between organizations it is readily acknowledged that command relationships are usually seasoned with negotiation, and it is also true that organizational

cultures, generally conceived of as both pervasive and specific to one particular organization, have been studied. Neither of these two directions of
enquiry has, however, focused attention on the formation of communities of
interest across several organizations, let alone organizations located in different countries.

Different mechanisms operate in the emergence of different types of transnational communities of interest. Professional, and what has here been called
business communities develop where new kinds of skill or expertise are
needed and new positions are created in formal organizations. Through
interaction and the perception of like others a group identity forms, which
facilitates interaction and the exchange of information. Chinese bankers or
accountants establish contact with their counterparts in London in order
to compare modes of operating, thus contributing to the transnational
expansion of a professional community. But while corporations as well as
inter-governmental and transnational organizations are the seedbed of transnational professional and business communities, the reverse can also be true;
that is, a new community of practice can push not only for the creation of new
positions in existing organizations, but even for a new organization. The
transnational policy community that formed around the goal of forest preservation thus became instrumental in the establishment of a new certification
agency (see Bartley 2003 and Bartley and Smith in this volume). The epistemic
communities concerned with global warming and with renewable energy have
similarly been instrumental in the formulation of new legislation and in the
establishment of new production lines. Such processes, however, should not
be pictured as harmonious problem-solving efforts. Power is involved in
creating and structuring expert communities, in defining shared goals, and
in pushing for new regulation. A survey of the topics that transnational policy
communities are concerned with may read like a list of recognized global
problems, but it says next to nothing about the way these problems are, or are
not, going to be solved.

This leads directly to the question of the importance of transnational
communities as elements of the evolving global order. Generally speaking,
the consciousness of sharing a relevant personal characteristic with a group of
other people has a bonding effect; it creates social cohesion. Wiesenthal (2000:
48) argues that "natural" communities and "spontaneous" associations provide markets and organizations with the important resource of trust. The
socially integrating power of shared identity is, of course, internal to the
group. Shared identities define boundaries between "us" and "them," and
they can polarize and have a disintegrating effect on the larger social whole.

This holds especially for communities based on ascribed rather than achieved personal characteristics. Religion and ethnicity are often the basis of geographically circumscribed multi-bonded groups that come into conflict, as in the case of different ethnic groups in the former Yugoslavia or the religiously based neighborhoods of Sunnis and Shiites in Baghdad. But despite the fact that religion and ethnicity can still be important elements of individual identity, even beyond geographically circumscribed communities, the binding power of an ascriptive community is in most cases relatively weak on the transnational scale. At international meetings of whatever sort, people of like occupation or of like political convictions will feel they have more in common than those who are of the same religion or nationality. With increasing geographical scope, weakly bonded communities of interest prevail over strongly bonded traditional communities. The narrowly bonded transnational communities forming on the basis of shared achieved characteristics, such as knowledge, skills, office, position, or policy preference, have neither the power of internal integration nor the same externally polarizing effects as traditional primary groups. If anything, they provide crosscutting webs of loose couplings.

But this does not mean that community elements are functionally expendable in a globalizing world. Though scientists now typically work in organizations, cognitive innovations are still produced by scientific communities; for this reason Gläser (2006) calls them "productive communities." The national as well as international contacts a research organization has are held by specific scientists, and are lost to the organization if he or she leaves it. It is by virtue of the personal collegial relations maintained by its individual researchers that research organizations are linked into a given scientific field. Transnational communities play an important role also in the formation and operation of international markets (such as the global currency market), international production networks, inter-governmental networks, global public policy networks, and international regimes – that is, the forms of social coordination that dominate our image of the globalizing world. Though not organized for a specific purpose, transnational communities produce emergent effects by virtue of the fact that the expertise, skills, or convictions which are their basis guide the autonomous behavior of the community members. This is the way in which policy communities impact on policy development and link corporate actors into a policy network. Transnational epistemic communities, as well as communities of practice can generally be important agents of change. This also holds for business communities that not only sustain and regulate market processes, but create new markets. Professional communities help to diffuse, and can even be the driving force of innovations, which in turn can impact on, and change, the performance of the group. Such performance changes can also have significant remote effects; it does not seem too far-fetched, for instance, to see a link between the professional orientation characteristic of American lawyers and the adversarial culture of the USA.

Though it is often easier to identify an international organization, a transnational corporation, an inter-organizational network, a joint venture, and the contractual relations constituting a production chain than to identify transnational communities, there are good theoretical reasons to pay close attention to the role of "community" in the emerging global structures – the global economy, global governance, and the socio-cultural aspects of an emerging "world society." This holds not only for the communities of interest that have been the focus of this chapter, but also for transnational ethnic and religious communities. Both establish links among people across national boundaries and independent of nationality, and are thus part and parcel of the process of globalization – for better and for worse.

NOTES

1. It is in this sense that Wiesenthal (2000) includes community (*Gemeinschaft*) along with market and organization in his discussion of governance forms.
2. This definition is based on Gläser (2006: 310).
3. This is reminiscent of the Marxian distinction between *Klasse an sich* and *Klasse für sich*.
4. This is not the only characteristic that communities share with other forms of social coordination; trust, for instance, is as important for the functioning of markets as it is for solidarity among community members.
5. The use of "Community" in the early stages of European integration was soon recognized as a misapplication to a process that started as an effort to create a common market but which is slowly growing into a polity, and is now called a "Union."
6. See the special issue "Online Communities" of *Organization Studies* 28, 3 (2007).
7. Not all properties people can share lend themselves in the same way to community formation; studying cultural variance in the social relevance of ascribed and achieved personal characteristics would be an interesting task for social anthropology.
8. This connection is closer for government officials who are members of a policy community and for CEOs in a business community, in which the organizational role shapes values and skills, than for scientists in a scientific community, whose expertise antedates (and survives) their occupation of a given position.
9. As Wiesenthal puts it (2000: 47), "Alle beobachtbaren Sozialformen scheinen unter dem Dach des jeweils 'führenden' Prinzips auch die übrigen Prinzipien zu beheimaten" ("All observable social forms appear to include within the sphere of a particular 'leading principle' all other principles as well," translation by the author).

REFERENCES

Adler, E. 1992. "The emergence of cooperation: National epistemic communities and the international evolution of the idea of nuclear arms control," *International Organization* **46** (1): 101–45.

Bartley, T. 2003. "Certifying forests and factories: States, social movements, and the rise of private regulation in the apparel and forest product field," *Politics & Society* **31**: 433–64.

Buckler, S. 2007. "Theory, ideology, rhetoric: Ideas in politics and the case of 'community' in recent political discourse," *British Journal of Politics and International Relations* **9** (1): 36–54.

Crouch, C. 2005. *Capitalist diversity and change: Recombinant governance and institutional entrepreneurs.* Oxford University Press.

Epstein, P. J. 1997. "Beyond policy community: French agriculture and the GATT," *Journal of European Public Policy* **4** (3): 355–72.

Etzioni, A. 1993. *The spirit of community: Rights, responsibilities, and the communitarian agenda.* New York: Crown.

Etzioni, A. (ed.) 1995. *New communitarian thinking: Persons, virtues, institutions, and communities.* Charlottesville, VA: University Press of Virginia.

Fuchs, D. 2005. *Understanding business power in global governance.* Baden-Baden: Nomos.

Geiger, T. 1960. *Die Gesellschaft zwischen Pathos und Nüchternheit.* Copenhagen: Universitetsforlaget.

Gläser, J. 2006. *Wissenschaftliche Produktionsgemeinschaften: Die soziale Ordnung der Forschung.* Frankfurt a.M: Campus.

Haas, P. M. 1992a. "Banning chlorofluorocarbons: Epistemic community efforts to protect stratospheric ozone," *International Organization* **46** (1): 187–223.

Haas, P. M. 1992b. "Introduction: Epistemic communities and international policy coordination," *International Organization* **46** (1): 1–35.

Hillery, G. A. 1955. "Definitions of community: Areas of agreement," *Rural Sociology* **20**: 111–23.

Jessop, B. and Ngai-Ling, S. 2006. *Beyond the regulation approach: Putting capitalist economies in their place.* Cheltenham: Edward Elgar.

Jordan, G. 1990. "Sub-governments, policy communities and networks. Filling the old bottles?," *Journal of Theoretical Politics* **2** (3): 319–38.

Kessler, J. 2007. *Globalisierung oder Integration: Korrespondenzprobleme bei der empirischen Erfassung von Globalisierunsprozessen.* Bremen: TransState Working Papers No.53.

Knorr Cetina, K. 1999. *Epistemic cultures: How the sciences make knowledge.* Cambridge, MA: Harvard University Press.

Knorr Cetina, K. 2005. "How are global markets global? The architecture of the flow world," in Knorr Cetina, K. and Preda, A. (eds.), *The sociology of financial markets.* Oxford University Press, pp. 38–61.

Kogut, B. and Metiu, A. 2001. "Open source software development and distributed innovation," *Oxford Review of Economic Policy* **17** (2): 248–64.

Mayntz, R. 2001. "*Die Bestimmung von Forschungsthemen in Max-Planck-Instituten im Spannungsfeld wissenschaftlicher und außerwissenschaftlicher Interessen: Ein Forschungsbericht.*" MPIfG Discussion Paper 01/8. Cologne: Max Planck Institute for the Study of Societies.

Mayntz, R. 2003. "New challenges to governance theory," in Bang, H. P. (ed.), *Governance as social and political communication*. Manchester University Press, pp. 27–40.

Quack, S. 2007. "Legal professionals and transnational law-making: A case of distributed agency," *Organization* **14** (5): 643–66.

Rhodes, R. A. W. 1990. "Policy networks. A British perspective," *Journal of Theoretical Politics* **2** (3): 293–317.

Wenger, E. 1998. *Communities of practice: Learning, meaning, and identity*. New York: Cambridge University Press.

Wenger, E. 2001. "Communities of practice," in *International Encyclopedia of the Social and Behavioral Sciences*, Vol. 4. Amsterdam: Elsevier, pp. 2339–42.

Wiesenthal, H. 2000. "Markt, Organisation und Gemeinschaft als 'zweitbeste' Verfahren sozialer Koordination," in Werle, R. and Schimank, U. (eds.), *Gesellschaftliche Komplexität und kollektive Handlungsfähigkeit*. Frankfurt a.M.: Campus, pp. 44–73.

Part II

Classical communities with a transnational extension

3 The multiple layers of a transnational "imagined community": the notion and reality of the ethnic Chinese business community

Heidi Dahles

Introduction

In this chapter I shall critically explore the notion and reality of a transnational Chinese community and its role in transnational business activity. Chinese businesspeople, whether of mainland or diasporic background and operating in the global economy have been constructed as a close-knit and far-flung transnational community (cf. Redding 1990; Castells 1996; Weidenbaum and Hughes 1996; Ong and Nonini 1997; Suryadinata 1997; Douw 1999; Ong 1999; Chan 2000; Yeung and Olds 2000; Yeung 2002; Coe *et al.* 2003; Gomez and Hsiao 2004). Ethnic affiliation and cultural affinity have been regarded as principles organizing flows of capital, goods, knowledge, and people within this transnational community and across national borders, superseding national differences. Management gurus such as Kotkin (1993) have identified ethnic ties – allegedly more sentiment-based than other forms of social relations – as key to Asian business success. Ethnic Chinese businesses in particular are regarded as spearheads of Asia's economic growth, as well as a major global force. As the story goes, the large Chinese diaspora, with its global presence, enjoys special privileges when it comes to business ventures across national borders in general and into mainland China in particular. Coupled with a capacity for hard work and trust based on a Confucian value system that honors blood ties and (ritual) kinship, the Chinese business community seems to be a distinguishing feature of Chinese in contrast to Western capitalism, and to have engendered economic success where others have failed (Redding 1990).

Critics of the widely discussed assumption that a common ethnic identity and shared value system constitute a bond among the Chinese across national borders have pointed out that profit maximization motivates cooperative efforts among Chinese businesspeople and that their economic activities do not differ from any other capitalist venture (Jesudason 1989; Gomez 1999; Gomez and Hsiao 2004). From an institutional perspective, capitalist ventures are imbedded in ethnicity, culture, and identity, but these contextual factors are not static and unchangeable. Instead, they are socially constructed (see Djelic and Quack in this volume). They can be manipulated by governments, individuals, and organizations in pursuit of their own goals and, consequently, can become resources for the advancement of material and political interests (Yeung and Olds 2000: 15–16). While the institutional approach does not deny that Chinese businesspeople establish close-knit transnational communities, it rejects the proposition that these communities are based on ethnic affiliation as such. The ethnic Chinese are viewed as a community that is both socially constructed and mediated through institutional and policy frames, resulting in a loosely connected patchwork of partly converging and partly conflicting practices and principles.

Two communities that should prove this case in point are the Malaysian and the Singaporean ethnic Chinese. Under British rule united in the Malay Union, Malaysia and Singapore split into two separate nation-states in 1965. The separation was a consequence of ethnic disturbances between the Chinese and Malay populations. Singapore became a city-state and the only place outside of Greater China where the Chinese constitute the majority of the population. In Malaysia, the ethnic Chinese came to establish a substantial minority of 26 percent of the total population. Both ethnic Chinese communities are identified in terms of a shared "diasporic" condition and colonial legacy (Cohen 1997; Ong and Nonini 1997; Ong 1999; Dahles 2008a). However, while the Singaporean Chinese are regarded as the epitome of the Asian Miracle, their Malaysian counterparts constitute one of the least assimilated Chinese groups in Southeast Asia (Ong and Nonini 1997: 24–25; Butler *et al.* 2000: 261). In the late 1980s, when China re-entered the world economy, the ethnic Chinese in Southeast Asia realized their potential to act as a bridge between China and their respective countries of residence (Bolt 2000: 121). The Singaporean and the Malaysian Chinese business communities were among those who took their business to China. Their ventures, however, showed both striking similarities and sharp differences. Their shared history on the one hand, and diverging current positions in two separate nation-states on the other, make a comparison of the two ethnic Chinese communities worthwhile, as it may challenge the claim of a Chinese transnational (business) community based on ethnic affinity.

At an empirical level, this chapter focuses on the strategies employed and assets invested by Singaporean and Malaysian Chinese businesspeople in order to understand how they establish and pursue business in China. In particular, the analysis will compare the role of family linkages, non-family-related *guanxi* (good connections), and their respective nation-states in terms of facilitating or hampering their business ventures. At a theoretical level, the concept of transnational *community* will come under critical scrutiny (see Djelic and Quack, and Mayntz in this volume). Questions will be raised concerning the often unchallenged assumption that economic success relies on close-knit business communities intrinsically defined by ethnic affiliation and shared cultural values (see also Mayntz in this volume). To what extent is ethnic Chinese entrepreneurship a community-based phenomenon? To what extent do the ethnic Chinese constitute a community that takes precedence over national affiliation?

The chapter is structured as follows. After developing the current theoretical debate on ethnic Chinese businesses, it proceeds with some remarks on the available data. In subsequent sections, which include a portrayal of the development of Singaporean and Malaysian investments in China, the empirical findings are first presented and then discussed against the background of the theoretical framework. In the concluding section, some theoretical ideas on transnational business communities and ethnicity will be developed for further investigation.

Ethnic Chinese transnational business ventures: a theoretical framework

Inspired by Max Weber's work on Confucianism, efforts have been made to interpret ethnic Chinese economic accomplishments in terms of "Confucian capitalism" or "Chinese capitalism" (Redding 1990). This has often been described in terms of a communal form of capitalism in contrast with the liberal capitalism based on individual achievements that emerged in the West. Chinese capitalism is believed to be rooted in colonial times when – due to population pressure and poverty – many Chinese left their homes in the coastal provinces of Southern China to make a living in other parts of Southeast Asia. This collective historical background generated discourses of the sojourner and the diasporic entrepreneur. Although these discourses are extremely diverse, they imply that migration tends to entail experiences of displacement, host community hostility, racial discrimination, and limited opportunities for upward mobility (Cohen 1997: ix), but also fresh prospects stemming from new economic niches and possibilities for capital accumulation by engaging in middlemen occupations (Ong 1999: 13), as well as split loyalties stemming from ambivalence towards the country of residence (Ong and Nonini 1997: 24–25). As one's livelihood is easily jeopardized in such a situation, the reliance on family and shared ethnicity for labor, capital, information, and transactions may be the only viable option for minority immigrants (Redding 1990; Kotkin 1993; Fukuyama 1995; Douw 1999; Butler *et al.* 2000; Tsui-Auch 2005: 1191). This "culturalist" approach constructs the ethnic Chinese as an "imagined" community, and argues that Chinese familism facilitated the growth of their enterprises and the emergence of ethnic business networks that came to extend across the globe and provide the glue of what has come to be known as the transnational Chinese community.

However, some have questioned whether such large numbers of ethnic Chinese businesspeople share a bond based on a common ethnic identity in general and with the Chinese in China in particular. In an analysis of large incorporated Chinese-owned businesses in Malaysia Gomez (1999) identified a number of factors characteristic of Chinese business operations, a combination of which has sustained the growth of major Chinese-owned firms. These factors include entrepreneurial intelligence, access to relevant knowledge and other resources, and patronage relations with influential political players (Gomez 2003: 123). Gomez's approach emphasizes the impact of political power on economic actors and shows that culture is often utilized as an instrument for the protection of material and political interests, which may generate a parochial orientation in business ventures (Gomez and Hsiao 2004). This approach contests the existence of a transnational ethnic Chinese community based on a common culture, shared identity, and value system. Instead, culture and ethnicity are social phenomena that may be created, controlled, and manipulated by governments, businessmen, and community organizations in pursuit of their own goals. In other words, for scholars to understand the social significance of communities, they have – to use the language of Elias – to be recontextualized and reinserted within the framework of societal and political institutions (Elias 1974; see also Djelic and Quack in this volume).

This skepticism as regards culture as the organizing principle of transnational Chinese entrepreneurship also resonates in the institutional literature, in which the focus shifts away from community towards network-based benefits (Yeung 2002: 187–89; Dahles 2004, 2005). Ethnic Chinese businessmen accumulate social capital by maintaining membership of a number of – partly overlapping – networks, which enables them to circumvent failing vertical linkages, such as uncooperative bureaucrats. This development fits well with Simmel's picture of a world in which increasing individualization does not mean the disappearance of community, but rather the possible multiplication of overlapping community circles with different bases (Simmel 1971; see also Djelic and Quack in this volume). *Guanxi*-based personal trust is an expansive and inclusive principle that provides the "institutional thickness" that characterizes (ethnic) Chinese business networks in a globalizing business environment (Chan and Tong 2000: 74; Tan and Yeung 2000: 240; Yeung and Olds 2000: 15–16). Such networks may incorporate ties with officials in institutional environments conducive to Chinese business, but they may also exclude such linkages and enable ethnic Chinese businesspeople to operate despite bureaucratic obstacles.

The Chinese family may nevertheless play an important role in business networks as a provider of resources, such as capital for business start-ups, education and hands-on training of successors, and good connections, in other words, "traditional" *guanxi*. While Chinese families may have lost their position of overall capital provider to institutes of formal education providing professional training and to governments intervening in markets and controlling economic assets (Dahles 2004), they have also become part of larger networks of loosely connected sets of firms (Numazaki 2000: 172). Therefore, the role of inter- and intra-family linkages expanding beyond local boundaries and national borders as providers of (transnational) network relations as a way of facilitating calculated risk-taking must not be underestimated – whether based on affective ties or mutual benefit. In addition to family relations, non-family *guanxi* as offered by peers (former classmates, college friends, former co-workers, and so on) has come to figure as a significant support system among ethnic Chinese entrepreneurs in transnational business ventures (Dahles 2004, 2005), so creating a community-based network.

To summarize, for the purpose of establishing a framework for the analysis of Singaporean and Malaysian Chinese business ventures into China, I shall draw a distinction between state patronage on the one hand, and two entrepreneurial strategies in terms of (i) calculated risk-taking by employing "traditional" *guanxi* (family, lineage, and ethnic connections) and (ii) non-family *guanxi* (peer support and professional connections) on the other. If the "culturalist" approach is valid, both Singaporean and Malaysian Chinese businesspeople will be employing very similar cross-border strategies in taking their business to China and do so relatively undisturbed by their respective nation-state; if the "institutionalist" approach turns out to be more relevant, there should be sharp contrasts between Singaporean and Malaysian cross-border strategies, in particular regarding family dependence and bureaucratic interference.

Methodology

Underlying this chapter are two databases consisting of case studies of small and medium-sized enterprises in Singapore and in Kuala Lumpur (capital city of Malaysia). The case studies were prepared with the purpose of mapping intra- and interethnic relations in their transnational business ventures (in particular into China), whether long-standing or recently established. The Singaporean database includes 32 small and medium-sized companies with business in China or plans to do business there in the near future (see Appendix 3.1). The largest of these companies has 209 employees; the majority employ between 10 and 20 staff. Most of the companies located their business ventures in Southeastern China; only a few went as far as Beijing. The Malaysian database (source: Zwart 2006; see Appendix 3.2) consists of 21 case studies of small and medium-sized companies with investments in mainland China or plans to explore business possibilities in China in the near future.

The research methods applied in both the Singaporean and the Malaysian case may be characterized in terms of organizational ethnography, which is a way of doing fieldwork (Dahles 2008b). Fieldwork entails long-term involvement with the people under study with the aim of obtaining an in-depth understanding of the ways in which they construct their world and give meaning to their lives. The case studies in the current database were prepared in the course of fieldwork in Singapore and Kuala Lumpur, extending inter-mittently across a period of five years. The aim of these ethnographic case studies was to obtain an in-depth understanding of the ways in which ethnic entrepreneurs establish themselves (either independently or in coalition with foreign companies) across national borders. For this purpose, interviews and participant observation were designed to identify the resources that Chinese entrepreneurs applied during start-up, consolidation, and – in a few cases – relocation phases. The case studies presented in the next section represent "critical cases" (Yin 1989) for the purpose of examining whether and in what ways Chinese entrepreneurs rely on their ethnic affiliation and shared culture or rather draw on multiple resources, including family and non-family-based *guanxi*, including government patronage. These cases

Appendix 3.1 Overview of (planned or operational) cross-border ventures of the sample Singaporean Chinese businesses

No.	Sector	Entered China through	Other business locations
1	Business-to-business	Government linkages	**Malaysia**, Hong Kong
2	Trade		**Malaysia**, Hong Kong, Indonesia
3	Retail and wholesale Japanese owned	Non-family *guanxi*	Japan, **Malaysia**
4	Business-to-business		Relocated to **Malaysia**
5	Manufacturing	Government linkages	**Malaysia**
6	Business-to-business		**Malaysia**
7	Manufacturing	Family *guanxi*	**Malaysia**
8	Trade	Non-family *guanxi*	**Malaysia**, USA, New Zealand
	Hong Kong owned		
9	Trade		USA
	US owned		
10	Trade		Taiwan, **Malaysia**
	Taiwan owned		
11	Trade		New Zealand, Netherlands
12	Manufacturing German owned	Non-family *guanxi*	Hong Kong, **Malaysia**
13	Manufacturing		**Malaysia**, Indonesia, Philippines, Thailand
14	Manufacturing	Family *guanxi*	Indonesia, **Malaysia**
15	Agriculture	Government linkages	**Malaysia**
16	Business-to-business		**Malaysia**
	Malaysian owned		
17	Retail and wholesale		Thailand, **Malaysia**, USA
	US owned		
18	Manufacturing		Relocated to Middle East, Australia
19	Manufacturing		**Malaysia**
20	Trade	Family *guanxi*	Relocated to **Malaysia**
21	Trade		Relocated to **Malaysia**
22	Retail		**Malaysia**
23	Trade	Family *guanxi*	none
24	Trade		**Malaysia**, Thailand
25	Trade		Relocated to **Malaysia**
26	Manufacturing		**Malaysia**, Hong Kong, Indonesia, Thailand
27	Trade		**Malaysia**, India, Indonesia
28	Manufacturing		Relocated to India
29	Trade	Government linkage	**Malaysia**, Hong Kong
30	Business-to-business	Government linkage	Relocated to **Malaysia**, USA
31	Business-to-business		Relocated to **Malaysia**, Australia
32	Business-to-business		Relocated to UK

Note: Fieldwork by the author (and assistant) in Singapore in 2002–04.

Appendix 3.2 Overview of (planned or operational) cross-border ventures of the sample Malaysian Chinese businesses

No.	Sector	Entered China through	Other business locations
1	Manufacturing	Family *guanxi*	None
2	Manufacturing		Kuwait, Hong Kong, **Singapore**, Philippines, Indonesia, New Zealand
3	Manufacturing	Family *guanxi*	None
4	Retail	Family *guanxi*	Hong Kong, Taiwan, **Singapore**, Thailand
5	Trade Singaporean owned		**Singapore**
6	Manufacturing		**Singapore**, Philippines, India
7	Retail Hong Kong owned	Non-family *guanxi*	Hong Kong, **Singapore**, Australia, Indonesia, Germany
8	Manufacturing	Family *guanxi*	Hong Kong, Taiwan, Thailand, **Singapore**, Japan
9	Business-to-business		none
10	Manufacturing		Taiwan
11	Business-to-business	Family *guanxi*	none
12	Manufacturing	Family *guanxi*	USA, UK, Taiwan, Korea
13	Manufacturing	Family *guanxi*	Hong Kong, **Singapore**, Australia, Scotland
14	Business-to-business Japanese owned	Non-family *guanxi*	Japan, **Singapore**, Philippines, Thailand
15	Trade	Family *guanxi*	Hong Kong, **Singapore**, USA, UK, Brazil, Indonesia, New Zealand, Australia, Sweden, Thailand
16	Business-to-business Taiwanese owned	Family *guanxi*	**Singapore** and other ASEAN countries and India
17	Business-to-business		Hong Kong, Macao
18	Manufacturing	Family *guanxi*	Hong Kong, **Singapore**, Taiwan
19	Business-to-business		**Singapore**, Hong Kong, Taiwan, all ASEAN countries
20	Trade Japanese owned		Relocated to **Singapore**
21	Business-to-business		**Singapore**

Note: Zwart (2006)

were selected because they present striking similarities or sharp contrasts when Singaporean and Malaysian entrepreneurs are compared. If we encounter similarities and maintenance of common identity between Chinese from Singapore and Malaysia, the "culturalist" thesis finds support. If this is not the case, we need a more complex and differentiated concept of transnational ethnic communities.

Venturing into China: the Singaporean and Malaysian cases compared

China policies

While political relations between Malaysia and Singapore were strained after the separation in 1965, economic interdependence remained strong, not least because of manifold relations between the Chinese populations of the two countries. For Singapore, Malaysia has always been the most important partner in terms of trade and direct investment (Yeung 2002: 194–95). Conversely, Singapore is Malaysia's second most important trade partner (after the USA). Chinese firms in Singapore and Malaysia maintain long-standing trade relationships with partners in mainland China that may go back to colonial times when Chinese traders imported goods from China to cater to the growing Chinese migrant communities in the Malay Peninsula.

In mainland China, the economic reform and modernization program beginning in 1979 attracted Chinese overseas investors who had their ancestral roots there (Tan and Yeung 2000). The Singapore government was among the first to invest in China (Yeung 2002: 195). While economic exchange between Singapore and China increased, official relations between the two countries remained distant due to the threat emanating from China's support of the communist parties in all countries in the region. While Malaysia was among the first Southeast Asian nations to enter into diplomatic relations with China (in 1974), economic relations did not develop until the 1990s. Partly, this was due to the communist threat. More important, however, were intra-Malaysian ethnic relations. The Malaysian government objected to economic relations that would strengthen the economic position of its ethnic Chinese population as this might undermine the New Economic Policy (NEP) – launched in the 1970s – which was aimed at improving the economic position of the Malay population vis-à-vis the ethnic Chinese. Whereas in the 1980s the Malaysian government criticized their ethnic Chinese entrepreneurs for trading with China through Singaporean agents, in the 1990s Malaysia executed an amazing turnabout in its relations with China. Malaysian Prime Minister Mahathir started to encourage ethnic Chinese entrepreneurs to act as a bridge between the Malaysian economy and other Asian economies, including the mainland Chinese market. This new strategy has to be understood as part of the "Look East" policy for Malaysian foreign investments – targeting Japan in particular – in order to counteract the increasing Western impact on the Malaysian economy and cultural values (Bolt 2000: 122).

Since the establishment of diplomatic relations between Singapore and China in 1990, there has been a rapid increase in capital investments in China. China is among the most important countries for Singaporean investment abroad, and Singapore is among the largest foreign investors there (Bolt 2000: 135–36; Kumar *et al.* 2005). Singaporean government-led companies (GLCs) in joint ventures with third-country firms or Chinese state investment agencies have become involved in massive projects, such as the development of ports, industrial parks, and infrastructural projects, which require huge injections of financial capital (Chan and Tong 2000). While for the latter investments the term "political entrepreneurship" has been coined to describe the role of the Singapore government as one of the most important institutional forces behind Singaporean investments in China (Tan and Yeung 2000: 239), small companies benefited from family relationships that had been maintained through a long period of political hostility between China and Singapore (Kuah 1999: 143). The Malaysian government has been more conservative in its dealings with China. It was only when the China policy of neighbor Singapore started to bear fruit that Malaysia actively pursued economic relations with China. In the course of the 1990s alone, Malaysian trade with mainland China quadrupled (Bolt 2000: 122).

Venturing into China

The preferential use of personal resources such as family ties and various forms of ethnic affiliation (expressed through lineage, dialect group, hometown associations, and so on) and the intermingling of economic and sentimental reasons for doing business in China are among the characteristics of a strategy that "culturalist" scholars describe as "typically Chinese," and which I shall label as "traditional" *guanxi*. A variant of this entrepreneurial strategy is the utilization of non-family *guanxi*, in terms of which friends and professional relations have come to replace or supplement blood and ethnic ties. This variant has gained in importance with increasing pressure to send children to prestigious schools and overseas universities and for people to enroll in postgraduate programs in the course of their professional careers. Contacts established through these schools and programs may become an integral part of a person's social capital, to be used strategically whenever the opportunity arises (Dahles 2004, 2005). Conversely, the emergence of Singapore and Malaysia as regional centers of business services and high-tech industries gave rise to myriad new business strategies, such as subcontracting and other cooperative relations with either GLCs or multinational corporations (MNCs). The use of both government patronage and personal assets reflects Chinese entrepreneurs' adaptable approach to doing business and may be described in terms of pursuing new opportunities and mutual interests, as institutionalist scholars argue. The data presented below allow us to identify differences in the ways in which ethnic Chinese businessmen who use the two strategies separately or in combination respond to business problems in China. For each of the two strategies (traditional *guanxi* and non-family *guanxi*), two exemplary cases from Malaysia and Singapore will be presented (in box format) and compared with a view to identifying striking similarities or contrasts between the two categories of the same ethnic but diverging national background.

The "typically Chinese" way

When asked about their reasons for venturing into mainland China, ethnic Chinese entrepreneurs in Singapore and Kuala Lumpur produced answers that showed a mixture of calculation and sentiment. The majority referred to the economic opportunities that this huge country seemed to offer, but they also mentioned the advantages of having relatives in China, speaking the language, and their familiarity with and the pleasure taken in "Chinese ways of doing business." One of my third-generation Chinese informants, John Lee,[1] director of the Singaporean manufacturing firm "Wings Asia," firmly believes that his proficiency in Cantonese will provide him with an excellent start for his planned business venture into China, although he is entirely without connections there. Conversely, Clarence Kong, finance manager of the high-tech VBU Software Developers in Kuala Lumpur relates that his firm entered China through distant relatives of the deceased founding father of the enterprise, who hailed from Xiamen in Fujian province, Southern China. In his case, family linkages paid off and the business venture proved successful. In other cases, expectations of ancestral ties and ethnic linkages providing a smooth entrance into China landed entrepreneurs from Singapore and Kuala Lumpur in trouble (as illustrated by Cases 1 and 2).

In Case 1, Jimmy Tong firmly believes in shared ethnicity as a factor of trust and business success when carving out the internationalization strategy for his enterprise. When he encounters failure, he blames officialdom instead of failing ethnic ties. And when his distant kin leave him in the lurch, he holds the shortcomings of the political system responsible for low levels of education or the lack of respect for intellectual property. Jimmy Tong is not an isolated example of an ethnic Chinese holding on to the "community" discourse as a vehicle for business ventures, as Case 2 below illustrates.

Case 1: Trust in ethnicity

Jimmy Tong, a chemist with a degree from a Taiwanese university, started his factory manufacturing a floor cleaning product in 1993. He had to start from scratch because no one else in his family had ever been an entrepreneur. Like his grandfather, who had emigrated from Guizhou (China), his father and brothers were all fishermen in Sabah, a province in East Malaysia. His business went well, however, and soon Jimmy was able to get a bank loan to buy a bigger factory.

Success in the domestic market generated a wish to expand across the Malaysian border. Remembering his grandfather's stories about Guizhou, he decided to tackle the huge market of mainland China through partners who knew the country better than he did. Therefore, he re-established long-lost ties with his distant kin. His plan was to have his relatives take care of the imports and sales, including customs clearance. However, the plans went awry. First of all, Chinese customs demanded that the product be tested before being allowed to enter China. Jimmy refused as he feared that these tests would reveal the secret formula of his floor cleaner and the Chinese would imitate his product. Secondly, his relatives failed to handle this matter adequately for lack of education, experience, and good connections.

After seeing his first attempt fail, Jimmy plans to enter China through a Hong Kong agent, who was introduced to him by his Singaporean agent. Going through Hong Kong seems a safer option to him: "Singapore and Hong Kong is almost the same [as Malaysia]. Because the people there are more rich and their education is higher [than in China]. So, we feel comfortable there. ... The last time, it was managed by the British, just like here [in Malaysia]."

(Interview 2004)

As Case 2 (in support of Case 1) illustrates, a firm belief in the reliability of family ties exists among ethnic Chinese, irrelevant of where kin are located and how distant the blood ties may be. The betrayal by distant kin in China is blamed on the weakness of these blood ties, not on the failure of kinship as grounds for trust. Interestingly, the Luhs did not lose faith in the basic strategy they used to establish cross-border business coalitions, namely building on family relations. Hence, instead of persuading businesspeople to shift their cross-border business strategies from a kin-based approach to a "rationalist" one, kin maintains its role in Chinese cross-border business strategies.

Comparing the Singaporean and Malaysian cases, the interconnectedness of Malaysian and Singaporean families across the border is striking, underlining their shared colonial history under British rule. In the case of the Luh family one may argue that it is as much Malaysian as it is Singaporean. Where close family ties are lacking, as in the example of Jimmy Tong, an intertwining of ethnicity and history replaces kin, inducing Jimmy Tong to put his trust in his Singapore

---

> ## Case 2: Trust in distant kin
>
> ### Principal Refrigerating & Air Conditioning
>
> This company was established in 1965 by the brother of its present owner as a firm trading in household items. The business was subsequently transformed into a successful exporter of refrigeration spare parts. Principal R&A is a family business owned by Mr. Luh, a Singaporean Chinese, and managed by his Malaysian Chinese wife. The firm is embedded in the Luhs' extended family network, forty members of which are involved in the business as branch managers, staff or associates. Principal R&A has Singapore as its home base and offices in Kuala Lumpur and Johore Bahru (Malaysia). These offices are managed by Mrs. Luh's brothers. Principal R&A was one of the first small entrepreneurs from Singapore to enter China, as early as 1988. The Luh couple established business links with distant kin in Hong Kong, who ran a few companies across the border. The Luhs entrusted them with the capital to start trade offices in mainland China. The Hong Kong relatives took the money to China but invested it in their own manufacturing businesses, which went bankrupt. After this failure, the Luhs decided to play it safe. They consolidated their Singapore business and started to expand their Malaysian branch offices through Mrs. Luh's close kin. "One has to be careful doing business in China," says Mrs. Luh, "in Malaysia with close relatives, we don't expect bad surprises." Although Mrs. Luh is aware of the different positions of the ethnic Chinese in the two countries, she denies that there are any cultural differences between the Singaporean and the Malaysian Chinese. After all, she remarked, "Malaysia and Singapore used to be a British colony."
>
> (Interview 2002)

and Hong Kong agents. Singaporeans and Malaysians demonstrate the same ignorance about China, having little clue how much things have changed since their (grand-)parents left, while the old China is revived over and over again in the stories they tell. Singaporean and Malaysian businesspeople naïvely put their trust in and make business decisions based on an "imagined community" that draws on frozen images of the past. These images are brutally destroyed once they encounter present-day China. As a consequence, they may change from defining their identity as rooted in mainland China to locating their roots in colonial Southeast Asia under British rule.

Putting trust in non-family *guanxi*

Among young entrepreneurs in Singapore and Malaysia connections established during a period of study abroad (which implies that they are English-language educated) with former employers and colleagues, and professional associations play a rather prominent role. These connections directly or indirectly provide a vehicle for launching businesses across the border into Southeast

Asia, China, and the Asia Pacific region, often with the ultimate aim of starting a successful venture in the United States. While many young Singaporeans and Malaysians leave the country to pursue tertiary education overseas, which, besides diplomas and certificates, yields them an international network of peers, there is also a home-based source of such connections. For decades, the governments invited foreign multinational corporations to invest and to locate their regional head offices in Singapore and Kuala Lumpur. When the Singaporean government started to promote the establishment of an "external wing" of the domestic economy, these MNCs took on the role of intermediaries in introducing Singaporean entrepreneurs to foreign markets. The preferred role of Singaporean businesspeople as subcontractors of foreign multinational corporations provided crucial assets in venturing beyond Singapore. Malaysian entrepreneurs had to fend for themselves much more than their Singaporean counterparts as their government did not instigate measures to support ethnic Chinese businesses. This also applied to government trade missions across the border to which the Singaporean GLCs invited local entrepreneurs. Basically, it was a risk-avoidance strategy that allowed small companies to surf the wave of their main clients' expansion, benefiting from their local knowledge, their networks, and contacts with foreign state agencies, as Case 3 below illustrates.

Recently, both Singaporean and Malaysian Chinese companies working for large Japanese or Western MNCs were more or less forced to do business across the border when their clients decided to cut costs by outsourcing or relocating some of their production units in low-pay countries in the region. This applies in particular to Japanese companies targeting China. Due to strained political relations between Japan and China that have deep historical roots, Japanese enterprises prefer to work through their subsidiaries in Southeast Asia. However, benign diplomatic relations at nation-state level may not render sufficient *guanxi* at firm level, as illustrated by Case 4.

The establishment of good connections by nurturing highly skilled employees through in-house training and subsequently entrusting them with the management of a subsidiary across borders may at first sight seem to be a new pattern that diverges from the ethnicity- and family-based strategies of the Luhs or Jimmy Tong. Knowledge-based approaches seem to do away with outdated notions that have sometimes hampered Singaporean and Malaysian business success in China. However, on closer inspection, these new and innovative strategies are again embedded in the "ethnic community" discourse. After all, Com-Elect endeavored to develop a highly skilled workforce by targeting Chinese co-ethnics from Singapore, Malaysia, Hong Kong, and

---

Case 3: MNC-based *guanxi*

Com-Elect Special Products

This company was established in 1990 with only three staff members, including the founder, who also acted as owner-manager. The firm produced components such as semiconductors, metal finishings, and circuit boards under contract to Singapore-based MNCs in the electronics sector, including Philips, AMD, and Hitachi. The company did well and employed twenty people by 1995. Upon obtaining ISO certification, Com-Elect entered into a process of expansion and restructuring. Permanent sales offices were established in Malaysia, Thailand, the Philippines, and Indonesia. The staff of these offices, consisting of sales representatives and technical personnel, were trained in Singapore and came back regularly for audits. In Singapore, in addition to the manufacturing, quality control, and marketing divisions, an R&D team was set up in 2000, consisting of engineers from Singapore, Malaysia, Hong Kong, and China. An employment agent was entrusted with the recruitment of highly trained and specialized experts, all of whom were Singapore Chinese. In 2002, the company, with forty employees, shifted production to Suzhou, the Singapore GLC-operated industrial park in China. The Suzhou plant did not involve local partners; manpower was relocated from Singapore to China to start operations. Eventually, the Singaporean production workers were substituted by Chinese workers to cut production costs. At the time of the interview, the Chinese branch was still in operation and, according to its general manager Mr. Tang, doing well. The transfer of the industrial park to the Chinese authorities did not seem to have affected his firm negatively. On the contrary, with cheap production in China he was able to invest in his R&D division at home.

(Interview 2002)

China and socializing them in Singaporean business culture by means of recurring audits in the city-state. It seems that Singaporean companies adhere to the belief that skills, knowledge, and expertise should be shared, as long as these assets remain in Chinese hands. Having said that, utilizing *guanxi* with foreign companies on behalf of China ventures does not diverge from the "ethnic community" discourse either. After all, the Japanese parent firm of Universal Technology KL reasoned that Japanese direct investments in China were doomed to fail and therefore turned to its Singaporean/Malaysian subsidiary to mediate its China venture, referring explicitly to the ethnic affiliation of the Malaysian manager.

In summary, the ventures of Singaporean and Malaysian firms into China combine traditional and modern ways of establishing business. They may trust in ethnic ties, rely on family relations and professional networks, follow government-sponsored trade missions, or take advantage of the relocation of their main clients. Often, they utilize all of these opportunities at the same time. But whatever strategy they follow, ethnicity as a binding factor

---

Case 4: Misjudgment of *guanxi*

Universal Technology KL

The Malaysian branch of Universal Technology KL is a subsidiary of the Singaporean regional office of the Japanese corporation that trades in machinery and electronic equipment all over Southeast Asia. The firm has a long-standing presence in the region: twenty-seven years in Singapore and eight years in Kuala Lumpur. The Kuala Lumpur branch was established by a friendly takeover of their local agent. Mr. Lee Kam Seng, third-generation ethnic Chinese, trained as an architect, with working experience in the construction and trade sectors. He lived in England and Germany for a couple of years and was headhunted by the Japanese to become their local agent. When Universal Technology Japan took over his agency, he was appointed general manager.

The Japanese head office, tempted by the success stories of East Asian firms doing business in China, began to cherish great expectations concerning such a move. In order to enhance their business opportunities, they decided to leave the start-up in mainland China in the hands of their Malaysian branch manager. After all, they assumed that both the good relations between China and Malaysia on the one hand, and Mr. Lee's Chinese roots on the other, would facilitate easy entry into the huge Chinese market.

Mr. Lee had no experience of China whatsoever when he was sent to Beijing in 2000 to start the Universal Technology office. He was overwhelmed by the system which was still subject to government intervention at all levels. At the time, foreign companies were forced to enter into joint ventures with local firms. According to Mr. Lee, the company he had to collaborate with looked like a private firm but was actually a front for a state-owned enterprise. This collaboration did not contribute to a smooth market entry. On the contrary, it prevented him from attaining the targets set by his Japanese bosses. "What you have sold them [to the Chinese partners], they sold elsewhere; they changed their minds and came back to claim warranties from you or asking for a refund. So, due to the fact that we were just a new setup in their country and we didn't want to lose, we tried to accommodate – until we failed." All in all, Mr. Lee's career as branch manager in China was short-lived.

(Field notes, Kuala Lumpur, 2004)

---

constitutes a persistent theme – either cherished by the Chinese business-people themselves or reproduced by governments or foreign investors. Does this imply that Chinese transnational communities are based on ethnic affiliation, as the "culturalist" perspective claims? The last two sections will attempt to answer this question.

Relocating the comfort zone: analysis

In this section I shall address the relationship between the imagined transnational community of ethnic Chinese and the national communities of which they are citizens. How do the ethnic Chinese in Singapore and Malaysia juggle between multiple loyalties? How do they capitalize on complementarities and tensions between transnational and national loyalties in developing business strategies (see also Morgan and Kubo; Harvey and Maclean; Fetzer; and Ramirez in this volume)? At first sight, there are many similarities between the ways in which Singaporean and Malaysian companies organize their ventures into China and respond to problems and failures. Overall, their expectations at the start of such ventures tend to be that their membership of the "imagined community" of ethnic Chinese, their proficiency in Mandarin and/or local dialects, and – sometimes – their family linkages in mainland China will provide them with business advantages. In our case studies, almost all located their start-ups in Southeast China – traditionally the area from which the Southeast Asian ethnic Chinese originate. Their risk-reducing strategies during the start-up phase were usually characterized by attempts to utilize different sources of *guanxi*, such as connections, whether family- or non-family-based. In times of crisis, upon business failure, or for ventures into new and unknown markets, they either diversified or relocated business to their closest neighbor: Malaysian entrepreneurs turned to Singapore and Singaporean entrepreneurs to Malaysia (see Appendices 3.1 and 3.2). Of the fifty-five Singaporean firms in my sample, twenty-six have a subsidiary or branch office in Malaysia, and fourteen Malaysian firms have a branch or representative in Singapore. Both Singaporean and Malaysian firms use Hong Kong subsidiaries or head offices as brokers to facilitate moves into China, or leave Chinese business entirely to their Hong Kong counterparts. Frequently, contract law, based on the British legal system that has survived decolonization in many former British colonies, was mentioned as an important advantage and, at the same time, a binding factor for doing business in countries with a common British colonial past, an institutional legacy of both the Singaporean and the Malaysian developmental regimes (Dahles 2008a). Upon closer analysis, however, there are striking differences in terms of cross-border ventures and crisis/failure management between Singaporean and Malaysian Chinese entrepreneurs.

Comparing the ways in which the Singaporeans and Malaysians in my sample prepared for their business ventures into China, the idea of a shared Chinese identity and ancestral linkages as a binding factor was more pronounced among the Malaysian businesspeople. Ten of our Malaysian interviewees explicitly mentioned their family-based *guanxi* as a motive for taking their business into China. Only three Singaporeans cited these linkages as significant for their China venture; some even dismissed the suggestion that Chinese identity of any kind would facilitate business success in China. "I may look Chinese, but I am a Singaporean," commented Henry Chan, a software producer with offices in Shanghai and Kuala Lumpur. And Johnny Lim, a Singaporean iron and steel producer, said: "China is very Chinese; by comparison, Singapore is not Chinese at all" (interview 2003). For Lim, his awareness of the cultural differences between the two countries resulted in successful deals with Chinese partners. For others, the same awareness became a reason to pull out of China. "We do things different here in Singapore," was a much repeated comment in this context.

The differences between Malaysians and Singaporeans in how they approach family-based *guanxi* as a business-related asset is also visible when it comes to actually utilizing family linkages in the process of establishing and operating a business. Seven Malaysians but only three Singaporeans mention family members being involved in their China venture (see Appendices 3.1 and 3.2). This may be related to the different positions of the ethnic Chinese in Singapore and Malaysia. Ethnic Chinese businesspeople, in particular in the SME segment, suffered under the restrictions imposed on them by the NEP and were thrown back on their family-based resources because of lack of economic capital and patronage linkages with power-holders (Kahn 1996: 69). Encouraged by Chinese nationalists in their attempts to keep Chinese norms and values alive, these small entrepreneurs developed a strong sense of Chinese identity that facilitated their business ventures into China once economic and political conditions were conducive to this (Zwart 2006). In Singapore, the government orchestrated both investments in China and the notion of a shared Chinese identity. In fact, the Singapore government recreated the "imagined community" after having attempted to destroy it in its formative years as a nation-state. This suggests that the political construction of ethnic "imagined communities" does not require a territory, either existing or projected (in contrast to Anderson 2006; see also Djelic and Quack in this volume). For Singaporean entrepreneurs, ethnic and family ties, though not irrelevant, seemed to be less important to the success they hoped to reap from their China ventures.

In terms of the strategic utilization of non-family-based *guanxi*, it is worth noting that more Singaporeans than Malaysians mentioned former college friends as partners in or supporters of their China business ventures. This difference may be related to Singaporeans being more affluent and therefore able to pursue an education either in Singapore or overseas. This yields them a network of peers some of whom eventually rise to positions of political or economic power. In Malaysia, such high-powered networks can be found only among the English-educated Chinese entrepreneurial elite, not among the small and medium-sized business owners (Lee 2003: 38–39). On the other hand, both Malaysians and Singaporeans are equally endowed with opportunities to enter China in the slipstream of foreign-owned companies. A number of our interviewees run a foreign-based subsidiary or branch office in Malaysia or Singapore and act as broker for the owner in China. As already mentioned, Japanese firms prefer their Southeast Asian subsidiaries to launch the business in China, as do Western companies for the purpose of bridging cultural differences. Taiwanese firms turn to Southeast Asian subsidiaries, for that matter, to circumvent political restrictions. While only a decade ago Singaporean businesses may have enjoyed an advantage as possible brokers, Malaysia has now caught up as a Southeast Asian business hub. In turn, both Singaporean and Malaysian firms use Hong Kong subsidiaries or head offices as brokers to facilitate moves into China or leave Chinese business to their Hong Kong counterpart entirely.

One difference between Singaporean and Malaysian businesspeople is the extent to which their respective national governments are involved in their China business ventures. Among our Malaysian interviewees, only one referred to government policy and the lifting of restrictions on Chinese education, language, and culture as a source of encouragement for their China venture. No financial or material government support was extended to the Malaysian firms that ventured into China. Among the Singaporeans, on the other hand, a number of government linkages on their route to China were mentioned. Firm owners and managers listed government funding for product development and expert input, repeated government tenders, financial support under special programs, government scholarships, invitations to trade missions, and even government loans. However, these privileges were shared by only five of our interviewees. It seems that the "happy few" who meet all the eligibility requirements for small and medium-sized businesses benefit from government schemes most. The vast majority of interviewees contended that self-reliance is necessary for Singaporean companies to survive and prosper, whether at home or in cross-border ventures. "Here one cannot just borrow money from the government; one needs to be already very successful to qualify for the government help," one of our informants commented.

Conclusions

The number of Singaporeans and Malaysians expanding their businesses to China has increased significantly since the 1990s. The new generation of ethnic Chinese entrepreneurs is attracted to China because they are looking for new markets, product diversification, and low-cost production sites. To enter China in a risk-avoiding way, they establish cooperative ventures with close or distant kin, joint ventures with other ethnic Chinese private firms, Chinese agents, state-owned companies, and foreign MNCs based on mutual interest. The primacy of ethnicity and family linkages as success factors in cross-border ventures in general and into China in particular forms a persistent discourse permeating business decisions and cross-border strategies. From a macroeconomic perspective, China is a very promising market due to sheer numbers (of both potential consumers and labor), but microeconomic experience often teaches otherwise. China is difficult to penetrate, as the multi-layered state bureaucracy requires cautious handling. The internationally less experienced Singaporeans and Malaysians may not be well equipped to deal with the complexities of doing business in China. Ethnic ties may facilitate a smooth entrance, but often seem to be part of the manifold obstacles that ethnic Chinese investors encounter in China and lead to failure. Doing business "the Chinese way" may take the disenchanting form of mainland Chinese partners disregarding contracts and corrupt local governments delaying licenses indefinitely.

Ethnic Chinese born, raised, and educated in Singapore or Malaysia are often not sufficiently aware of the changes that China has undergone in recent decades. Their image of Chinese identity is characterized by two cardinal mistakes. First, they think that their personal resources establishing their Chinese identity are identical with those of the older generation who have first-hand recollections of China. Second, they think that mainland China has remained the same as it was when their parents maintained connections with their place of birth or ancestral village. However, it is several decades since the older generation was actually involved in mainland China. In the meantime, both Singapore and Malaysia have developed into modern nation-states with a British colonial history and a multicultural present. Memories of a Chinese past are based on frozen images and stereotypical representations of China in the ethnic Chinese imagination. The assumption that looking Chinese, speaking the language, and sharing "Asian values" constitutes a sound basis for business success has turned out to be rather naïve. Societal transformations in both China and Southeast Asia make part of the social capital which the ethnic Chinese assume they possess redundant in the present situation.

While the ethnic Chinese in Singapore and Malaysia share a diasporic condition and the same colonial legacy, the differences between them are intertwined with the diverging politics of identity in Singapore and Malaysia. The deconstruction of these politics involves an analysis of the role of state patronage towards ethnic groups, social engineering of majority and minority statuses, and the social construction of an imagined community. The Singapore government was overoptimistic in its expectation that the Singapore economy could be transplanted to mainland China, so solving the problem of the tiny home market. The government-orchestrated self-presentation of the Singaporean businessman (or woman) as a cultural hybrid versed in both Western and Asian cultural repertoires and able to mediate between and benefit from both worlds collapsed in the face of mounting business problems. Cultural affinity, speaking the language, understanding business practices, and even obtaining government support turned out to be insufficient guarantee of lasting success. In terms of ethnic loyalty, the lesson learned by the Singaporean entrepreneurs was that Chinese identity represents rather a disadvantage than an advantage in China. This lesson has contributed to a changing attitude towards the ethnic Chinese in Malaysia, their closest neighbors. Many of those who delete China from their foreign venture planning (re-)turn to Malaysia instead. The relationship between the Singaporean and Malaysian Chinese is ridden with problems that reflect the tense relations between the two nation-states, but Malaysia also represents a comfort zone to turn to in order to recover from business failures in mainland China and to reconsider business strategies for the future. Because of the close relationship comprising a shared past and a separate present, love and hatred, similarities and differences, acceptance and rejection, the social capital of both Singaporean and Malaysian ethnic Chinese is well suited for joint business ventures.

In Malaysia, on the other hand, many entrepreneurs take pride in their alleged Chinese identity and management practices. This attitude has to be understood against the background of their ambivalent position in the Malaysian nation-state, a position that for decades forced them to draw on their ethnic and family-related resources, extending across national borders into Southeast Asia and even mainland China. When business ventures into China became possible and even encouraged by the Malaysian government, ethnic and family connections were strategically employed for business start-ups. However, this reliance on traditional *guanxi* declined in the process. Malaysian entrepreneurs – finding out the hard way that business conditions in Malaysia were not so bad after all – did not relocate their businesses, but reconsidered their assumption about national identity. The crises and failures they experienced in China fueled their identification with the Malaysian nation-state. Redefining Malaysia in terms of a post-colonial society with a British legal heritage, they came to focus their cross-border business activities on countries with a similar legal system. In the words of Djelic and Quack in Chapter 1 of this volume, they "shifted their order of priorities with respect to community-affiliation."

In the final analysis, the concept of a transnational Chinese community does not denote a homogeneous and static entity, but one which comprises multiple loyalties and at the same time is rapidly being transformed into a "meta community," a loosely connected patchwork of partly diverging but nevertheless inter-related subcommunities (see Djelic and Quack in this volume). It is clear that *community* is identified not in the primordial terms of shared ethnicity but in the situational and contextual terms of a common history that comprehends ancestral roots in (Southern) China and a sojourner past as much as a shared colonial experience. This aspect has not been acknowledged by current institutionalist theorists who attribute the success of Chinese businesses to overlapping networks rooted in economic, social, and political relations. One dimension to be included in this framework – giving it historical depth – is embeddedness in institutional legacies (Morgan and Quack 2005). This embeddedness may be strategically employed, abandoned, even silenced and again revitalized under rapidly changing conditions in the global economy (see, for example, Harvey and Maclean; Morgan and Kudo; Ramirez; and Fetzer in this volume).

Acknowledgments

The data collection was implemented under the sponsorship of the NWO-related Aspasia program, entitled "Organizational Culture in Transborder Regions," which was coordinated by the author in 2000–05. The author wishes to acknowledge the contribution of Dr. Helen Kopnina who collected the case studies of small and medium-sized Singaporean Chinese enterprises in the period 2002–03 as part of the Aspasia program. Conversely, Dr. Esther Zwart established the mirroring database on Malaysian Chinese small and medium-sized enterprises in Kuala Lumpur in the period 2003–05. Her research project, which resulted in a dissertation entitled "In Pursuit of Comfort. The Transnationalization Process of Malaysian Chinese Small and Medium Enterprises" (Zwart 2006), was part of the above-mentioned Aspasia program.

NOTE

1. All personal and company names used in this chapter are pseudonyms.

REFERENCES

Anderson, B. 2006 [1983], *Imagined communities*, London and New York: Verso.

Bolt, P. J. 2000. *China and Southeast Asia's ethnic Chinese: State and diaspora in contemporary Asia*. Westport, CT: Praeger.

Butler, J. E., Brown, B. and Chamornmarn, W. 2000. "*Guanxi* and the dynamics of overseas Chinese entrepreneurial behaviour in Southeast Asia," in Li, J. T., Tsui, A. S. and Weldon, E. (eds.), *Management and organizations in the Chinese context*. Houndmills: Macmillan, pp. 245–68.

Castells, M. 1996. *The rise of the network society*. Oxford: Blackwell.

Chan, K. B. 2000. "State, economy and culture: Reflections on the Chinese business networks," in Chan, K. B. (ed.), *Chinese business networks: State, economy and culture*. Singapore: Prentice Hall and Nordic Institute of Asian Studies, pp. 1–13.

Chan, K. B., and Tong, C. K. 2000. "Singaporean Chinese doing business in China," in Chan, K. B. (ed.), *Chinese business networks: State, economy and culture*. Singapore: Prentice Hall and Nordic Institute of Asian Studies, pp. 71–85.

Coe, N. M., Kelly, P. F. and Olds, K. 2003. "Globalization, transnationalism, and the Asia-Pacific," in Peck, J. and Yeung, H. W. C. (eds.), *Remaking the global economy: Economic-geographical perspective*. London: Sage, pp. 45–60.

Cohen, R. 1997. *Global diasporas*. London: Routledge.

Dahles, H. 2004. "Venturing across borders. Investment strategies of Singapore-Chinese entrepreneurs in mainland China," *Asian Journal of Social Sciences* **32** (1): 19–41.

Dahles, H. 2005. "Culture, capitalism and political entrepreneurship: Transnational business ventures of the Singapore-Chinese in China," *Culture and Organization* **11** (2): 45–58.

Dahles, H. 2008a. "Entrepreneurship and the legacies of a developmental state: Singapore enterprises venturing across national borders," *Journal of Developmental Entrepreneurship* **13** (4): 485–508.

Dahles, H. 2008b. "Organizational ethnography," in Clegg, S. and Bailey, J. R. (eds.), *International Encyclopedia of Organization Studies*, vol. 3. London: Sage, pp. 1066–67.

Douw, L. 1999. "The Chinese sojourner discourse," in Douw, L. Huang, C. and Godley, M. R. (eds.), *Qiaoxiang ties: Interdisciplinary approaches to "cultural capitalism" in South China*. London: Kegan Paul, pp. 22–44.

Elias, N. 1974. "Forward: Towards a theory of communities," in Bell, C. and Newby, H. (eds.), *The sociology of community: A selection of readings*. London: Frank Cass, pp. ix–xli.

Fukuyama, F. 1995. *Trust: The social virtues and the creation of prosperity*. New York: Free Press.

Gomez, E. T. 1999. *Chinese business in Malaysia: Accumulation, accommodation and ascendance*. Richmond: Curzon Press.

Gomez, E. T. 2003. "Ethnic enterprise, economic development and identity formation: Chinese business in Malaysia," in Gomez, E. T. and Stephens, R. (eds.) *The state, economic development and ethnic co-existence in Malaysia and New Zealand*. Kuala Lumpur: CEDER, pp. 121–45.

Gomez, E. T. and Hsiao, H. -H. M. 2004. "Introduction: Chinese business research in Southeast Asia," in Gomez, E. T. and Hsiao, H. -H. M. (eds.), *Chinese business in South-East Asia: Contesting cultural explanations, researching entrepreneurship*. London: Routledge Curzon, pp. 1–37.

Jesudason, J. V. 1989. *Ethnicity and the economy: The state, Chinese business, and the multinationals in Malaysia*. Singapore: Oxford University Press.

Kahn, J. S. 1996. "Growth, economic transformation, culture and the middle classes in Malaysia," in Robison, R. and Goodman, D. S. G. (eds.), *The new rich in Asia. Mobile phones, McDonalds and middle-class revolution*. London: Routledge, pp. 49–78.

Kotkin, J. 1993. *Tribes: How race, religion, and identity determine success in the new global economy*. New York: Random House.

Kuah, K. E. 1999. "*Anxi* connection: Ancestor worship as moral-cultural capital," in Douw, L. Huang, C. and Godley, M. R. (eds.), *Qiaoxiang ties: Interdisciplinary approaches to "cultural capitalism" in South China*. London: Kegan Paul, pp. 143–57.

Kumar, S., Siddique, S. and Hedrick-Wong, Y. 2005. *Mind the gaps: Singapore business in China*. Singapore: ISEAS.

Lee, K. H. 2003. "Political positions of the Chinese in post-independence Malaysia," in Wang, L. C. and Wang, G. (eds.), *The Chinese diaspora: Selected essays*, Vol. II. Singapore: Eastern Universities Press, pp. 36–65.

Morgan, G. and Quack, S. 2005. "Institutional legacies and firm dynamics: The growth and internationalization of British and German law firms," *Organization Studies* **26** (12): 1765–86.

Numazaki, I. 2000. "Chinese business enterprise as inter-family partnership: A comparison with the Japanese case," in Chan, K. B. (ed.), *Chinese business networks: State, economy and culture*. Singapore: Prentice Hall and Nordic Institute of Asian Studies, pp. 152–75.

Ong, A. 1999. *Flexible citizenship: The cultural logics of transnationality*. Durham, NC: Duke University Press.

Ong, A. and Nonini, D. M. (eds.) 1997. *Ungrounded empires: The cultural politics of Modern Chinese transnationalism*. New York: Routledge.

Redding, S. G. 1990. *The spirit of Chinese capitalism*. Berlin: Walter de Gruyter.

Simmel, G. (1971). *On individuality and social forms*, edited by Donald Levine, University of Chicago Press.

Suryadinata, L. (ed.) 1997. *Ethnic Chinese as Southeast Asians*. Singapore: ISEAS.

Tan, C.-Z., and Yeung, H. W. C. 2000. "The internationalization of Singaporean firms into China: Entry modes and investment strategies," in Yeung, H. W. C. and Olds, K. (eds.), *Globalization of Chinese business firms*. Houndmills: Macmillan, pp. 220–43.

Tsui-Auch, L. S. 2005. "Unpacking regional ethnicity and the strength of ties in shaping ethnic entrepreneurship," *Organizational Studies* **26** (8): 1189–216.

Weidenbaum, M. and Hughes, S. 1996. *The bamboo network: How expatriate Chinese entrepreneurs are creating a new economic superpower in Asia*. New York: The Free Press.

Yeung, H. W. C. 2002. "Transnational entrepreneurship and Chinese business networks: The regionalization of Chinese business firms from Singapore," in Menkhoff, T. and Gerke, S. (eds.), *Chinese entrepreneurship and Asian business networks*. London: Routledge Curzon, pp. 184–216.

Yeung, H. W. C. and Olds, K. 2000. "Globalizing Chinese business firms: Where are they coming from, where are they heading?," in Yeung, H. W. C. and Olds, K. (eds.), *Globalization of Chinese business firms*. Houndmills: Macmillan, pp. 1–30.

Yin, R. K. 1989. *Case study research: Design and methods*. Newbury Park: Sage Publications.

Zwart, E. 2006. In *pursuit of comfort. The transnationalisation process of Malaysian Chinese small and medium enterprises*. Dissertation. Vrije University Amsterdam.

4 From cross-border exchange networks to transnational trading practices? The case of shuttle traders in Laleli, Istanbul

Mine Eder and Özlem Öz

This chapter investigates the complexities inherent in the organization of economic activity within the context of transnational communities by focusing on the interplay between Istanbul's garment producers, shopkeepers, and so-called "shuttle traders" (mostly from the post-Soviet republics) in Laleli (a district of central Istanbul). These traders have played an active role in the emergence of an informal transnational economy in the district since the early 1990s. An in-depth analysis of the case of Laleli and the complex web of relationships between producers, shopkeepers, and shuttle traders allows us to comment on the features of a constantly changing marketplace which is highly informal as well as transnational in character, with social, spatial, organizational, and economic dimensions. What kind of formal and informal trading networks, for instance, emerge as our gaze shifts from small garment producers and shopkeepers in Istanbul to shuttle traders and kiosk managers in Russia? What kind of dynamics evolve through these transnational encounters shaping networks and markets? Do such activities trigger the emergence of a transnational community by means of the Laleli market? If they do, what sort of transnational community is evolving there and why? Only by addressing such questions, we suggest, can we begin to develop a better understanding of the formation and dissolution of transnational communities and their impact on the political and economic landscape.

The chapter starts with a brief discussion of theoretical foundations, addressing different concepts of transnational communities found in the literature and underlining the need for more detailed study of emergent and fragile forms of communities originating from unspectacular and informal cross-border trading activities. The next section examines the political economy of the emergence of Laleli as a transnational and informal market. In the concluding section the implications of the study for the broader literature on transnationalism and transnational communities are discussed. Both published and unpublished documents on Laleli have been analyzed, and these analyses are supported by ongoing ethnographic research on the Laleli market, which started in 2002 (see Eder *et al.* 2002). In 2007 the authors jointly conducted additional interviews with several shopkeepers in Laleli, as well as with producers working for the Laleli market, to update some of the research material.

Theoretical background

This chapter is located at the intersection of two different but inter-related debates on transnational communities. While the debate on transnational migration refers predominantly to communities whose members share an identity and sense of belonging based on common ethnic or national origin, the debate on transnational business communities considers the formation of identity and a sense of belonging across different ethnic or national constituencies (Djelic and Quack, Mayntz in this volume).

Researchers in migration studies, such as Alexander Portes (2000: 254) use the term "transnational community" to describe "migration from below." These authors refer to more or less closed networks that emerge among migrants and their home-country relatives involving various, often small-scale economic activities. The literature on Asian business networks (for a critical review see Dahles in this volume) has taken up a similar issue and highlighted how diaspora communities form the basis for large-scale transnational business enterprises and networks. More recently, AnnLee Saxenian (2005) has shown that members of ethnic diasporas are a powerful force in transferring knowledge between distant economic regions such as Silicon Valley and emerging economic centers in China and India. While these studies are not always explicit concerning whether the phenomena under examination are networks and communities – a distinction which is indeed often difficult to draw (Mayntz in this volume) – they share the view that ethnicity, family, and nationality constitute a shared identity and sense of belonging within a community of people who operate from different places across the world (Rath 2000). The capacity of such migrant communities to shape market rules has been depicted by a rich literature on the history of long-distance and cross-border trade ranging back to medieval times (Greif 2006; Quack forthcoming).

In contrast, the literature on transnational business communities focuses on the development of common practical, cognitive, and normative frameworks among people of different ethnic or national origins (Morgan 2001: 113). This approach, prominent in the present volume, has been used predominantly to study the development of transnational communities within and across multinational corporations (Morgan 2001), and in the analysis of the global network of interlocking corporate directorates (Carroll and Fennema 2002; 2004; 2006; Kentor and Jang 2004; Harvey and Maclean in this volume) and international politics (Adler 2005; see Plehwe in this volume for an overview). Such communities might involve individuals physically crossing borders or alternatively they might be "imaginary" like some recently emerging community types (for example, virtual/online communities) (Featherstone *et al.* 2007). Members of such communities are likely to exhibit multiple group and community affiliations, which are argued to provide members with a richer repertoire of reflexive sense-making practices, while also possibly leading to "communities of limited liability," whose members may come and go and thus exhibit varying degrees of involvement over time (Djelic and Quack in this volume). Most of this literature starts from relatively clearly defined economic actors and recurrent cross-border interactions that give rise to a shared sense of identity and belonging within the group, however fragile.

The sort of transnational community emerging from rather informal cross-border petty entrepreneurial activities and trade studied in this chapter has rarely been addressed in these two growing bodies of literature. What makes the case of Laleli shuttle traders interesting is that it is not only really transnational in character (involving people from different national, regional, and ethnic backgrounds creating new forms of economic business networks possibly linked to an emerging transnational community), but also departs from typical studies of transnational ethnic business networks in which all members are assumed to share the same ethnic affiliation and culture. We shall discuss the peculiarities of the type of transnational economic activity observed in Laleli in this light. At the same time, Laleli represents an opportunity to witness a transnational community of exchange practices gradually emerging whose members "share certain skills in some domain of human endeavour, and engage in a process of collective learning by communicating with each other" (Mayntz 2007: 6), while their macroeconomic environment undergoes a major transformation. Another purpose of this chapter is to explore these interactions between micro-level community formation and macro-level economic change.

First, we build on the argument that transnational communities are complementary to and mutually constitutive of macro changes in the global economy. As we will show, for instance, the emergence of transnational encounters and interactions between the shuttle traders from the former

Soviet republics and the growing number of producers/shopkeepers of Laleli were integrally tied to the overall impoverishment and deregulation in the Communist world following the collapse of the Berlin Wall, as well as the unprecedented level of informalization and liberalization in Turkey's economy. These transnational interactions, in turn, began to shape the economic geography of the region due to the dynamic mobility of people, goods, and services.

Secondly, this chapter suggests that equating transnationality with transmigrant families and individuals narrows the field and limits "what and who can be seen as transnational" (Crang *et al.* 2003: 452). This is particularly important for our discussion of shuttle traders in Laleli as they hardly constitute a transnational "immigrant" community. Few shuttle traders migrate to Istanbul, though they continue to shuttle back and forth. Although there has been a considerable increase in marriages between Turkish men and women from the former Soviet Union, as well as a significant influx of migrant workers employed informally in the sex industry or in domestic service, shuttle traders continue to be "permanently in-between": located in the home country but traveling abroad frequently to bring back goods, as well as new style and fashion ideas. Hence, "transnationality is multiply inhabited by circuits, flows, trajectories and imaginaries" (Crang *et al.* 2003: 449).

Expanding the horizons of the concept of transnationality, however, brings its own risks. Clearly, demolishing a singular understanding of transnationalism, and recognizing the hybridity or "in-between-ness" of individuals and the complexities of these flows are welcome developments. But such studies also risk going to the other extreme, coming adrift from history and political economy or suffering from what Mitchell (1991) called the "hype of hybridity." Everyday practices and economic relationships in which social identities emerge and evolve are often neglected. Unfortunately, it is this overemphasis on agency and subjectivity, this focus on "ephemerality and motion" instead of "grounding" that ultimately renders each transnational community local and unique, leaving no room for exploring systematic, repeated dynamics in transnational activities and communities. Within the specific context of Laleli, the cultural encounters between the shuttle traders and the shopkeepers/producers have clearly shaped identities and self-perceptions on both sides, challenging the established, social/conventional wisdoms while creating new stereotypes and biases (such as the depiction of all post-Soviet women as "Natashas," a pejorative term used for migrant sex workers). But these encounters cannot be detached from the pull and push factors that make them possible. As we shall see, despite its unique characteristics, transnational shuttle trading in Laleli has been driven by familiar forces of migration, poverty, trade prospects, and changing regulatory frameworks.

That is why looking at Laleli as a "transnational social space" à la Faist (2000) might provide some access points for addressing some of these structure-agency debates, avoiding both the homogeneous depictions of transnationalism and the risk of "deconstructing ourselves into relativist hell" (Bailey 2001: 422). Space, for Faist, cannot be equated with physical place alone, and the concept of transnational social spaces explores the principles by which geographical propinquity, which implies the embeddedness of ties in one locality, is supplemented or transformed by transnational exchanges. This further raises the question of the transaction mechanisms embedded in social ties and structures, such as reciprocity, exchange, and solidarity (Faist and Özveren 2004: 4). Here, Faist (2000: 202–10) proposes three types of transnational social space, each with its own linkages. Kinship groups are predicated on ties of reciprocity; "transnational circuits" based on instrumental exchange ties such as trade networks; and "transnational communities" based on solidarity with collective identity (such as ethnicity). Though there are clear overlaps among these concepts (such as a trading community based on ethnicity or a community reinforced by kinship ties), these distinctions raise relevant questions for rethinking shuttle trading in Laleli.

According to Faist's categorizations, post-Soviet shuttle traders and Laleli shopkeepers constitute a typical "transnational circuit" based on instrumental exchange as both sides use the existing opportunity structures to profit from trade. Such a depiction also explains, as we shall see, the fragility and volatility of these exchanges, which are contingent on changing customs and tariff regimes, the political environment, and currency values. More than fifteen years into this trade, however, during which time some of these exchanges have become regularized and more organized, we can argue that, despite the absence of these solidarity and kinship ties, there has been a slow and gradual move towards the *making* of a transnational community in Laleli, albeit a very loose "community of practice." This process can also explain why some of these trade ties have survived numerous financial crises, regulatory changes, and/or political crises, becoming resilient over time.

From a transnational circuit to a fragile community of practice?

The transformation of Laleli from a residential neighborhood into a trading hub began in the early 1970s (Keyder 1999) when Hungarians, Yugoslavs,

Czechs, and Poles started "shopping tourism" in the area. Making use of the discrepancies between the official and market exchange rates, these traders – who can be seen as early architects of this transnational circuit of goods and people – started to engage in barter in the Grand Bazaar. Algerians, Libyans, and North Africans were also lured to Istanbul in the 1980s, largely to circumvent their own highly protected domestic markets. It was the influx of Middle Easterners into the district, fuelled by the skyrocketing of oil prices in the 1970s, which removed the last residential traces from the neighborhood and completed its commercialization. Oil-rich Arabs flooded into the district as precious metals and the silk trade flourished. Signs, shops, the goods on sale, and restaurants all catered to tourists and traders coming from Lebanon, Libya, and the Gulf States. While the dwindling of oil money capped some of the inflow in the 1980s, Laleli settled into the role of a district with medium-sized, medium-quality hotels, with small to medium-sized shops and lower quality goods. But by then both the city and the district of Laleli had begun to acquire transnational characteristics.

Yugoslavs and Poles were the pioneers of cross-border trade in Eastern Europe in the early 1980s. Russians were buying Turkish leather from Poles long before the 1990s. Poles continued to come to Istanbul for shopping tourism, though their share in the suitcase trade waned, and from the 1990s, purchases by Russian shuttle traders began to dwarf those by other Eastern Europeans.

While Poles were the major actors in the 1980s, Yugoslavs were more small-scale traders in these early years of shuttle trading. Up to the 1980s, they would exchange cigarettes and whisky for leather coats and gold jewelry. They would also bring porcelain and crystal goods to exchange for leatherwear and garments (Yenal 2000: 26). In the 1980s, Yugoslavs brought electrical and electronic equipment that was in demand in Turkey to exchange for suitcases of garments. But they were known to have sold these goods mostly to their friends and neighbors rather than in open air markets. It is nevertheless clear that the origins of shopkeeping for shuttle traders actually go back to this period when Bosnian and Macedonian immigrants played a pioneering role thanks to their fluency in Slavic languages.

Transformation of Laleli: an overview

Two major changes began to transform the social and urban landscape in Laleli once again in the 1990s, turning the district into a genuine arena for the transnational circuit of goods and people. One was the boom in shuttle trading between Turkey and the former Soviet Union; the second was the intensification of domestic migration from Southeast Turkey, mostly of Kurdish origin, bringing in a new kind of shopkeeper (alongside the earlier Balkan migrant shopkeepers). With most of the shops, goods, and signs catering to the Russian clientele the district came to be known as "little Russia." As already noted, the encounters between these shopkeepers and the shuttle traders constituted a new "transnational social space." As the small suitcase traders shuttled back and forth between Laleli and the former Soviet Union, a multi-billion-dollar trade, with backward and forward linkages, began to emerge, creating new business practices, social networks, and a new transnational circuit. Before we turn to the community-forming aspects of this trade, however, we need to analyze the pull and push factors and the major transformations associated with the collapse of the Soviet Union and the opening of the borders between the former Soviet republics and Turkey which ultimately led to this shuttle trade, starting a new transnational circuit.

Why this booming trade?

The collapse of the Soviet Union ushered in major changes in Turkish–former Soviet relations.[1] Turkey's foreign policy, for example, began to move from a Cold War, security-based platform focusing on bilateral relations with the USA and the EU, towards a more "regional," more layered, and soft power-based policy – what Kirisci calls a shift from a post-Cold War warrior to a benign regional power (Kirisci 2006). From the 1990s on, the Turkish government began to get actively involved in strengthening economic and cultural ties, particularly with the "new" former Soviet Turkic republics, such as Turkmenistan, Uzbekistan, Kyrgyzstan, and Azerbaijan. Secondly, with the new-found freedom of travel and desire to consume, Turkey became a convenient country enabling many post-Soviet tourists to explore, travel, and establish business ties. As a result, the volume of trade and human mobility began to increase at an unprecedented rate. The number of visitors from the Balkans and the Soviet Union was a little over one million in the 1990s, but reached 2.4 million at the end of the decade and 6.2 million by 2005 (Kirisci 2005).[2]

An overview of the trade data reveals that Turkey has also intensified trade ties with its neighbors, including Greece, Bulgaria, Syria, and Iran (see Kirisci 2006). But this regional economic deepening is most evident with the former Soviet Union in general and the Russian Federation in particular. This is partly linked to Turkey's increasing energy demands and Russia's dependence on Turkey for the transit of natural gas and oil.[3]

Meanwhile, the intensification of flows of goods and people between Turkey and the former Soviet Union has taken place against a background of radical liberalization and informalization in Turkey's political economy. Since the trade liberalization that started in the 1980s and the rather premature financial liberalization in the 1990s, the Turkish economy has increasingly lowered its regulatory barriers to foreign direct investments, equity flows, and commodities. Intensive deregulation in the economy has also created a fertile environment for informalization. Though the causes of informality in Turkey are beyond the scope of this chapter (see Eder and Çarkoğlu 2008), it is important to note that Laleli as an informal transnational business district has largely been seen as a vibrant new reflection of Turkey's famous entrepreneurial spirit.

These macro-level changes in the regional political and economic landscape, and the intensification of flows of goods and people between Turkey and the former Soviet countries, can help to explain how shuttle trading began to emerge in the early 1990s and intensified throughout the decade. As foreign travel became possible in the former Soviet Union, the patterns of informal shuttle trading also began to change. Initially, citizens of the former Soviet Union would cross the border carrying various items, such as machinery, cameras, and stolen goods from state warehouses. They bartered these goods for leather and garments. Turkey was not the only destination. Norway, Germany, and Finland were among the favorite bartering sites. While Poles, Czechs, and Hungarians went to Istanbul to trade, Georgians, Azerbaijanis, and Armenians traveled along the Black Sea coast to enter the country. Though in much smaller numbers, what started as trips by Russians to various makeshift harbor bazaars on Turkey's Black Sea coast, such as Trabzon and Hopa, gradually shifted to Istanbul, becoming more centralized, organized, and diversified. These "tourist traders" initially brought various goods (household products, clothing, electronic goods, and so on) into Turkey literally in their suitcases and declared them as their personal belongings to avoid customs on the way home. By the mid-1990s, however, Russians had stopped bringing goods from their own country, becoming regular shuttle traders in the process.

Though the recent oil boom in the Russian economy, with its glitzy shops and haute couture establishments, makes it hard to believe, the birth of shuttle trading accompanied an intense contraction of the Russian economy in the early 1990s (some 20 percent between 1991 and 1993), which caused severe financial difficulties on ordinary families. People made redundant from defense jobs, women who used to work in now closed or bankrupt industries, and public servants who were not being paid – in short, people from a whole range of occupational groups – began to engage in shuttle trading. First, shuttle traders (mostly women), like the Soviet customers, were inexperienced and not concerned with quality, buying mostly cheap and low-quality products. Turkey was among the favorite destinations for this initial demand, along with Poland and China.

As this trade became more professionalized and organized, cargo companies took over the transportation of goods. A typical shuttle trade transaction therefore involves a shuttle trader contacting a tourism agency in their hometown. The agencies often work jointly with cargo companies (sometimes they are one and the same). Reservations are made for a few days in a Laleli hotel, just enough to complete the shopping. The shuttle trader then flies into Istanbul, is ferried to a hotel, and starts to make purchases. The shopkeepers have either received the orders in advance or will push their subcontractors to meet the deadline for producing the required clothing or goods. These goods are then packaged by the cargo companies (or by the trader, depending on the volume). The shopkeeper is mainly responsible for delivering the demanded goods. In order to ensure timely delivery, several subcontractors are often used. Once again, developing a working relationship with subcontractors is vital. The cargo company then delivers the goods either directly to the open market or to the requested shop in the trader's hometown.

Outward appearances at Laleli belie the size and importance of this trade. At its peak in 1995, the volume of suitcase trade reached an estimated $10 billion. Even today, it stands at approximately $3 billion a year. The shuttle trade is also important for the Russian economy, though it is only one of many important new informal trading networks. Before the August 1998 ruble crisis, the official Goskomstat estimate of the volume of shuttle trade in Russia in 1998 was approximately $4.5–5.0 billion per quarter, falling to $2.0–2.5 billion per quarter after the crisis. Turkey's share in this overall volume is estimated to be around 40–50 percent (Goskomstat 1999). Even after the ruble crisis, shuttle trade accounted for 10.3 percent of Russia's foreign trade turnover (Goskomstat 2000). At its peak in 1993–94, an estimated 10–15 million Russians were involved, and in 1999 the turnover of unregistered shuttle trade reached an estimated $11.5 billion, comparable to the total revenue derived from Russian exports in that year (Goskomstat 1999). With the upturn of the Russian economy – largely thanks to rising oil prices – and the Putin government's insistence on increasing customs tariffs and on formalizing this trade in light of prospective WTO membership, these numbers have declined considerably. Nevertheless, shuttle trading remains an important part of people's livelihoods on the periphery of the post-Soviet region.

In short, the transformation of the Laleli district from a sleepy residential area adjacent to the old city into a bustling shopping district with intensive transnational encounters and informal exchanges coincided with the explosion of trade with the former Soviet republics, as suitcase or shuttle trade came to represent all unregistered commerce between Turkey and the former Soviet republics.

The architects of an emerging "transnational community of practice"

What is particularly interesting in the case of Laleli is the wide range of actors who make this transnational circuit of goods and people possible, including shopkeepers, textile producers, and transnational shuttle traders, as well as cargo companies, tourism and employment agencies, and hotel owners and managers. Over time, however, and despite considerable market volatility and uncertainty, some of these business networks and practices have become quite established.

On the production front, for instance, three distinct types of *production relations* can be observed in Laleli. The first took the form of the "forward integration" of small Istanbul textile producers into the Laleli market in the early 1990s. These small firms mainly targeted the lower end of the market and tended to shift their focus rather opportunistically, giving priority to either Laleli or the domestic market, depending on their relative prospects. From the mid-1990s onwards, however, this structure changed drastically, when shuttle traders began to demand higher quality goods and the textile producers of Istanbul targeting the upper end of the market also saw opportunities in Laleli. Shopkeepers saw the likely benefits of integrating production into their operations, leading to the emergence of the second type of production relations in Laleli, namely the "backward integration" of Laleli shopkeepers into production. They transformed themselves into full-fledged textile firms. In fact, a number of firms originating in Laleli later developed into large and well-known companies in both national and international markets (for example, Colin's, now a large-scale jeans producer) (Yükseker 2003, 2007).

The emergence of the third and most recent type of relationship was triggered by the entry of larger Istanbul textile and leather garment firms into the Laleli market. Observing that Laleli had its ups and downs, and hence was rather a risky market, the priority of these firms was to engage in regular export activity. Seemingly they were unable to resist the potential high returns offered by Laleli during boom periods. The constant lure of the market allowed the producers to use Laleli as a safety-valve, designing and producing some of their goods for Laleli while continuing their formal export activities and/or producing for the domestic market. These growing links between textile production and the Laleli market were crucial in the routinization of this trade and began to "lock-in" certain types of informal business networks on a longer-term basis.

There are different modes of operation in the Laleli district, mirroring the case of the manufacturers mentioned above. For example, a number of shopkeepers started as small traders in nearby districts (for instance, Mahmutpasa) and moved early and somewhat opportunistically to Laleli (typically without being involved in production). As already noted, however, business in Laleli is extremely volatile and price sensitive. Almost all of the interviewees have either gone bankrupt once in the Laleli market or have had to scale down significantly due to changes in demand. Most transactions take place in cash (US dollars), though short-term credit or late, after-sale payment schemes are also common. In response to this intense volatility, the shopkeepers adopt a number of strategies. They try to compete on both quality and pricing. The era of "easy" Russian and Eastern European customers is long gone and customers are no longer as numerous as they were. Profit margins have declined significantly, pushing the inexperienced one-timer traders out of the market. "We used to get seven dollars profit for each skirt we sold," said one shopkeeper; "now we're happy if we can get a dollar for each skirt." The 1998 crisis also seems to have had a tremendous impact on the production side. Small and large manufacturing firms working as subcontractors with Laleli shops went under, as the shopkeepers were not able to pay for the goods or returned most of them. "The Russian traders themselves could not pay us, so we could not pay our subcontractors, which created a terrible domino effect," explained one shopkeeper.

Another modus operandi in Laleli includes those firms that have improved their businesses substantially over the years by making good use of the opportunities provided by the Laleli market. One leather clothing firm we interviewed, for instance, has increased its presence in the district to four retail stores, with another in Zeytinburnu, and a tannery (production unit) in Corlu.

Shopkeepers

It would be going too far to assert that the Laleli shopkeepers and producers form a community, as competition among them is intense, particularly since the decline in profit margins. However, at the risk of some oversimplification, three distinct groups may be observed among the shopkeepers; affiliation with which helped them to weather the various crises. One is the migrant community, whose members largely moved to Laleli in the early 1990s, mostly from the Balkans, particularly the former Yugoslavia and Bulgaria. Those in this group tend to run family businesses and continue to bring in friends and relatives from their home regions. This is also the group which has the least problem adjusting to the Laleli market, as most speak Russian or other Slavic languages. The Balkan community is also particularly active in gold and jewelry.

The second group's basis of solidarity is Islamic. This group of traders has a high ratio of members from the same towns and villages, who tend to resent the "negative image" often attached to the Laleli market largely due to the tourism and prostitution in the area. "I had to change the location of my shop in Laleli," explained one religiously devout shopkeeper. "It was right across from a hotel and I was worried about the effect it might have on my younger brother, who works for me. I did not want him to see what was going on." This group is highly conservative but still ready and willing to exploit the opportunities offered in the market.

The third group are the Kurds, who mostly migrated to Istanbul in the early 1990s, probably due to the escalation of the military conflict in Southeast Turkey.[4] This group of newcomers is widely accused by more established traders in the district as being after "easy money" and engaging in "one-off trading" rather than establishing long-term, sustainable shopkeeper–trader relations. "They still do not know how to trade," explained a shopkeeper who was also from the Southeast. "They are the ones who have given the district a bad name. They sell old stuff as if it was new, overcharge the customers, and cause people to lose trust." Kurds are also accused of involvement in prostitution and drug trading in the area.

Solidarity among the Laleli shopkeepers therefore did not play a particularly important role in the survival of businesses, but rather the informal business networks and interactions between the shopkeepers and the shuttle traders. Only those shops that have developed long-term partnerships with their Russian counterparts appear to have survived the crisis. Because of the substantial collapse of the credit system and the unprecedented rise in credit defaults, money-lending and other forms of informal lending began to increase. But although the 1998 crisis was a major blow to relations of trust between traders and shopkeepers, those who survived the crisis were able to establish more long-term relationships. Their ability to survive by means of long-term credits, giving goods with no advance payment, or postponing payment until the next trip showed how this informal market could quickly adjust to a changing environment. It is this flexibility that gives the shop-keepers their edge. This also explains why shopkeepers and producers keep returning to this market even after several bankruptcies, helping to routinize this transnational trade over time.

Shuttle traders

The profile of, in particular, shuttle traders from the former Soviet Union also provides interesting insights into the nature of informal networks.[5] These shuttle traders – known locally as *chelnokis* – are predominantly women, mostly in their thirties and well educated. The initial traders started up with as little as $2,000 worth of merchandise, while a medium-size trader would have $10,000–20,000 worth of goods for sale, often at more than one sales outlet. The maximum amount is estimated to be $50,000 (Melnichenko *et al.* 1997: 4). At the peak of shuttle trading, professional traders made as many as twenty trips per year. The proximity of Turkey, easier entry thanks to the convenient sticker visa issued at the border, Laleli's high density of hotels and cargo companies, the attractive price/quality ratio, and the wide selection of items on sale were all cited as reasons favoring Istanbul compared to other destinations.

The education and gender gaps between the Turkish male shopkeepers and female Russian traders were also striking. With the exception of Balkan migrants, who tend to be university graduates, most Laleli shopkeepers have a limited education. Some worked as street vendors for years before opening a shop; some are former textile workers who long labored in sweatshops; others were involved in other small enterprises, such as grocery stores. Kurdish migrants were mostly unemployed or were agricultural workers. Despite this educational gap, the same economic reasons brought about this transna-tional encounter between the shopkeepers and the traders, making them truly a transnational community of practice with (quite) limited liability (see Djelic and Quack in this volume).

What is remarkable about the Laleli marketplace is the speed with which these transnational networks have emerged, overcoming all the cultural and linguistic barriers described above. To be sure, the initial encounters between women from the former Soviet Union and Turkish/Kurdish shopkeepers and producers were fraught with misunderstandings and mistrust. These initial encounters between the relatively poorly educated and dark Turkish shopkeepers and mostly blonde, highly educated Russian women are partly responsible for the negative reputation acquired by the Laleli district as a "red light" neighborhood: the shopkeepers often treated these women as potential prostitutes rather than as legitimate traders, seeing them as naïve and over-charging them or offering them flawed or damaged goods. The shuttle traders reciprocated to some extent, regarding their counterparts as "uneducated brutes," as one interviewee put it, and not paying on time or even not paying at all for goods received. Most shopkeepers pointed out how educated and beautiful their Russian customers were, which also explains why these traders were easily stigmatized as "Natashas," a term largely used for prostitutes. While there is some evidence that prostitution was used to accumulate start-up capital at the beginning of shuttle trading, with the increasing professionalization of trading very little overlap has remained, though the negative reputation of the district lingers.[6] Some of these women did indeed migrate to Istanbul; some working as domestic workers, some in Laleli shops as clerks or shop assistants on an informal basis. The shopkeepers tended to favor them because of their language skills and familiarity with the customers and consumer tastes. The links between the shuttle traders who travel back and forth and the Soviet migrant workers are very loose and limited, however. In fact, some shuttle traders resent any implication that they are somehow related, which underscores the diversity of actors in Laleli's transnational market.

Over time, however, both the shopkeepers and the shuttle traders have been able to overcome these stereotypes and to establish professional and prag-matic business relations. The immense potential for "arbitrage" – for example, selling a jacket bought for ten dollars in Turkey for a hundred dollars at home – explains the initial speed and ease with which these networks emerged. As this trade has matured and settled, albeit with relatively declining profit margins, surviving financial crises and several bankruptcies, these transnational networks have grown more resilient, with each side adapting to changing demands and costs to lay the foundations of a fragile transna-tional community (for more details, see Yükseker 2004). Establishing trust, as we shall see, was crucial in the gradual, but nevertheless tumultuous transfor-mation of this market.

Other actors in the network

The suitcase trade clearly involves more than the shopkeepers and the traders. A whole series of related businesses have sprung up in Laleli, including tourism agencies, hotels, and, most importantly, cargo companies, which service the shuttle trade. Cargo companies play a crucial role in sustaining this mode of trading. Indeed, as the *chelnokis* have developed long-term informal networks with Laleli shopkeepers, bulk trading through informal cargo companies and/or tourist operators has become increasingly common. These companies work closely with travel agencies, which bring the customers and book hotels for them. Most cargo companies also have joint ventures with Russian, Moldavian, and Romanian counterparts. Each partner is responsible for the products up to their national border. The shopkeepers often stated that the "real money" is being made in the cargo business. Some cargo companies have developed to such an extent that they now own their own charter planes. The business is risky, however, as it involves dealing with customs officials and establishing the necessary networks for the "problem-free" passage of goods; that is, knowing the right people in the right places. Often, police, inspectors, and customs officials become an organic part of these informal networks, which also helps explain the resilience of these trade flows despite constantly changing regulatory frameworks. The shopkeepers do not work directly with the cargo companies but simply deliver the goods wanted by the client to the designated cargo company. Another related area of activity is the warehouses where customers can leave their goods for one dollar a day. The so-called "cargo boys," on the other hand, help the customers carry their goods from the shops to the cargo companies, which are all conveniently located in Laleli.

Hotels in Laleli are also crucial for the shuttle trade. There are an estimated 500 hotels in the district, some regulated by the municipality, others by the Ministry of Tourism. Most hotels work closely with travel agencies in Russia, which in turn tend to have partners in Turkey. (These agencies offer special packages that include a round-trip ticket to Istanbul and a few nights' accommodation for approximately $300.) The hotels have very different rates, with some offering as much as a 60 percent discount on a daily basis. Most hotels in Laleli have converted their conference rooms into warehouses for shuttle traders. This allows the customers to leave their goods at the hotel and then transfer them to the cargo company with which the travel agency works (see Figure 4.1).

The way in which economic agents establish business ties and build trust in Laleli is also distinctive. In contrast to the theories espoused in the relevant literature (for example, Granovetter 1985), buyers and sellers in Laleli do not have long-established historical relations embedded in a common culture. Instead, business ties and trust developed among economic agents in Laleli can best be described in terms of game theory, as the likelihood of continued

Figure 4.1   A truck being loaded with shuttle traders' purchases at the end of a shopping day
Source: Taken by the authors during the fieldwork in Laleli, January 2007.

relations between the parties depends on their previous commercial interactions (Öz 2004). Arguably, this is partly due to the market's transnational and informal nature.

In general, the system works smoothly, but in cases of failure there is not much shuttle traders can do, as none of the operations we have described is attended by paperwork. The key role of "trust" is evident here, too. Indeed, the functioning of the entire chain of operations depends on it. "You need to establish a relationship based on trust between all the parties," one interviewee stressed; "you need a trustworthy cargo boy, for instance, to make sure that the goods your customers have purchased reach them on time." Under these circumstances, networks are created – and recreated if necessary – to ensure that the required level of trust is maintained.

The growing level of trust is also evident in the transformation of business practices. Instead of continuously making short trips to Istanbul and placing their orders, some experienced traders have started to fax or phone bulk orders to shopkeepers. If they are regular customers, no payment is demanded until the goods are delivered. Less experienced traders still come to Turkey by plane or bus, do not buy in bulk, and usually pay before shipment.

In short, Laleli has indeed become a center of gravity, the success of some traders drawing in others. One interviewee, who has specialized at selling jeans in Laleli on and off for seventeen years, twice going bankrupt during that period, declared that he had never even considered leaving Laleli. This is mainly because the profit margins are considerably higher than in the domestic market and the Laleli producers/shopkeepers would not like to be left out if sales pick up again. ("Let us not forget that if Laleli made us bankrupt, it also made us rich," in the words of another interviewee). All this in turn explains why Laleli rather than another possible location, such as Trabzon (a city on the Black Sea coast, considered to have helped to pioneer this kind of trade), ended up attracting shuttle traders. The type of transnational economic activity that has emerged could not find a base in Trabzon, but Laleli offered better links with the local and national economy as well as a more welcoming, cosmopolitan atmosphere for shuttle traders.[7]

Conclusions

In this chapter, we have investigated how informal and scattered cross-border business and social encounters between so-called shuttle traders and shopkeepers in a local market, such as the Laleli market in Istanbul, can gradually give rise to a transnational community. We have argued that it is too early to assert that Laleli shopkeepers, shuttle traders, producers, cargo companies, and hotel managers constitute a transnational community of practice. At best, participants in the Laleli market can be described as an *emerging* community of trading practice. The fact that this trade has become routinized over time and that some of these business networks have managed to survive despite highly volatile market conditions and financial crises, however, suggests that there are identifiable trends in that direction. Indeed, what started as the burgeoning of a "transnational circuit" of goods and people as the informal trade between Turkey and the post-Soviet republics began to expand, and tourists/traders began to enjoy their new-found freedom after the collapse of the Soviet Union, has now settled into still fragile, but resilient transnational trading networks and routinized business practices.

It is important to point out, however, that there are lingering barriers to community formation. One is the fragile and transient nature of these networks. Although some of this shuttle trade has been routinized and organized over the years, with producers and shopkeepers establishing so-called "permanent customer profiles," changing macroeconomic environments, financial crises, and, most importantly, constantly changing customs regulations have systematically threatened the stability of these networks. Secondly, these particular transnational networks are fragile, due to their informal or semi-formal nature. Almost all transactions take place in cash, and the credit system is based on verbal promises and handshakes rather than enforceable contracts. Though the goods traded are not illegal, the manner in which they cross the border does involve extensive informal bargaining, bribery of customs officials, and other "arrangements" to ensure safe passage of the goods. Finally, since this trade is based on frequent but very short visits to Istanbul by shuttle traders (an average trip lasts about three days), the traders and shopkeepers do not have time to participate in local community events or in any other fashion in the life of the district. Though socializing and non-business interactions between shopkeepers and traders are common, the shuttle traders appear to view Laleli more as a destination of convenience than as a place of community engagement.

Nevertheless, Laleli combines a number of features traditionally ascribed to local communities (including a territorial location, physical proximity, and direct and regular contact) and some typical features of transnational communities, such as the position of members at the crossing of different webs of affiliation and a rich repertoire of reflexive practices arising from multiple group adherence. The potential for community formation is underscored by the fact that this market and its participants have survived for more than fifteen years, and that Laleli still serves as a hub for transnational traders. The fact that the market has also prevailed despite a whole series of cultural ambiguities, stereotyping, and misunderstandings also shows that some of the barriers to community formation can be overcome. Furthermore, the story of the Laleli market and the shifting business strategies of Laleli shopkeepers and shuttle traders suggest not only the fragility and volatility but also the flexibility, adaptability, and stubborn resilience of these encounters. There are numerous examples of sporadic transnational shuttle trading and shopping districts around the world, including cross-border trading (Polish suitcase traders to Germany), informal bazaars in Trieste and Novi Bazaar, and the Chinese market in Budapest. Some have declined over the years as opportunities disappeared, while others, such as Laleli, have continued to reap the benefits.

What explains the resilience of the Laleli market? In this chapter we have suggested that participants in Laleli's transnational market have been driven largely by a combination of macroeconomic factors, such as poverty and lack of sufficient jobs at home on the part of the shuttle traders, and the lack of domestic demand and markets on the part of the shopkeepers. Relatively loose implementation of domestic and international trade rules, easier visa requirements, and complicit negligence by the respective states as this informal trade continues to create opportunities and jobs on both sides have also kept this market alive. In short, despite its dramatic ups and downs, the potential for profitable trading remains, however fragile and informal.

Another important factor that explains the resilience of this trade has to do with the establishment of business networks and routinization over time. We have suggested that despite continuing market volatility and uncertainties, the participants in the trade have become quite organized and have established their business routines over time. Both traders and shuttle traders have become familiar with market dynamics on both sides and have begun to organize accordingly. Producers have also mastered the nuances of demand from post-Soviet markets and have adapted to it. Again, we do not want to overemphasize the permanence of these business networks. Even a tiny regulatory change or a different approach to the enforcement of customs regulations, for instance, would be sufficient to interrupt this trade. Nevertheless, it is clear that shopkeepers, shuttle traders, and cargo companies continue to work together and find it worthwhile to keep the Laleli market alive. They recognize a mutual dependence, or better, a convergence of interests. However, it may still be too early to suggest that these business networks have matured enough to transform themselves into a community. For this reason, it might be more accurate to call the actors of the Laleli market an *embryonic* transnational community with limited liability as they are still crucially dependent on market incentives.

Finally, the experience of Laleli illustrates the complex process through which transnational economic activities are organized. We have argued that to understand new forms of mobility, particularly the emergence of transnational communities – or a transnational "community of practice" – we need to consider the historical as well as the macro dimensions of the issue and to develop a better understanding of how these business networks are socially embedded. Only through closer observation of the participants in the market, and of how these networks emerge, operate, and change over time can we get a better understanding of how such communities, however fragile, form and develop.

Clearly, the transactions described in this chapter do not fit easily into the existing literature on international migration and "conventional" transnational communities, in which some sort of solidarity, based on kinship, ethnicity, nation, or race, is assumed. These activities cannot be reduced to sporadic instrumental exchanges or "circuits" either, as they have clear social, cultural, and spatial dimensions, though given the volatility and fragility of these networks it is tempting to do so. For this reason, looking at Laleli as a "transnational social space" and as an "emerging community of practice" can serve as a means of challenging common binary distinctions such as globalization "from below" versus globalization "from above," communities versus networks, and transnational communities versus circuits. These issues warrant further investigation. Only then, perhaps, could we begin to "ground" our understanding of transnationalism and transnational community and explore the links between changes in global political economy and the everyday micro-experiences of individuals, in this case the shuttle traders, shopkeepers, producers, and others in Laleli.

Acknowledgment

Özlem Öz would like to thank the Turkish Academy of Sciences, TUBA, for their financial support.

NOTES

1. The information in this section is based on Eder *et al.* 2002, and the interviews conducted by the Russian partner in the project, Professor Andrei Yakovlev.
2. In the case of entries from the Balkans, the numbers increased from 60,000 in 1980 to 850,000 in 1990 and 2.7 million in 2005 (Icduygu 2006). For the former Soviet countries, the number increased from a meager 40,000 in 1980 to 222,000 people in 1990 and a staggering 3.5 million in 2005.
3. In 2006, Turkey imported 19 billion cubic meters of Russian natural gas, 13 billion from Bulgaria, and the rest from the Blue Stream pipeline across the Black Sea, including 6.7 billion cubic meters from Iran, and 5.8 billion from Algeria and Nigeria. Energy exposure to Russia is now 60 percent and is expected to increase even further, to 80 percent (cited

in Kirisci 2006: 85). Rising energy prices around the world also explain why Turkey's imports from the Russian Federation increased from 0 in 1990 to around $1.2 billion in 1993, hovering at that level throughout the 1990s only to jump to $3.8 billion in 2002, $5.4 billion in 2003, $9 billion in 2004, $12 billion in 2005 and a whopping $19 billion in 2006. Although exports to Russia are not as impressive and suffered from the ruble crisis in 1998, which made Turkish products very expensive for consumers, the numbers still reflect the expansion of Turkey's exports to the Russian Federation, rising from 0 in 1990 to $1.2 billion in 1995 and $2 billion in 1997, only to fall back to $580 million in 1998. Exports subsequently recovered, hovering around $2 billion in 2004 and 2005 and jumping yet again in 2006 to $3.2 billion (www.foreigntrade.gov.tr, accessed May 2, 2007).

4. The correlation between the escalation of the Kurdish separatist conflict in the region and the influx of Kurds to Laleli is not conclusive, but eminently plausible given the high level of internal migration.

5. Even though our sample of shuttle traders was small, our findings overlap considerably with Andrei Yakovlev's research on Russian traders. See "Redefining Contagion," Eder *et al.* (2002).

6. For an excellent analysis of the gender dimension, see Yenal (2000). In fact, there are two distinct areas in Laleli and its vicinity. One is central Laleli, where most shuttle trading takes place, and the other is Aksaray and Kumkapi where most of the bars and dingier establishments are located.

7. This can also be linked to the part of the literature in which transnational communities are often discussed in relation to global cities, the city being seen here as a node at which various types of global networks, including transnational communities, intersect (Castles 2002: 1159–60).

REFERENCES

Adler, E. 2005. *Communitarian international relations.* London: Routledge.

Bailey, A. 2001. "Turning transnational: Notes on the theorisation of international migration," *International Journal of Population Geography* 7: 413–28.

Carroll, W.K. and Fennema, M. 2002. "Is there a transnational business community?," *International Sociology* 17: 393–419.

Carroll, W.K. and Fennema, M. 2004. "Problems in the study of the transnational business community: A reply to Kentor and Jang," *International Sociology* 19: 369–78.

Carroll, W.K. and Fennema, M. 2006. "Asking the right questions: A final word on the transnational business community," *International Sociology* 21: 607–10.

Castles, S. 2002. "Migration and community formation under conditions of globalization," *The International Migration Review* 36 (4): 1143–68.

Crang P., Dwyer, C. and Jackson, P. 2003. "Transnationalism and the spaces of commodity culture," *Progress in Human Geography* 27 (4): 438–56.

Eder, M. and Çarkoğlu, A. 2008. "Economic vulnerability and urban informality in Turkey" (under revision for publication in *Comparative Political Studies*).

Eder, M., Çarkoğlu, A., Yakovlev, A. and Chaudry, K. 2002. *Redefining contagion: Political economy of suitcase trade between Turkey and Russia.* Unpublished final IREX Research Project Report, www.ecsoc.msses.ru/pdf/yakov.doc.

Faist, T. 2000. *The volume and dynamics of international migration and transnational social spaces*. Oxford University Press.

Faist, T. and Özveren, E. (eds.) 2004. *Transnational social spaces: Agents, networks and institutions*. Aldershot: Ashgate.

Featherstone, D., Phillips, R. and Waters, J. 2007. "Introduction: Spatialities of transnational networks," *Global Networks* 7: 383–91.

Goskomstat. 1999. *Russian Statistical Yearbook*. Moscow.

Goskomstat. 2000. *Russian Statistical Yearbook*. Moscow.

Granovetter, M. 1985. "Economic action and social structure: The problem of embeddedness," *American Journal of Sociology* **91** (2): 481–510.

Greif, A. 2006. *Institutions and the path to the modern economy: Lessons from medieval trade*. Cambridge University Press.

Icduygu, A. 2006. *Labor dimensions of irregular migration in Turkey*. Research report. Florence: European University Institute RCAS.

Kentor, J. and Jang, Y. S. 2004. "Yes, there is a (growing) transnational business community: A study of global interlocking directorates 1983-98," *International Sociology* **19**: 355–68.

Keyder, C. 1999. "A tale of two neighborhoods," in Keyder, C. (ed.), *Istanbul between the global and the local*. New York: Rowman and Littlefield, pp. 173–87.

Kirisci, K. 2005. "A friendlier Schengen visa system as a tool of soft power: The experience of Turkey," *European Journal of Migration and Law* 7: 343–67.

Kirisci, K. 2006. *"Turkey's foreign policy in turbulent times,"* Challiot Papers, No. 92 (September). Paris: European Union Institute for Security Studies.

Mayntz, R. 2007. "Global structures: Markets, transnational organizations, networks–and communities?," Paper presented at 23rd European Group for Organizational Studies (EGOS) Colloquium, Vienna, July 5–7.

Melnichenko T., Bolonini, A. and Zavatta, R. 1997. *"Russian shuttle trade: General characteristics and its interconnection with the Italian market."* Unpublished research paper. Bologna: Economisti Associati.

Mitchell, T. 1991. "The limits of the state: Beyond statist approaches and their critics," *American Political Science Review* **85** (1): 77–96.

Morgan, G. 2001. "Transnational communities and business systems," *Global Networks* **1**: 113–30.

Öz, Ö. 2004. *Clusters and competitive advantage: The Turkish experience*. Houndmills: Palgrave Macmillan.

Portes, A. 2000. "Globalization from below: The rise of transnational communities," in Kalb, D., van der Land, M., Staring, R., van Steenbergen, B. and Wilterdink, N. (eds.), *The ends of globalization*. New York: Rowman and Littlefield, pp. 253–72.

Quack, S. forthcoming. "Global markets in theory and history: Towards a comparative analysis," *Kölner Zeitschrift für Soziologie und Sozialpsychologie*, Special Issue.

Rath, J. 2000. *Immigrant businesses: The economic, political and social environment*. Basingstoke: Macmillan.

Saxenian, A. 2005. "From brain drain to brain circulation: Transnational communities and regional upgrading in India and China," *Studies in Comparative International Development* **40** (2): 35–61.

Yenal (Yükseker), D. 2000. *Weaving a market: The informal economy and gender in a transnational trade network between Turkey and the former Soviet Union.* Dissertation. Department of Sociology, Binghamton University.

Yükseker, D. 2003. *Laleli–Moskova mekigi: Kayitdisi ticaret ve cinsiyet iliskileri.* Istanbul: Iletisim.

Yükseker, D. 2004. "Trust and gender in a transnational market: The public culture of Laleli," *Istanbul Public Culture* 16 (1): 47–65.

Yükseker, D. 2007. "Shuttling goods, weaving consumer tastes: Informal trade between Turkey and Russia," *International Journal of Urban and Regional Research* 31 (1): 60–72.

Part III

Professional communities with a transnational extension

5 Transnational boards and governance regimes: a Franco-British comparison

Charles Harvey and Mairi Maclean

Introduction

This chapter assesses the argument that a transnational community of elite corporate directors, bonded by shared values and assumptions, and spanning leading international companies, is emerging as a consequence of globalization and the harmonization of corporate governance practices. Governance regimes are inextricably connected to the interplay between national business systems and the processes, albeit nascent, of transnational community-building. The past decade has witnessed extraordinary global change, fuelled by heightened competition, and marked by extensive transnational corporate restructuring.

Internationalization has raised questions concerning the extent to which best practice in governance regimes may be transported from one national business system to another (Djelic 1998; Whitley 1999). This has generated much research on the prospects for international convergence (Pedersen and Thomsen 1997; Rhodes and van Apeldoorn 1998; Carati and Tourani Rad 2000; Aguilera and Jackson 2003; Toms and Wright 2005; Maclean and Harvey 2008), to which the growing internationalization of the boards of leading global companies might be deemed to be contributing (Conyon and Muldoon 2006; Scherer *et al.* 2006; Staples 2007). Against this supposed trend, however, it can be seen that actors involved in rule-setting at international level often remain embedded in national and local cultures and environments, from which they extend their behaviors and strategies into the global domain (Djelic and Quack 2003a).

A community, from our perspective, is a defined set of individuals with shared values, assumptions and beliefs, whose interests, whether material, aesthetic or ideological, are bound together. Communities bind individuals into a collective whole. Membership requires admission and commitment to the well-being of the collective. A community is far more than a loose collection of individuals (see Mayntz, Djelic and Quack in this volume).

Companies can be thought of as organizational communities, which are themselves members of wider corporate communities bound by shared values, assumptions, and beliefs. Corporate communities have been conceived historically as nationally rooted, elemental within national business systems; but with the progressive internationalization of big business it might be argued that a new transnational corporate community is in the process of formation. The leaders of corporate communities, of whatever description, are the members of the boards of directors of the largest, most powerful firms within them. In this sense, members of business elites might be thought of, potentially, as community leaders, with a special responsibility for the well-being of the community as a whole, not simply of their own organizations.

In assessing the nature, extent, and significance of transnationality amongst elite company directors, we draw upon evidence from a cross-national study of business elites and corporate governance in France and Britain (Maclean *et al.* 2006; 2007; Harvey and Maclean 2008). The research has been conducted by the authors since 1999. At its core is the analysis of governance changes within the top 100 companies in France and the UK between January 1, 1998 and December 31, 2003, complemented by prosopographical research into the social backgrounds, education, networks, and careers of the 2,291 directors of these companies, of whom 1,231 were affiliated primarily to French companies and 1,041 to British companies. The research is both quantitative and qualitative. The quantitative dimension of the project allows concepts such as social capital and networking to be explored systematically; while interviews with business leaders and governance experts provide a second rich seam of material.

In what follows, we suggest that while governance reform has proceeded apace in both countries, nevertheless pre-existing structures and practices remain at national, regional, and local levels, retaining much of their intrinsic integrity, whilst interacting with new, transnational influences (Djelic and Quack 2003b; Clift 2007). Eric Hobsbawm (cited in Bauman 2000: 192) gives expression to this intrinsic duality:

What we have today is in effect a dual system, the official one of the "national economies" of states, and the real but largely unofficial one of transnational units and institutions . . . [U]nlike the state with its territory and power, other elements of the "nation" can be and easily are overridden by the globalization of the economy. Ethnicity and language are the two obvious ones. Take away state power and coercive force, and their relative insignificance is clear.

Governments, Bauman (2000: 192) asserts, unable to balance the books with the resources they command, have an understandable *parti pris* "to collaborate with the 'globals.'" The creation of genuine transnational communities at board level, however, despite some evidence of community isomorphism (Marquis *et al.* 2007), appears nascent and far from complete. This may be because boardrooms, like the corporate systems in which they are embedded, have their own distinctive traditions and "habitus" (Bourdieu 1990), rooted in particular socio-cultural contexts and generating self-perpetuating practices (Granovetter 1985; Schatzki 1996). It may also have to do with the distinction made by Tönnies (2002 [1897]) between *Gemeinschaft* and *Gesellschaft*, the first relating to families and kinship with a high level of trust and shared mores, and the second to companies, seemingly driven by self-interest, as articulated by Djelic and Quack in this volume. Our view is that the incremental changes observed in favor of transnational communities will continue, ultimately with profound consequences. Equally, however, national and local diversity in the mindsets, dispositions, and predilections of elite transnational directors is likely to persist for many decades to come, resisting isomorphic pressures towards conformity in the substance and application of corporate governance in the international domain (for parallels, see Morgan and Kubo and Ramirez in this volume).

   The current financial crisis casts a long shadow of uncertainty over the global regulatory landscape. For the last decade or more, the status and power of the nation-state have been in decline (Bauman 2000). More recently, however, there has been a dramatic reversal of fortunes. We have seen spectacular falls from grace, epitomized by the Madoff case in 2008, with some businesses collapsing like houses of cards, built on greed. State intervention and nationalization are once again on the agenda in the West. Following crises of confidence not seen for more than a hundred years, banks have been bailed out throughout the Western world. In the UK, Northern Rock and Royal Bank of Scotland (RBS) are now essentially under public ownership. We live, as Bauman (2007) asserts, in "liquid times," when "identification" or a sense of belonging may become ever more important for "individuals desperately seeking a 'we'" to whom to belong (Bauman 2004: 24). Communitarianism, in Bauman's (2000: 170) view, is a natural response to "the accelerating 'liquefaction' of modern life." Alternatively, in turbulent times, communities may disperse, as social anchors are cast adrift. International communities stand today at a crossroads: either to continue along the path towards a future, modern, international economy; or to be pushed backwards, such that individual national economies become more traditionalist and protectionist. We may be witnessing a recentering of national systems of governance and nationally based communities as a means of reducing risk. This may follow if countries choose to turn inwards, recalling the "beggar thy neighbor" policies of the 1930s, which contributed to the Great Depression (as well as to the rise of fascism and the outbreak of hostilities in World War II). On the other hand, an internationally coordinated response to the global crisis might lead to the process of transnational governance potentially becoming much stronger and more powerfully backed and relayed. In this case, the current movement towards international convergence could continue and might even be reinforced. The idea of a new "Bretton Woods" conference, broached in autumn 2008 by British Prime Minister Gordon Brown, implies just such a strengthening of the mechanisms and institutions of international regulation and governance.

If we consider these two alternatives with regard to transnational communities in the making, then according to the first scenario, the old order of competing nation-states with firms securely rooted in national business systems would remain securely entrenched and pre-eminent. According to the second scenario, the old order of competing national business systems would be gradually superseded by a new transnational corporate community. A third scenario is also possible, however: transnational corporations might be members simultaneously of two or more communities, just as an individual might be active within multiple communities (Djelic and Quack in Chapter 1 of this volume). As Bauman (2004: 13) states: "Few of us can avoid the passage through more than one genuine or putative, well-integrated or ephemeral 'community of ideas and principles.'" For elite corporate directors, one of these might be the new transnational corporate community in the making. Combining a strong local embeddedness with an opening to broader transnational communities in the making might turn those elite directors in time into "rooted cosmopolitans" (Djelic and Quack in Chapter 1 of this volume).

Competing capitalisms and transnational communities

The notion that the raw forces of capitalism are bounded and directed according to different rules in different countries owes much to the work of Michel Albert (1991), who explored the notion of two vying capitalist systems: the neo-American model founded on individual achievement and short-term financial gain; and the Rhenish model, of German extraction but with strong Japanese connections, which prizes collective success and consensus. The active market for corporate control, which typifies the Anglo-American model, is regularly contrasted with the far weaker market for corporate control, characteristic of the Rhenish model (Franks *et al.* 1990; Prowse 1995; La Porta *et al.* 1998; Goergen and Renneboog 2001; Hall and Soskice 2001). The French national business system is generally considered to be situated towards the middle of the spectrum, and is often typified as a variant of the Continental European model of managed capitalism (Rhodes and van Apeldoorn 1998), whilst the UK system is positioned towards the US end of the spectrum (Scott 1990; Cheffins 2001; Goergen and Renneboog 2001; Toms and Wright 2002).

National business systems and international communities might be seen as two theoretical notions in (apparent) opposition to one another, yet nevertheless in interaction. As Djelic and Quack suggest in Chapter 1 of this volume, transnational communities might be viewed as a means of collective "sensemaking" in the domain of transnational governance (Weick 1995), bringing together national and transnational fields and influencing policy debates and outcomes in both spheres. Colin Crouch (2005) writes that the context of globalization clearly calls into question the feasibility of individual business systems, which it transcends. Building on the varieties of capitalism literature (Hall and Soskice 2001), Crouch emphatically rejects the notion that governments might have to choose between just two viable forms of capitalism. In recent times, change has been relentless at both national and international level. It is arguably the Anglo-American type of capitalism which has come to the fore in the international arena, promoting a shareholder-value ethos, which infuses much governance reform, at the expense of more stakeholder- and network-based business systems – thereby privileging notions of *Gesellschaft*, perhaps, at the expense of notions of *Gemeinschaft* or community.

French companies have been compelled, for example, by the strength of global competition, to provide value for their shareholders, to become more transparent, and to focus more resolutely on financial issues and return on capital. At the same time, the foreign ownership of French listed companies has risen dramatically, such that foreign, particularly Anglo-American, institutional investors, own approximately 43 percent of the share capital of CAC-40 firms (Morin 2000; Maclean 2002; Mauduit 2003). The boards of directors of leading French firms increasingly include non-national members, reflecting the changing composition of the shareholding body.

As Mayntz highlights in this volume, the study of globalization has focused on markets, firms, and networks, whilst overlooking the study of transnational communities. While it is generally recognized that the world's largest companies are driving globalization and global governance practices (Scherer *et al.*

2006), comparatively little attention has been paid to the globalization of corporate boards and the individuals who populate them. Gillies and Dickenson (1999) found that 36.3 percent of the world's eighty largest transnational corporations had one non-national on their boards in 1993, while Staples (2007, 2008) established that by 2005 three-quarters of these companies had at least one foreign board member. The "communities of practice" literature (Lave and Wenger 1991) emphasizes the importance of social relations between participants (Thompson 2005). The members of boards of directors of global firms, who are frequently decision makers in other organizations, form social networks which may be characterized as "small worlds" (Conyon and Muldoon 2006). Drawing on the work of Alfred North Whitehead, Cobb (2007: 585) argues that process and internal relations – such as the governance processes of boards of directors and the relations which exist between members – matter more to the organization than "substantialism" and external relations, which "dehumanize employees and counter their desire for community." Boards themselves are subject to path dependency, "carry[ing] with them vestiges of their history and traditions" (Lynall *et al.* 2003: 416). Their composition and behaviors are therefore likely to remain reasonably stable over time.

Enduring differences in governance regimes

Such change as has occurred in the French system, moreover, has not been in one linear direction. Certainly, leading French companies are taking corporate governance much more seriously than hitherto. In this they are backed by the Nouvelles Régulations Economiques (NRE) of 2001 and the *loi sur la sécurité financière* on financial market regulation, which established the new Autorité des Marchés Financiers (AMF) in 2003. The NRE builds on the Viénot (AFEP/CNPF 1995; AFEP/MEDEF 1999), Marini (1996) and Bouton Reports (MEDEF/AFEP 2002) – themselves inspired by the British Combined Code (2003) and the various reports which inform it. The NRE comprises a wide-ranging set of corporate governance measures, whose primary objectives would appear to be informed by the shareholder-value paradigm, bringing France closer to the Anglo-American model. It encourages the separation of Chairman and CEO functions, traditionally united in the Président Directeur Général (PDG); restricts the number of board memberships held concurrently to five; strengthens the board vis-à-vis top management; facilitates the participation of minority shareholders through, inter alia, the introduction of new technologies (electronic voting and video-conferencing); and reinforces transparency of ownership by bolstering disclosure requirements. Likewise, the AMF, which unites the existing prudential institutions, the COB (Commission des Opérations de Bourse) and CMF (Conseil des Marchés Financiers), is designed to improve the efficiency of the French system, and to render it more comparable to those of other countries.

The ethos that traditionally has underpinned the French business system, however, lies in the "social interest" of the firm, enshrined in the *arrêt Freuhauf-France* of 1965. This may be defined as a belief in the common good uniting the interests of workers and employers; a belief that economic and social affairs are inseparable; and an expectation that employers should heed their responsibilities as well as their rights (Weber 1986; Maclean 2002). In other words, the notion of social interest is imbued with a deep-seated concern for communities – employees, employers, neighbors, government, and so on. Despite its apparent shareholder-value ethos, the NRE originated in the cause of *intérêt social*, initiated by former socialist premier Jospin to redress the balance in favor of stakeholders by discouraging "abusive lay-offs" in pursuit of higher profits. The NRE grants rights to stakeholders to challenge managerial decisions (Frison-Roche 2002; Clift 2007), though in practice such powers may prove illusory. Action by minority shareholders may collide with the fundamental principle governing French company law, which prioritizes the company interest. French business leaders remain largely autocratic, and challenges to an incumbent PDG by the board are rare; merely to take a vote on a decision, Alcouffe suggests, would be considered "bad manners" (cited in Clift, 2007). The response to the events at Société Générale, France's second-largest bank, in 2008, when a rogue trader was discovered to have amassed losses of €4.9 billion, is indicative. While the bank's CEO, Daniel Bouton, offered to resign twice at board meetings, on both occasions he was unanimously supported by his fellow directors despite the scale of the débâcle.

Elsewhere, we conceptualize a governance regime as existing on three inter-related levels – practical, systemic, and ideological – in which the rules, regulations, and practices at the uppermost level are more visible and open to change than the systems, ideologies, or "habitus" at the two lower, less visible levels (Maclean *et al.* 2006). The most visible and easily apprehended features are formal practices, rules, and regulations, positioned close to the apex. In legal or constitutional terms, we might think of the ways in which companies are set up and dissolved, the composition of boards of directors, and the ground rules for financial reporting. Each of these is relatively simple to observe and document. Conversely, underlying ideologies, assumptions and deep-seated values, on which rules and practices draw, are located closer to the base of the pyramid, being more difficult to circumscribe and pin down. It follows that changes at the organizational level, such as changes to corporate governance practices introduced in response to legislation or governance reports, are only ever likely to be stable if matched by parallel changes in assumptions, values, and beliefs at the sedimentary, ideological level.

The proposition that flows from this is that while there may be some international convergence of corporate governance policies and practices as a result of isomorphic pressures (DiMaggio and Powell 1983), as between France and Britain over the past fifteen years, their implementation and consequences for action will continue to differ because of the lesser potentiality for change that exists in business systems and dominant ideologies. Key features continue to differentiate the governance regimes of France and Britain, which are fundamental to what is generally regarded as "best practice" in corporate governance. These include the extent of separation in the roles of CEO and Chairman, and the independence of non-executive directors from top management – the extent to which board members are able to challenge company executives when appropriate.

According to the latest thinking on the composition and conduct of corporate boards, the interests of shareholders are best safeguarded when strategic moves proposed by top executives are scrutinized by the board in its entirety (Hermalin and Weisbach 1998; Young 2000; Aguilera 2005; Hendry 2005; Roberts *et al.* 2005), in consultation, if necessary, with key investors. To avoid the destructive, catastrophic situations that have embroiled companies across the world, Northern Rock and Société Générale included, governance systems are seen to be needed that might help to prevent situations from spiraling out of control. In this context, it is often recommended that power should be more evenly distributed throughout a board, and that all directors should be well informed and directly engaged in the decision-making process. This is seen to require the separation of the roles of Chairman and CEO, and the appointment of non-executive directors who are genuinely independent of top management.

Progress towards this "ideal" has been most rapid in the UK due to regular changes to the Combined Code. Following the Higgs review (2003), which argued that the "gene pool" of non-executive directors should be widened to promote independence, the criteria for qualifying as a genuinely independent director were articulated as follows: not having been employed by the company in a five-year period prior to appointment; having no close ties with the company's advisors, directors, or senior employees; not serving on the board for longer than ten years; and not serving as the representative of a single large shareholder or group of shareholders. If a non-executive director is appointed to a listed company who does not satisfy these requirements, the annual report must specify the reasons in accordance with the fundamental principle of the Combined Code, "comply or explain." UK companies have tended to opt for "comply" rather than "explain" with respect to most aspects of the Combined Code, such that by 1998 the functions of Chairman and CEO had been separated in 91 of the top UK 100 companies, rising to include all 100 by 2003–04.

In France, the prevailing situation is different because corporate governance regimes, in their reality and essential dynamics, are more the product of history, embraced in systems and mindsets, than conformance to a set of universally espoused principles (Roe 1994). The option exists under French company law to separate the roles of Chairman and CEO, but in many quarters the belief persists that effective decision-making requires that power be concentrated in the hands of the PDG. In 1998, 23 of the top 100 French companies had separated the roles of Chairman and CEO. By 2003 this had risen to 37. This might be seen as a major evolution, with an increase of 62 percent in leading companies separating out the roles of Chairman and CEO. On the other hand, it might also be interpreted as highlighting the importance of cultural reproduction as a mechanism for moderating pressures for change (Bourdieu and Passeron 1990; Bourdieu 1996), comparing as it does with the figure of 100 percent in Britain, and thereby suggesting a relative unwillingness to change on the part of the French. Several companies that had split the roles of Chairman and CEO later chose to reunite them, as in the cases of Alstom and Suez. There is an understandable reluctance to abandon the perceived advantages of long-standing institutional arrangements (Rhodes and van Apeldoorn 1998). This applies also to interlocking director-ships. Many of the most powerful PDGs continue to hold multiple non-executive directorships, as French directors continue to value corporate networking as a mechanism for coordinated action and fruitful engagement with their peers and the state (Burt *et al.* 2000; Yeo *et al.* 2003).

The natural affinities in outlook of Britain and other Anglo-American countries (Australia, Canada, New Zealand, and the USA) have ensured that these have borrowed significantly from the Combined Code, whereas French companies have clearly struggled with key governance concepts such as the independence of directors. This is understandable. In Britain, there is a manifest divide between the owners and managers of companies, shareholdings are dispersed, and institutional investors control just over 70 percent of equity. There is a standard corporate form that matches a standard governance code, whereas in France there is enduring diversity in relations between owners and managers (Bloch and Kremp 2001; Grant and Kirchmaier 2005). Some companies conform to the Anglo-American norm, but many others differ in remaining family owned or state owned, or in having close relationships with other companies. Directors are often appointed to boards specifically to represent a family, institution, or interest group, and therefore cannot be classified as "independent." Our research highlights differing perceptions of independence in Britain and France. Whereas Higgs (2003) views independence as a commodity that may be certified and audited, one French interviewee and governance expert doubts whether non-executive directors in France will ever be fully independent, given the importance of the community-based ties which unite them:

The notion of the independent director is an empirical notion. I often prefer to speak of "professional" directors rather than "independent" directors. In French practice, to be a director is a complement of activities. It is linked to the ties with capital; it is linked to the ties of friendship; it is linked to all kinds of things.[1]

The issue of independence, while difficult and problematic in France, is also likely to be problematic elsewhere, not just outside the Anglo-American countries. Being independent at the outset is one thing; remaining independent over a longer stretch of time is another. As one Chairman of a top 100 British company explained at interview: "Independence is all about a frame of mind. You can be independent according to the rules and weak at the same time, in which case you are of no value." He warned against appointing individuals to boards simply because they may be deemed "independent":

Of course there's been an improvement in independence, but again, you've got to be very, very, careful that the extension of the "gene pool" of non-executives doesn't suddenly mean that for the sake of ticking off the independence criteria, you actually get people who don't contribute much. Or worse, some pools, like those of government, can even be downright dangerous. A board is about facilitating the creation of sustainable value for shareholders, not about adopting every short-term fashion.[2]

While board independence from management is believed to improve board effectiveness (Westphal 1999; Roberts et al. 2005), the prevalence of CEO-board social ties in France means that board members exhibit considerable "class solidarity," characterized by an "enforceable trust" (Portes and Sensenbrenner 1993; Kadushin 1995). Enforceable trust is the means by which "social capital is generated by individual members' disciplined compliance with group expectations" (Portes and Sensenbrenner 1993: 1325). Trust serves as an "expectational asset'" (Knez and Camerer 1994), cementing relationships and building confident expectations regarding the future (De Carolis and Saparito 2006). One question that arises from the present context is what happens to community-building and group expectations of trust when the group is not homogeneous, from the same background, network, or family, but is on the contrary international; and when the values and assumptions impacting upon individual board members stem not from the same national source but from different national traditions, contexts, and habitus (Djelic and Quack in Chapter 1). In such circumstances, rather than a pre-existing, a priori network, board members have to deal with an a posteriori network or community in the making, identity being in this sense something which is invented or created rather than discovered (Bauman 2004).

The internationalization of boards in Britain and France

France is one of the European countries in which the level of employment by foreign companies is at its highest, approximately 25 percent of the French workforce being employed by foreign-owned companies, more than in the USA, the UK, or Germany.[3] An estimated 20,000 jobs are created annually through inward investment, which arguably exceeds those lost through company relocations to low-wage countries (Basani and Lechypre 2004).

As the ownership of French companies has become more distributed internationally, board membership has become more diversified by country of origin, although perhaps to a lesser degree than might be expected. Table 5.1 reveals that French and UK boards, with 15.0 and 16.5 percent of members being foreign nationals, respectively, are far from being transnational in composition. Yet the absolute numbers involved in both cases – 189 sitting on French boards and 173 on British – constitute substantial minorities. Two questions emerge. First, how do such large numbers of people become members of boards in other countries? Second, does this constitute evidence of the emergence of a transnational corporate community?

To help answer these questions, we have classified the foreign directors of French and British companies by director type (see Table 5.2). The basic division is between executive and non-executive directors, and each is divided further to reflect the different ways in which foreigners become members of the boards of big companies. Interesting similarities and differences emerge.

Table 5.1 Nationality profiles of the business elites of France and Britain in 1998

Country	Directors of French companies		Directors of British companies	
	No.	%	No.	%
France	1 071	85.00	20	1.90
UK	40	3.17	877	83.52
Italy	45	3.57	1	0.10
Germany	25	1.98	10	0.95
USA	15	1.19	62	5.90
Spain	13	1.03	4	0.38
Netherlands	11	0.87	14	1.33
Belgium	9	0.71	4	0.48
Switzerland	9	0.71	3	0.29
Japan	6	0.48	6	0.57
Canada	3	0.22	8	0.76
Australia	0	0.00	6	0.57
Hong Kong	0	0.00	8	0.76
South Africa	0	0.00	7	0.67
Others	13	1.03	20	1.93
Total	1 260		1 050	

Note: The data relate to 2,291 individuals, of whom 1,031 were directors of British top 100 companies, 1,241 were involved in French top 100 companies, and 19 were involved in both French and British companies.

Sizeable minorities in both countries are made up of top executives retained on a combined board following a cross-national merger. These executives are often found in clusters in genuinely cross-national boards. They can be distinguished from foreign executive directors recruited through the international labor market on account of their specialist skills, expertise, and knowledge. Such individuals, who constitute a higher proportion of the British cohort, tend to be spread more thinly across the system, often being the only foreigner within a top executive team. Equally pronounced similarities and differences exist with respect to non-executives, who are in the majority in both countries – 61.9 percent in France and 51.7 percent in Britain. A far higher proportion of the French cohort is made up of non-independent directors, many of whom are shareholder representatives, reflecting the historic ties binding companies and financial groups in Continental Europe. In both countries, however, large and comparable proportions of foreign directors consist of independent non-executives. These individuals, drawn from the highest ranks of their own national business communities, are recruited

Table 5.2 Foreign directors of top 100 French and British companies in 1998, by director type

	France (%) (n = 189)	UK (%) (n = 173)
Executive directors		
Joined from acquired companies	17.9	17.1
Recruited internationally	20.2	31.2
Non-executive directors		
Non-independent directors	27.4	14.3
Independent directors	34.5	37.4

because of the exceptional levels of cultural, social, and symbolic capital they might bring to the boardroom table.

The findings reported in Tables 5.1 and 5.2 provide mixed evidence regarding the emergence of transnational boards and communities. On the one hand, genuinely mixed nationality boards remain a rarity in both France and Britain. Foreign-born executives are found in some companies in some numbers, but often this configuration represents a blip following a merger. Of the ten British executive directors of French companies in 1998, only two remained in post six years later, the others, while still in employment, having returned to work for British companies. The evidence of active international markets for executive and non-executive talent is likewise ambiguous. The six-year survivor rates for foreign executive directors in top 100 companies are lower than for nationals in both France (53 percent against 62 percent) and Britain (47 percent against 59 percent). Meanwhile, many independent non-executive directors are recruited precisely because of their commanding knowledge of their own national business systems and regulatory regimes rather than their more general knowledge of international business – for example, five out of six Japanese non-executive directors of French companies fall into this category. These points illustrate that the international expansion of large firms does not automatically lead to the progressive emergence of transnational boards or business communities. On the other hand, the evidence presented on the international recruitment of top executives and independent non-executives suggests the emergence of an elite transnational business community with shared values, assumptions, and beliefs, and whose interests are increasingly perceived as being linked together.

The British economy is one of the most internationalized in the world. As one interviewee, a business leader and, more latterly, Cabinet Minister, highlighted, two-thirds of Confederation of British Industry (CBI) members are foreign.[4] Successive British governments, unlike their French counterparts, have chosen not to make British ownership of leading firms an important issue. The energy sector is symptomatic in this regard. Whereas the British chose to fragment national utility monopolies on privatization, the French have followed a different path, encouraging domestic monopolists such as EDF to exploit their favored position by expanding vigorously abroad (Maclean *et al.* 2007). As one British interviewee put it: "Business and the government don't pull the boat in the same direction in this country."[5]

One example of a genuinely international company is arguably Airbus, a European consortium comprising French, German, British, and Spanish actors. Airbus has traditionally operated a system of "passports" at board level, ensuring that all four nationalities were represented according to agreed ratios; though the company is trying to progress to a system in which appointments are determined by the quality of candidates rather than nationality, as one participant explained at interview:

The reality is that there is at that level some agreement between the shareholders in terms of how many people from different nationalities are on the board. So in fact the British have two people on the executive committee, the French and Germans three, and the Spanish have one. But in principle we have moved to a business where it is best man for the job. Certainly, when you go beneath the management board itself, then we are working in a transnational sense, and it is best man for the job. I have people working in France and Germany and the States in actual fact, so it's a transnational job. I have to manage teams in France, Germany and the US as well as the team I would normally manage in the UK.[6]

The transnational character of Airbus UK has stood it in good stead, helping it to weather economic downturns, as the same interviewee explains:

A prime example of our learning from our French and German partners is post September 11th, when a lot of UK aerospace companies made very instant reactions to reduce and downsize the workforce. In Airbus in the UK, we followed the lead of what was happening in France and Germany, and worked together with the trade unions to develop a jointly agreed plan in terms of what we called flexibility measures that we could introduce to try and preserve long-term employment. So, you could see a French and German influence on us, which was in stark contrast to the way other UK plcs were making their decisions, and I think, from my perspective, that actually has proved to have been the right thing to have done.[7]

The sale by BAE Systems in 2006 of its shareholding in EADS (European Aeronautics Defence and Space Company) has nevertheless "upset" the balance of nationalities at Airbus. Previously, the distribution of shareholdings according to nationality had been 4 percent Spanish, 20 percent British, with the balance being split equally between the French and Germans. This, by all accounts, had worked very well, but the removal of the British stake altered this balance. One British manager observed that the tenor of the company was becoming progressively "more French," underlining the point that ownership does indeed matter.[8]

Transnational communities, of course, are not limited to the boards of individual companies, but frequently cut across them. An example of a successful community doing this is provided by one interviewee, the human resource director for Europe of a top French company, who explained how he had developed a network of international human resource directors across Paris, called the HR Exchange:

We have created an association which is a somewhat informal association, but with incorporation in order to get some funds. We meet once every six weeks on the subject of common interests, so it's a place of exchange of good practices. We wanted to have a small group of people who were really able to liaise and talk to each other without playing politics ... We are international HR people, we have members in our group who are not French nationals, who are British nationals working in Paris.[9]

Our research has revealed that French and British boards differ in the "hierarchy" of directors' nationalities that apply. While Britain's main source of foreign directors is, not unexpectedly, the USA (60 directors, amounting to 5.8 percent), ahead of France in second place (20 directors, or 1.9 percent), and the Netherlands in third (1.3 percent), France's number one source for foreign directors in 1998 was in fact Italy (45 directors, equal to 3.6 percent), narrowly ahead of the UK (40 directors, or 3.2 percent), with Germany in third position (2 percent), and the USA in fourth place, with just 15 of a total of 1,260 directors coming from the USA (Maclean *et al.* 2006). Examining France's top 40 boards, Korn/Ferry found that by December 2002, foreign membership of CAC-40 boards stood at 24 percent, comprising 133 board seats out of a total of 551. The companies with the most internationalized boards were Dexia, 60 percent of whose members were non-French, followed by Alstom (56 percent), Orange, Suez, and Aventis, whose boards were all 50 percent non-French; reflecting their origins and involvement in mergers, and the high percentage of company turnover achieved abroad: 62 percent in the case of Alstom, 55 percent for Orange, 51 percent for Suez, and 48 percent for Aventis (Korn/Ferry 2002).

At top executive level, however, French boards in particular were notably less international, with just three members of the super-elite of the hundred most powerful directors in France in 1998 being non-French: Lindsay Owen-Jones

(British), Viscount Etienne Davignon (Belgian), and Stefano Meloni (Italian). British companies are more internationalized at the top level, with twelve of the super-elite being non-British, of which five are from the USA, two from New Zealand, and one each from Australia, Denmark, Ireland, the Netherlands, and Sweden. These figures would appear to affirm the power of cultural reproduction, suggesting that, at the uppermost level, the French are slightly more reluctant to let go of the reins than the British, who embrace diversity slightly more. That said, three-quarters of the top foreign directors in the British power elite come from the Anglo-American family of countries, with just three coming from elsewhere: Per Gyllenhammar (Sweden), Jan Leschli (Denmark), and Jan Peelen (the Netherlands). Though British boards may appear to be more internationalized at the uppermost level, they do so from a position of relative strength, with a strong corporate governance model which has widely influenced the governance regimes of the Anglo-American family of countries globally.

The internationalization of boards which has taken place requires, of course, a common language, which is English, corroborating Hobsbawm's observation cited earlier in this chapter that language can be overridden by globalization. Language, as Djelic and Quack point out in this volume, is also critical to notions of a common national identity. To move beyond one's mother tongue in a community in the making is therefore to open oneself up to new possibilities for transnational belonging. In a personal interview, one former Chairman and CEO of a leading French company explained that English had been adopted as the corporate language in 1990 because the company headquarters had begun to resemble "Babel Tower":

It was like a Babel Tower. We had the British, the Germans, the Spaniards and the Americans. The decision we took in 1990 was to say that English is our corporate language, so every time we speak between countries we use English – bad English, but English. A Frenchman who sends me an email generally sends me it in English because I may forward it to an English colleague, or a German colleague, so it's by far easier.[10]

This decision has been reiterated in numerous top Parisian boardrooms in recent years, the use of a common language facilitating communication in board meetings and emails. It has not gone unchallenged, however, and not just from the Académie Française, a staunch defender of the linguistic "purity" of French. In 2005, French trade unionists won an important victory over the imposed use of English at General Electric Medical Systems. The union claimed successfully that this breached the 1994 Toubon law, which requires all foreign expressions to be translated into French inside the workplace, as a result of which the company must now provide French translations of all vital documents (Bremner 2005). This ruling challenged the trend for French and international companies in France to use English as their first language, providing a small but telling example of how the French may revert to type, even in the face of an apparent *fait accompli*.

The European consortium Airbus has likewise adopted English as a common language; though as one interviewee pointed out, "this is fine for board meetings, but I believe that to go beyond this, especially for socializing with other directors, you do need a working knowledge of French and German."[11] Another interviewee agreed, lamenting at interview the fact that he had never learned to speak French:

The thing I most regret is that I was never given a French lesson. If I could speak four or five languages . . . the opportunities are so great. I'm lucky that I'm in the television business, which is predominantly English, but I have friends who can speak four or five languages in any accent, and it is a huge advantage.[12]

Language is clearly an essential element in the transnational community-building process, allowing shared socialization. In a similar vein, the spread of business education and its partial homogenization across the globe, including the increased training of board members in many countries, may lead to more broadly shared common cognitive frames, which might in time go some way towards representing, at least in part, a functional equivalent to the "family," "ethnic," or "national" cement of more traditional communities. One interviewee spoke enthusiastically of the thirteen-week senior executive program he had attended at the Massachusetts Institute of Technology (MIT). Intensive executive courses often lead to a deep bonding process across different nationalities and ethnic groups. He described his fellow students as "a rich group of individuals, very cosmopolitan." The program had given him an overall understanding of the way that business was transacted, leading to his career as a top manager really taking off in a life-changing manner: "If you had told me before I went to MIT how I would feel afterwards, I would have paid for it myself."[13]

A further important dimension has to do with the process of the professionalization of boards, which is part and parcel of the process of governance reform. An increasing number of board nominations and key appointments are now in the hands of professional head-hunters. Associations such as the CBI or Institute of Directors (IoD) in Britain or MEDEF in France have an important role to play in sustaining the development of a transnational "common culture," through fostering shared cognitive and behavioral patterns at directorial level, irrespective of nationality. That said, the wheels of change turn slowly, and it is also the case that such well-respected, enduring institutions have a role to play in transmitting the culture of their host nation. A visit to the IoD, for example, occupying an impressive building in Pall Mall, central London, confirms its inherently "British" nature and "clubbish" atmosphere.

Our research also sheds light on the mechanisms through which the members of the elite join forces to make common cause at supranational level. Pivotal in this regard are business associations, which cover every sector of the economy from nuclear power and rail transport to construction and food services. The boards of these associations invariably are dominated by directors of leading companies. Working through a small professional staff they aim, through sustained lobbying, to change the institutional landscape to their collective advantage. We have identified 595 directors of the top 100 companies in France as having a governance role within a business association for some time during the fifteen-year period down to the end of 2003. Many have in addition held prominent roles within the European Commission, the OECD, and the World Bank. Others were active within bodies such as the European Round Table of Industrialists and the World Economic Forum that promote wider business goals and ideological positions (for a different but complementary story see Plehwe in this volume). Viewed in this light, the transnational community of directors in the making is clearly linked to the process of transnational regulation, reflecting a particular form of regulatory effort with transnational scope.

Conclusion

"Communities," Bauman (2000: 169) observes, "come in many colours and sizes, but if plotted on the Weberian axis stretching from 'light cloak' to 'iron cage', they all come remarkably close to the first pole." This metaphor of a community as a "light cloak" is appealing. Consequential change is often evolutionary rather than revolutionary. Djelic and Quack describe such change as "stalactite" (2003b: 310), drawing on the analogy of miniscule droplets of water running down the wall of a cave. While each is insignificant in itself, over time the results are likely to be stupendous, leading ultimately to a radical transformation of the cave as a whole.

So it may be with the development of transnational communities. From our analysis of the composition and *modus operandi* of the business elites of

France and Britain, it is our contention that business elites, including those of large transnational enterprises, continue to be forged primarily within the context of national communities. We observe that such leaders are attuned to the demands and requirements of competing across international boundaries, and as such are flexible in their tactical responses; but nonetheless their community affiliations remain primarily national, regional, or local. This said, there is nevertheless evidence of systemic change and a growing recognition of shared values, assumptions, and beliefs at the transnational level. As Djelic and Quack observe in this volume, similarity and homogeneity do not represent a sine qua non for community-building. In today's globalized world, the notion of community merits projection into the analysis of transnational phenomena. Elite directors are active within multiple communities, one of which may be the new transnational corporate community in the making. It is our view that the trend towards multinational boards is one that will continue, contributing over time to the possible emergence of a transnational community of business elites.

Acknowledgments

The authors wish to thank the Leverhulme Trust and Reed Charity for funding the research which has informed this paper. They also wish to thank the directors and governance experts from Britain and France who kindly agreed to be interviewed, and the editors for their insightful comments.

NOTES

1. Interview with French Senator, French Senate, January 14, 2004, Paris.
2. Interview with Chairman of top 100 British company, June 23, 2008, London.
3. Interview with Human Resource Director of leading French company, May 26, 2003, Paris.
4. Interview with business leader and Cabinet Minister, May 3, 2006, Bristol.
5. Interview with business leader and Cabinet Minister, May 3, 2006, Bristol.
6. Interview with former Managing Director of Airbus UK, February 4, 2003, Bristol.
7. Interview with former Managing Director of Airbus UK, February 4, 2003, Bristol.
8. Interview, November 29, 2007, Bristol.
9. Interview with Human Resource Director of leading French company.
10. Interview with former Chairman and CEO of leading French company, Paris, January 2003.
11. Interview with former Managing Director of Airbus UK.

12. Interview with Chairman of leading entertainment company, September 5, 2003, London.
13. Interview with former Director of Operations and Customer Services of leading British company, Windsor, January 2, 2009.

REFERENCES

AFEP/CNPF. 1995. *Le Conseil d'administration des sociétés cotées*. Paris: IEP (Viénot Report I).

AFEP/MEDEF. 1999. Rapport du Comité sur le gouvernement d'entreprise présidé par M. Marc Viénot (Viénot Report II).

Aguilera, R. V. 2005. "Corporate governance and director accountability: An institutional comparative perspective," *British Journal of Management* **16**, supplementary edition: 39–53.

Aguilera, R. V. and Jackson, G. 2003. "The cross-national diversity of corporate governance: Dimensions and determinants," *Academy of Management Review* **28** (3): 447–65.

Albert, M. 1991. *Capitalisme contre capitalisme*. Paris: Seuil.

Basani, B. and Lechypre, E. 2004. "Délocalisations: la grande peur française," *L'Expansion* No. 691/November: 36–39.

Bauman, Z. 2000. *Liquid modernity*. Cambridge: Polity.

Bauman, Z. 2004. *Identity: Conversations with Benedetto Vecchi*. Cambridge: Polity.

Bauman, Z. 2007. *Liquid times: Living in an age of uncertainty*. Cambridge: Polity.

Bloch, L. and Kremp, E. 2001. "Ownership and voting power in France," in Barca, F. and Becht, M. (eds.), *The control of corporate Europe*. Oxford University Press, pp. 106–27.

Bourdieu, P. 1990. *The logic of practice*. Stanford University Press.

Bourdieu, P. 1996. *The state nobility: Elite schools in the field of power*. Cambridge: Polity Press.

Bourdieu, P. and Passeron, J.-C. 1990. *Reproduction in education, society and culture*. Second edition. London: Sage.

Bremner, C. 2005. "French hail victory over English," *The Times*, January 12, **37**.

British Combined Code. 2003. *The combined code on corporate governance*. London: Financial Reporting Council.

Burt, R. S., Hogarth, R. M. and Michaud, C. 2000. "The social capital of French and American managers," *Organization Science* **11** (2): 123–47.

Carati, G. and Tourani Rad, A. 2000. "Convergence of corporate governance systems," *Managerial Finance* **26** (10): 66–83.

Cheffins, B. R. 2001. "History and the global corporate governance revolution: The UK perspective," *Business History* **43** (4): 87–118.

Clift, B. 2007. "French corporate governance in the new global economy: Mechanisms of change within models of capitalism," *Political Studies* **55** (3): 546–67.

Cobb, J. B. 2007. "Person-in-community: Whiteheadian insights into community and institution", *Organization Studies* **28** (4): 567–88.

Conyon, M. and Muldoon, M. R. 2006. "The small world of corporate boards," *Journal of Business Finance and Accounting* **33** (9–10): 1321–43.

Crouch, C. 2005. *Capitalist diversity and change: Recombinant governance and institutional entrepreneurs*. Oxford University Press.

De Carolis, D. M. and Saparito, P. 2006. "Social capital, cognition, and entrepreneurial opportunities: A theoretical framework," *Entrepreneurship, Theory and Practice* **30** (1): 41–56.

DiMaggio, P. and Powell, W. W. 1983. "The iron cage revisited: Institutional isomorphism and collective rationality in organizational fields," *American Sociological Review* **48** (2): 147–60.

Djelic, M.-L. 1998. *Exporting the American model: The postwar transformation of European business.* Oxford University Press.

Djelic, M.-L. and Quack, S. 2003a. "Introduction," in Djelic, M-L. and Quack, S. (eds.), *Globalization and institutions: Redefining the rules of the economic game.* Cheltenham: Edward Elgar, pp. 1–14.

Djelic, M.-L., and Quack, S. 2003b. "Conclusion," in Djelic, M.-L. and Quack, S. (eds.), *Globalization and institutions: Redefining the rules of the economic game.* Cheltenham: Edward Elgar, pp. 302–33.

Franks, J. Mayer, C., Hardie, J. and Malinvaud, E. 1990. "Capital markets and corporate control: A study of France, Germany and the UK," *Economic Policy*, **5** (10): 189–231.

Frison-Roche, M.-A. 2002. "Le droit français des sociétés cotées entre *corporate governance* et culture de marché," in Plihon, D. and Ponssard, J.-P. (eds.), *Le Montée en puissance des fonds d'investissement.* Paris: la Documentation française, pp. 77–92.

Gillies, J. and Dickenson, M. 1999. "The governance of transnational firms: Some preliminary hypotheses," *Corporate Governance: An International Journal* **7**: 237–47.

Goergen, M. and Renneboog, L. 2001. "United Kingdom," in Gugler, K. (ed.), *Corporate governance and economic performance.* Oxford University Press, pp. 184–200.

Granovetter, M. 1985. "Economic action and social structure: The problem of embeddedness," *American Journal of Sociology* **91**: 481–510.

Grant, J. and Kirchmaier, T. 2005. "Corporate control in Europe," *Corporate Ownership and Control* **2** (2): 65–76.

Hall, P. and Soskice, D. 2001. "An introduction to varieties of capitalism," in Soskice, D. and Hall, P. (eds.), *Varieties of capitalism: The institutional foundations of comparative advantage.* Oxford University Press, pp. 1–70.

Harvey, C. and Maclean, M. 2008. "Capital theory and the dynamics of elite business networks in Britain and France," in M. Savage and K. Williams (eds.), *Remembering elites.* Oxford: Blackwell, pp. 105–20.

Hendry, J. 2005. "Beyond self-interest: Agency theory and the board in a satisficing world," *British Journal of Management* **16**: 55–63.

Hermalin, B. E. and Weisbach, M. S. 1998. "Endogenously chosen boards of directors and their monitoring of the CEO," *American Economic Review* **88** (1): 96–118.

Higgs, D. 2003. *Review of the role and effectiveness of non-executive directors.* London: Department of Trade and Industry.

Kadushin, C. 1995. "Friendship among the French financial elite," *American Sociological Review* **60** (2): 202–21.

Knez, M. and Camerer, C. 1994. "Creating expectational assets in the laboratory: Coordination in 'weakest link' games," *Strategic Management Journal* **15**: 101–19.

Korn/Ferry International. 2002. *Gouvernement d'entreprise en France en 2002.* Paris.

La Porta, R., Lopez-de-Silanes, F., Schleifer, A. and Vishny, R. W. 1998. "Corporate ownership around the world," *Journal of Finance* **54**: 471–517.

Lave, J. and Wenger, E. 1991. *Situated learning: Legitimate peripheral participation*. Cambridge University Press.

Lynall, M. D., Golden, B. R. and Hillman, A. J. 2003. "Board composition from adolescence to maturity: A multitheoretic view," *Academy of Management Review* **28** (3): 416–31.

Maclean, M. 2002. *Economic management and French business from de Gaulle to Chirac*. Basingstoke: Palgrave Macmillan.

Maclean, M. and Harvey, C. 2008. "The continuing diversity of corporate governance regimes: France and Britain compared," in Strange, R. and Jackson, G. (eds.), *International business and corporate governance: Strategy, performance and institutional change*. Basingstoke: Palgrave Macmillan, pp. 208–25.

Maclean, M., Harvey, C. and Press, J. 2006. *Business elites and corporate governance in France and the UK*. Basingstoke: Palgrave Macmillan.

Maclean, M., Harvey, C. and Press, J. 2007. "Managerialism and the post-war evolution of the French national business system," *Business History* **49** (4): 531–51.

Marini, P. 1996. *La modernisation du droit des sociétés*. Paris: La Documentation Française (Marini Report).

Marquis, C., Glynn, M. A. and Davis, G. F. 2007. "Community isomorphism and corporate social action," *Academy of Management Review* **32** (3): 925–45.

Mauduit, L. 2003. "Du capitalisme rhénan au capitalisme américain, la mutation de l'économie s'accélère," *Le Monde*, July 29.

MEDEF/AFEP. 2002. *Pour un meilleur gouvernement des entreprises cotées*. (Bouton Report). Paris: MEDEF.

Morin, F. 2000. "A transformation in the French model of shareholding and management," *Economy and Society* **29** (1): 36–53.

Pedersen, T. and Thomsen, S. 1997. "European patterns of corporate ownership: A twelve-country study," *Journal of International Business Studies* **4**: 759–78.

Portes, A. and Sensenbrenner, J. 1993. "Embeddedness and immigration: Notes on the social determinants of economic action," *American Journal of Sociology* **98** (6): 1320–50.

Prowse, S. 1995. "Corporate governance in an international perspective: A survey of corporate control mechanisms among large firms in the US, UK, Japan and Germany," *Financial Markets, Institutions and Instruments* **4** (1): 1–63.

Rhodes, M. and van Apeldoorn, B. 1998. "Capital unbound? The transformation of European corporate governance," *Journal of European Public Policy* **5** (3): 406–27.

Roberts, R., McNulty, T. and Stiles, P. 2005. "Beyond agency conceptions of the work of the non-executive director: Creating accountability in the boardroom," *British Journal of Management* **16**: S5–S26.

Roe, M. J. 1994. "Some differences in corporate governance in Germany, Japan and America," in Baums, T., Hopt, R. and Buxham, R. M. (eds.), *Institutional investors and corporate governance*. Berlin: De Gruyter, pp. 23–88.

Schatzki, T. R. 1996. *Social practices: A Wittgensteinian approach to human activity and the social*. Cambridge University Press.

Scherer, A. G., Palazzo, G. and Baumann, D. 2006. "Global rules and private actors: Toward a new role of the transnational corporation in global governance," *Business Ethics Quarterly* **16** (4): 505–32.

Scott, J. 1990. "Corporate control and corporate rule: Britain in an international perspective," *British Journal of Sociology* **41** (3): 351–73.

Staples, C. L. 2007. "Board globalisation in the world's largest TNCs 1993–2005," *Corporate Governance: An International Review* **15** (2): 311–21.

Staples, C. L. 2008. "Cross-border acquisitions and board globalization in the world's largest TNCs, 1995–2005," *The Sociological Quarterly* **49**: 31–51.

Thompson, M. 2005. "Structural and epistemic parameters in communities of practice," *Organization Science* **16** (2): 151–64.

Toms, S. and Wright, M. 2002. "Corporate governance, strategy and structure in British business history, 1950–2000," *Business History* **44** (3): 91–124.

Toms, S. and Wright, M. 2005. "Divergence and convergence within Anglo-American corporate governance systems: Evidence from the US and UK, 1950–2000," *Business History* **47** (2): 267–91.

Tönnies, F. 2002 [1897]. *Community and society*. Mineola, NY: Dover Publications.

Weber, H. 1986. *Le Parti des patrons: le CNPF (1946–1986)*. Paris: Seuil.

Weick, K. E. 1995. *Sensemaking in organizations*. London: Sage.

Westphal, J. 1999. "Collaboration in the boardroom: Behavioural and performance consequences of CEO–board social ties," *Academy of Management Journal* **42** (1): 7–24.

Whitley, R. 1999. *Divergent capitalisms*. Oxford University Press.

Yeo, H-J., Pochet, C. and Alcouffe, A. 2003. "CEO reciprocal interlocks in French corporations," *Journal of Management and Governance* **7** (1): 87–108.

Young, S. 2000. "The increasing use of non-executive directors: Its impact on UK board structure and governance arrangements," *Journal of Business, Finance & Accounting* **27** (9–10): 1311–42.

6　Private equity in Japan: global financial markets and transnational communities

Glenn Morgan and Izumi Kubo

Introduction

One of the main developments in financial markets over the last decade has been the growth of private equity. Thomson Financial reported that approximately 25 percent of all mergers and acquisitions in 2007 were private equity-funded buyouts, compared to 3 percent a decade ago. In 2006, almost $135 billion of private equity was invested, up a fifth from the previous year. The amount of funds actually raised by private equity globally was $232 billion in 2005, up three-quarters on 2004 (International Financial Services [IFSL] 2006). In 2006, private equity firms expanded into Asia outside Japan, investing $28.9 billion in the first nine months of the year, up 78 percent. In Europe, private equity deals were up 70 percent in the first half of 2006. Private equity has become a worldwide movement. In 2005, North America accounted for 40 percent of global private equity investments (down from 68 percent in 2000) and 52 percent of funds raised (down from 69 percent). Europe increased its share of investments (from 17 percent to 43 percent) and funds raised (from 17 percent to 38 percent). The Asia Pacific region's share of investments increased from 6 percent to 11 percent during this period, whilst its share of funds raised remained unchanged at 8 percent.

This expansion was based on a series of financial innovations as regards the structuring of debt and equity and the ability to create secondary financial markets in which risk could be parceled out in new ways in contexts in which there appeared to be a growing glut of savings (particularly from Asia) and a growing number of borrowers (particularly in the USA and the UK). This created a complex network of actors and institutions that became dependent on each other in ways which, as the current financial crisis has revealed, were not clearly anticipated or controlled. Since late 2007, the environment for new private equity deals has gradually deteriorated, collapsing precipitously with the onset of the deep crisis in the banking system beginning in September

2008. This collapse has meant that private equity cannot raise funds for the sorts of leveraged deals in which it previously engaged, nor can it release funds from existing investments since the market for exiting (through IPOs, auctions, trade sales, or secondary sales to other private equity firms) has also collapsed. However, the acquisitions made in the boom years remain in place. The dynamic of the industry is therefore shifting from processes of acquisition, financial engineering, and sell-off to a process more focused on the consolidation and management of existing investments (Morgan 2009). Therefore, private equity itself has not collapsed, even if some funds are struggling with the new economic conditions.

In this chapter, we are interested in whether private equity can be usefully described in terms of the formation of a transnational community, in contrast to being simply a "global industry." The first part of the chapter examines the idea of transnational communities and considers how private equity might be viewed as such a community. The second part focuses on the growth of private equity in the Japanese context. Our general point is that the development of private equity in Japan depended on key actors being part of a wider transnational community in which the norms, practices, and procedures of how to undertake private equity activity were established. Individuals and organizations in Japan participated in and identified with this transnational community in their efforts to establish private equity in the Tokyo financial markets. They did so in ways that adapted those practices to the specific characteristics of Japanese financial markets.

In many ways, Japan can be considered an extreme case. It has traditionally been seen as one of the most closed industrial societies across a variety of dimensions, including its financial markets. Since the early 1990s, this has begun to change. Part of that change in the last few years has involved the growing role of private equity in the Japanese financial system. These changes reflect the interaction of internal forces with external international ones, of political factors with economic ones, of markets with hierarchies and networks, and of path dependency (Morgan and Kubo 2005a) with institutional change. It is within this complex set of forces and processes that private equity as an emergent transnational community with a Japanese subpopulation has played a role.

Transnational communities

In the introductory chapters to this book, Djelic and Quack and Mayntz make clear that the constitutive nature of "community" does not lie in propinquity/locality nor in the permanence of social relations nor in shared ascriptive characteristics. Instead, Djelic and Quack emphasize that it can be defined in terms of "mutual orientation and dependence of members, a common identity or common project, a form of active engagement and involvement, and a sense of belonging." They argue that this community is not all-encompassing as regards the lifeworld of the individuals or groups that constitute it; rather, such individuals and groups may belong to a variety of different communities with varying degrees of permanence. There is no protean "community" waiting to be given agency; there are only social processes that give rise to communities that have agency. In this sense, the study of communities is a study of process and emergent features: how is belonging generated and sustained, and with what effects?

Mayntz describes these as communities of interest in which shared characteristics constitute the identity of the collective. She identifies a range of different communities of interest: scientific, epistemic, policy, communities of practice, professional, and business ones. The governance of these communities varies because of the nature of the actors who are brought together, and the purpose of the community and its shared values.

In traditional analyses of community, the nature of boundaries and borders was significant. Communities defined themselves through the nature of the boundary that they drew between themselves and their practices and those of others who remained outside. Similarly, communities were often forged at least in part by a response to labeling by others. Transnational communities in the sense defined by Djelic and Quack and by Mayntz are likely to have relatively porous borders; entry to the community is not strictly controlled, actors can move in and out relatively easily. Some actors may commit relatively long-term, and invest in specific assets that lock them in to the community (for example, by becoming organizers and proponents of it), whilst others may vary in their level of commitment and investment (Morgan 2001b).

The term "transnational community" therefore points to the existence of cross-cutting networks of firms, individuals, associations, technologies, and rules of action that define a certain common set of activities and processes across national boundaries (Morgan 2001a). From this perspective, what Sorge (2005) defines as the "horizon of action" transcends the national space and brings into view, and into the action space of the individual and the organization, activities in other institutional contexts. The national context is not abolished but nested in sets of relationships that are transnational in scope. As actors recognize this process more explicitly, they engage in building the material, regulative, and social infrastructure of such communities, which in turn reinforces this new horizon of action (Djelic and Quack 2003; Djelic and Sahlin-Andersson 2006).

Transnational communities and international financial markets

Compared to twenty years ago, when banking and finance were clearly national in structure and strategy, there is today an important tier of international financial institutions (for parallels, see Ramirez in this volume). Investment banking, for example, has emerged as a distinctive type of institution that links together a wide range of expertise in banking and finance, capital markets, trading and dealing. Whilst we can still identify nationally distinctive features, the basic model of the large-scale investment bank is shared by US, UK, French, German, Dutch, Swiss, and Japanese institutions. The fact that they are each others' most important customers has been a powerful force towards compatibility and the standardization of their various technological, contractual, and market interfaces. It has pushed them towards the sharing of facilities, such as mechanisms for the clearing and settlement of international accounts. The more they interacted, the more they required the construction of a level playing field so that no participant in a market was unfairly advantaged (see Morgan 2001a). As a result, they were to an extent regulated in similar ways through the capital adequacy standards of the Basel agreements, which aim to standardize the basic risk profile of any institution defined as a bank. In terms of products, they shifted predominantly to capital market activities and interaction with other financial institutions as their main mode of activity and away from a predominant emphasis on deposit taking and lending. Around these banks were large numbers of more specialized actors that established particular niches: on the finance side, private equity, hedge funds, investment companies, rating agencies, advisers, lawyers, and so on.

The discourse of transnational communities, however, draws us beyond this sort of account towards a focus on individuals, their interactions, and their collective formations (see, for example, Plehwe in this volume). Where there are global firms, there are new emergent models of individual, group, and community. In terms of international financial markets in the period from the 1990s through to around 2007, a number of aspects can be identified in relation to the nature of recruitment, career development, skill sets, and networks. Global firms in the financial sector tended to require individuals who were relatively mobile across national borders so that they could attend to international clients, join international project teams, participate in the opening of new offices across emerging economies, and learn about new financial products and regulatory issues through common training systems. They also required individuals with a certain common level of education that enabled them to communicate about problem-solving tasks using a shared vocabulary and technical knowledge. This commonality increased the potential of individuals to move between similar firms in terms of career development and along the way to develop networks of loose ties with the individuals with whom they had worked. The financial markets in which they engaged were increasingly virtual, based on electronic media that link sites across the world into a common trading network in which the actors became standard participants in a predictable process of global interaction (see Hussain and Ventresca in this volume). These individual, group, and network linkages constituted a distinct level of analysis, separate from that of firms and industry structures. They overlaid and interacted with firm-level structures and regulatory boundaries but they were not defined by them.

In turn, these transnational processes interacted with what may be labeled the "stickiness" of place and locality (see, for example, Harvey and Maclean, and Ramirez in this volume). As firms, regulations, markets, individuals, groups, and networks shifted their horizon of action to the transnational, they did not disengage from place but rather created a tension between local embeddedness and transnational processes and community formation. The differences between contexts lay partly in the institutional and regulatory framework, partly in the knowledge base and the networks necessary for different business models, and partly in the ability to develop new organizational forms. These historical differences did not disappear in the process of transition but created distinctive path dependencies.

In the financial sector, transnational communities are revealed most clearly in centers such as New York and London where firms with different national origins employ individuals from diverse national backgrounds. Other cities with strong financial markets – such as Paris, Frankfurt, Singapore, Hong Kong, and Tokyo – share similar characteristics to varying degrees. The same firms appear in the different cities, individuals move between these cities, the practices of financial markets are common, subject to some regulatory variation, and finally the actors are connected by an intense technological infrastructure (Hussain and Ventresca in this volume).

To summarize, the sphere of international financial services can be considered as one of both flows and fixity. Flows cross national borders and are the forces that facilitate the formation of broader transnational communities (for example, Schrad in this volume). Fixes pin activities down to certain locations and material processes through national systems of law and regulation (for example, Ramirez in this volume). Flows include flows of capital, flows of new organizational forms, flows of financial products, and flows of individuals. Points of fixity include the international financial institutions themselves, the system of law and regulation within national contexts, the technology systems established to coordinate flows, and the international regulatory systems. It is out of the conjuncture between flows and fixity that forms of transnational communities emerge as the horizon of action for specific actors changes and they begin to participate as relays, linking national contexts with international processes.

Private equity

In this section, we briefly summarize the development of private equity as a model of financial investment. Our claim here is that the term "private equity" signifies a particular set of practices and processes. Although some features of private equity can be traced back a long way, by the late 1990s the term identified a particular set of financial market processes, actors, and techniques. In the period 2001–07, these features that had initially emerged in the UK and the USA were replicated in a number of other countries. They were replicated by the transfer of firms and individuals across national borders and by actors within these new contexts learning, imitating, and adapting the model to their particular circumstances. The result was the creation of a transnational community of private equity. This community identification was reinforced by the way in which the model itself drew forth strong resistance from trade union groups and employees, and also led to increased monitoring by international financial regulators. Private equity was often forced to come together as a community in order to defend itself against outsiders who sought to control and reduce its influence. Indeed, it was the segment of the financial markets that was most politicized in the period leading up to the current crisis.

What are the characteristics of private equity? The basic organizational form of a private equity house is a private partnership between what are termed the general partners.[1] The private equity firm seeks capital from large institutional investors to set up a fund that has defined objectives and a defined timetable. These investors, who commit to a specified (limited) amount of capital, are known as the limited partners. The final, crucial element of the model, particularly as it operated in the 2000s up to 2007, is "leverage." Leverage means that the private equity company puts up a relatively small amount of funds (usually around 20–30 percent of the total price) from its general and limited partners into the purchase price for an acquisition and then borrows the rest (70–80 percent) by selling bonds in the financial markets. In order to borrow, it relies on its relations with leading investment banks that underwrite bond issues. Bond markets have become increasingly sophisticated as debt is packaged up and sold off ("securitized") into financial instruments with distinct levels of risk reflected in interest rates and covenants on conditions. For example, if one of the big ratings agencies was to downgrade debt because it felt that other conditions were making default more likely, then the interest rate to be paid on the debt would increase to reflect increased risk. The owner of the bond can sell it on in the financial markets, where its value will vary according to the performance of the firm originating the bond, the dynamics of the sector, and the broader economic environment. For big deals, a lead bank may be supported by a number of other, smaller participants. The private equity model, therefore, depends on relatively stable and low interest rates, a large and risk-sensitive population of investors seeking alternative investments, and high market liquidity.

When a firm is acquired, the private equity company installs a new management and board of directors that focus on increasing the value of the company so that at the end of three to seven years, it can be sold on at a profit. There are various financial engineering techniques that facilitated this up to 2007 related to tax liabilities and restructuring debt obligations. Private equity managements argue that there is a stronger alignment of principals and agents than in public companies as the interests of principals are not as diverse and agents (senior managers) are expected to have committed substantial amounts of their own wealth to the company. There are multiple exit routes for private equity, ranging from relaunching a company on public markets (IPO), selling it to another private equity firm, arranging a management buyout, or arranging a private auction.

In a survey conducted by Private Equity International (May 2007), 31 of the top 50 (and 7 out of the top 10) private equity firms (measured by the amount of capital raised in the last 5 years) were from the USA, 2 from Canada, 11 (including 3 in the top 10) from the UK, 5 from Western Europe (2 from the Netherlands, 3 from Sweden, and 1 from Paris), and 1 from the Asia Pacific (Sydney). In terms of investment, 40 percent of private equity investment in 2005 went into the USA (0.4 percent of GDP), 22 percent into the UK (1.3 percent), 7 percent into France (0.4 percent),

3 percent each for Sweden (1 percent), Spain (0.3 percent) and Germany (0.1 percent), and 2 percent each for the Netherlands (0.5 percent) and Japan (less than 0.1 percent). A total of 43 percent of investments went into Europe as a whole in 2005 and 11 percent into Asia Pacific.

This increased global activity had implications for the establishment of a transnational community around private equity. Private equity firms recruited locals from different potential markets both to work in their head offices as part of the scanning process and also to be active in subsidiary offices established in various countries. Some of these locals eventually established their own private equity firms in their home context, using the skills, knowledge, and networks of contacts that they had acquired from this experience.

An important effect of the global spread of private equity offices and firms was that local participants in the system helped draw local investors and savers more tightly into the private equity world. Private equity firms suck in savings from institutional investors wherever they can find them. US institutional investors were early in diversifying into this area, with UK pension funds following. The size of investment and its speed of growth was slower in parts of Europe where pensions are funded on a "pay as you go" basis rather than through investment, but this is changing as a result of demographic and political pressures. Savings in Asia have, however, become particularly important. In the case of Japan, this arises from a high savings ratio that is required in order to compensate for a weak state welfare system and a corporate pension system that is limited in its efficacy. Thus funds flow from the personal sector into banking institutions for circulation into global investment opportunities (particularly given weak prospects for investment returns elsewhere in the market). In some countries (particularly the Middle East but also in other resource-rich countries and in China), the development of sovereign wealth funds has become an important source of funding for private equity, along with investments by growing numbers of wealthy and upper middle class individuals and families.

Private equity works as a network of activity. It requires banks that can provide access to savers, institutions that can develop financial instruments, financial markets where such instruments can be traded, brokers to engage in the trading process, investors willing to take on risks, lawyers to draw up contracts, rating agencies to score bonds, and so on. These networks of activity are partly densely concentrated in London and New York, but they are also dispersed and localized in other financial centers, such as Paris, Tokyo, Frankfurt, Shanghai, and Los Angeles. These networks are partially linkages between multinational firms in the financial sector, including lawyers and accountants, but they are also partially linkages between local firms or between local firms and multinational ones.

The development of these networks was accompanied by the creation of two other networks. The first was the network of national financial regulators brought together in various forms at the Bank of International Settlements (the Basel Group), the G7 finance ministries, the IMF, and the World Bank. Until 2007, the regulators were content to keep a watching brief over developments in the financial markets, including the growth of private equity. Whilst some regulators expressed concern about the level of leverage in private equity and its dependence on low interest rates and liquid credit markets, they were generally passive and allowed the financial markets to decide levels of funding and the viability of deals. Nevertheless, their oversight helped constitute the private equity transnational community, providing a forum in which national associations of private equity came together to cooperate on influencing financial regulation and trying to ensure that it did not create hindrances to their business model.

The second international network that emerged consisted of left-wing politicians (particularly inside the EU) and trade unions. Across the USA, Europe, and elsewhere, these groups became increasingly critical of private equity, arguing that it cut jobs, reduced expenditure on research and development, sold off core assets (such as property), lowered the quality of products and services, unfairly used the tax system to maximize gains to private equity partners, and overall generated massive inequalities in the distribution of rewards. Many trade unions developed parts of their websites to oppose private equity and to give their members information about its impact.[2] As with financial regulators, this pressurized private equity to cooperate on both a national and an international scale in order to defend its business model.

In short, we propose that there is an emerging transnational community structured around private equity. In Mayntz's terms this community combines different sorts of communities. It is partly epistemic (sharing certain assumptions about the world, how to measure performance and profitability), partly a professional community (in which certain standards of financial management and managing employees are set), partly a community of practice (in which actors learn from each other and evolve their techniques and processes), and partly a business community that organizes itself nationally and cross-nationally (for example, in the European Venture Capital Association, which has members from across the EU and lobbies in the EU context for private equity). Those participating in this community, no matter whether they are based in the USA or elsewhere, share a common understanding of how to set up a private equity business, how to acquire firms and engage with their development, common processes for funding private equity (mainly institutional investors seeking alternative investment classes and banks organizing loans to private equity), common structures for payment and rewards (to general and limited partners), common mechanisms for realizing gains (IPOs, trade sales, and sales to another private equity fund). Similarly, private equity has become a global public policy issue because of the common regulatory problems which it creates and the political backlash which has occurred; it has been identified as a distinct community of interest by politicians, trade unions, the media, and the public (for a parallel, see Bartley and Smith in this volume).

The Japanese financial system: continuity and change

Traditionally, in the post-War period Japanese firms met market challenges through restructurings that were organized within *keiretsu* groupings (groupings of firms based on long-term relationships and interlocking ownership structures organized either through bank-centred horizontal networks or through vertically structured networks between buyers and suppliers). Human resource costs could be cut through the transfer of employees among associated firms. New technologies, new management skills, and capital resources could be coordinated through the *keiretsu* in order to rebuild a poorly performing firm. This process was built around the preservation of the company and the employees through forms of long-term lending and assistance. As the bulk of the shares was held inside the group, shareholders did not constitute a distinct group with different interests. The Tokyo stock market was active and shares were churned, not in order to exercise control over firms but in order to gamble on unpredictable share movements (Morgan and Kubo 2005b). Capital markets were weakly developed in terms of corporate governance. The state continued, through the Ministry of Finance, to control interest rates and favor certain institutions over others. There was little open competition between financial institutions over products, prices, or quality. Financial institutions served their own *keiretsu* companies mainly through bank loans. During the bubble economy of the 1980s, lending practices became increasingly lax and loans were provided that even in the long run had little chance of providing an adequate return.

When the bubble economy collapsed, banks were left holding worthless loans because companies were now incapable of paying back the funds that had gone to create speculative price hikes in assets such as land and securities. This meant that one of the core sets of institutions in the Japanese system – the banks – was effectively bankrupt (Gao 2001). If they had been allowed to collapse, they would have brought many industrial companies down with them. For nearly a decade in the 1990s, therefore – the so-called "lost decade" – governments, politicians, bankers, and industrialists maneuvered in order to find a way out of this problem (Pempel 1998; Laurence 2001; Amyx 2004; Vogel 2006). Part of the solution was that *keiretsu* members had to sell off their interlocking shares in the market, even at considerably reduced prices. The loosening of control over shares, the financial weakness of a lot of firms in this period, and the push for reform and the opening up of the Japanese capital markets that came from international pressures and emerging new local coalitions of interest led to a steady rise in mergers and acquisitions activity, where firms either too weak to survive on their own or struggling to grow and expand due to lack of assets were taken over by stronger firms. In a small number of cases, this led to competitive bidding with other companies, but in the main mergers and acquisitions took place without much hostility. What was also significant here was that gradually mergers and acquisitions were being financed not by bank lending but by financial institutions using the markets for bonds and loan syndication.

Alongside these processes came the gradual emergence of what has been described elsewhere as an investment banking nexus (Morgan and Kubo 2005a). This consisted of US banks, some European institutions, and some reorganized Japanese banks that were now increasingly focused on making money out of the capital markets. Key to investment banking is its ability to drive processes of financial restructuring in companies, whether by supporting new forms of financing, developing IPOs, encouraging mergers and acquisitions activity, stimulating more capital market activity, or trading. Japan has moved slowly in this direction in two senses: first, as its own banks have sought slowly to restructure; and second, as it has opened up to allow foreign investment banks, particularly US ones, to enter. The result has been a very slow reorganization of the capital markets. Most Japanese firms are still controlled and organized by their senior managers, supported by inactive friendly investors. Restructuring is still mainly driven from inside the firm or at most from inside the *keiretsu*. On the other hand, there is now some space for more active dealing and restructuring through the capital markets, as well as some discussions about shareholder value and improved performance for shareholders (for detailed studies of recent changes see Aoki *et al.* 2007). It is in this context that we need to consider the development of private equity in Japan.

Table 6.1 Size of the private equity market as a proportion of GDP, 2005–07 (billion USD)

	2005		2007	
	Assets	Proportion of GDP (in %)	Assets	Proportion of GDP (in %)
USA	53.3	1.2	443.8	3.2
UK	29.6	1.3	107.1	3.9
France	9.1	0.4	31.5	1.2
Japan	6.8	0.15	22.9	0.5

Data from Thomson Financial, IFSL, IMF, and Venture Enterprise Centre.

Table 6.2 Allocation of alternative investments by institutional investors, 2007 (in % of total investments)

	USA	Europe	Japan
Domestic equities	44%	33%	11%
Fixed income	25%	29%	69%
Foreign equities	15%	28%	6%
Alternative investments	9%	8%	1%
Other	7%	2%	11%

Note: Total differing from 100% is due to rounding.
Source: Euromoney (winter 2008), p. 26.

According to the Association of Private Equity in Japan, the total size of assets controlled by the twenty-eight private equity companies in Japan was 9 trillion yen as of the end of November 2006. The estimated size of the private equity funds varies between different sources but remains relatively small in Japan as a percentage of GDP when compared to other advanced economies (Table 6.1).

This reflects the broader issue that Japan lags significantly behind other countries in terms of the willingness of its institutional investors to engage with alternative investment assets (of which private equity is one).

The first buyout with a leveraged private equity-type finance scheme involved ICS Kokusai Bunka Kyoiku Center (International Culture and Educational Center) in December 1998 (Sasayama and Muraoka 2006: 38). Private equity became more active from 2003 onwards. Private equity funds accounted for 2.4 percent of total mergers and acquisitions volume in 2002, reaching 10.9 percent in 2006 (*Euromoney*, winter 2007: 24). The largest participants in private equity deals between 1998 and 2006 are listed in Table 6.3.

Table 6.3 Major participants in largest PE deals in Japan, 1998–2006

Firm	Origin	Established	Major deals
Cerberus	USA	1998	Aozora Bank, Nagasakiya, Kokusai Kogyo
Loan Star	USA	1998	Tokyo Star Bank, Tokyo City Finance, First Credit
Ripplewood HD	USA	1999	LTCM, Phoenix Resort, Nihon Colombia Record
Nomura Principal Finance	Nomura Securities	2000	Misawa Home, Millennium Retailing, House Tembos, Toshiba Tangaroi
Daiwa Securities SMBC Principal Investments	Daiwa Securities	2001	Myojo Electric, Ogihara Group, Daiwa Seiko, Maruzen, Mitsui Coal Mining
Nikko Principal Investments	Nikko Securities	2000	Seibu Holdings, Bell-system24, Genesis Technology
Phoenix Capital	Mitsubishi UFJ	2002	Mitsubishi Motor, Takizawa Iron Works, Gold Pac, Tiac, Sokia
Permira Advisors	UK	2005	Arysta Life Science
Bain Capital	USA	2005	
KKR	USA	2006	
Goldman Sachs	USA	2006	Sanyo Electric, E-access

Source: Tanaka (2006: 14).

The restructuring in Japan in which private equity has played a part derives from broader problems arising due to the recovery from the bubble economy years and the "lost decade." A number of private equity deals have arisen as a result of government efforts to restructure the financial sector. One of the earliest examples came in 2000, when Ripplewood, a US fund in consortium with other financial institutions, acquired the nationalized Long Term Credit Bank from the Japanese government. As part of the deal, the Japanese government agreed to buy back problem loans owed to LTCB (Amyx 2004: 340) so that eventually Ripplewood was able to put the bank up for IPO in 2004. This was identified as a "landmark" in private equity business in Japan because the deal had gone through the full cycle, from purchase through restructuring to successful sell-off. A more extensive instance of the same process occurred in 2002, when the Japanese government established IRCJ (Industrial Revitalizing Corporation of Japan). IRCJ's goal was to "purchase nonperforming loans from the non-main banks and then work out debt restructuring or liquidation programs in conjunction with the main bank" (Amyx 2004: 244). IRJC had a 10 trillion yen commitment from the government and it purchased 4 trillion yen in debts (Ono 2007: 81); it extracted the bad debts from a business, reformed it, and then sold it on. This official guarantee which offered for sale businesses without debts encouraged private equity funds to take them over. IRCJ was involved in forty-one deals, including the supermarket Daiei and toiletry products manufacturer Kanebo. More recently, private equity has been particularly involved in an increasing number of management buyouts in Japan, such as the 2008 40 billion yen management buyout of pharmaceutical company Showa Kayaku, supported by private equity funds Polaris Principal Finance (part of Mizuho Bank) and Tokio Marine Capital. This reflects the fact that private equity funds have moved from restructuring underperforming companies under the aegis of state control to involvement in buyouts of mature businesses as profitable firms restructured. In addition, a possible area of private equity growth (shared with a number of other countries) is the SME sector in Japan. There are 2.7 million SMEs in Japan; 30 percent have a corporate structure and 30 percent are profitable; 50 percent of the latter – totaling around 120,000 SMEs – are experiencing a lack of succession planning for top management (*Euromoney* winter 2007: 27), making them open to offers from private equity, which enables the owners to realize their personal wealth in the business and pass on the management issues to outsiders.

In this period, a relatively rich infrastructure of investment banks and deal intermediaries, as well as law firms and accounting firms specializing in mergers and acquisitions deals, has emerged in Japan. Seven of the top ten global private equity firms established offices in Japan. Japanese private equity firms such as MKS Partners, Advantage Partners, and Unison Capital were established. These three Japanese firms were founded in 1982 (as a venture capital company, which was transformed into a private equity firm in 2002), 1992, and 1998 respectively, after their founders had accumulated professional experience of private equity in US or UK firms based in Japan and overseas. Private equity investment practices in Japan were learned and imported from non-Japanese firms (Hizume 2008: 25).

Companies and venture businesses requiring investment increasingly identified private equity funds as possible funding sponsors. As a result, finding deal opportunities was relatively easy, although competition among private equity funds was increasingly tough (Soeda 2004: 103). Investors in Japanese private equity funds are international as well as domestic. Perceptions of mergers and acquisitions deals and the role of private equity in Japan have started to change. Gradual legal changes, such as the revision of commercial law in 2001 and 2002, then reform of company law in May 2006, have allowed US-style financial tools to emerge that provide greater flexibility for private equity activity and funding. Associated with this, new forms of bank loans based on the distinction between senior debt and mezzanine finance became available due to the progress of financial engineering techniques and their importation into Japan.

The main area of difficulty for private equity in Japan, however, concerns shareholders and stakeholders. On the one hand, there has been some adoption of shareholder-value discourse in Japanese companies. This seeks to legitimize senior managers' reducing the workforce, intensifying working conditions, and reducing benefits (for example, pensions), all characteristic of how private equity extracts value in the UK and US contexts (Morgan 2009). On the other hand, in Japan this conflicts significantly with the stakeholder model of the firm and the continued commitment to defending the firm against takeovers threatening it as a community (see Aoki *et al.* 2007). Although necessary restructuring processes mean that Japanese firms have spun off through management buyouts or other parts of their organization and these have become possible private equity targets, the capacity of private equity to restructure them financially in order to make the high level of profits that characterized the US and UK private equity firms at their 2006 peak has been limited.

Private equity in Japan: part of a transnational community?

In this section, we look at how these developments in Japan related to broader transnational developments around private equity over the past decade. It is important to note in this respect that although the Japanese financial sector has always been very distinctive, it has nevertheless interacted with and participated in international financial markets – to varying extents – since the 1970s. For example, from this period, Japanese banks invested in US-based leveraged buyouts (the equivalent of the private equity model of the current period). Commitment to the funds was 200 billion yen at the beginning of the 1980s, then rapidly became 500 billion yen in 1984 and almost 2,000 billion yen in 1988. After the crash of the leveraged buyout market in 1990, commitment went down to 500 billion yen but Japanese financial institutions continued to invest overseas in vulture funds and later in IT-based venture capital funds, recovering to reach more than 2,000 billion yen in 1995.

As part of this process, Japanese banks had sent trainees to the USA to monitor their investments and to obtain information on mergers and acquisitions and joint venture opportunities. As new financial techniques were developed in the New York and London markets, Japanese bankers took them on board. Some banks attained a high presence in the mergers and acquisitions debt-financing market; for instance, the London branch of Fuji Bank (now Mizuho Bank) was the top debt supplier to buyout business, followed by Goldman Sachs, Bankers Trust, and Morgan Stanley in 1998 (Kitamura 2004: 2). Fuji Bank accumulated acquisition finance knowledge in London and became the leading debt financier in the emerging mergers and acquisitions market in Japan in 1996. Through their London operations Fuji Bank also learnt about MBO deals, debt financing and leverage, differences between the legal systems of the UK and other European countries, varying bank attitudes towards MBO financing in the different European countries, and how to hedge risk through the use of debt covenants. When the UK buyout market crashed in the early 1990s because of interest rate rises, many Japanese banks found their profits falling on debt financing and withdrew from the UK market. However, Fuji Bank remained, so that when the MBO market emerged in Japan, it was able to use its skills and knowledge to exploit growth potential. It established its debt financing operation in Japan quickly by transferring experienced bankers from London to Tokyo. This resulted in the first MBO deal of ICS Kokusai Bunka Kyoiku Center in 1998 and the first MBO deal with a private equity fund in the purchase of Nihon Kojyundo Kagaku (chemical company) in 1999 (Kitamura 2004: 138).

Another factor that contributed to the spread of private equity in Japan was the financial crisis following the collapse of the bubble economy in the 1990s. This caused many banks to withdraw from these overseas commitments. Banks that had entered project finance markets in New York and London and accumulated knowledge there were involved in the repeated mergers that have occurred since the late 1990s in order to create mega banks freed from the debt overhang. As a result, many project finance teams were dissolved (Matsuki et al. 2004: 115) and these specialized bankers in project finance and structured finance departments lost their prestige and positions. This specialist group became potential candidates to help establish the new US private equity funds (such as Carlyle, Ripplewood, and Loan Star) that began to enter Japan at this time, as well as seeking funding to launch their own independent private equity funds.

Many employees of the Japanese buy-out funds were former bank employees, especially from bankrupted ones. It could be said that this was a large spin-off from the major banks. In other words, Japanese bankers were able to take the risk but it was necessary to work in other firms to conduct this kind of business. (Kitamura 2004: 3)

Table 6.4 Board members of large private equity funds

PE firm	Top management	Previous position
Advantage Partners (AP)	Taisuke Sasanuma, Richard Forsom	Bain & Co. consultant
Unison Capital	Nobuyoshi Ebara	Goldman Sachs partner
MKS Partners	Nobuo Matsuki	Schroder Ventures CEO
Phoenix Capital	Yasushi Ando	MTFG, IM planning department
Renaissance Capital	Yoshiyuki Fujii	Cerberus Japan Chairman, BNP; Paribas Japan chairman
Nippon Mirai Capital	Akira Yasujima	IBJ private equity manager
	Minoru Honzawa	ING Baring, head of strategic trading department
IRCJ	Atsushi Saito	Nomura Securities, vice CEO
	Kazuhiko Toyama	
	Akitoshi Nakamura	Boston Consulting
	Jun Matsumoto	Ripplewood Japan, senior executive
	Yoshihira Watanabe	GMAC Commercial Mortgage, vice CEO
		Cerberus Japan, director
RHJ International Japan (ex-Ripplewood)	Hiroshi Nomiya	Mitsubishi Corp.
Carlyle	Tamotsu Adachi	GE Capital Japan
	Kazuhiro Yamada	Sumitomo Mitsui Bank (SMBC)

Source: Imada 2006; **50**: 158.

Contrary to the usual situation in Japan, therefore, skilled labor was not locked into tight internal labor markets but was actually available on the external labor market.

In contrast to most Japanese firms and employees, in this sector many top private equity managers have circulated around the industry, trained at rival companies, and have been mid- or top-level entry recruits from competitors. They are well known to the press, to the firms, and to each other as a result of these processes. Private equity funds tend to be run by 10–15 professional Japanese managers (see Table 6.4). Their backgrounds vary but their careers all tend to have progressed through successive jobs in the financial industry. As already indicated, many of these managers have had experience working in foreign financial institutions and all of them are fluent in English. They are the first-generation managers in the Japanese private equity industry and the vehicle by means of which business practices and private equity financial skills are transferred from overseas markets.

Most private equity firms in Japan were established in the late 1990s or at the beginning of the 2000s. Overseas firms have been particularly prevalent in the last decade. In the private equity industry, three Japanese funds are known as the "Big Three," namely Advantage Partners (AP), Unison Capital, and MKS Partners. Three US private equity funds – Ripplewood, Carlyle, and Cerberus – are known as the non-Japanese "Big Three." These six private equity firms constitute the core of the private equity industry in Japan.

These firms are led by relatively young managers, aged between 35 and 45. When deals are successful, they are highly paid on the basis of performance-driven incentive systems, still relatively unusual in the Japanese context. This makes them visible in the media where they are treated as "young millionaires of the financial industry," and seen as rich and arrogant, although the lower performance of private equity deals in Japan and the different tax and legal regimes mean that this is in no way comparable to the huge wealth accumulated by partners in large US and UK private equity firms. Nevertheless, in Japan, which in terms of distribution of wealth and income is more egalitarian than the USA and the UK, these earnings still have the ability to shock public opinion. Another reason for these lower earnings is that private equity funds in Japan have found that job cuts are difficult to achieve because of the Japanese institution of long-term employment for core employees. For this reason it has been hard to realize projected returns by job cuts and resultant work intensification. In other Asian countries, where employment rights are less protected and restructuring can be achieved rapidly, private equity was able to deliver profit levels comparable with those in the USA and the UK during the high point of the private equity boom. In Japan, however, there is no record of a deal which has delivered more than 20 percent profit (Fukagawa 2003).

In the financial crisis that began in September 2008, risk money, and especially the debt market, have shrunk, meaning that private equity funds have not been able to find the leveraged capital they require. Activist hedge funds have sold holding stocks. The Childrens' Investment Fund (TCI) sold its 9.9 percent stake in J-Power in October 2007 and Steel Partners reduced its assets by 30 percent. On November 20, 2008, the *Nikkei* newspaper reported that MKS Partners, one of the largest Japanese private equity funds, was preparing to close down in 2009. Large US private equity funds such as KKR and TPG are struggling to find good investment opportunities (Kikuchi 2008: 27).

Conclusions

Private equity affected only a small part of the Japanese economy in the period up to 2007. This was due to the particular Japanese context. In other words, private equity activity in Japan differs from that in the USA and the UK. In Japan, private equity has been one of the mechanisms through which the industrial restructuring consequent upon the collapse of the bubble economy has occurred. Private equity has been involved in restructuring some of those businesses that have had their debt taken out by the action of governments and banks. It is possible that private equity will spread further in Japan, particularly as a result of the restructuring of large firms as well as amongst SMEs where succession problems are emerging due to the ageing population. However, the speed of change is slow and has now been halted by the financial crisis.

On the other hand, for this part of the Japanese system there are definite transnational connections. At one level, these connections emerge from the need of funds to seek overseas investors as well as overseas investment opportunities. Japanese private equity is not locked in to the Japanese system but has a more transnational set of connections. These are necessary in order to access financial markets, skills, and knowledge about how to evaluate investment opportunities and how to engage in the sorts of financial engineering necessary to make private equity viable. Since this knowledge also exists in overseas financial institutions, it is no surprise that such overseas firms have sought a foothold in Japan. This provides an important source of dynamism in Japan, in terms of both stimulating a labor market for expertise in this area and also diffusing such financial techniques. A central part is being played in this by Japanese bankers who acquired overseas experience in the 1980s. This expertise lost its value inside Japanese banks during the mega merger and consolidation period after the collapse of the bubble economy when these individuals sought work overseas. However, they have become the building blocks of the new industry because they can act as intermediaries between insiders in Japan and outsiders in the broader private equity network, moving into overseas banks in Japan, setting up their own private equity businesses, or simply moving around between different Japanese financial institutions. They are supported now by an increasing infrastructure of specialist intermediaries that can facilitate private equity deals. As Japanese banks themselves realize the potential rewards from acting as intermediaries in these deals, they too have started to support a gradual extension of capital market restructuring activity, so drawing more overseas companies into the system. Thus the Japanese private equity system, small though it is in Japanese terms and relatively insignificant as it remains compared to the major role played by private equity in restructuring firms in the USA and the UK, is being reinforced by these transnational connections. Particular individuals have been the relay mechanisms for some of these processes. Some firms have facilitated the transfer of the capital and know-how which have made this work. Reforms of corporate law and firms' changed expectations have also fed into this process, both under pressure from international investors. Clearly, all this may disintegrate or wind down under the pressure of the current financial crisis, though it may be that as private equity firms in the USA and the UK adopt new methods to deal with this new situation, they too may spread through the transnational community into Japan.

From this perspective, what has happened with private equity in Japan resembles what has happened there with a number of other things. Terminology that has substantial legitimacy in the West – like "shareholder value" – was borrowed and adapted to Japanese requirements. Clearly this has entailed some problems, particularly when as part of the borrowing process foreign financial institutions enter the scene. Ripplewood showed that, in at least one case, a foreign private equity firm took the task of restructuring seriously and this had a substantial and unexpected impact on some Japanese firms.

All this suggests that insofar as there is an emerging private equity transnational community, Japan is still very much on the margins. However, in comparison to a decade ago, even that is a remarkable change. There are now international banks in Japan and an investment banking nexus has emerged. Japanese financial institutions are increasingly part of this international system in terms of regulation, methods of organizing investment banking, procedures for measuring risk, and ways of engaging profitably with capital markets. The fact that private equity has gained a foothold reveals the significance of this.

What this suggests is the need for at least four further types of research in the area of private equity. The first would be research that looked more closely at the sort of private equity deals that have been conducted in Japan. How far do they follow the model of financial engineering, restructuring of assets, and reorganization of principal and agent relationships characteristic of the USA and the UK? Second, how do Japanese private equity funds engage outside of Japan and with what effect? Third, how do private equity funds outside their heartland in the UK and the USA operate and how far are they engaged in a process of adapting the private equity structure to replace existing business models or to reform them? More comparative research on the impact of private equity is clearly necessary to understand the interaction between national processes of economic change and international processes of diffusion and flows. Finally, how are these processes changing under the impact of the financial crisis?

Does the concept of transnational community provide any help with this task? There can be no definitive answer at present. The idea of a transnational community does point to the significance of emerging common modes of acting and organizing, as well as to the material conditions that underpin these processes. However, it is immediately obvious once one adopts a comparative perspective that the "community"-like nature of these phenomena varies across nations and regions, as well as across sectors. If one uses the concept as a way of sensitizing research to processes of adaptation and change, then it certainly can be useful (see Djelic and Quack, and Mayntz in this volume). International financial markets furnish an appropriate access point for studying the processes of transnational community formation, primarily because these markets are fast moving, innovative, have global consequences, and are also fixed to place and locality in distinctive ways. Thus social processes are continuously in flux and the community nature of phenomena is transient yet powerful in its impact.

NOTES

1. There are exceptions – for example, 3i in the UK. In the aftermath of the financial crisis, a number of private equity firms have looked to secure additional finance through going public but conditions have not been propitious for this though some large investors have taken significant stakes.
2. See, for example, the Private Equity buyout watch website of the Geneva-based International Union of Foodworkers (www.iufdocuments.org/buyoutwatch/) or the French CGT website on private equity (www.collectif-lbo.org/). For an example of political opposition see, for example, the draft report by the Socialist Group in the European Parliament, *Capital Funds – A Critical Analysis* (March 2007).

REFERENCES

In English

Amyx, J. A. 2004. *Japan's financial crisis: Institutional rigidity and reluctant change*. Princeton University Press.

Aoki, M., Jackson, G. and Miyajima, H. (eds.) 2007. *Corporate governance in Japan: Institutional change and organizational diversity*. Oxford University Press.

Djelic, M.-L., and Quack, S. (eds.) 2003. *Globalization and institutions: Redefining the rules of the economic game*. Cheltenham: Edward Elgar.

Djelic, M.-L., and Sahlin-Andersson, K. (eds.) 2006. *Transnational governance: Institutional dynamics of regulation*. Cambridge University Press.

Gao, B. 2001. *Japan's economic dilemma: The institutional origins of prosperity and stagnation*. Cambridge University Press.

International Financial Services (IFSL). 2006. *Private equity*. City Business Series. IFSL: London.

Laurence, H. 2001. *Money rules: The new politics of finance in Britain and Japan*. Ithaca, NY: Cornell University Press.

Morgan, G. 2001a. "The development of transnational standards and regulations and their impacts on firms," in Morgan, G., Kristensen, P. H. and Whitley, R. (eds.), *The multinational firm*. Oxford University Press, pp. 225–52.

Morgan, G. 2001b. "Transnational communities and business systems," *Global Networks* **1** (2): 113–30.

Morgan, G. 2009. "Private equity in the UK," *Transfer: The European Review of Labour and Research*. Brussels: ETUI.

Morgan, G. and Kubo, I. 2005a. "Beyond path dependency? Constructing new models for institutional change: The case of capital markets in Japan," *Socio-Economic Review* **2** (3): 55–82.

Morgan, G. and Kubo, I. 2005b. "Where do institutional complementarities come from? The case of the Japanese stock market." Paper presented at EGOS (European Group for Organizational Studies) Colloquium, Berlin, June 30–July 2.

Pempel, T. J. 1998. *Regime shift: Comparative dynamics of the Japanese political economy*. Ithaca, NY: Cornell University Press.

Sorge, A. 2005. *The global and the local*. Oxford University Press.

Vogel, S. K. 2006. *Japan remodeled: How government and industry are reforming Japanese capitalism*. Ithaca, NY: Cornell University Press.

In Japanese

Fukagawa, T. 2003. "Sekai kara mita nihon no private equity" [Private equity in Japan from a global point of view]. RIETI seminar, www.rieti.go.jp.

Hizume, N. 2008. *Private equity fund no doko to Nihon kigyo ni yoru senryakuteki katsuyo* [Trend of private equity funds and strategic use of private equity funds by Japanese companies]. Nomura Research Institute, November 2008, pp. 18–29.

Imada, E. 2006. *Zukai de wakuru Toshi Fund* [Investment Funds at a glance]. Nihon Jitsugyo Suppansya.

Kikuchi, M. 2008. *Nihon no fund business no genjo to mitooshi* [Current situation and forecast of the private equity fund business in Japan]. Tokyo: Bank of America/Merrill Lynch Japan Securities.

Kitamura, M. 2004. *Ginko ga okonau buy-out business* [Buyout business conducted by banks]. Tokyo: Chuo Keizai sya.

Matsuki, N., Ohashi, K. and Honda T. 2004. *Buy-out fund* [Buyout funds]. Tokyo: Chuo Keizaisha.

Ono, N. 2007. *Kigyo fukkatsu* [Corporate restructuring]. Tokyo: Kodansha.

Sasayama, K. and Muraoka, K. 2006. *M&A finance*. Tokyo: Kinzai.

Soeda, M. 2004. *Private equity investment: Its logic and practice*. Tokyo: Sigmabase Capital.

Tanaka, Y. 2006. *Private equity in Japan*. Tokyo: Morgan Stanley Japan.

7 Formal organizing and transnational communities: evidence from global finance governance associations, 1879–2006

Asma A. Hussain and Marc J. Ventresca

Introduction

The global economic, political, and social landscape underwent a remarkable transformation in the latter half of the twentieth century (Giddens 1984, 1990; Hirst and Thompson 1996; Boli and Thomas 1999; Drori *et al.* 2003; see also Foucault 1970, 1979 on general epistemic shifts). These changes had an impact on many aspects of economic and social life. One of the most profound developments has been the proliferation of transnational organizing through formal structures. The extraordinary growth in global voluntary associations, in particular, and the timing of the emergence of these associations in the global sphere have not been adequately explained by existing theories in organizational analysis and other social sciences. Therefore, an alternative theoretical approach is required to understand how and why associational forms of organization of economic and social activity have moved into the transnational space.

In this chapter we shall address these concerns by looking at the historical emergence of global finance governance associations and note the existence of archipelagos of agencies that govern finance in different ways. These voluntary associations include legally incorporated associations that exist within local legal jurisdictions as well as loosely structured networks and movements that are disembodied entities that exist and coordinate using electronic media. Incorporated associations display local rootedness with implications such as legal liability of its members, the right to own property and enter contracts, and the right to open a bank account and officially lodge a complaint.

Much of the earlier work on understanding global organization focused on particular factors related to technology, knowledge, or expertise, and worked within the framework of existing nation-state jurisdiction. However, the heterogeneity within this global space reveals how, through the governance mechanism of global associations, finance has evolved into a global concern embodying particular logics and following a specific historical trajectory.

Global finance refers to finance-based knowledge and tools and their application to global capital formation processes. Global finance governance associations are the governance mechanism of the global field of finance, which comprises organizations specifically devoted to finance-related activities. The empirical case of global finance associations includes organizations that are worldwide in their membership and not linked to a particular national context.

By examining this proliferation of formal organizations we build up an argument concerning how global finance associations begin to comprise communities of practice, action, and influence. The emergence of these organizations is not a unilateral process – rather, these actors shape and are shaped by their jurisdictions. Moreover, observable flows and dynamics are themselves shaped and permeated by culture, norms, and institutions (Djelic and Sahlin-Anderson 2006). Therefore meanings and logic embedded in institutions help us to develop a greater sense of how transnational communities may evolve.

The field of finance is an important case for the study of globalization because of its international scope. This should not prevent us from taking into account the field's heterogeneity in form and content, as displayed by a variety of finance associations and governance agencies. The association formation process demonstrates how governance associations define the scope of finance activity and how meaning is attributed to this activity. A major concern related to global civil society is how they mobilize resources and the impact they have on national policies. Global finance associations are an interesting case because of their political usage and influence on policy-making. The concept of finance as a form of corporate control noted by Fligstein (1990) and others has diffused into the global sphere where associations that embody finance-based ideas are beginning to use it as a form of control at a global level. The scope of governance of some international associations is moving beyond the field of finance due to their significant impact on national policies (see Sinclair 1994; Stiglitz 2002; Barnett and Finnemore 2004). This differentiates it from other fields of global activity because it is more directly affected by larger global political and historical developments.

Figure 7.1 depicts the founding patterns of global finance governance associations from 1879 to 2006. Global finance, like many other global sectors, is a recent phenomenon, with much of the activity taking place after World War II. Closer examination of the population reveals heterogeneity within the

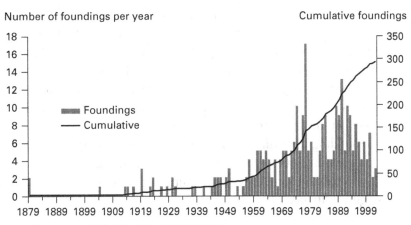

Figure 7.1   Global finance association foundings, 1879–2006

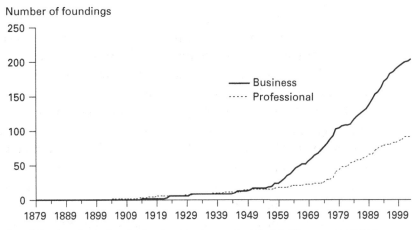

Figure 7.2   Cumulative foundings of professional and business-oriented global finance associations

field. At a high level we note that the population comprises two distinct types of finance governance associations: professional[1] and business[2] associations (see Figure 7.2).[3] "Business finance associations" act as global financial intermediaries that cater to the more practical applications of finance ideas to businesses. Global intermediaries reduce domestic turbulence by seeking wider contexts for investment opportunities (Hirst and Thompson 1996). This subpopulation is a rich mix of a wide variety of different types of associations, with members ranging from nation-states, funds, banks, and credit organizations to stock exchanges and other financial intermediaries. As a result, this space is varied in terms of themes and agendas.

The other subpopulation to note is that of "professional finance associations" that cater to the promotion of finance as a discipline by enhancing cooperation between finance professionals globally and facilitating the development of specialized financial expertise (Lounsbury and Lee 2005). The existence of subpopulations within the field based around distinct ideas, as well as their different founding patterns and the overall timing of developments in the field, form the basis of this chapter.

Founding dynamics among these governance associations can help explain how ideas become organized through "formal organization." Multiple interconnected and sometimes contending logics influence the historical shaping of global finance.

Theorizing formal organizing and transnational communities

Since the 1980s, much research on organizations has been preoccupied with the exponential growth of organizations in the twentieth century. Prominent among contributions to the study of globalization and its organizational consequences are studies at the intersection of organization theory and world polity institutionalism (Thomas *et al.* 1987; Ventresca *et al.* 2003). The abstract claim of the world polity approach developed by John Meyer and colleagues is that formal organizations and discourse are the twin indicators of world polity (Meyer *et al.* 1987, 1997). The observation is that more and more activity at the global level is moving out of the domain of nation-states into a transnational space, and that this is an indicator of a world culture that provides a framework for legitimate action.

Global associations can take many forms and represent different levels of local rootedness. However, they differ from associations in the national context in that they represent ideas and aims that extend beyond local jurisdictions. Global voluntary associations are groups of individuals who voluntarily enter into an agreement to form an association to accomplish a purpose. The neocorporatist tradition argues that the association has a different potential for generating social order as compared to state bureaucracy, market, or community. Streeck and Schmitter (1985) argue that associations represent organizational concertation compared to communities which in their view are based on spontaneous solidarity. This analysis is based on national contexts, where associations are seen as intermediaries between state and civil society. In the global space, global associations are fast forming a new arena for global action that extends beyond the national context.

The work on world culture is, importantly, a bridge to considering work on "community" in the transnational space, rather than "society" in the (neo-) liberal conception – in short, attending to frameworks of meaning and organization that support community formation.

Traditional concepts of community reflect the tensions in Tönnies's famous typology of *Gemeinschaft* and *Gesellschaft*. Community here represents an integrated notion based on functionalist ideas. Durkheim proposed an alternative approach where a community is not a physical structure but instead is described by human relations and connections. Literature on communities looks at a number of different types, including communities of interest (Hillery 1955: 27), epistemic communities (Haas 1992), policy communities, and communities of practice, including professional ones (Wenger 1998). While traditional concepts of community are based on social solidarity, more recent work has highlighted ideas of commonality and similarity to explain communities.

Fourcade's (2006) insights summarize ideas related to the formal organization of a profession at a global level and how it grows and becomes dominant. This development is a process of "creative destruction" – the result of a "dialectical relationship between economics and the economy" (Fourcade 2006). We draw from the main argument in Fourcade (2006) to theorize how more diffuse patterns of occupations, expertise, logic, and policy engagement become globalized. Elias suggests the recontextualization of "community" into state-building (Elias 1974: xxxi–xxxii), as community evolution and social context are closely connected. Transnational identities and activity in finance, as per Fourcade, need to be recontextualized within wider global processes.

The symbolic dimension of communities implies that community formation is based on common meaning systems, symbols, and logics. Symbolic construction allows communities to evolve in the absence of interaction and physical proximity (see also Mayntz in this volume). Benedict Anderson (2006) argues that nations emerge as "imagined communities." In the context of global finance, "imagined communities" are emerging (from a heterogeneous space) around similar ideas on the professionalization and rationalization of finance – that is, a transcendental view of "finance" encompassing ideas of systemic management of finance activity. Djelic and Quack (see Chapter 1 of this volume) draw attention to the "multi-level forms of affiliation and association, complementarities, as well as conflicts in social roles and identities" experienced by members of communities.

Building on our idea of archipelagos, global finance associations share little in the way of day to day interaction, but do share a common vision of purpose and practice.

The rise of global finance governance associations

The evolution of global finance can be traced back to the nineteenth century when modern global finance governance associations began to emerge.[4] The late nineteenth century was also a period of increased global commercial activity and much formal organizing (Hirst and Thompson 1996; Boli and Thomas 1999). Association foundings peaked in numbers in the 1970s and then again around the 1990s (see Figure 7.1). Earlier foundings are recorded in the 1870s, compared to similar organizations in other fields, such as health, for example, that records the formation of its first international organization in 1650 (Inoue and Drori 2006), and science, where global activity was recorded in the mid-nineteenth century.

The globalization theme

Changes in the names of associations indicate changes in scope and membership. The American Petroleum Credit Association became the International Petroleum Credit Association and eventually the International Energy Credit Association (IECA). Similarly, the Information Systems Audit and Control Association and Foundation was originally called the EDP Auditors Association of the USA. Associations repackage their content by using names that reflect cultural shifts towards globalization.

Associations change memberships by expanding geographically. For example, the Organization of Latin American and Caribbean Supreme Audit Institutions was formerly the Latin American Institute of Auditing Sciences. The reverse has also been observed. Following Fourcade (2006), we note that there have been generic international organizations. Their names imply that they were either "American" or "international" associations. Post-World War II region-based global associations, based on notions of regional development, emerged; for example, the Arab Fund for Economic and Social Development states its aim as to "contribute to the financing of economic and social development in Arab states and countries through financial development projects" (UIA 2005/2006: 121).

Thematic stratification

The field of global finance associations is heterogeneous, with two main subpopulations, professional and business associations (see Figure 7.2). As

Number of foundings

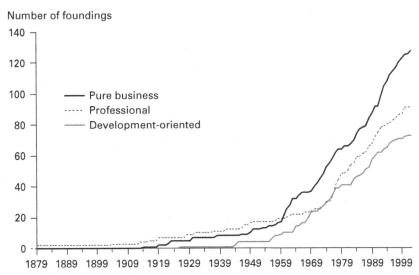

Figure 7.3   Cumulative foundings of "pure" business, development-oriented, and professional global finance associations

already noted, "business finance associations" work on the common theme of the systematic application of financial expertise as a formal technique of problem solving based on quantitative analysis. Close examination of the population reveals another two subtypes. These two types differ in the way in which a formal systematic activity such as finance is extended beyond its conventional applications. Figure 7.3 shows that business associations can be either "pure" or "development-oriented." "Pure business associations" signify the application of formalized financial ideas to business, based on economic notions of profit maximization. A modification of this towards the application of finance-based ideas to economic and social development is captured in the emergence of "development-oriented" finance associations.

Taking a step back to view the entire population, the discovery of the subpopulation of professional finance associations is an interesting one. Whereas one would expect the globalization of finance to be based on traditional ideas of the proliferation of economics-based ideas, we are confronted with a set of associations representing a different logic.

The development of professional identity and jurisdiction is usually a historical process comprising active boundary work and legitimacy projects (Abbott 1988). Professional finance associations are directly linked to the profession and practice of finance as a high status activity that is coming to be of primary importance in the modern world, supplanting law and earlier forms of business expertise, such as accounting (see Ramirez in this volume). Finance, when professionalized, is linked to a "universalized" culture, based on Western-style economic analysis and tools and management practices, wherein the specialized knowledge and tools are systematically applied to solve traditional problems of management and economics (Smiddy and Naum 1954).

Figure 7.4 shows the proportion of the global finance association population that is either governmental or non-governmental. Even though the proportion of non-governmental organizing in finance has predominated, the proportion of governmental organizations increased during the post-World War II period. Figure 7.5 shows the change in transnational organizing in the context of business finance associations. The figure highlights first that global finance associations were mainly non-governmental initiatives. In the 1920s, development-oriented associations emerged that were still non-governmental in nature. In the 1920s and 1930s governmental associations appeared that aimed at finance-based business collaborations. After World War II development-oriented governmental associations emerged. After the 1970s, we can observe that the development-based concerns moved out of the governmental sphere and the proportion of non-governmental development-oriented finance associations continued to increase. The development theme in the

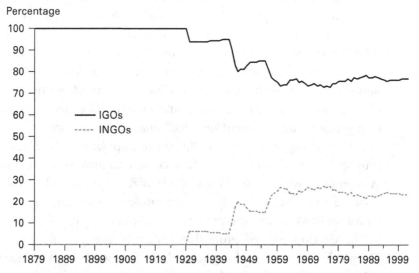

Figure 7.4   Proportion of governmental and non-governmental global finance associations, 1879–2006
Note: IGO = international governmental organization; INGO = international non-governmental organization

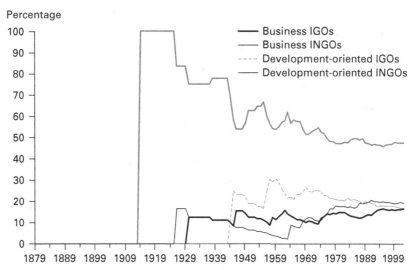

Figure 7.5   Proportions of governmental and non-governmental, pure business, and development-oriented global finance associations

transnational organizing of finance started off as being a non-governmental concern, and then became prominent in governmental organizations; since the 1970s it has been moving into the non-governmental sphere.

Globalization of finance: arguments and hypothesis

As finance globalized, patterns of capital and economic exchange changed in the global arena (Obstfeld and Taylor 2004) and consequently there was a change in the flow, density, and complexity of capital drivers that led to the development of more differentiated finance organizations. In the Durkheimian view of the social world, changes and shifts in logic come about through shocks that upset the established equilibrium. In the case of modern world history these shocks, in the form of wars and the Great Depression, have upset the equilibrium of the economic system and capital mobility (Obstfeld and Taylor 2004), thereby affecting transnational finance activity. Our initial observation is:

Hypothesis 1: Global capital drivers create a functional need for specialized finance activity and positively affect the foundings of professional and business finance associations.

Global finance is also dependent on institutional infrastructure. The formation of central banks indicates infrastructural development because "more day to day activities came into the orbit of finance via the growth and development of banking systems in many countries" (Lavelle 2004). This infrastructural development owed much to the proliferation of American-style economic models across the globe. To support these institutions there was a need for financial expertise and knowledge. Moreover, the "popularity of comprehensive, governmental economic planning prompted by Keynes and like-minded economists before, during and after World War II convinced many that governments, guided by well-trained economists, were in a unique position to plan and promote development on a national scale" (Chabott 2003: 224). This leads us to believe that:

Hypothesis 2: Infrastructural changes will positively impact the formation of business and professional associations.

There are increasing indications of a global finance culture that is being promoted by a community of financial experts from core nations and major international institutions such as the IMF and the World Bank (Stiglitz 2002). International organizations such as the World Bank, the IMF, and the IFC (International Finance Corporation) have become a medium for much social activity by emphasizing a "universal culture base of shared norms and core values (such as human rights, antislavery, equality, and satisfaction of basic needs)" (Drori *et al.* 2006). Ideas embodied by these organizations are easily diffused and accepted because they are not specific to particular settings (Strang and Soule 1998). These global ideologies form the basis of "soft laws" (Drori *et al.* 2006) and a global culture that exists beyond national jurisdictions (Boli and Thomas 1999).

These ideas are steeped in the neoliberal discourse in which the basic premise is that markets should be left to function on their own without intervention by the state. The collapse of the Bretton Woods regime marks the historical shift towards economic liberalization with the failure of the fixed exchange rate regime. As the dominant idea in the neoliberal discourse is the reduction of the role of the state, a transnational, non-governmental approach to finance may be expected, which we observe in the form of finance governance associations.

Therefore we note that:

Hypothesis 3: The cultural trend of liberalization will positively affect business association foundings but will not significantly increase the founding rates of professional associations.

The emergence of finance as a global activity has also been affected by the wider cultural processes of globalization that have had similar effects on all aspects of social activity. Meyer *et al.* (2006) identify our society as emerging as an arena of rationalization, where rationalization is systemization accelerated by the "scientization" of society, the consequences of which can be seen as follows:

> If the world surrounding an issue is scientized (categorized, ordered, codified, and universally lawful), and if the uncertainties it contains can and must be analyzed and responded to rationally (analyzed and modeled into patterns), then organization of that issue – any issue – is a very natural consequence. (Meyer *et al.* 2006: 37)

The professionalization of a field involves the development of a body of sacred knowledge that defines a shared meaning system (Abbott 1988) that provides an identity for the members of the field. This identity and meaning creation process is central to the notion of community formation around specific ideas and aims. Professional associations shape and define appropriate practices of interaction through rights of membership (Galvin 2002). Lounsbury and Lee (2005) note that financial associations play an important part in promoting global finance practice by bringing experts together to promote it. Therefore, the implication of globalization for finance is its formalization as a professional discipline (see Morgan and Kubo in this volume, though, for the difficulties and limits of such a process).

Hypothesis 4A: Global cultural and rationalization trends will positively affect the foundings of global professional associations.
Hypothesis 4B: Global cultural and rationalization trends will not affect the foundings of business associations.

Finally, it is important to explore why there are differences in the patterns of emergence of business and professional associations. The emergence of stock exchanges is not influenced by the conventional arguments of liberalization; instead, it indicates an increase in the number of platforms where financial knowledge is being meaningfully applied to practical problems. They are indicators of the degree of financialization of national economies and the broader commercial involvement of finance ideas. Therefore, we contend that business associations are more directly related to national political agendas, but that professionalization agendas are less connected to regional political ideas and represent dominant ideologies spreading from the West.

Hypothesis 5A: Professional global finance associations are more affected by the rise of global finance activity and the evolution of a global finance culture emanating from "core nations."
Hypothesis 5B: Business global finance associations are more affected by global financialization of business activities.

Methods and data

We follow the neoinstitutionalist tradition of quantitative methods in our analysis of cross-national time series data and event count data on world polity processes (Schofer and McEneaney 2003). The focus on a longitudinal observation plan is crucial in studying the various arguments put forward to explain the foundation of global associations. Our approach reveals (i) that the "associational transnational" organization of finance shows evidence of historical time dependence and (ii) that by comparing different time periods we see the limits of technical functionalist accounts of transnational organization, that is, efforts to explain by means of the argument that there was a need to organize in a particular way at a particular point in time.

The event of interest in this analysis is the founding of a transnational finance association (both business and professional associations). We created an original dataset on founding dates and other features of all active global finance associations from 1879 to 2006. The data on global finance association foundings are coded from the Yearbook of International Associations 2005/2006,[5] published by the Union of International Associations.[6]

Dependent variables

We use two dependent variables, one for each of the global finance subpopulations observed: *professional association foundings cumulative* and *business association foundings cumulative*, which are the cumulative counts of professional and business associations, respectively.

Independent variables to test hypotheses

Hypothesis 1: We use the variable *global capital mobility* to explore global functional forces. These time series data are a measure of the ratio of foreign-owned capital to output.[7]

Hypothesis 2: Infrastructural development in global finance, the need for specialized organizations informed by the proliferation of Western-style economics, is captured using the variable *Central Bank foundings cumulative*, as in Pollilo and Guillén (2005). This is an annual cumulative count obtained from a comprehensive roster of central bank foundings maintained by the Bank for International Settlements.[8]

Hypothesis 3: Three dummy variables to measure the impact of the Bretton Woods regime using the categorical variables: *Gold Standard Regime*

(1880–1914), *Interwar Regime (1914–45)*, and *Post-Bretton Woods Regime (1971–date)*.

Hypothesis 4: Core nations global professional finance association foundings measures the rationalization and professionalization of finance in core nations. It measures cumulative professional finance association foundings in the USA and the UK.

Hypothesis 5: Global science association foundings cumulative measures global trends in rationalization and universalism with a cumulative annual count of all science organizations founded during the period of the study (Schofer 1999, 2004). *Stock exchange foundings cumulative* measures the global trends for specialized business expertise by an annual cumulative count of the number of stock exchanges founded up until and including each year.

Models and analysis

The founding of a new global finance association is a Poisson process in which the rate of arrival λt is determined by a function of the covariates. The model assumes that the rate is constant, the events are independent, and there is no observed heterogeneity. The founding process of global finance associations experiences contagion effects that are common to organizational foundings (Hannan and Freeman 1987). To cater for the time dependence in rate, contagion, and unobserved heterogeneity within periods of observations, we used the negative binomial regression models, as recommended by Barron (1992).

Results

Table 7.1 presents a summary of the results of the negative binomial models of the association founding counts[9] of the two subpopulations of global finance associations and a summary of the hypothesis, and the support for them provided by the models. The result of the negative binomial analysis is given in Appendix 7.1.

Business association foundings are positively affected by changes in global capital flows and capital mobility, infrastructural development, and sector-specific cultural trends. Global rationalization trends are insignificant in the model, thus supporting Hypothesis 4B. The emergence of a global finance culture that is based on the notions of rationalization and professionalization is not enough to explain why business-based finance associations came into

Table 7.1 Summary of results

| Hypothesis | Description | Business Associations | | Professional Associations | | |
		Direction of influence on foundings	Hypothesis	Direction of influence on foundings	Hypothesis
1	Global capital flows	Positive	Supported	Positive	Supported
2	Sector-specific infrastructure	Positive	Supported	Positive	Supported
3	Sector-specific cultural trends	Positive	Supported	No effect	Supported
4A	Global rationalization			Positive	Supported
4B	trends	No effect	Supported		
5A	Western culture			Positive	Supported
5B	Financialization of business	Positive	Supported		

Appendix 7.1 Modeling finance association foundings: results of negative binomial analysis predicting founding rates of professional global finance associations, 1879–2006[a]

Covariate	Business finance associations	Professional finance associations
Constant	−1.56 (2.96)	2.06* (3.85)
Global capital mobility index$_{t-1}$	−1.92 (1.86)	−5.02* (2.71)
Central Bank foundings cumulative$_{t-1}$	−0.01 (0.03)	−0.07 (0.05)
Gold Standard Regime (1880–1914)	−3.23** (1.30)	−2.72* (1.43)
Interwar Regime (1914–45)	−1.02** (0.50)	−0.72 (0.75)
Post-Bretton Woods Regime (1971–date)	0.05 (0.38)	1.15* (0.87)
Global science association foundings cumulative$_{t-1}$	0.02** (0.01)	0.02* (0.01)
Stock exchange foundings cumulative$_{t-1}$	0.06* (0.01)	−0.01 (0.13)
Core nations global professional finance association foundings$_{t-1}$	−0.10** (0.04)	0.10* (0.07)
Log-likelihood	−120.24	−90.75
$\Delta\chi^{2b}$	8.64	7.92
Δdf^{b}	2	2
N = 127 years		

Notes: [a] Standard errors are in parentheses.
[b] Relative to the previous model.
* $p < .10$
** $p < .05$
*** $p < .01$

being. Business association formation is positively affected by the rise in formal global science activity and a formalized rational global culture. Hypothesis 5B is supported as business associations were positively affected by the formation of stock exchanges.

The global flow of capital and infrastructural development increased professionalization activity but cease to be significant as field-specific forces come into play to explain the logic of professionalization. Hypothesis 3 is supported by the analysis as there was an increase in professional finance activity after the collapse of Bretton Woods, whereas the periods before Bretton Woods were not conducive to the formation of professional finance associations. Rationalization of the world as shown by "scientization" or the institutional penetration of science through formalized global proliferation of science as a rationalized activity (Schofer 1999) is shown to have promoted the emergence of new global professional finance associations, thereby supporting Hypothesis 4A.

Hypothesis 5A sums up the arguments about the rise of professional global finance associations by looking at how global stock market growth and professional activity in core nations affect the foundings of professional associations. The proliferation of professionalization projects in global finance is directly connected to political cultural regimes, rationalization, and scientization trends and a universal culture based on Western-style models and is not influenced by infrastructural developments such as the emergence of state banks or the proliferation of stock exchange activity across the world.

A community of global finance governance associations in the making

This chapter tracks the formalization and rationalization of finance in the modern world because the governance of finance has transformed itself in a number of ways. This transformation into the governance of global finance has several dimensions. Traditionally the field was governed by nation-states that remain relevant but now share the governance space with other actors. A second observation is that economists – as a profession – increasingly took on a transnational scope (from more nationally bound groups). Thirdly, other groups began to develop their professional identity and became relevant to the governance of the field. The two last evolutions are also connected with the increased role and presence of transnational organizations and associations. Therefore the cumulative result is a linear process of a decrease in the influence of economists and nation-states and an increase in the influence of finance professionals. This complicated transformation resonates with what has happened in other fields (Djelic and Sahlin-Andersson 2006).

The results of our empirical analysis confirm the ideas we set out initially and also open up areas for new ideas and discussion. We note that the global finance field is heterogeneous, with different types of organizations. The subpopulation of business associations is heterogeneous, comprising banking and trade associations, associations of stock exchanges, and development-oriented business associations. We also note that business-oriented finance associations track the standard path of the development of global finance post World War II, much influenced by functionalist need-based factors.

Professional associations differ from business-oriented finance associations, however, in their timing and pattern of emergence, their core purpose, and the factors that have influenced their historical emergence. They represent "communities of practice" much in line with Wenger (1998). These are governance associations of professionals that share little in the way of day to day interaction, but share a common vision of purpose and practice – a rationally administered world, still organized by expertise-specific "communities of practice" (see Ramirez on accounting associations in this volume). This is a departure from the concept of "finance" initially based on American concepts of economics and trade. Fourcade (2006) looks at the "genesis and structuration of new modes of governance – rules and regulations and the organizing, discursive and monitoring activities that sustain, frame and reproduce them." These insights summarize much of the manner in which one profession (economics) grew and became dominant globally. We are not talking about one profession, but rather a body of knowledge (theories, practices, accountabilities, expertise, and policy engagement) that comes under the banner of "finance" (see also Morgan and Kubo in this volume). These associations embody the notions of profession-building and governance of professional arenas (Abbott 1988).

Finance is embodied in rational organizations with loose linkages. In the evolution of these archipelagos of finance associations and in their development and transformation, we find the mechanism by which global finance came to be. Thus these clusters of associations or archipelagos can be thought of as evolving "imagined communities" that begin to appear in a global space, departing from the concept of a monolithic global community and creating the imagery of an archipelago of agencies. We depart from traditional ideas of community-building and propose here that territory and physical proximity, as well as direct interaction, are neither necessary nor defining components of the concept of community (see also Djelic and Quack in Chapter 1 of this volume). We note that through the creation of common meaning systems and logics, transnational communities begin to emerge across associations. In this chapter we have observed how this phenomenon had an impact on the structuration and governance of financial activity as global finance associations clustered together around a particular logic, and how these clusters followed different trajectories of evolution.

Conclusion

This chapter seeks to contribute to the recent upsurge in organizational studies of global organizing in broad policy sectors (Djelic and Quack 2003; Ventresca *et al.* 2003). By building on frameworks and arguments at the intersection of work on transnational communities, structuration, and world culture and global organization, we have examined issues surrounding the founding dynamics of global finance governance associations in the nineteenth and twentieth centuries.

We have looked at the associative form of organizations that are a voluntary "coming together" of actors around specific ideas and a common purpose. These associations are interesting cases since this type of formal organization is a distinctive venue for action as well as a "marker" or "indicator" of action.

In tracking the foundings of these associations, the aim was not to investigate how finance became important in modern capitalism; instead, we looked at this sector as one specific case in which activities came to be organized transnationally through formal organizational clusters around specific themes, ideas, and logics.

First, this chapter presents a framework for understanding transnational organization and community formation through a historical view. The framework allows us to approach the structuration of global finance over a period of time. Though this approach is common in neoinstitutional literature, we extend it to include broad political and historical factors.

Beyond the structure of the field of finance the content of the dominant discourses in finance was demonstrated by the two subpopulations that link to broader global dynamics. Professional finance associations are directly linked to the professionalization of finance. Finance in this sense is linked to a universalized culture, enshrined in Western-style economic analysis and tools, which is based on the growth of key international agencies and their ideologies. Business finance organizations, on the other hand, represent all the ancillary expertise connected with business and accounting. These are also shaped by the same globalizing rationalities and cultural processes but the drivers of these are less tied to developments in global finance and more to the financialization of various domains.

Extending this analysis further, we have attempted to explore how different logics are shaped in different ways and how these processes interact over time to form a collective phenomenon. The different historical evolutions of business and professional finance suggest the importance of disaggregating and paying attention to how different logics are affected by different forces.

Functionalist explanations of the above-mentioned observations are based on material resources, demand, social diffusion processes, and the formalization of finance as driven by the globalization of economics-based ideas. However, the empirical study does not fit this pattern. By examining how functional as well as cultural factors have affected the rise of finance associations this work builds on neoinstitutional work but extends it by examining how these two sets of arguments interact with each other and which one provides better explanations.

The two subpopulations represent different logics and emerge differently, and their growth helps explain the community formation process across associations. In our view interaction does not imply community but common ideas and logics are key to community emergence. In the case of finance we note that there is no single population but instead archipelagos in which finance associations incorporate ideas such as accounting, professionalization, and development. Where there is debate, energy, and opportunity, associations form and "imagined communities" or archipelagos subsequently emerge. Here the image is not that of an integrated community but of emerging clusters. Therefore it is useful to extend traditional theories of community formation to incorporate ideas of emerging archipelagos, in analogy with Simmel's notion of multiple and intersecting circles of social interaction and community formation (Djelic and Quack in Chapter 1 of this volume). In conclusion, this chapter builds on earlier work on the study of globalization that is pervasive in the neoinstitutional literature and the literature on transnational communities, and presents a more comprehensive theoretical and methodological framework. The approach adopted here is macro-phenomenological, but it also pays attention to micro-processes and variations. The comparative approach reveals that unitary explanations of globalization and transnational communities can benefit from adopting a more detailed comparative approach.

Acknowledgments

We acknowledge the helpful comments of Gili Drori, Evan Schofer, Holger Sommerfeldt, and Patrick Panitz. The editors and other contributors to this volume also made useful suggestions at the original EGOS workshop and in subsequent reviews. In addition, we thank Jerry Davis and Klaus Weber for generous sharing of data.

NOTES

1. Examples include the Chartered Institute of Management Accountants – England (CIMA), Financial Executives International (FEI), and the Association of Corporate Treasurers (ACT).
2. Examples include the International Co-operative Banking Association, the European Banking Federation, and the European Association of Cooperative Banks (EACB).
3. Different internal forms and logics are also noted in other fields. In the field of global science there are professional and socially oriented associations (Schofer 1999), and health has professional, development-oriented, human rights-oriented, and charity-based associations (Inoue and Drori 2006).
4. Earlier "transnational organizing" was also notable. The West Indies Committee, founded in 1750 and later a Trading Company, was a key political and economic development agency in the formation of early UK finance institutions; see also Carruthers (1996) on the origins of the London Stock Exchange.
5. Edition 42.
6. Inactive or disbanded associations are not included. The proportion of these associations is small and therefore will not affect the results (Boli and Thomas 1999).
7. These data come from Obstfeld and Taylor (2004), Figure 2.1, with the permission of Alan Taylor.
8. www.bis.org.
9. The association foundings were modeled using time-series data of cross-national counts of such foundings.

REFERENCES

Abbott, A. 1988. *The system of professions: An essay on the division of expert labor*. University of Chicago Press.

Anderson, B. 2006 [1983]. *Imagined communities*. London and New York: Verso.

Barnett, M. and Finnemore, M. 2004. *Rules for the world: International organizations in global politics*. Ithaca, NY: Cornell University Press.

Barron, D. N. 1992. "The analysis of count data: Overdispersion and autocorrelation," *Sociological Methodology* **22**: 179–220.

Boli, J. and Thomas, G. M. (eds.) 1999. *Constructing world culture: International non-governmental organizations since 1875.* Stanford University Press.

Carruthers, B. 1996. *City of capital: Politics and markets in the English financial revolution.* Princeton University Press.

Chabott, C. 2003. "Development INGOs," in Boli, J. and Thomas, J. M. (eds.), pp. 222–48.

Djelic, M.-L., and Quack, S. 2003. *Globalization and institutions: Redefining the rules of the economic game.* Cheltenham: Edward Elgar.

Djelic, M.-L., and Sahlin-Andersson, K. 2006. *Transnational governance: Institutional dynamics of regulation.* Cambridge University Press.

Drori, G. S., Meyer, J. W. and Hwang, H. (eds.) 2006. *Globalization and organization: World society and organizational change.* Oxford University Press.

Drori, G. S., Meyer, J. W., Ramirez, F. O. and Schofer, E. (eds.) 2003. *Science in the modern world polity: Institutionalization and globalization.* Stanford University Press.

Elias, N. 1974. "Foreword: Towards a theory of communities," in Bell, C. and Newby, H. (eds.), *The sociology of community: A selection of readings.* London: Frank Cass, pp. ix–xli.

Fligstein, N. 1990. *The transformation of corporate control.* Cambridge, MA: Harvard University.

Foucault, M. 1970. *The order of things: An archeology of the human sciences.* London: Tavistock Fourcade-Gourinchas.

Foucault, M. 1979. "On governmentality," *Ideology & Consciousness* **6** (Autumn): 5–21.

Fourcade, M. 2006. "The construction of a global profession: The transnationalization of economics," *American Journal of Sociology* **112** (1): 145–94.

Galvin, T. L. 2002. "Examining institutional change: Evidence from the founding dynamics of U.S. health care interest associations," *Academy of Management Journal* **45** (4): 673–96.

Giddens, A. 1984. *The constitution of society.* Berkeley: University of California Press.

Giddens, A. 1990. *The consequences of modernity.* Cambridge: Polity Press.

Haas, P. M. 1992. "Introduction: Epistemic communities and international policy coordination," *International Organization* **46** (1): 1–35.

Hannan, M., and Freeman. J. 1987. "The ecology of organizational founding: American labor unions, 1836–1985," *American Journal of Sociology* **92**: 910–43.

Hillery, G. 1955. "Definitions of community: Areas of agreement," *Rural Sociology* **20**: 111–23.

Hirst, P. and Thompson, G. 1996, *Globalization in question: The international economy and the possibilities of governance.* Cambridge: Polity Press.

Inoue, K. and Gili, D. 2006. "The global institutionalization of health as a social concern: Organizational and discursive trends," *International Sociology* **21** (2): 199–219.

Lavelle, K. C. 2004. *The politics of equity finance in emerging markets.* New York: Oxford University Press.

Lounsbury, M. and Lee, B. 2005. "Decoupling and the cultures of global finance," *International Studies of Management and Organization* **34**: 116–34.

Meyer, J. W., Boli, J. and Thomas, G. M. 1987. "Ontology and rationalization in the Western cultural account," in Thomas, G. M., Meyer, J. M., Ramirez, F. and Boli, J. (eds.), pp. 12–37.

Meyer. J. W, Drori, G. S. and Hwang, H. 2006. "World society and the proliferation of formal organization," in Drori, G. S., Meyer, J. W. and Hwang, H. (eds.), pp. 25–49.

Meyer, J. W., Boli, J., Thomas, G. M. and Ramirez, F. O. 1997. "World society and the nation state," *American Journal of Sociology* **103**: 144–81.

Obstfeld, M. and Taylor, A. M. 2004. *Global capital markets: Integration, crisis and growth.* New York: Cambridge University Press.

Polillo, S. and Guillén, M. 2005. "Globalization pressures and the state: The worldwide spread of Central Bank independence," *American Journal of Sociology* **110** (6): 1764–802.

Schofer, E. 1999. "Science associations in the international sphere 1875–1990: The rationalization of science and the scientization of society," in Boli, J. and Thomas, G. M. (eds.), *World polity information: A century of international non-governmental organization.* Stanford University Press, pp. 249–66.

Schofer, E. 2004. "Cross-national differences in the expansion of science," *Social Forces* **83** (1): 215–48.

Schofer, E. and McEneaney, E. 2003. "Methodological strategies and tools for the study of globalization," in Drori, G. S., Meyer, J. W., Ramirez, F. O. and Schofer, E. (eds.), pp. 23–42.

Sinclair, T. J. 1994. "Passing judgment: Credit rating processes as regulatory mechanisms of governance in the emerging world order," *Review of International Political Economy* **1** (1): 133–59.

Smiddy, H. F. and Naum, L. 1954. "Evolution of a 'science of managing' in America," *Management Science* **1**: 1–31.

Stiglitz, J. E. 2002. *Globalization and its discontents.* New York: Norton.

Strang, D. and Soule, S. A. 1998. "Diffusion in organizations and social movements: From hybrid corn to poison pills," *Annual Review of Sociology* **24**: 265–90.

Streeck, W. and Schmitter, P. C. 1985. "Community, market, state–and associations? The prospective contribution of interest governance to social order," *European Sociological Review* **1** (2): 119–38.

Thomas, G. M., Meyer, J. M., Ramirez, F. and Boli, J. (eds.) 1987. *Institutional structure: Constituting state, society and the individual.* Newbury Park, CA: Sage.

UIA (Union of International Associations). 2005/2006. *Yearbook of International Organization.* Brussels: UIA.

Ventresca, M., Szyliowicz, D. and Dacin, M. 2003. "Institutional innovations in governance in the global field of financial markets," in Djelic, M. L. and Quack, S. (eds.).

Wenger, E. 1998. *Communities of practice: Learning, meaning, and identity.* Cambridge University Press.

8 Promoting transnational professionalism: forays of the "Big Firm" accounting community into France

Carlos Ramirez

Introduction

The constitution of professional communities is generally thought to take place at national level. The establishment of a profession usually involves negotiations with the nation-state, which allows professionals to exercise their unique and specific knowledge under a regime of self-regulation as long as they guarantee to provide high-quality services. Although the form and degree of self-regulation has varied between countries, generally being more extensive in Anglo-American countries than in Continental European ones (Burrage and Torstendahl 1990), professions have been allowed to set up jurisdictions and to define the boundaries within which they claim exclusive competence and non-interference from other professional or occupational groups.

Critical accounts of professions have highlighted the fact that their boundaries, internal structure, and functions are historically contingent (Abbott 1988; Freidson 2001). Professions are therefore neither internally coherent nor externally clearly bounded. Instead, they should be viewed in terms of an ongoing struggle between different groups about the nature and boundaries of the knowledge for which they claim exclusive jurisdiction and from which they derive a privileged social status. This conception has become prevalent in the investigation of national professional communities. One might wonder whether it also applies to communities that have emerged as a consequence of the globalization of the market for certain professional services.

Professional services are indeed increasingly provided and traded across borders (Suddaby et al. 2007). This is particularly true of business services, such as accounting, consultancy, and law, fields in which "global players" – that is, multinational professional service firms – now serve corporate customers from a large number of offices in different countries. Accountancy is a profession that can truly boast global players (Strange 1996). Deloitte, KPMG, Ernst & Young, and PricewaterhouseCoopers – also known as the "Big Firms" or the "Big Four" – have a leadership position that extends beyond merely commercial aspects. These organizations head professional rankings in terms of the fees they charge and have managed to build a quasi-cartel in the multinational client segment, to which they sell much more than accountancy and auditing services (or used to, before the Enron scandal and ensuing legislation). They also provide almost all the accountancy profession's representatives on international accounting and auditing standard-setting bodies. Beyond their official role in the production of international expertise, they are further assumed to be part of networks spanning the business and political milieus, whose influence is not always considered to be in the public interest (Catchpowle *et al.* 2004).

While some attention has been given to the Big Firms' cooperation in terms of mutual interests, such as trade liberalization in the context of the World Trade Organization (Arnold 2005), relatively little consideration has been given to the transnational professional communities that might be developing around these firms and the projects that their members might be pursuing in competition or cooperation with national professional communities. The absence of such studies is even more surprising since the promotion of specific approaches to professional work (Freidson 1986 and 2001) might be one of the central channels through which multinational professional services firms exert their influence. The lack of such detailed studies stands in stark contrast to the overall importance attributed to professionals as key actors in globalization processes (Meyer *et al.* 1997; Djelic and Sahlin-Andersson 2006).

This chapter aims to fill some of the research gaps. It shows how a transnational professional community of accountants and auditors has emerged around the big accountancy firms. The chapter focuses on how the big accountancy firms and the professional community around them have attempted to spread their version of professionalism to France, which hitherto has followed a very different path in the professionalization of accounting. By linking up with and gradually transforming the elite of a previously insulated national professional community the transnational professional community around the big accountancy firms has effectively expanded its regulatory leverage across national borders.

The big Anglo-American accountancy firms as a transnational community

The homogeneity of the "Big Firm" category is for the most part an assumption. It has not been the subject of much scholarly investigation, and then often with the purpose of criticizing such firms (Arnold and Sikka 2001; Arnold 2005). If a community is to be defined by the sharing of a common identity, the definition of the Big Firms is problematic. First, these firms are no longer traditional professional accountancy partnerships but complex and hierarchical organizations, offering multidisciplinary services – some of them regulated – under the same brand name. Each of the four firms has a unique history and structures its activities in a particular way (Jones 1981, 1995; Spacek 1989; Wootton and Wolk 1992; Allen and McDermott 1993; Matthews *et al.* 1998; Wootton 2003). While affiliation to the firm seems, in the case of accountants, to be more prevalent than affiliation to the profession (Grey 1998), the sense of a "Big Firm" identity distinct from and superimposed on the "KPMG" or the "Deloitte" identity might therefore be questioned. Second, vehicles for collectively promoting such a Big Firm identity do not exist as such. Besides the fact that the interests and positions of the firms composing the Big Four may not always coincide, these firms seem to have taken much care to ensure that they are not seen as an exclusive lobby group. When the Big Firms are represented at such forums as the European Contact Group or the Transnational Auditors Committee of the International Federation of Accountants, it is always in the company of other firms that are their immediate – but distant – subordinates in the professional rankings.[1] By the same token, members of the Big Firms elected or seconded to the different governing and technical committees of the national professional bodies, or to the national and international audit and accountancy standard-setters, always act in their capacity as professionals and not as representatives of their firm or of a Big Firm consortium.

There is therefore no particular "professional project" (Larson 1977), motivated by the demand that a specific professional identity be recognized, that these firms could try to develop. Rather than in terms of a community, the Big Firm phenomenon would seem to be more readily categorizable in terms of "markets," "organizations," or "networks" (see Mayntz in this volume). The Big Four have indeed cartelized the market for the provision of audit services to the top listed companies. Moreover, according to Suddaby *et al.* (2007), they constitute an organizational field in terms of DiMaggio's and Powell's

(1983: 148) definition. Also, a Big Firm is in fact a network of firms whose professionals participate in broader networks spanning the business and political spheres. However, professions are also "loose amalgamations of segments pursuing different objectives in different manners and more or less delicately held together under a common name at a particular period in history" (Bucher and Strauss 1961: 326). As far as the accountancy profession is concerned, among members of the Big Four there is certainly a sense of having much more in common with other Big Firm professionals than with members of other communities in the profession. Of course, this sense of belonging might be felt differently at the different hierarchical levels of the Big Firm or vary in accordance with interactions with members of other Big Firms. At the same time, communities do not necessarily need physical proximity in order to be built (see Mayntz in this volume) but the "sharing of cognitive and value schemes often associated with complex socialization processes that are translated into common expertise, shared interests, and projects" (see Djelic and Quack in this volume). From this point of view, what is interesting in relation to the Big Firms is that community-building in fact means the building of a transnational community.

First, although local particularities might have persisted in the approach to professional work (Cooper *et al.* 1998), the Big Firms can boast of being the only transnational accountancy and audit firms. Indeed, the standardization of recruitment, training, promotion, work, and quality control procedures, as well as the inculcation of professional behavior, investigation of which by organizational studies constitutes what we know about accountants' professional identities (see, for instance, Dirsmith *et al.* 1997; Covaleski *et al.* 1998; Anderson-Gough *et al.* 2005), define a specific professional culture that the Big Firms have managed to reproduce worldwide and which differs from that of other accountancy and audit firms, even those belonging to an international network.

Second, these firms have from an early stage acted together at the international level, either to lobby in favor of their interests (Arnold 2005; Suddaby *et al.* 2007), or to advance their conception of professional work. Indeed, not only do the Big Firms compose a community of interests, but they also constitute what Haas defined as an epistemic community, that is, "professionals with recognized expertise and competence in a particular domain and an authoritative claim to policy-relevant knowledge within that domain or issue-area" (Haas 1992: 3). Partners in what was then the Big Ten were at the forefront of the constitution of the International Accounting Standards Committee, which in 2000 became the International Accounting Standards Board. The representatives of the Big

Firms are also indispensable to the functioning of the International Auditing and Assurance Standards Board, for which they provide the "best practices" in auditing that are later translated into standards. On these boards they are often the only representatives of the accountancy profession, and what is more, although they have to share their influence with members who do not come from an accounting firm, the latter have in general been trained as accounting and auditing specialists at one of the Big Firms. The international standard-setters could thus be considered as a sort of "club" largely comprising Big Firm partners or their "old boys/girls" (Chantiri 2000; Quack 2007).

Third, these firms have – at least until the Enron scandal and subsequent legislation – managed to integrate the different accounting and auditing activities into a global array of services specifically tailored to the needs of multinational companies. Auditing, for example, has been progressively rede-fined in terms of risk assurance and integrated into a set of other services (Robson *et al.* 2007).The multinational dimension of the Big Firm community is thus here combined with multidisciplinarity, contributing to the establish-ment within the accountancy profession of the Big Firm professional as a member of the community of specialists of multinational companies.

The constitution of the Big Firms as a transnational community does not take place only at the global level. There is also a local dimension, as the Big Firms have a history of spreading worldwide by "colonizing" local scenes, trying to exert their power and impose their conception of professionalism at the national level (for parallel observations on private equity see Morgan and Kubo in this volume). They thus perfectly exemplify the role authors such as Morgan (2001), Djelic and Quack (2003), or Djelic and Sahlin-Andersson (2006), have assigned to certain transnational communities as instrumental in transnational institution-building and national institutional change. The Big Firms' global expansion has taken various routes depending on the firm, but in most cases it was initiated very early and relied first on the expatriation of personnel to service the subsidiaries of Anglo-American companies (Jones 1995; Matthews *et al.* 1998). As these outposts grew and came to undertake work falling under local professional regulations, the question of the recruit-ment of native accountants and their promotion to partnership level was inevitably raised. In their expansion abroad, the conception of professionalism that the Big Firms conveyed has sometimes been at odds with the local professional culture. It is this confrontation of professional cultures that this chapter explores. It examines the French profession since 1970 to see how the representatives of Big Firms in France have evolved from "off-shore" plat-forms to become the French component of a transnational community, but also to analyze the progressive replacement of the local professional elite by these big multinational firms. It thus deals primarily with national aspects of transnational community-building.

Before we set the scene for the confrontation between the French and multinational professional elites, it is important to bear in mind that in the Anglo-American world the term "professional elite" has essentially been associated with firms rather than individuals. Among the characteristics of the Big Firms, most relevant for our study is the importance of the partnership form for the organization of professional practice. The association of practitioners working under the same name has made a significant contribution to the growth of business and the possibility of tailoring firm size to client size. In stark contrast, French accountants, because they wished to resemble more established professionals and because the French market for accountancy and audit services was too narrow, stuck to a form of practice that was essentially "parochial" (that is, local and personal).

An island to be conquered: the French professional community of accountants

The professional project of French accountancy practitioners before World War II to gain official recognition for their activity was based on imitation of the formal characteristics of other professions that were more advanced in terms of "social closure". The accountants decided to follow the example of the legal profession (advocates and notaries) in their attempt to "serve the public." This was all the more logical and necessary because the French accountancy elite included many individuals who had failed to make a career in the professions they were imitating (Ramirez 2001). As a result, the professional associations promoted values and conceptions of practice that tended to equate excellence in the craft of accountancy with individual practice and the practice of accountancy and auditing exclusive of any other professional specialism. Sole practitioners, because they could maintain proper control over the work they delegated to subordinates, were deemed best able to meet the requirements of independence and competence that are essential to professional activity. Like law practitioners, it was considered that professional accountants should serve their business clients but also maintain a certain professional distance (Ramirez 2001).

Achieving professional status in France is dependent on state recognition, usually in the form of granting a monopoly. From this standpoint it was a long time before accountants and auditors' associations were properly rewarded for their lobbying efforts. If one takes the case of statutory auditing or *commissariat aux comptes*, legislation passed as early as 1867 made provision for *commissaires* to certify companies' accounts.[2] However, the Act said nothing about how the competence and independence of those *commissaires* would be guaranteed. As a result of the lack of formal guidance on that question, and also on the scope of auditors' investigations, the audit institution became a laughing stock. Shareholders, politicians, essayists, and even British professionals (Brown 1905) would describe in outraged or jocular terms the way in which *commissaires* were recruited from managers' own families, or were ageing shareholders with only the most rudimentary knowledge of accounting. In particular, audit fees were so low, especially by Anglo-American standards, that the sort of tasks carried out by practitioners could best be described as perfunctory. French auditing was therefore more a function than a proper profession. The very notion of the large audit firm in particular, with a sizeable number of partners and staff, appears to have been alien to the French auditing tradition, which was more closely related to a professional field in which size was not correlated with prestige. In comparison with its Anglo-American counterparts, one distinctive feature of the French profession was therefore the connection between large companies and the small practices which sold audit services to them.

At the end of the 1960s the French accountancy profession was still small and the vast majority of its members were modest bookkeepers. The *commissariat aux comptes*, officially established in 1867, had to wait until 1969 to attain the status of a full-fledged profession, at least in form (see below). A culture of auditing compatible with a financial market-based economy was yet to be inculcated in French business people (Ramirez 2005: 495–98). Within the profession, the dominant approach to practice remained rooted in values such as individualism and social prestige. Professional institutions had been constructed around the figure of the professional working on his (and occasionally her) own, or with a few partners. Due to slow development, the supply side of the market for audit services was principally populated by individuals with good social connections but limited means of providing a thorough examination of their clients' accounts.

The major turning point for the French profession came at the end of the 1960s, when the government decided to launch an initial series of reforms aimed at enabling France's financial markets to play a larger role in the context of further integration of the national economy into the European Economic Community. As far as auditors were concerned, a decree formally establishing a new professional body in France, the *Compagnie nationale des commissaires aux comptes* (CNCC), was published on August 12, 1969, and awarded its members a monopoly over statutory audits. New requirements were set in terms of qualifications and ethical standards so as to put the French profession on a par with its counterparts in the other industrialized countries of Western Europe (Ramirez 2009). The reform was completed in 1985 when the official audit fee scale was amended so that it was no longer based on the size of the company audited but on the number of hours actually worked. By that time, France's transition from a situation in which the financial markets were under strict state control to a more open, free-market oriented economy was well under way. Between 1984 and 1989, in a period nicknamed the "Little Bang," the Paris stock exchange had its own revolution, and by 1989 was the second most open stock exchange in Europe (Schmidt 1996).

The transformation of the "debt" economy of the early 1980s into a "market" economy on the threshold of the twenty-first century would be inconceivable without reliable auditing of the accounting information supplied by listed companies, and therefore impossible without a powerful auditing profession, that is, a body of independent, competent professionals. The reforms of the end of the 1960s seemed to equip France with such a profession. However, the increasing internationalization and opening up of the French economy to financial flows essentially represented a boon for professional firms that already enjoyed a strong reputation worldwide.

The encounter between the Big Firm accounting community and the French accounting profession

France's increasing opening up to capital flows tolled the death knell of the old-style *commissariat aux comptes*, which now had to make way for another type of audit practice that could mobilize sufficient technical and human resources to meet the challenge of globalization. This section recounts the reaction of local professionals, and their powerful patron, the state, to the growth of the French representatives of the Big Firms as a response to the need for new professional practices.

Trying to resist: the French profession and the Big Firms in the 1970s – the Asterix syndrome

The Anglo-American firms had set up shop in Western Europe as early as the beginning of the twentieth century, but most of their business concerned the auditing of British or American parent companies and providing management consultancy services. The British were the first to open offices in France: Price Waterhouse in 1917, Peat in 1920, Cooper Brothers in 1929, and Ernst and Whinney the same year. Arthur Andersen came to Paris in 1955, followed by Touche Ross in 1961. With the exception of Arthur Andersen, which in keeping with the *one-firm concept* had based its development on internal growth (Spacek 1989) and recruitment of French staff (graduates of the *grandes écoles*), the Big Firms retained a marked Anglo-American flavor (Ramirez 2005: 500). For a long time (Jones 1995: 118–20), Price Waterhouse's French office – which was to become the firm's European headquarters – was manned by staff seconded from the British or American firms, and its clients were Anglo-American. There were hardly any local clients, as the financial markets played a very small role in the reconstruction of Europe. Jones (1995: 118–20) also describes recurring problems in finding "quality staff" locally, which led to a reliance on expatriates. The more limited size of continental offices, too, was initially insufficient to develop economies of scale and specialized services.

This prevalent non-local approach changed, by and large, after 1970, not so much because the Big Firms were attracted by the prospect of auditing local companies in compliance with the regulation of *commissariat aux comptes* (as we have just said, the modernization of the Paris stock exchange came later, in the 1980s), but because of considerable growth during the economic crisis in the demand for contractual audit engagements by large French groups planning IPOs in London or New York. Demand for management consultancy services was also on the increase. In 1970, Price Waterhouse was engaged to assist the Saint Gobain company in the preparation of consolidated accounts under US GAAP (generally accepted accounting principles). Two years later, Cooper Brothers performed the same service for Rhône Poulenc. Flotation on foreign stock markets and raising capital on Euromarkets were unthinkable without a sign-off by one of the Big Firms, the only ones with an international reputation. From the second half of the 1970s, the number of engagements by large French companies, and also government agencies, began to rise (Ramirez 2005). There was two-figure growth in the fee income registered by the multinational audit firms. Meanwhile, the Big Firms began to "Frenchify" their personnel. The number of graduates of the three largest Paris business schools who were recruited rose threefold, on average, in the course of the 1970s (Ramirez 2005: 502). The transnational community of the Big Firms thus expanded due to its integration of local elements. The Big Firms managed to penetrate the French system of producing elites by recruiting graduates from the *grandes écoles*, and began to establish networks in the local business milieus. They nevertheless still lacked the possibility of converting this cultural and social capital into sufficient leverage to displace the local professional elite.

This local elite at first tried to resist the encroachment of the Big Firms. Resistance included public manifestations of discontent by professional leaders and legal attempts to block the right of the Anglo-American firms to practice statutory auditing. Both rested on a different interpretation of what auditing ought to be. In a pamphlet of December 2, 1970, Jean Sigaut, who was to become the head of the professional body for auditors, depicted Anglo-American methods as alien, whereas "what France must do is develop *commissariat aux comptes* methods." He added: "We will not accept the assumption that methods are good because they are American," going on to compare the situation he was criticizing and the system of capitulations in the Ottoman Empire that allowed foreigners to use only their own consuls at a time when the Sublime Porte was falling into decline. Sigaut concluded: "We are being called shopkeepers protesting against supermarkets, as if this comparison had any meaning in our field of business" (Ramirez 2005: 503).

The attempt to hinder the Big Firms' incursion into regulated markets also took the form of French representatives of the Big Networks being debarred from engaging in accountancy-related activities under their international name. On February 1, 1974, the Paris *Compagnie des commissaries aux comptes*'s regional disciplinary chamber issued its ruling in the case against MacCarthy, Smith, Samaran, Lathom-Sharp, and Tauss, who were Price Waterhouse partners at the firm's Paris office.[3] The chamber noted that Price Waterhouse, whose offices were in the Avenue de l'Opéra, was "a de facto association with no existence as a legal entity, whose members are co-opted in, pay no entry fee and receive no severance indemnity." In France, this association was directed by H. Lathom-Sharp and S. Samaran, who were both registered *commissaires aux comptes* in compliance with the August 12, 1969 decree. The chamber also observed that the firm's main business was auditing (*révision comptable*) "at rates that are five times higher than the official scale" (Ramirez 2005: 503). Faced with the possibility of official reprimands and warnings, the Price Waterhouse partners concerned decided to resign from their positions as *commissaires aux comptes*. These decisions obliged the Anglo-American firms operating on French territory to speed up the promotion of French partners and register under "Frenchified" names.[4] Arthur Andersen, for example, audited under the name Guy Barbier et Associés, while Price Waterhouse's French audit firm was called Blanchard, Chauveau et Associés.

The impassioned reactions of the leaders of French institutions show that this period was still dominated by a conception of professionalism in accordance with which independence and individualism were presented as cardinal virtues. The whole professional field still clearly exhibited the legacy of a hierarchical organization in which the elite consisted of small firms or sole practitioners. *Commissariat aux comptes* for large companies was thus distinct from auditing, and reserved for a small community of Parisian practitioners who had long-standing associations with the companies whose accounts they verified. Although the big Anglo-American firms had initiated "Frenchification" of the personnel in their local subsidiaries and had increased the proportion of French companies in their portfolios, sometimes substantially, they still remained "off-shore platforms" with respect to the community constituted by France's professional accountancy elites, not to mention to the French professional rank-and-file. It is to the analysis of the transformation of the Big Firms into a new local professional elite that we now turn.

Trying to compete: the demise of an independent French profession in the 1980s

After 1980, it became obvious that the French professional elite would not be able to resist the expansion of the Big Firms with only makeshift protectionist measures. The decision to adapt professional practice was not made at the initiative of the traditional professional elite, which represented the *commissaire aux comptes*/sole practitioner model. Indeed, this initiative did not come from a professional body but from an ad hoc organization formed by a band of "young Turks" amongst the professional community that set up the *Association française pour le développement de l'audit* (AFDA) in 1982. Planned in principle since the late 1970s, the AFDA's aims were supported by the authorities, as expressly stated in the two reports commissioned by the French Ministries of Finance and Justice in 1982 and 1984 (the Aubin report and the Huet report). The AFDA was initially a collective promotional body, seeking to raise the quality of the flagship French *commissaire aux comptes* firms to equal that of their Anglo-American counterparts. Article 6 of the AFDA's articles of association stated that it was "open to all candidates whose professional activity includes the use of audit techniques to a substantial degree." No client could provide more than 10 percent of the firm's total fee revenues, and no more than 20 percent of total fee revenues could come from a foreign organization. Finally, the firm should not be substantially dependent on a foreign decision-making center for the appointment of partners or staff training. For a successful launch, the AFDA was relying on the Socialist government's major economic projects (*grands chantiers*). On coming to power, the Left had been faced with a considerable need for expert services, largely exceeding the capacities of the government audit office, the *Inspection des finances*, and the national audit office, the *Cour des comptes*, particularly for the valuation of businesses due to come under state control as part of the nationalization program. The AFDA was to act as a kind of shortlist from which the authorities would select the firms to be awarded audit engagements.[5]

The AFDA's initiative worked simultaneously against the professional organizations, since it was operating on the margins of their own activity, forming a kind of elitist club whose members would be given engagements denied to other professionals, and against the model of the old-fashioned *commissaire aux comptes*/sole practitioner without sufficient resources to comply with international auditing standards. With the AFDA's stated purpose of developing "audit," not *commissariat aux comptes*, resistance to the spread of the Big Firms in France took the form of a plan to create an alternative model on the same pattern, in terms of recruitment, practices, and firm organization. AFDA members expected that this model would be able to compete, even if only locally.

AFDA members represented more than one billion francs in fee revenues, employed 2,000 professional staff, and were auditors to 600 listed companies. However, from the outset the viability of a purely national undertaking was contested. First the government, which had supported the project, rather than calling exclusively on AFDA firms to value companies being nationalized (and later reprivatized in 1986 when the Right returned to power) engaged them to work in collaboration with the French representatives of the Big Firm networks.[6] In late 1986, ten projects were thus distributed between "French" and "foreign" firms. Once "inside the door" some firms representing Anglo-American practices in France remained as auditors to the newly privatized entity (Ramirez 2005: 518–20). Then it was the turn of the French firms representing Anglo-American networks to become indignant, this time at what some saw as disguised protectionism. In several interviews to the professional press, French partners of the Big Firms insisted that their capital was owned by French partners, that decision-making procedures (including those concerning recruitment, promotion, and training) were local and that the only remaining foreign link consisted in the technical agreements regarding the quality of service provided to clients (Ramirez 2005: 518). Finally, the exclusion of French representatives of Anglo-American firms was even denounced within the AFDA. Some partners in AFDA member firms considered that the association, instead of learning from what the Big Firms had to offer, was at risk of "ghettoization," carrying out pseudo-Anglo-American style audits that could not measure up to the "real thing," with the danger that client companies would no longer want them (Ramirez 2005: 519).

The right-wing government's privatization campaign, introduced when it returned to power in 1986, seemed to confirm these predictions. By this time the AFDA was already losing ground in the face of the Big Firms' competition. The economic transformations described earlier had made the *commissariat aux comptes* market attractive to large Big Network member firms, by now almost wholly French in terms of recruitment.[7] In the late 1980s many of the main French companies changed statutory auditors. This was also a time when professional elites underwent a profound transformation. The Big Firms pursued a proactive policy of takeovers of French traditional *commissaires aux comptes* practices that were well established as auditors of large groups (Ramirez 2005: 520–21). Some AFDA member firms also eventually decided to merge with a Big Firm. In 1989 Arthur Andersen merged with Frinault Fiduciaire, a *commissariat aux comptes* firm that was the statutory auditor of a significant number of large companies. Frinault, once a representative of the traditional elite of sole practitioners, had first been tempted by the AFDA adventure and had become one of its founder members. Its absorption by the American Arthur Andersen sealed the alliance between the major Anglo-American firms and the old French professional elites, and between *commissariat aux comptes* and audit, through convergence towards the latest working methods.

The demise of the AFDA as top French companies fell into the hands of the Big Firm auditors rang the death knell for a French profession that was both independent and powerful. In the end, the AFDA community was unable to assert itself as the new professional elite because it would have had, on the one hand, to distance itself from part of the traditional French professional elite and, on the other, to offer a credible local alternative to the global community constituted by the Big Firms. The acceptability of the latter as the new French professional elite had gained ground. By the late 1980s their offices in France bore little resemblance to the "outposts" most of them had been just fifteen years earlier, when expatriate partners dealt principally with the local subsidiaries of Anglo-American companies. They now more closely resembled the French component of a multinational ensemble. At the same time, the community of the Big Firms in France did not differ from those in other countries, as the same standards of socialization, training, and work applied.

However, it was also rooted in the French meritocratic system as it had been increasingly trying to attract candidates with a *grande école* background. Still, however "Frenchified" it might have been, this community remained estranged from the local profession.

Limited integration: blending transnational professionalism and French accounting in the 1990s

During the 1990s, the large multinational firms continued to expand on the French audit market with further acquisitions of French firms. In fact, this market, in which they built up a cartel for the listed companies segment, was a springboard for the establishment of firms on related markets, such as management or legal and tax consultancy. This commercial strategy made the Anglo-American firms the specialists in intellectual services to large businesses (Ramirez 2005). The native French firms were reduced to either hyperspecialization, general services for smaller businesses, or association on the sidelines of the Big Firms' work, for instance in joint appointments as auditors. Besides their economic success, the Big Firms developed their integration in France's elite networks, especially through their recruitment policy. Their auditors now mostly came from the large Paris business schools, the prestigious Sciences-Po, and the reputed Paris-Dauphine University (Ramirez 2005: 524). The Big Firms thus adapted perfectly to the *grandes écoles* system and to the rise of business *grandes écoles* such as the *École des hautes études commerciales* (HEC) as providers of French elites.[8] The "Frenchification" of their personnel had led the Big Firms in France to espouse local ways of producing these elites, as well as adapting them to suit their own needs. Although they were full-fledged members of professional institutions, the Big Firms did not prioritize the recruitment and training of rank-and-file accountancy students. Masses of trainees continued to study for their professional exams while working in smaller practices, while many Big Four recruits regarded their time at Ernst, KPMG, Deloitte, or PWC as a specialization, a sort of postgraduate course opening up the doors to the finance departments of their firm's clients. The pyramidal organization of the multinational firms, and the resulting "up or out" career system, thus developed "alumni" networks of former Ernst, KPMG, Deloitte, or PWC personnel, an elite which, like in any other country, circulated between the auditing and business worlds in France (on the French business elite, see Harvey and Maclean in this volume).

The dominant position of the Big Firms on the market for accountancy and audit services to large companies, together with their increasing integration into

France's system of producing elites, does not mean that the community they represent has been recognized by all French professionals as their new elite. The Big Firms have made no attempt to conquer French professional institutions overtly and directly. Not only do they lack legitimacy in the eyes of rank-and-file French practitioners, but a strategy based on vote-winning can prove too volatile and therefore risky. The representatives of the Big Firms have instead elected to bypass professional institutions and establish their own exclusive vehicles for wielding power. The Big Firms were joined by leading French firms on the audit services market (principally former AFDA members such as Salustro-Reydel and Mazars) in forming the Arnaud Bertrand Committee at the beginning of the 1990s. Named after a deceased KPMG partner, this committee has often been seen as a sort of parallel council where affairs affecting the large audit firms are discussed and lobbying strategies are decided.[9] The advent of the Big Firms as the new professional elite has thus yielded new channels for exerting influence and new connections between different professional communities. The reorganization of the market for audit and accountancy services on the basis of size, with the result that large companies can be serviced only by large firms, has led to a coalition of the Big Firms with other local firms, which the former consider as legitimate interlocutors because they also work with such companies to advance the interests of their own professional segment.

However, the feature that contributes most to the estrangement of the Big Firms from the majority of the domestic profession, paradoxically, is the fact that they have managed to penetrate to the very heart of French accounting and auditing. These are indeed domains in which the production of national standards is totally (in the case of audit) or increasingly (in the case of accounting) governed by the importation of international standards. The Big Firms can provide the kind of technical expertise in these standards that is most valued by the leaders of the professional institutions in France, because it is something that remains elusive to them. Partners of the Big Firms have thus managed to sit on the professional standards committee of the *Compagnie nationale des commissaires aux comptes* and have become a vital element in the integration of international audit standards into French audit regulations. They have also officially become members of the CNC (*Conseil national de la comptabilité*), the French accounting standard setter, after participating in its activities for some years (Colasse and Standish 1998). Having designed and promoted the *Plan comptable général*, the CNC, which became the *Autorité des normes comptables* (ANC) in 2009, now devotes most of its work to consolidated accounts and the introduction of IFRS in France. In the past, the CNC could rely on assistance from the multinational firms' technical directors for this purpose. In 1996, following a reform of the institution, one of those firms' senior partners was made director of the standard-setting body. This position, which was traditionally held by a high-ranking civil servant, was taken by Georges Barthès de Ruyter, who had been a partner of Frinault Fiduciaire, and subsequently of Arthur Andersen, and Chairman of the Board of the International Accounting Standards Committee. He was later succeeded by Antoine Bracchi, former senior partner of Ernst & Young in France.

The Big Firms have thus been instrumental in the globalization of French accountancy and auditing, while at the same time using the monopoly they enjoy over this global dimension to dominate the French profession. The Big Firms now occupy a special position within this profession. They are inside the profession because their staff is French and because they are involved in the profession's development – technically through accounting and auditing standard-setting, and politically through a series of "parallel" committees. They are also outside the profession, however, because they represent international networks and do not head the national professional institutions. Ultimately, the leaders of these institutions have been obliged to accept the Big Firms' presence as a necessary evil for the prestige of independent French accountancy and auditing.

One episode illustrates the estrangement of the Big Firm community from representatives of the more rank-and-file French practitioner. It is the "Big Firm strike" that occurred in 1993. This had its origins in the publication of the first Le Portz report (July 1993) on "ethics and the listed company auditor." Yves Le Portz was commissioned by the *Commission des opérations de bourse* and the *Compagnie nationale des commissaires aux comptes* to lead a working party whose purpose would be to study the development of consultancy services provided by entities operating alongside audit firms in multidisciplinary networks and to determine the measures necessary to guarantee the independence of judgment of these audit firms' professionals. Le Portz suggested that the CNCC should regulate on the prohibition of those services whose provision would jeopardize the auditor's judgment. Although it did not mention any multidisciplinary firm in particular, the report was clearly trying to loosen the Anglo-American firms' grip on the market for professional services and was against a conception of audit as being one of the many services offered by these firms. When, at the beginning of 1993, the *Compagnie des commissaires aux comptes* did cross the Rubicon by integrating these recommendations into its body of audit standards, the Big Firms' representatives went on "strike," refusing to continue sitting on the *Compagnie's* professional standards committee.[10]

Conclusion: the regulatory power of transnational professionalism

At the beginning of the story told in this chapter, the representatives of the Anglo-American firms in France were "offshore platforms," where expatriates catered mainly to the needs of the subsidiaries of their parent firm's clients. By the late 1990s, however, the French professional landscape resembled that of many other industrialized countries. There was now a correlation between size and hierarchical rank, which had come to be a matter primarily of organizations rather than individuals. We have addressed two aspects of the constitution of a transnational community, both explored at the national level. The first aspect concerns the building of the large multinational firms as a transnational community. From this point of view the expansion of the Big Firms on the French market for professional services is an episode in a longer history of going global. The episode unfolded into a process of "Frenchification" aimed at turning mere outposts manned by foreign personnel into the French component of a multinational ensemble (see Morgan and Kubo in this volume for the opposite strategy adopted by Japanese private equity firms setting up outposts in global financial centers in order to link into a transnational community). The second aspect has to do with the replacement at the head of the French profession of an elite of individuals who had a conception of professionalism that was essentially local and individual, based on a monopoly over auditing excluding the provision of any other service, by an elite of international firms whose manner of functioning and mode of insertion in national economic and social environments derives from a professional tradition developed initially in the Anglo-American countries.

The story we have told about French accountants provides us with a good opportunity to reflect on the impact for professions of the existence of "communities within the (professional) community."[11] In the case of professions working with multinational corporations, a community of transnational professionals has emerged in the wake of the constitution of a market for expertise in such corporations. If we accept Freidson's definition of professional knowledge as the transformation of formal knowledge through practice (Freidson 1986), professionals develop a knowledge that corresponds to the particular clientele for which they practice, and the particular type of problems that this clientele submits to them. In the case of the accountancy profession, transnational professionals have managed to import their particular knowledge of multinational companies and their problems into the very same fabric of accountancy and auditing standards. Their active participation in the setting up and functioning of the IASB and the IAASB was rewarded by increased leverage in relation to national standard-setters when international standards have been gradually introduced in national regulations, at least as far as the consolidated accounts of listed companies are concerned (Quack 2007). Participating in the production of standardized knowledge implies here not only a comprehension of problems acquired from study but also practical experience of these problems. Big Firms' professionals, especially those directly involved in standard-setting, have thus helped to draw a "circle" within which they exist in isolation from most of the other members of the accountancy profession. In the case of the former, it seems to be a virtuous circle as the Big Firms acquire expertise in the creation of standards that they can sell to their clients, and in turn their clients' "problems" nurture further reflection on accounting and auditing standardization. In the case of the latter, it is certainly a vicious circle as most non-Big Firm professionals, because of their insufficient familiarity with the world of multinational companies, have been virtually excluded from the production of accounting and auditing knowledge in its most prestigious form.

In countries in which accounting and auditing standards are essentially designed for the production and certification of the information needed by financial investors, the situation described above does not seem to raise many problems. In the USA or the UK, standard-setting bodies have been the preserve of the Big Firms since the beginning. The separation between the transnational and the local is seen as more natural than in countries, such as France, in which accounting has the status of a public good and traditionally serves the purpose of providing information to much wider social categories, including the state. In these countries, the domination of international accounting and its experts over standard-setting creates a separation that is certainly seen as less natural and as imported from abroad.

NOTES

1. The Transnational Auditors Committee (TAC) nominates five of the eighteen members of the International Auditing and Assurance Standards Board. The European Contact Group was set up in 1993 to represent the interests of the six major accountancy firms in Europe. It is officially registered as an interest representative body by the European Commission (source: International Federation of Accountants and European Commission).
2. France is peculiar in that it has two separate professional institutions for accounting and auditing. The *Ordre des experts-comptables* was established in 1942 and its members are principally in charge of account-keeping or supervising the account-keeping of corporate

bodies, while *Commissaires aux comptes* who register with the *Compagnie nationale des commissaries aux comptes* (CNCC, see below) enjoy a legal monopoly over auditing. A provision of the 1968 law reforming the *expert-comptable* profession allowed all registered members also to register in the *commissaire aux comptes* profession. France also has a clear-cut division between practitioners and accountants working in industry. Only the former are considered as members of an organized, independent profession.

3. A similar ruling was issued against Peat Marwick Mitchell.

4. As noted in the *International Accounting Bulletin* (August 2, 1983, pp. 21–23), by 1983 Arthur Andersen was almost entirely French, and any remaining perception of the firm as "American" was due to the structure of the worldwide Arthur Andersen network. Apart from Arthur Andersen, the "most French" firms were Arthur Young and Touche Ross. The situations of the other Big Firms varied. Price Waterhouse and Coopers & Lybrand were well established in France, with respectively 24 partners (17 of whom were French, compared to 2 in 1970) and 15 partners (10 of whom were French). Peat Marwick Mitchell had 13 audit partners, including 7 Frenchmen. Deloitte Haskins & Sells and Ernst & Whinney were the least well-established Big Firms in France, and the least advanced in terms of "Frenchification," with respectively only 13 partners (including 5 Frenchmen) across the whole French firm (audit and other activities such as management consultancy, and tax and legal consultancy), and 10 partners (including 3 Frenchmen).

5. AFDA's supervisory board included a prominent member of the *Conseil d'Etat* (Supreme administrative court), Claude Lasry (Ramirez 2005: 513).

6. In November 1982, a question put by a senator to Jacques Delors, Minister of Finance (*Journal des débats du Sénat*, November 19, 1982, pp. 5624–25) referred to the ongoing nationalisations as a "goldmine" for the Anglo-Americans, who, it was claimed, had been consulted in preference to French professionals. The Minister of Finance confirmed the facts, but insisted that these firms employed French people and that the engagements were one-off contracts, in contrast to appointments as statutory auditors. Their success in a competitive framework was, in the Minister's view, related to "the companies' needs to call on international financial markets, where certification by French firms is not yet recognised, and also the quality of the service provided, made possible by the scale and experience of these firms."

7. The late 1980s were boom years for auditing; the word "audit" was used for procedures and practices sometimes quite unrelated to accountancy and financial audits. In the March 1986 edition of the professional publication *La profession comptable*, the editorial referred to a famous politician's declarations in *Le Monde Informatique* that an "audit" of the scale of the deterioration of France's technological independence should be organized. In the public sector, the government was considering having audits carried out to check that they were making good use of public subsidies. In the same period, local authority audits were also on the increase, especially when the political majority changed. Arthur Andersen and Arthur Young in particular were pioneers in this kind of engagement.

8. Further proof of this penetration is the fact that the Big Firms have successfully made use of typically French connections between the highest levels of the French civil service and the business world. For example, in 1991 J. Bédier, a product of the *Ecole nationale d'adminis-tration* who was the Minister of Industry's principal private secretary, joined Deloitte Touche Tohmatsu as head of development (Ramirez 2005: 526).

9. Around the same time as it was opening the doors of its professional standards committee to the large multinational firms, the *Compagnie nationale des commissaires aux comptes* also set up a special IPO department in 1989, whose members include representatives of firms that audit France's main industrial and commercial groups.

10. This voluntary non-attendance had dramatic consequences, for it deprived the French professional institution of the indispensable technical back-up required to keep up with the production of standards appropriate to large companies' needs and compatible with international standards. A modus vivendi was eventually reached to settle the conflict. In fact, this arrangement allowed the Big Firms to carry on with their expansion. As a second Le Portz report stated in 1998, although the recommendations of the first report had been transposed into regulations, in practice, without a detailed inventory of the services provided by large firms to their clients, it was very difficult to assess these regulations' actual impact.

11. I am echoing Goode's famous article (Goode 1957) on professions as communities within the larger community constituted by society itself.

REFERENCES

Abbott, A. D. 1988. *The system of professions: An essay on the division of expert labor*. University of Chicago Press.

Allen, D. G. and McDermott, K. 1993. *Accounting for success: A history of Price Waterhouse in America, 1890–1990*. Boston: Harvard Business School Press.

Anderson-Gough, F., Grey, C. and Robson, K. 2005. "Helping them to forget: The organizational embedding of gender relations in two large audit firms," *Accounting, Organizations and Society* **30** (5): 469–90.

Arnold, P. J. 2005. "Disciplining domestic regulation: The World Trade Organization and the market for professional services," *Accounting, Organizations and Society* **30** (4): 299–330.

Arnold, P. J. and Sikka, P. 2001. "Globalization and the state–profession relationship: The case of the Bank of Credit and Commerce International," *Accounting, Organizations and Society* **26** (6): 475–99.

Brown, R. C. A. 1905. *A history of accounting and accountants*. Edinburgh: Jack.

Bucher, R. and Strauss, A. 1961. "Professions in process," *American Journal of Sociology* **66** (4): 325–34.

Burrage, M. and Torstendahl, R. (eds.) 1990. *The formation of professions: Knowledge, state and strategy*. London: Sage.

Catchpowle, L., Cooper, C. and Wright, A. 2004. "Capitalism, states and accounting," *Critical Perspectives on Accounting* **15** (8): 1037–58.

Chantiri, R. 2000. *Contribution à l'analyse des processus d'élaboration des normes comptables: une étude comparée des processus français et britannique*. Dissertation. Université Paris IX – Dauphine.

Colasse, B. and Standish, P. (1998). 'De la réforme 1996–1998 du dispositif français de normalisation comptable,' *Comptabilité Contrôle Audit* **4** (2), 5–27.

Cooper, D. J., Greenwood, R., Hinings, B. and Brown, J. L. 1998. "Globalisation and nationalism in a multinational accounting firm: The case of opening new markets in Eastern Europe," *Accounting, Organizations and Society* **23** (5–6): 531–48.

Covaleski, M., Dirsmith, M., Heian, J. and Samuel, S. 1998. "The calculated and the avowed: Techniques of discipline and struggles over identity in Big 6 public accounting firms," *Administrative Science Quarterly* **43**: 298–327.

DiMaggio, P. J. and Powell, W. W. 1983. "The iron cage revisited: Institutional isomorphism and collective rationality in organizational fields," *American Sociological Review* **48** (2): 147–60.

Dirsmith, M. W., Heian, J. B. and Cowaleski, M. A. 1997. "Structure and agency in an institutionalised setting: The application and social transformation of control in the Big Six," *Accounting, Organisations and Society* **22**: 1–27.

Djelic, M.-L., and Quack, S. 2003. *Globalization and institutions: Redefining the rules of the economic game.* Cheltenham: Edward Elgar.

Djelic, M.-L., and Sahlin-Andersson, K. 2006. "Institutional dynamics in a re-ordering world," in M. L. Djelic and Sahlin-Andersson, K. (eds.), *Transnational governance: Institutional dynamics of regulation.* Cambridge University Press, pp. 375–97.

Freidson, E. 1986. *Professional powers: A study of the institutionalization of formal knowledge.* University of Chicago Press.

Freidson, E. 2001. *Professionalism: The third logic.* Cambridge: Polity Press.

Goode, W. J. 1957. "Community within a community: The professions," *American Sociological Review* **22** (2): 194–200.

Grey, C. 1998. "On being a professional in a 'Big Six' firm," *Accounting Organizations and Society* **23**: 569–87.

Haas, P. M. 1992. "Introduction: Epistemic communities and international policy coordination," *International Organization* **46** (1): 1–35.

Jones, E. 1981. *Accountancy and the British economy 1840–1980: The evolution of Ernst & Whinney.* London: Batsford.

      1995. *True and fair: A history of Price Waterhouse.* London: Hamish Hamilton.

Larson, M. S. 1977. *The rise of professionalism: A sociological analysis.* Berkeley: University of California Press.

Le Portz, Y. (1993). 'Rapport du groupe de travail sur la déontologie des commissaires aux comptes dans les sociétés qui font appel public à l'épargne,' Compagnie Nationale des Commissaires aux Comptes, Commission des Opérations de Bourse, pp. 1–50.

Matthews, D., Anderson, M. and Edwards, J. R. 1998. *The priesthood of industry: The rise of the professional accountant in British management.* Oxford University Press.

Meyer, J. W., Boli, J., Thomas, G. and Ramirez, F. O. 1997. "World society and nation state," *American Journal of Sociology* **103**: 144–81.

Morgan, G. 2001. "Transnational communities and business systems," *Global Networks: A Journal of Transnational Affairs*, **1**: 113–30.

Quack, S. 2007. "Cross-border interaction in multi-level governance. The case of professional associations as standard setters." Paper presented at workshop on "Multi-level governance," Centre for the Study of Globalization and Regionalisation, University of Warwick, May 17–19.

Ramirez, C. 2001. "Understanding social closure in its cultural context: Accounting practitioners in France (1920–1939)," *Accounting, Organizations and Society* **26** (4–5): 391–418.

Ramirez, C. 2005. *Contribution à une théorie des modèles professionnels: le cas des comptables libéraux en France et aux Royaume-Uni*. Dissertation. Ecole des hautes études en sciences sociales, Paris.

Ramirez, C. 2009. "Reform or rebirth? The 1966 Companies Act and the problem of the modernisation of the audit profession in France," *Accounting Business and Financial History* **15** (2): 127–48.

Robson, K., Humphrey, C. *et al.* 2007. "Transforming audit technologies: Business risk audit methodologies and the audit field," *Accounting Organisations and Society* **32** (4–5): 409–38.

Schmidt, V. A. 1996. *From state to market? The transformation of French business and government.* New York: Cambridge University Press.

Spacek, L. 1989. *The growth of Arthur Andersen & Co., 1928–1973: An oral history.* New York: Garland.

Strange, S. 1996. *The retreat of the state: The diffusion of power in the world economy.* Cambridge University Press.

Suddaby, R., Cooper, D. J. and Greenwood, R. 2007. "Transnational regulation of professional services: Governance dynamics of field level organizational change," *Accounting, Organizations and Society* **32** (4–5): 333–62.

Wootton, C. W. 2003. "An historical perspective on mergers and acquisitions by major US accounting firms," *Accounting History* **8** (1): 25–60.

Wootton, C. W. and Wolk, C. M. 1992. "The development of the 'big eight' accounting firms in the United States, 1900 to 1990," *The Accounting Historians Journal* **19** (1): 1–27.

Part IV

Virtual communities

9 Gift-giving, transnational communities, and skill-building in developing countries: the case of free/open source software

Anca Metiu

Transnational communities and the North–South divide

Individual skills are a priority in development policies concerned with bridging the socio-economic divide between the global North and South. Increased disenchantment with the models that have dominated relations between the North and the South since the end of colonialism – whether top-down or bottom-up (Stohr 1981) – has yielded the notion that a more productive way of developing the South is to help the people living there to acquire skills and know-how (Sen 1997; Karnani 2006). While there does seem to be agreement on this, the search is still on for the most effective social formations to help close the gap, as is the quest for the mechanisms most suitable for developing the South.

Top-down and bottom-up approaches

The top-down approach to bridging the North–South divide assumes that development starts in a few dynamic sectors and geographical regions, from which it hopefully spreads to other sectors and areas (Stohr 1981), trickling down through trade, multinational corporations, and government organizations. Thus, large-scale organizations (private or government) were installed to serve as the "motor" of development in the South (Stohr 1981). Prominent in this approach are multinational corporations, conceptualized as superior repositories and vehicles for organizing knowledge, and playing an important role in transferring knowledge and skills between countries (Kogut and Zander 1993; Gupta and Govindarajan 2000). Non-governmental organizations have also come to play a significant role in North–South relations; the aid they dispense to Southern countries is frequently portrayed as a form of altruism, an act of charity that enables wealth to flow from rich to poor, reducing poverty and empowering the poor.

However, top-down approaches have yielded poor results in terms of knowledge, skills, and capabilities (Sen 1997; Sogge 2002; Karnani 2006), and in all likelihood they have undermined the South's efforts to emancipate itself. A major reason for this is that development discourse continues to perceive the recipients of aid paternalistically – for example, as "different" from Westerners – and thus to reproduce the social hierarchies prevalent under colonialism (Manji and O'Coill 2002; Sogge 2002; Thompson 2004). In the end, many top-down development initiatives "have failed due to increased dependency and inadequate human capital to fill the role of the external body when it withdraws from the project" (Nel *et al.* 2001: 4).

In contrast to the top-down approach to development, a bottom-up strategy was promoted as a way of escaping from the current spiral of increasing disparities and underdevelopment in which many countries seem caught (Stohr 1981). If development comes from below, growth will be based on "increased and integrated resource mobilization in a regional context" (Stohr 1981: 61); the involvement of local communities can improve their social and economic well-being. Instead of power being concentrated in the hands of few large private or government organizations, it is distributed at the level of individuals and communities. Such endogenous development emphasizes the role of inter-firm cooperation, business associations, unions, and government in developing, in collaboration, specific skills, resources, and institutions (the "rules of the game").

However, this strategy has also been fraught with problems; community self-reliance initiatives may not be able to sustain themselves easily, especially when local capacity and resources are lacking, coupled with a poor understanding of the broader environment (Hulme and Edwards 1997; Nel *et al.* 2001). In the absence of the requisite human and social capital among local agents, as well as of inputs from external (usually North-based) entities, the prospects for the widespread emergence of self-initiated, community-based projects is limited and, where they do emerge, their long-term prognosis is doubtful (Hulme and Edwards 1997; Nel *et al.* 2001; Sogge 2002).

Thus, it seems that securing effective and lasting change at the local level requires a focus on skill development, as well as blending top-down and bottom-up approaches (Stohr 1990; Scott Fosler 1991; Simon 1992; Nel *et al.* 2001). The social formations that are best adapted to a mixed strategy are partnerships, twinning arrangements, networks, and communities because they presuppose involvement and foster local ownership of the issues while providing links with the North. For instance, political and advocacy networks enable global groups of activists, by means of the Internet, to circulate information and political work and strategies (Tarrow 2005). While intensely transnational in their exchanges, the focus of these networks remains on their localities and their specific issues, such as organizing slum dwellers to obtain housing (Sassen 2002). Coming even closer to our question about bridging the North–South divide, studies of Chinese- and Indian-born engineers who have worked in Silicon Valley show the role of transnational communities of immigrants in transferring technical and institutional know-how between distant regional economies (Saxenian 2005, 2006). This suggests that transnational communities could play an important role in building knowledge and skills at the local level.

Transnational communities

According to Adler, a community is a "joint enterprise that is constantly being renegotiated by its members and is held together by relationships of mutual engagement" (2005). This process view of transnational communities, focusing on relationships, interactions, and exchanges, suggests a fruitful avenue for analyzing the mechanism that may make these communities effective in bridging between the South and the North. In contrast with other social formations, such as markets, hierarchies, and networks, which are based on exchange, command, and negotiation respectively, communities are held together by perceptions of shared identity and a sense of belonging (Djelic and Quack in this volume), as well as by feelings of solidarity (Jessop and Sum 2006; Mayntz in this volume).

Communities of practice may be particularly effective in building the skills of people in the South because such communities are "groups of people who share a concern, a set of problems, or a passion about a topic, and who deepen their knowledge and expertise in this area by interacting on an ongoing basis" (Wenger *et al.* 2002: 4). However, despite the theoretical promise that communities of practice may hold for North–South development, it is reasonable to ask whether a community built around skills and interests could really develop among geographically dispersed individuals whose backgrounds and contexts differ immensely. Could solidarity develop in these conditions? We can approach this question by recalling that the main mechanism for creating social solidarity is gift-giving. Furthermore, the gift's greatest power lies in creating solidarity among people whose social relationships are disturbed or unsettled (Gouldner 1973; Caplow 1984), as are North–South relations.

Gift-giving and community-building

Gift exchange is the moral cement of society and of culture, and thus of community formation (Malinowski 1922; Mauss 1967). Malinowski's seminal work on the gift was based on his observations of how the inhabitants of the Trobriand Islands in the Western Pacific exchanged shell necklaces and armbands in a cycle of reciprocal gift-giving that held together over two dozen islands spread over hundreds of miles of ocean. In Malinowski's view, the enormous expenditure and effort involved in these annual gift-giving expeditions was justified by the benefits in terms of establishing and maintaining peaceful relations with trading partners.

Gift-giving as analyzed by anthropologists are group dealings based on reciprocity. The exchanges build trust and over time they provide societal "glue" (Simmel 1950; Mauss 1967: 34). In this sense, a theory of the gift is a theory of human solidarity (Douglas 1990). Apart from creating and maintaining social ties (Mauss 1967), the gift's other functions include: expressing one's superiority (Simmel 1950; Gouldner 1960); maintaining a certain status hierarchy (Malinowski 1922; Mauss 1967); and fostering rule-following without visible means of enforcement (Caplow 1984). Its many functions make the gift a "total social phenomenon" (Mauss 1967).

There are two aspects of the gift as a mechanism for community formation that are of interest in terms of North–South relations. The first is the principle of reciprocity that is always present in gift-giving (Mauss 1967). Reciprocity is essential in North–South relations because it means recognizing the other as an equal partner and sometimes as a potential ally (Komter 2005). Indeed, gifts signal the nature of the relationship and mark the identity of givers and receivers; to accept a gift is to accept a certain identity (Schwartz 1967). The gift is also an affirmation of the giver's personality, and symbolizes the giver's view of the recipient (Komter 2005).

At the same time, in North–South relations reciprocal exchange can be asymmetrical. When one is in a position to give only a little, one will also receive little, "to the point of excluding the weak and the needy from cycles of gift giving" (Komter 1996: 314). In a study of gift-giving in the Netherlands, Komter (1996) found that unemployed and retired people tend to give less than all other categories, and also that they receive less. Based on these studies, one would expect the South's paucity of resources to exclude it from the reciprocity cycle. Furthermore, the aid given to poor countries may be seen as

a "put-down," a means of maintaining power and social status (Simmel 1950; Gouldner 1960; Mauss 1967).

Nevertheless, the gift is able to create social ties even within the framework of resource asymmetries. In such conditions some gifts, such as education, are viewed as developmental and not as condescending (Caplow 1984). Furthermore, there are "pure gifts" in which no reciprocity is expected (Malinowski 1922). In his discussion of gratitude, Simmel (1950) argued that it is the pure gift that is given with no expectation of reciprocity that in fact holds society together because such a gift binds people most strongly to their benefactors. In the North–South context both forms of gift – pure gifts and reciprocal gifts – are needed, but also problematic. Because aid (a "pure gift") has been perceived as paternalistic by Southern recipients, and because direct reciprocity is difficult in conditions of asymmetric resources, it is likely that the forms of gift that would be most effective in North–South relations are those in relation to which the expectation of reciprocity is indefinite.

A second aspect of gift-giving important for North–South developmental relations is its local nature. It is a point of historical interest that the first systematic study of the gift was also one of the only ones that has portrayed a dispersed community of islanders (Malinowski 1922). Recent research has pointed out that most gift-giving is local. In a study of an American suburb, the only gift-giving beyond the territorial limits of the town took place on the basis of ethnic identity (Eckstein 2001). At the same time, the current development of communication and coordination technologies is extending the reach of gift-giving (Wellman and Haythornthwaite 2002) because they enable far-reaching exchanges between North and South communities (Sassen 2002; Walsham *et al.* 2007).

Based on this analysis of the characteristics of the gift that are relevant for North–South relations, we can conclude that even in conditions of acute asymmetric resource access and geographic dispersion, gifts still have the potential to be developmental. Thus, the gift may form the basis for the emergence and functioning of transnational communities bridging the North and the South.

Free/open source software as a transnational community

Malinowski described how the gift kept together a community that was dispersed among an archipelago. Imagine now a Kula ring (or "Kula exchange") that involves not only a particular region, but the entire world, and in which gifts are exchanged not by means of canoeing from island to island, but through electronic networks. Instead of shell necklaces and armbands, the gifts are immaterial, digital: they consist of patches of software code that developers offer one another, and to anyone else who wants to download them. While the Kula gifts have no use value, the software's utility ranges from considerable to immense. Still, as in the case of the Kula, where the aim of the chiefs was to give away something of greater value than they received, software developers try to improve the software they receive. Similar to the way the shells were displayed prominently so that they would bring status to those bestowing them, the software code is posted on the Internet, for everyone to see and use, and bears the name of its creators, who thus gain in reputation. Dissimilarities notwithstanding, it is obvious that the same "fundamental human impulse to display, to share, to bestow" (Malinowski 1922: 135) animated the Trobrianders and the free/open source software developers.

Because of its origins, ethos, and global reach, free/open source software epitomizes a transnational community. Free/open source software corresponds to the most restrictive definitions of transnational communities, as it is rooted not only in shared interests or collective projects, but also in shared values (see Djelic and Quack in this volume). The free and open source software movement emerged in the 1980s, after companies producing software started to apply intellectual property laws to restrict access to the source code (see also Dobusch and Quack in this volume).[1] In response, Richard Stallman, then a researcher at MIT, created the Free Software Foundation, based on the idea that everyone should have free access to source code, so as to be able to modify software according to their needs, improve it, and redistribute it to others at no cost, in most cases. Stallman also started to develop a "free" operating system called GNU (a recursive acronym for "GNU's Not Unix") that could be downloaded at no cost, and created the GNU General Public License (GPL), which ensures that recipients of the software cannot restrict the use of that software or of derived works when they redistribute it. This so-called "copyleft" provision effectively ensures that a person cannot appropriate free software. Some of the most important success stories of the community comprise well-known products such as the Linux operating system, the Apache web server (leading the market with about 55 percent, followed by Microsoft at 35 percent), and the Perl scripting language.

The free/open source software ethos has always been transnational, aiming to reach users and developers throughout the world. The origins of the Linux operating system illustrate this aspect well. In 1991, Linus Torvalds, a Finnish student, started to develop the kernel of the operating system, which he licensed under the GPL. He then posted an email on a newsgroup, asking for suggestions and contributions from anyone interested in a free operating system. The response was overwhelming. The large and so far latent community of developers who shared the Unix ethos of sharing information and software was waiting for this. By 1993 over 100 programmers had contributed changes, version 0.99 had about 100,000 lines of code, there were over 20,000 users, and Torvalds started to delegate some code review duties. By 1998, there were over 10,000 programmers involved in newsgroups, testing and providing code improvements. Version 2.1.110 had about 1.5 million lines of code, and the number of users exceeded 7 million. By 2000, Linux had almost 3 million lines of code and 15 million users. By March 2005, it was estimated that there were 29 million users, in virtually every country around the world (www.linuxcounter.org).

In common with many other transnational communities, the free/open source communities combine features of epistemic, expert, and professional communities, as well as having an overarching identity and multiple local roots (Djelic and Sahlin-Andersson 2006: 390). For the purposes of our analysis, two of their dimensions are particularly important: they are communities of practice, and they display features of social movements (see Dobusch and Quack in this volume). In contrast with other social movements (such as Greenpeace and other environmental groups), the free/open source software community also develops products at the same time as it campaigns against established intellectual property rights. Thus, its aim is to mobilize not just any supporters, but users who have developed and/or are willing to further develop the technical and managerial skills that will enable them to be valuable contributors to the product.

Free/open source software as a community of practice

The free/open source software communities are communities of practice that include not only individuals sharing a similar profession (such as engineers), but also other people (such as students) interested in similar issues. Because the ability to produce stable, robust products is key to free/open source software success, the challenge for the community, which relies on a continual influx of newcomers, is to quickly turn some of these novices into full participants who can start making high-quality contributions. Through a process of legitimate peripheral participation newcomers acquire the skills that transform them into full community members (Lave and Wenger 1991).

One becomes a developer after having used the product for a while, having acquired the skills to signal bugs, write patches of code, and coordinate with others (Kogut and Metiu 2001). Because mathematics and programming are universal, the same practices are to be found everywhere free/open source software is used and developed.

The free/open source software development model is dependent upon volunteers who, for the most part, are not paid for their work or services to the community.[2] Nowadays, however, there are also large computer companies who pay programmers to contribute to open source software (IBM, Red Hat, Hewlett Packard). In principle, then, anyone with an Internet connection and a knowledge of programming can participate. The vast majority of interactions and coordination take place online, which only enhances the access to information and exchanges (for more details about the organization of free/open source software projects, see Kogut and Metiu 2001). The community is a meritocracy in the sense that the best code is included in the released versions. Not surprisingly, free/open source software products are complex, sophisticated, and innovative. For example, Red Hat Linux version 6.2 has more than 17 million lines of code, and researchers estimate that had it been developed in a software company, its cost would have exceeded $600 million (Wheeler 2004). Also, nearly 40 percent of large US companies and 65 percent of Japanese corporations use GNU/Linux in some form, and it may now run as much as 15 percent of the large server market overall (*Business Week* 2003).

Free/open source software as a social movement

Free/open source software is also a social movement, primarily because it poses "collective challenges (to elites, authorities, other groups or cultural codes) by people with common purposes and solidarity in sustained interactions with elites, opponents and authorities" (Tarrow 1994). This definition of social movements emphasizes the importance of solidarity and shared purpose, and distinguishes social movements from simple interest groups (see also Dobusch and Quack in this volume for an application of Tilly's [2004] dimensions of social movements to open content).

The philosophy of the movement is to grant freedom to computer users by replacing proprietary software with free software. This ideology comes in two "flavors," reflected in the combined name of the movement. Members of the free software movement believe that all users of software should have four freedoms: the freedom to run the program; to study and adapt it; to distribute copies of the program; and to improve it and release the improvements to the public (Stallman 2001). Proponents of free software hold that it is immoral to prohibit or prevent people from exercising these freedoms and that these freedoms are required to create a society in which software users can help each other and retain control over their computers.

At the same time, some adherents of the movement do not believe that proprietary software is immoral. These members, who identify themselves more closely with open source than with free software, consider that freedom is valuable insofar as it leads to better quality software. For many open source adepts, the motivation behind toning down the radical discourse of the free software movement is simply to gain more acceptance among neophytes and the business world. Regardless of their differences these two flavors contrast sharply with the prevailing business emphasis on software patents and the secrecy of proprietary software.

The two communities – the community of practice and the social move- ment – largely overlap. While the community of practice includes developers who have made contributions to projects, and who are actively involved in signaling bugs and helping each other gain knowledge and skills, the social movement is broader, including all users and individuals sympathetic to free/ open source software. Even the many developers who are not actively engaged in posing collective challenges to elites are knowledgeable about the main ideological stances of the community and interested in the institutional principles behind the movement. One study reports that out of the 1,540 developers surveyed, only 14 percent said the ideology was not important (FLOSS-US 2003), thus demonstrating the ideological commitment of many free/open source software developers. Thus, the community of practice and the social movement intersect strongly.

As with all social movements, the success of free/open source software rests on its ability to attract new members. Therefore, the community is actively engaged in helping people who are willing to install and use free/open source products. Thus, both as a community of practice and as a social movement, free/open source software's aim is to expand to as many users and developers in as many countries as possible.

Free/open source software in developing countries

From the beginning, there was an awareness in the movement that developing countries are most in need of free/open source software – that is, good quality software at almost no cost. An obvious reason for developing countries' interest in free/open source software is the prohibitive licensing costs of proprietary software outside of the developed world. For example, the cost of Microsoft Windows XP together with Office XP represents over 2.3 months of GDP/capita in Brazil and over 14 months of GDP/capita in India (Ghosh 2003). Even more importantly, proprietary software does not lead to the development of deep expertise in developing countries, as the servicing of this software is limited. In contrast, free/open source software builds the skills of local developers, as they can fix bugs, customize the software, and create solutions for integration with other software. Not surprisingly, following the lead of Brazil and under pressure from free/open source software advocacy groups, numerous countries in Latin America, Africa, and Asia have passed laws to convert from proprietary to free software. While the effectiveness of these laws is still being debated, it seems that many governments with limited budgets for information technology see resorting to free/open source software as a way of closing the digital gap between North and South.

At the same time, numerous obstacles stand in the way of free/open source software's expansion in developing countries. These include lack of infrastructure, lack of awareness of the benefits of this type of software development, and determined attempts on the part of large proprietary firms to introduce their software in firms and schools and thus create a population dependent on proprietary software. According to a British report on intellectual property rights, the various "fair use" or "fair dealing" provisions in copyright stated in international treaties (allowing copying for personal and educational use) "have generally not proved adequate to meet the needs of developing countries, particularly in the field of education" (Commission on Intellectual Property Rights 2002).

These obstacles partly explain the scarcity of developers from the South in a community that claims to be open and meritocratic.[3] At the end of 2002, 42 percent of developers listed in SourceForge (the largest repository of open source projects) came from Europe, 39 percent from North America, 7 percent from Asia, and 4 percent from Latin America; the location of the other 8 percent of developers could not be determined (Ghosh 2006). The distribution of Debian (one of the major Linux distributions) project leaders is similar: 48 percent come from the European Union and associated states, 30 percent from the USA and Canada, and the remaining 22 percent from other parts of the world (Ghosh 2006).

Limits on involvement are also laid down by skill levels. In this sense, free/ open source software adoption is not only a choice of software, but also a particular way of acquiring knowledge. The code and the knowledge acquired at no cost by anyone interested can be considered gifts. In the remainder of the chapter I will analyze the types of gifts exchanged in free/open source software communities, their effects on individual skill development, and their impact on the creation of chains of solidarity across the North and the South.

Methods

Data on free/open source software, especially at the level of various communities, are scarce and incomplete. In this chapter I rely on several types of data. The first is archival and qualitative data on the types of activities performed by various free/open source software user and developer groups in various countries. For example, I analyzed the Linux User Groups hosted on www. linux.org/groups/, and the activities in one of the main communities for women in free/open source software, LinuxChix (www.linuxchix.org). Second, I have used publicly available data on the activities of various free/open source software groups in both developed and developing countries, such as media, governmental, and non-governmental reports. An important component of this type of data is the European Union's two-year study of free/open source software in developing countries. The study was led by the Maastricht Economic Research Institute on Innovation and technology (MERIT) at the University of Maastricht, the Netherlands, and was based on surveys of 115 people in Argentina, 40 in Bulgaria, 541 in Brazil, 83 in China, 51 in Croatia, 71 in India, 77 in Malaysia, and 51 in South Africa. The results of the study were published in the *Free/Libre/Open Source Software: Worldwide Impact Study* (henceforth: FLOSS World 2007), a major part of which focused on skill development and employment generation.

Gift-giving and skill development in the free/open source software community

The data on user groups reveal that free/open source software is a vast exchange system in which a stunningly rich and diverse set of gifts is exchanged. The extent of the gift exchanges in the largest free/open source software community is illustrated by two facts about the Linux operating system: Linux users are distributed in 207 countries (http://counter.li.org/), and the Linux credit files mention developers from 35 countries as having contributed to the project (Tuomi 2004). Examination of the user groups also reveals the variety and extent of their online and offline activities, and thus their functioning as communities of practice and as centers for skill development for those participating on a regular basis.

Free/open source software user groups

Because software is digital, the vast bulk of gift-giving takes place online, on dedicated websites on which new software patches are posted, debates about technical issues and about the strategic moves of proprietary software firms take place, and advice is asked for and given. However, free/open source software users and developers are not disparate individuals whose only connection to the larger free/open source software community is an online group. Most of them are part of local user groups that have been instrumental in their becoming free/open source software users and developers.

For instance, Linux User Groups (LUGs) are informal groups of individuals, locally based, who are interested in learning more, as well as in teaching about free/open source software in general and Linux in particular. These groups meet regularly – usually once a month – in a university setting, community center, company facility, or even restaurant. Participation is free. While a certain amount of socialization is always involved, participants are mostly there to exchange information and technical tips. There may be presentations of company products, requests for help, and announcements of jobs or projects. Installfests are one of the more interesting, and most consequential, LUG activities. They are opportunities for experienced Linux users to help novices with the installation and configuration of Linux systems, and to teach new technical tips. Once one installs and learns how to use free/open source software, one may then become a coach for others, as well as a contributor to online discussions and products, signaling bugs and developing code. Some LUGs have developed into expertise clubs where one can find expert lecturers on free/open source software topics. Thus, the user groups are major settings in which giftgiving takes place. As we can see in Table 9.1, there are numerous groups of Linux users on all continents.

As of June 7, 2008, there were 772 LUGs in 103 countries. These numbers are very conservative: many user groups – perhaps the majority – have not registered with linux.org.

The extent to which local user groups are involved in the wide variety of gift exchanges can be illustrated by examining the regional chapters of LinuxChix, the most important women-oriented Linux community. Table 9.2 lists the main regional chapters and their activities.

Table 9.1 Linux user groups

Continent	Number of countries	Number of user groups
Asia	14	65
Australasia and Oceania	2	13
Europe	46	300
North America	2	281
South America	18	60
Africa	10	29
Middle East	11	24

Source: www.linux.org/groups.

Table 9.2 LinuxChix activities

	Courses/ knowledge base	Events	Task list	People	Meetings	Newbie corner	Volunteering	Feminism
LC India	✓	✓	✓	✓	✓	✓	✓	✓
Aussie Chix		✓		✓	✓			
New Zealand	✓	✓	✓	✓	✓	✓	✓	
LC Brazil	✓					✓	✓	✓
LC France		✓		✓	✓		✓	✓
LC Italy		✓		✓	✓		✓	
LC Poland				✓	✓		✓	
LC Canada (4 main cities)	✓	✓	✓	✓	✓	✓	✓	✓
LC USA (8 main cities)	✓	✓	✓	✓	✓	✓	✓	✓

Source: www.linuxchix.org/regional-chapters.html.

While most of the data come from developed countries, India and Brazil are also active. India in particular is involved in all types of activities, offering technical courses, strengthening women's managerial and legal skills, helping newcomers ("newbies"), and listing events of interest to group members. The data also document the tailoring of "gifts" to women's specific needs and interests. For example, several groups post feminist material and encourage discussion of such issues as the status of women in free/open source communities and discrimination in the workplace.

Given the extent of the knowledge one can acquire by participating in these groups, it is not surprising that their membership is growing constantly. As the data in Table 9.3 show, there are Debian (one of the major Linux

Table 9.3 Debian mailing list statistics

Continent	Number of countries	Number of members
Asia	6	1,593
Europe	19	25,007
North America	1	15 (USA n/a)
South America	n/a	n/a
Africa	n/a	n/a
Middle East	n/a	90

Source: http://lists.debian.org/stats/.

distributions) mailing lists all over the world. While data on South America and Africa are missing, anecdotal evidence confirms that there are Debian users on these continents, too. Also, the data in the table show that there are numerous members in both Asia and the Middle East.

The Debian mailing lists also give a sense of the strong growth in these communities over the past several years. For example, between January 2000 and January 2008, there was a threefold increase in the number of members in the two Chinese mailing lists (from approximately 320 to approximately 990). In the same period, the Spanish developer mailing list grew from zero to over 5,000. Also, the Indonesian mailing list grew from fewer than 10 members in 2002 to over 130 in 2008 (source: http://lists.debian.org/stats/). These data are suggestive of these groups' potential for further disseminating and enhancing the skills of developers in the South.

Types of skills in free/open source software groups

As the above-mentioned data show, the gifts exchanged in the free/open source software communities are complex. The main types of gift in these communities consist in contributions to free/open source software products: code patches, maintaining modules or entire products, bug signaling, and writing documentation. These technical contributions form the most visible part of the gift exchanges, and they have been the object of attention of researchers who have studied free/open source software from the perspective of a gift economy (Raymond 1999; Kollock 1999; Bergquist and Ljungberg 2001; von Krogh *et al.* 2003; Zeitlyn 2003).

At the same time, we can see that these highly visible technical contributions rest on a huge amount of information exchange, technical and ideological debates, advice and guidance to newcomers, advocacy within and outside of the community, organizing conferences, setting up local user groups, and online courses. Thus, while the ethos of the lonely "hacker" who writes code for days and nights on end is a central component of the free/open source software mythology, all these other activities form the "invisible work" (Star and Strauss 1999) that is crucial for the functioning of these communities.

It would be difficult to overstate the extent of the learning and teaching that take place in the free/open source software communities, both online and offline. An examination of LUG websites brings to light the multitude of activities performed in these groups. In the end, apart from technical skills via training courses, Installfests, conferences, and IRC (Internet Relay Chat) channels, members also learn a broader set of skills: managerial (how to coordinate and negotiate), legal (about the various types of licenses that protect the software produced by the community, as well as about public policy measures promoting or impeding the development of free software in various countries), and interpersonal (presentation skills and self-confidence).

Developers in all eight countries participating in the FLOSS World Study state that the types of skills that improve most with community participation are as follows: writing reusable code, awareness of legal issues, and ability to deal with criticism. Furthermore, developers consider that all three types of skills can be better learned within the framework of free/open source software than in formal courses (FLOSS World 2007). This suggests that the gift functions as an effective mechanism for knowledge transfer. In fact, the main reason developers say they join free/open source software groups is "to learn and develop new skills." Even more strikingly, the developers for whom learning was the main motive for joining also state that their main reason for staying in the community is to "share skills" (FLOSS World 2007). This finding illustrates perfectly the functioning of a community of practice, and the evolution, within it, of members' roles as their expertise grows: from newbie to expert user, developer, and mentor.

The importance of free/open source software skills for people's careers

Because free/open source software skills are important to a developer's career, reputation and better employment opportunities represent a key motivation for getting involved with free/open source software (Lerner and Tirole 2002). About 64 percent of the developers surveyed in the FLOSS World Study consider that proven participation in free/open source software development

Table 9.4 The role of free/open source skills in people's careers (in %)

Country	They provide a core skill for my professional career	They provide a useful supplement, but they are not a core skill	They are an end in itself[a] but play no important role	I don't know
South Africa	56.9	31.4	5.9	5.9
Malaysia	43.2	32.4	8.1	16.2
India	56.5	26.1	14.5	2.9
Croatia	44.0	40.0	12.0	4.0
China	41.3	40.0	12.0	6.7
Brazil	47.9	34.8	12.9	4.5
Bulgaria	62.6	22.5	15.0	0.0
Argentina	63.7	25.7	8.8	1.8
Europe	57.4	28.6	8.7	5.3

Notes: [a] "They provide fun, contact with others, help in using my time in a reasonable way, and so on."
Source: FLOSS World (2007: D31, Track 1, Skills Study: International Report, p. 16).

can make up for the lack of university degree or other formal certificate. Table 9.4 presents the results of the FLOSS World Study in terms of the career impact of the skills learned by developers in developing countries.

As Table 9.4 shows, a substantial proportion of developers in all the countries surveyed (ranging from 41.3 percent in China to 63.7 percent in Argentina) said that the skills learned from free/open source software activities are of central importance for their careers. A much lower percentage (ranging from 22.5 percent in Bulgaria to 40 percent in China and Croatia) said that free/open source software skills are a useful supplement, but not core. An even lower percentage (ranging from 5.9 percent in South Africa to 15 percent in Bulgaria) said that free/open source software skills play no important role in their careers. For comparison, it is worth noting that 57.4 percent of European developers do consider free/open source software skills as core to their career. The percentage in Europe tends to be higher because in developing countries most software development jobs involve routine tasks such as maintenance of software systems, and are rarely creative or challenging (Metiu 2006). Thus, in both developing and developed countries, free/open source software skills are seen as central to one's career.

In this section I have shown that free/open source software is an important means by which individuals in developing countries develop a multitude of skills. The other main consequence of the gift-giving community is that some of these skilled individuals will also become contributors to global projects, and thus become gift-givers in their turn.

Toward an ecology of communities

The impact of participation in free/open source software on the development of individual skills, in the South as well as in the North, seems indisputable. To what extent, though, are groups based in developing countries participating in these transnational exchanges of gifts? In other words, is there reciprocity in these exchanges, from a South–North perspective, or are the user groups in the South merely the beneficiaries of software developed in the North? Table 9.5 begins to provide an answer to this question. The data were reported in the FLOSS World Study (2007) on the basis of information collected from thirteen local forges,[4] as well as from SourceForge. The table portrays the number of users, projects, and "committers" (people who have the right to introduce new code in the existing product), as well as the number of mailing lists and LUGs in each country.

Most importantly, the data in Table 9.5 show that developers from the countries surveyed participate in these transnational exchanges. Thus, in most countries (with the exception of China) the number of registered users in

Table 9.5 Local communities: registered users and projects in local forges and SourceForge

Countries	Forges	Registered users	Registered projects	Committers	Mailing lists	Communities	LUGs
China	China	57,123	1,851	111	129	5	2
	SourceForge	36,517	851	82	n/a	n/a	n/a
India	India	3,237	461	72,355	18	n/a	n/a
	SourceForge	22,113	1,383	28,749	n/a	n/a	n/a
South Africa	South Africa	305	121	71	14	3	3
	SourceForge	5,706	494	102	n/a	n/a	n/a
Brazil	Brazil	15,617	2,132	n/a	96	20	n/a
	SourceForge	21,291	851	n/a	414	n/a	n/a
Argentina	Argentina	155	44	16	6	7	57
	SourceForge	5,439	849	132	n/a	n/a	n/a
Malaysia	Malaysia	2,016	26	n/a	3	17	12
	SourceForge	3,189	94	183	n/a	n/a	n/a
Croatia	Croatia	n/a	n/a	6	7	2	3
	SourceForge	1,286	104	14	n/a	n/a	n/a
Bulgaria	Bulgaria	983	183	68	11	6	1
	SourceForge	3,606	408	46	n/a	n/a	n/a

Source: FLOSS World (2007: D30, Track 2, Software Study: International Report).

SourceForge (the global forge), considerably exceeds the numbers in local forges. With the exception of China and Brazil, the number of registered projects in SourceForge is also larger than the number of projects hosted on local forges. These data – for all their limitations: for example, many projects registered in these forges are inactive – suggest that significant numbers of developers are active not only in local communities, but also in the larger transnational community. Even more tellingly, the number of committers – people who have the right to introduce new code into a software product – is impressive (especially, but perhaps not surprisingly given the use of the English language there, in India). Also, there are significant numbers of communities in many of the countries surveyed: Brazil, Malaysia, Argentina, and Bulgaria.

The finding that the free/open source software transnational community enables a whole ecology of local communities (see Bartley and Smith in this volume for an ecology of transnational certification communities), which in turn contribute both locally and to the global community is also corroborated by qualitative data. One of the main activities of local groups is to adapt free/open source software projects to local needs, which has a significant impact on the further adoption and development of free/open source products – and thus on skill upgrading – in these countries. Still, in some developing countries, strong groups of contributors to major global projects have developed. For example, within only two years of the Lanka Software Foundation beginning to give local developers the opportunity to work on interesting, creative projects, nearly 50 of the more than 1,200 committers in Apache are from Sri Lanka (Weerawarana and Weeratunga 2004). This example of rapid skill upgrading suggests that in the future we can expect that such groups can drive some of the technical evolution of free/open source software, echoing the way in which the Indian software industry has rapidly upgraded its skills from coding and maintenance to design and architecture (Arora and Gambardella 2004).

The effectiveness of learning in these settings would probably be much less were it not for the efforts of community institutions that help deploy free/open source software in the South. For example, the Free Software Foundation, through its sister organizations in Latin America and India, and other institutions, such as the Debian server and mailing lists, SourceWatch, and Linux Online, play a double role: as catalysts for gift-giving and community-building, and as advocates for shaping government policies in the areas of software development, information technology, and education. Acknowledging free/open source software's potential to fuel economic development, a new initiative among Brazil, China, and the European

Union is focusing on the creation of competence centers in a network that will share knowledge about free/open source software development (see www. qualipso.org/).

Free/open source software gifts: "pure gifts" or reciprocity?

The above analysis also suggests that it is the dual nature of the gifts exchanged – both as pure gifts and as reciprocal exchanges – that have enabled these communities to overcome the vast differences between their members' backgrounds. The striking feature of free/open source software is that it can be downloaded by anyone, anywhere, with no obligation to give anything back. Thus free/open source software gifts have the characteristics of "pure gifts." In this sense, free/open source software communities are generalized exchange systems because the rewards that an actor receives are not directly contingent on the resources provided by that actor (Ekeh 1974; Sahlins 1974). In these systems there is no one-to-one correspondence between what two actors directly give to and receive from each other. This aspect is essential in the spread of free/open source software around the world, including to regions whose poor resource access would not allow them to respond in kind.

The dual nature of the gifts is also expressed in the licenses guarding the commons (such as the GPL) that stipulate a very specific type of reciprocity whereby the user of the code is not expected to give anything back to the community, either in code or in any other form (for example, advocacy or teaching others). Only when users want to give to others what they have received, or what they have developed on the basis of the free/open source software code, are they obliged to share it as a gift. In other words, the institutional rules expressed in licenses are there to preserve the "commons" (Dobusch and Quack in this volume; Raymond 1998; Kollock 1999; Kogut and Metiu 2001) and to ensure that those with superior resources do share.

Thus, the dual nature of the gifts – reciprocity-based and "pure gifts" – matches the dual nature of the community, as a community of practice and as a social movement that flourishes when it attains the greatest number of users. The double nature of the gift also determines the identity of the community members: the core set of developers – usually the 20 percent who do most of the development (Kogut and Metiu 2001) – are those who are most deeply involved in the reciprocal exchanges; the much larger set of active users, bug signalers, and so on, and a larger group of users who rarely if ever contribute, are the recipients of a gift with no reciprocity obligation.

The dual aspect of the gift is especially effective in the North–South context. In contrast with aid, which has been seen as paternalistic, the gifts exchanged in the free/open source software community recognize the individuality and the potential of Southern developers and users. This is no small accomplishment: given what people in developing countries would have to pay for comparable proprietary software, free/open source software could be seen as a lavish gift, one with the potential to subordinate and humiliate the recipient (Malinowski 1922). Still, it is not seen as condescending for two reasons. First, free/open source software is a pure gift not only for people from the South, but also for millions of people in the North; thus, the South is not singled out as uniquely in need of software or skills. Second, there is always the possibility that some of the recipients will become gift producers as well; in this sense, reciprocity is effective because it recognizes the other as equal subject and partner.

Conclusion

This chapter shows how, in spite of huge negative odds – tremendous differences in levels of socio-economic development and context, as well as enormous physical distances – the voluntary exchanges of gifts among free/open source developers include the South and contribute to the development of individual skills in all regions. We have thus addressed two important aspects of the role of the gift in bridging the divide between North and South.

Gift-giving and the expansion of transnational communities

In retrospect, the finding that the gift is an effective mechanism for skill-building in transnational communities should not be surprising. After all, we know that communities are tied together by relations of belonging and solidarity (Tönnies 2001; Djelic and Quack in this volume; Mayntz in this volume), and that gift exchanges are at the root of social ties (Mauss 1967) and human solidarity (Douglas 1990). In the free/open source software community, the gift's generative power is revealed by the growing skills of developers in the South, the exchanges of gifts between developers from the North and the South, and the diffusion of free/open source software to the most remote parts of the world.

The variety of gifts exchanged in free/open source software – technical, legal, managerial – seems to imply that successful knowledge transfer should be seen as a broad goal encompassing not only purely technical aspects but also more general skills. Perhaps not surprisingly, some European NGOs have reoriented their Latin American aid policy to embrace the notion of building citizenship, developing civil society, and promoting democratization as the keys to long-term development (Grugel 2000).

The richness and diversity of the exchanges, combined with the more democratic way of transferring knowledge and skills, distinguishes this kind of transfer from other types of transactional exchange, with the effect that in free/open source software the knowledge transfer is perceived not as colonization, but as a gift. The gift's dual nature makes it a particularly effective mechanism for knowledge transfer in a context in which other forms of transfer – for example, the multinational enterprise, donations by aid agencies – have had mixed results. While these mechanisms are based on the assumption that the South's unequal resource access makes it difficult, if not impossible to envision a community – with all that the word implies, such as full mutual recognition, common interests and goals, reciprocal exchange – spanning the developed and the developing world, the free/open source transnational community accepts that every user, no matter where they are located, might contribute to the common good. At the same time, because it relies extensively on electronic communication networks, the free/open source software community holds great promise in an era of electronic communication and product digitalization, and for contexts in which the physical movement of individuals is restricted.

This chapter also shows the role played by social movements in transnational knowledge transfer. While the sharing of knowledge and information has been depicted as important in the diffusion of social movements (see Schrad in this volume, for example), gift-giving has not been explicitly studied in relation to the expansion of social movements and transnational communities. In the case of free/open source software, gift-giving and the social movement are coconstitutive. Without gift-giving – of code, knowledge, advice – local skills could not be built up and the transnational community would not span the entire globe. At the same time, without the ethos of the social movement, institutionalized in the licenses, gift-giving would not continue (see Dobusch and Quack in this volume for similar findings for the open content movement).

Gift-giving and North–South relations

We have also looked at the impact of a transnational community on developing countries. Free/open source software is a democratic way of building skills and of empowering people in groups previously excluded from global flows of knowledge. In this sense, free/open source software is a case of globalization from below (Portes 1999). Free/open source software successfully mixes the top-down and bottom-up approaches to development: pure gifts bestowed mostly by developers from the North, and skill-building, empowerment, and increasing participation from developers from the South.

Through its substantial impact on the skill level of developers from developing countries, free/open source software has the potential to reduce the digital divide that has exacerbated the disparity between rich and poor countries. Of course, free/open source software is not in itself sufficient to enable developing countries to improve their standing in the world economy. For that, much more is needed, including substantial investments in infrastructure and comprehensive institutional reforms (Wilson 2004; Walsham *et al.* 2007). However, as Linus Torvalds has said:

[T]he real advantage of open source ended up being able to build up your own knowledge base. And that is not cheap in itself – you'll likely pay as much for that as you'd pay for a proprietary software solution. The difference being that with the proprietary solution, you'll never catch up, and you'll have to pay forever, without ever learning anything yourself. (Cited in Weerawarana and Weeratunga 2004: 86)

While proprietary technology locks nations into a spiral of long-term dependence, free/open source software allows countries that do not have easy access to technology to participate in the global exchange of knowledge.

One important question is whether free/open source software's success in bridging North and South can be emulated by other communities. Environmental groups, for instance, have created networks of transnational cooperation across North and South, with intensive communication between the various groups, as well as substantial resource transfer from environmental groups in the North to those in the South (Rohrschneider and Dalton 2002; Betsill and Bulkeley 2004). Resource asymmetries notwithstanding, the free/ open source software community has two characteristics that help to create feelings of shared identity. First, they are communities of practice whose members not only exchange information and advice, but also codevelop products. Second, the community is guarded by a host of institutions: the licenses and numerous foundations (such as the Free Software Foundation) ensure that what is called free software is just that, and also promote free/open source software internationally. Thus, the free/open source software model is likely to work best for transnational communities that have strong features of both communities of practice and social movements.

In conclusion, while transnational communities do not represent a panacea for the development issues of the South, or for the integration of the North and the South, they offer a model of interactions and governance that can inspire other actors interested in bridging the North–South gap.

Acknowledgments

I would like to thank the participants in the Workshop on Transnational Communities held in Cologne in April 2008 for their comments and suggestions. Special thanks to Marie-Laure Djelic and Sigrid Quack for their valuable comments on an earlier version. Thanks also to Hae-Jung Hong for research assistance.

NOTES

1. Source code can be read and modified by the user, and is usually inaccessible in proprietary software.
2. The reasons for volunteering one's efforts in the creation of a common good include adherence to the ideology of free software (Stallman 2001), the desire to satisfy one's own needs (Raymond 1999; Lakhani and von Hippel 2003), enjoyment of the activity (Ghosh *et al.* 2002; Shah 2006), the need for affiliation and identity (Hertel et al. 2003), reputation and status within the community (Raymond 1999), and learning and reputation outside the community (Lerner and Tirole 2002).
3. The other missing group is women, who represent less than 1 percent of contributors to the Linux credit files (Tuomi 2004). For an analysis of women's participation in free/open source software, see the FLOSS Gender Report (2006) and Metiu and Obodaru (2008).
4. A software forge is a collaboration platform allowing collaborative software development over the Internet.

REFERENCES

Adler, E. 2005. *Communitarian international relations.* London: Routledge.

Arora, A. and Gambardella, A. 2004. "The globalization of the software industry: Perspectives and opportunities for developed and developing countries," NBER Working Paper No. W10538. Cambridge, MA: National Bureau of Economic Research.

Bergquist, M. and Ljungberg, J. 2001. "The power of gifts: Organizing social relationships in open source communities," *Information Systems Journal* **11** (4): 305–20.

Betsill, M. M. and Bulkeley, H. 2004. "Transnational networks and global environmental governance: The cities for climate protection program," *International Studies Quarterly* **48** (2): 471–93.

Business Week. 2003. "The GNU/Linux uprising" (March 3).

Caplow, T. 1984. "Rule enforcement without visible means: Christmas giving in Middletown," *American Journal of Sociology* **89**: 1306–23.

Commission on Intellectual Property Rights. 2002. *Integrating intellectual property rights and development policy: Report of the Commission on Intellectual Property Rights*. London: Commission on Intellectual Property Rights: www.iprcommission.org/papers/pdfs/final_report/CIPRfullfinal.pdf

Djelic, M.-L., and Sahlin-Andersson, K. 2006. *Transnational governance: Institutional dynamics of regulation*. Cambridge University Press.

Douglas, M. 1990. "No free gifts." Foreword to Mauss, M., *The gift: The form and reason for exchange in archaic societies*. London, Routledge, pp. ix–xxiii.

Eckstein, S. 2001. "Community as gift-giving: Collectivistic roots of volunteerism," *American Sociological Review* **66**: 829–51.

Ekeh, P., 1974. *Social exchange theory: The two traditions*. Cambridge, MA: Harvard University Press.

FLOSS Gender Report. 2006. Maastricht: UNU-Merit, United Nations University, www.flosspols.org.

FLOSS-US. 2003. FLOSS-US. *The free/libre/open source software survey for 2003*, by David, P. A., Waterman, A. and Arora, S. Stanford Institute for Economic Policy Research, Stanford University: www.stanford.edu/group/floss-us/report/FLOSS-US-Report.pdf.

FLOSS World. 2007. *FLOSSWORLD. Free/libre and open source software: Worldwide impact study*, by David, P. A., Ghosh, R., Glott, R., Gonzales-Barahona, J., Heinz, F. and Shapiro, J. Available at: http://flossworld.org/deliverables/D31%20-%20Track%201%20International%20Report%20-%20Skills%20Study.pdf.

Ghosh, R. 2003. "License fees and GDP per capita: The case for open source in developing countries," *First Monday* **8** (12): http://firstmonday.org/issues/issue8_12/ghosh/index.html.

Ghosh, R. 2006. "Sustaining a software ecosystem with free/open source software: Skills and local economic growth." Paper presented at the seventh "Asia Open Source Symposium," Kuala Lumpur, Malaysia, March 7.

Ghosh, R. A., Glott, R., Krieger, B. and Robles, G. (2002). *Free/Libre and Open Source Software: Survey and Study. FLOSS. Deliverable D18: Final Reportt IV: Survey of Developers*. University of Maastricht, The Netherlands: International Institute of Infonomics.

Gouldner, A. W. 1960. "The norm of reciprocity: A preliminary statement," *American Sociological Review* **25**: 161–78.

Gouldner, A. W. 1973. "The importance of something for nothing," in Gouldner, A. W., *For sociology*. London: Allen Lane, pp. 260–99.

Grugel, J. 2000. "Romancing civil society: European NGOs in Latin America," *Journal of Inter-American Studies and World Affairs* **42** (2): 87–107.

Gupta, A. K. and Govindarajan, V. 2000. "Knowledge flows within multinational corporations," *Strategic Management Journal* **21**: 473–96.

Hertel, G., Niedner, S. and Hermann, S. 2003. "Motivation of software developers in open source projects: An Internet-based survey of contributors to the Linux kernel," *Research Policy* **32**: 1159–77.

Hulme, D. and Edwards, M. (eds.) 1997. *NGOs, states and donors: Too close for comfort?* Basingstoke: Macmillan.

Jessop, B. and Sum, N.-L. 2006. *Beyond the regulation approach. Putting capitalist economies in their place.* Cheltenham: Edward Elgar.

Karnani, A. 2006. "Mirage at the bottom of the pyramid," William Davidson Institute Working Paper No. 835. Ann Arbor: University of Michigan.

Kogut, B. and Metiu, A. 2001. "Open-source software development and distributed innovation," *Oxford Review of Economic Policy* **17** (2): 248–64.

Kogut, B. and Zander, U. 1993. "Knowledge of the firm and the evolutionary theory of the multinational corporation," *Journal of International Business Studies* **24** (4): 625–45.

Kollock, P. 1999. "The economies of online cooperation: gifts and public goods in cyberspace," in Smith, M. A. and Kollock, P. (eds.), *Communities in cyberspace*. London: Routledge, pp. 219–40.

Komter, A. 1996. "Reciprocity as a principle of exclusion: Gift giving in the Netherlands," *Sociology* **30** (2): 299–316.

Komter, A. 2005. *Social solidarity and the gift.* New York: Cambridge University Press.

Lakhani, K. and von Hippel, E. 2003. "How open source software works: 'Free' user-to-user assistance," *Research Policy* **32**: 923–43.

Lave, J. and Wenger, E. 1991. *Situated learning: Legitimate peripheral participation.* Cambridge University Press.

Lerner, J. and Tirole, J. 2002. "Some simple economics of open source," *Journal of Industrial Economics* **50** (2): 197–234.

Malinowski, B. 1922. *Argonauts of the western Pacific.* London: Routledge.

Manji, F. and O'Coill, C. 2002. "The missionary position: NGOs and development in Africa," *International Affairs* **78** (3): 567–83.

Mauss, M. 1967. *The gift: Forms and functions of exchange in archaic societies.* New York: Norton.

Metiu, A. 2006. "Owning the code: Status closure in distributed groups," *Organization Science* **17** (4): 418–35.

Metiu, A. and Obodaru, O. 2008. "Women's professional identity formation in the free/open source software community." Essec Research Center Working Paper No. DR 08009. Paris: ESSEC Business School.

Nel, E., Binns, T. and Motteux, N. 2001. "Community-based development, non-governmental organizations and social capital in post-apartheid South Africa," *Geografiska Annaler. Series B, Human Geography* **83** (1): 3–13.

Portes, A. 1999. "Globalization from below: The rise of transnational communities," in Kalb, D., van der Land, M. and Staring, R. (eds.), *The end of globalization: Bringing society back in.* Boulder, CO: Rowman and Littlefield, pp. 253–70.

Raymond, E. S. 1998. "Homesteading the Noosphere," *First Monday* **3** (10): http://firstmonday.org/htbin/cgiwrap/bin/ojs/index.php/fm/article/view/621/542.

Raymond, E. S. 1999. *The cathedral and the bazaar: Musings on Linux and open source by an accidental revolutionary.* Sebastopol, CA: O'Reilly & Associates.

Rohrschneider, R. and Dalton, R. J. 2002. "A global network? Transnational cooperation among environmental groups," *The Journal of Politics* **64** (2): 510–33.

Sahlins, M. 1974. *Stone age economics*. London: Tavistock.

Sassen, S. 2002. "Global cities and diasporic networks: Microsites in global civil society," in Glasius, M. *et al.* (eds.), *Global civil society 2002.* Oxford University Press, pp. 217–40.

Saxenian, A. 2005. "From brain drain to brain circulation: Transnational communities and regional upgrading in India and China," *Studies in Comparative International Development* **40** (2): 35–61.

Saxenian, A. 2006. *The new argonauts: Regional advantage in a global economy.* Cambridge, MA: Harvard University Press.

Schwartz, B. 1967. "The social psychology of the gift," *American Journal of Sociology* **73**: 1–11.

Scott Fosler, R. (ed.) 1991. *Local economic development: Strategies for a changing economy.* Washington, DC: International City Management Association.

Sen, A. 1997. "Human capital and human capability: Editorial." *World Development* **25** (12): 1959–61.

Shah, S. 2006. "Motivation, governance, and the viability of hybrid forms in open source software development," *Management Science* **52** (7): 1000–14.

Simmel, G. 1950. "Faithfulness and gratitude," in Wolff, K. (ed.), *The sociology of Georg Simmel.* Glencoe, IL: Free Press, pp. 379–95.

Simon, D. 1992. "Conceptualising small towns in African development," in Baker, J. and Pederson, P. O. (eds.), *The rural–urban interface in Africa.* Uppsala: Scandinavian Institute of African Studies, pp. 29–50.

Sogge, D. 2002. *Give and take: What's the matter with foreign aid.* London: Zed Books.

Stallman, R. 2001. "Philosophy of the GNU project," www.gnu.org/philosophy/. Accessed August 2001.

Star, S. L. and Strauss, A. 1999. "Layers of silence, arenas of voice: The ecology of visible and invisible work," *Computer Supported Cooperative Work* **8**: 9–30.

Stohr, W. B. 1981. "Development from below: The bottom-up and periphery-inward development paradigm," in Stohr, W. B. and Fraser Taylor, D. R. (eds.), *Development from above or below.* New York: John Wiley, pp. 39–72.

Stohr, W. B. 1990. *Global challenge and local response.* London: Mansell.

Tarrow, S. 1994. *Power in movement: Social movements, collective action and politics.* New York: Cambridge University Press.

Tarrow, S. 2005. *The new transnational activism.* Cambridge University Press.

Thompson, M. 2004. "Discourse, 'development' and the 'digital divide': ICT and the World Bank," *Review of African Political Economy* **31** (99): 103–23.

Tilly, C. 2004. *Social movements, 1768–2004.* Boulder, CO: Paradigm Publishers.

Tönnies, F. 2001. *Community and civil society.* Cambridge University Press.

Tuomi, I. 2004. "Evolution of the Linux Credits File: Methodological challenges and reference data for open source research," *First Monday* **9** (6): http://firstmonday.org/htbin/cgiwrap/bin/ojs/index.php/fm/article/view/1151/1071.

von Krogh, G., Spaeth, S. and Lakhani, K. 2003. "Community, joining and specialization in open source software innovation: A case study," *Research Policy* **32**: 1217–41.

Walsham, G., Robey, F. and Sahay, S. 2007. "Foreword: Special issue on information systems in developing countries," *MIS Quarterly* **31** (2): 317–26.

Weerawarana, S. and Weeratunga, J. 2004. "Open source in developing countries." SIDA3460en (booklet). Stockholm: Sida–Swedish International Development Cooperation Agency, www.sida.se

Wellman, B. and Haythornthwaite, C. (eds.) 2002. *The Internet in everyday life*. Oxford: Blackwell.

Wenger, E., McDermott, R., and Snyder, W. M. 2002. *A guide to managing knowledge: Cultivating communities of practice*. Boston: Harvard Business School Press.

Wheeler, D. A. 2004. "Linux 2.6: It's worth more!" accessed at: www.dwheeler.com/essays/linux-kernel-cost.html.

Wilson, E. J. 2004. *The information revolution and developing countries*. Cambridge, MA: MIT Press.

Zeitlyn, D. 2003. "Gift economies in the development of open source software: Anthropological reflections," *Research Policy* **32** (7): 1287–91.

10 Epistemic communities and social movements: transnational dynamics in the case of Creative Commons

Leonhard Dobusch and Sigrid Quack

Is it impossible to imagine the lawyers ever on the side of innovation?

Lawrence Lessig (2003)

Introduction

When Victor Hugo in 1878, with an inaugural address at the Paris World exhibition, helped to initiate the Berne Convention for the Protection of Literary and Artistic Works (inured in 1887), he could hardly have imagined that, 120 years later, law professors, artists, and software producers would mobilize worldwide against the successor of the Berne Convention in favor of the free use of intellectual products such as texts, music, and software. The most recent and most obvious expression of this movement is the foundation of "Creative Commons" as a US-based non-profit organization in 2001, which has since extended its operation to over fifty different national jurisdictions. The aim of Creative Commons, according to its statutes, is to build a layer of "reasonable, flexible copyright" into the existing restrictive copyright law. Creative Commons develops licenses that enable people to dedicate their creative works to the public domain – or retain their copyright while licensing them as free for certain uses, on certain conditions.

The organization "Creative Commons," however, is only the most visible part of a wider transnational community that supports ideas of "free use" and "share alike" in the field of free and open source software (for example, the Free Software Foundation), artistic production, information (for example, the Wikimedia Foundation), and science (for example, diverse open access initiatives[1]). The broader issue at stake is free access to information and culture as a public good, not least to reduce inequalities between the industrialized and developing countries. The advent of the Internet and open source software has provided the means to achieve such a mission. These facilities have made the openness of innovation systems an economic factor in the software industry and in creative industries and thereby have raised questions about the appropriateness of existing intellectual property right laws.

In this chapter we aim to analyze the organizational and ideational features of Creative Commons as a transnational community. By transnational community, we refer to a social group of transnational scope, in which participating actors engage in interactions sufficiently close and regular to provide them with a sense of community and, to some degree, also of shared identity, which influences their behavior as a collective (see Djelic and Quack in Chapter 1 of this volume). Transnational communities have been suggested as important actors of transnational institution-building (Morgan 2001; Djelic and Quack 2003, 2008). We use a longitudinal approach to analyze the coevolution of two types of transnational communities assembled around and within the Creative Commons organization, which aims to establish a new set of transnational copyright standards. At the same time, we account for the multi-level nature of these communities by investigating organizational forms at national and international levels.

The results show that the transnational interactions between an epistemic community originating from a group of liberal US copyright lawyers and a social movement around the non-profit organization "Creative Commons" provided unforeseen momentum for their rule-setting project. While the rapid growth and transnationalization of the social movement enabled Creative Commons to successfully disseminate its private licenses among producers of digital intellectual goods, bypassing classical regulators and policy-makers, it also threatened the goals and internal decision-making of Creative Commons itself.

The chapter makes two contributions to the debate on transnational communities. First, it provides a synthetic perspective of the mobilizing capacity of different types of transnational communities and organizations which are too often studied in isolation from each other (cf. Vertovec 2001; Mayntz in this volume). Second, it highlights the comprehensive influence of transnational communities in international rule-setting, which rests in their capacity to intervene over the whole rule-setting cycle and is not, as often perceived, limited to agenda-setting or framing (see also Plehwe in this volume).

The chapter is structured as follows. In the first part, the theoretical concepts for the study of epistemic communities and social movements are outlined and compared. This is followed by a short discussion of methodological issues. The second part delineates the political and technological context of the study. In particular, it points to existing national and international regulations of copyright law and the challenges that the Internet poses to these regulations. The third and main part of the chapter consists of the case study of Creative Commons, including its history, organizational transformations, and transnational features. In the conclusion, we discuss the results and limitations of the case study in the context of other research findings and identify areas for further investigation.

Conceptual framework: transnational epistemic communities and social movements

Transnational epistemic communities and transnational social movements have a number of features in common, while diverging on others. Both develop around a common political project, something that people want to achieve together, an interest on which they converge, and shared principled beliefs that motivate them to pursue this project. In terms of size, composition, and means of mobilization, however, epistemic communities and social movements represent opposite poles of the continuum of transnational social formations reviewed by Vertovec (2001). These factors have consequences for the way in which these transnational communities pursue regulatory projects that not only concern their members but also have broader scope and ambitions.

Following Peter Haas (1992), a transnational epistemic community is a cross-border network of "professionals with recognized expertise and competence in a particular domain and an authoritative claim to policy-relevant knowledge within that domain or issue-area" (Haas 1992: 3). Epistemic communities may consist of professionals from a variety of disciplines, but they usually have a shared set of principled beliefs, common causal beliefs, shared notions of validity, and a common policy enterprise. According to most studies, epistemic communities provide knowledge and frame issues for politicians and decision-makers in international organizations and supranational institutions. In his work on epistemic communities in environmental politics, Haas (2007) also refers to non-state actors and social movements as recipients of the community's agenda-setting and framing efforts. There is, however, little discussion of the role of epistemic communities beyond this early stage of rule-setting projects, and the synergies or conflicts entailed in the possible interplay of epistemic communities and social movements have not been systematically considered.

While epistemic communities have been considered as potentially transnational from the beginning, social movements have been predominantly studied in local and national contexts. Sidney Tarrow (1998: 4) defines social movements as "collective challenges, based on common purposes and social solidarities in sustained interaction with elites, opponents and authorities." As such, they are distinct from political parties and interest groups. A key feature of social movements is "to mount common claims against opponents, authorities, or elites" based on common or overlapping interest or by tapping "more deep-rooted feelings of solidarity or identity" (Tarrow 1998: 4). The means by which social movements pursue their goals are campaigns, events, and what Tilly (2004) calls "WUNC displays," that is, participants' concerted public representation of Worthiness, Unity, Numbers, and Commitments. An essential element in social movement strategies is framing, that is, negotiating shared meanings and definitions with which people legitimate, motivate, and conduct collective activities.

The emergence of transnational social movements is seen as a result of and response to the changing global opportunity structure and arenas for mobilization – for example, the availability of and access to electronic means of communication (Della Porta and Tarrow 2005). In order to target international organizations or the policies of particular states, networks of activists often coalesce and operate across national frontiers (Keck and Sikkink 1998). Such a "planetization" of social movement activities, as Cohen and Kennedy (2000) call it, enhances the pooling of resources across borders and may lead to a "multiplier process whereby flows of pressure feed into each other on a cumulative and mutually reinforcing basis" (Cohen and Kennedy 2000: 320). The quality of Internet-based social mobilization, however, remains contested in the literature. Whereas Tarrow (2000) doubts that they have the same degree of crystallization in terms of trust and collective identity, others argue that online relationships can indeed constitute communities comparable to face-to-face ones (Ren *et al.* 2007) or provide a global extension to localized community relations (see also Miller and Slater 2000, Vertovec 2001). The latter view advocates that online and offline interaction and communication in social movements should be analyzed in concert rather than in isolation of each other.

In spite of the analytical distinctions summarized in Table 10.1, empirically social movements and epistemic communities might not only overlap but also be transformed in a number of ways; for example, members of epistemic communities might shift towards social movement activism or epistemic communities might evolve out of homogenizing subgroups in a broader social movement. These kinds of overlaps and interactions have so far been studied only rarely.

Table 10.1 Comparison of key features of epistemic communities and social movements

	Epistemic communities	Social movements
Common political project	Yes	Yes
Shared interests	Yes	Yes
Shared principled beliefs	Yes	Yes
Size	Limited	Large
Boundaries	Relatively clear	Fuzzy
Internal heterogeneity	Low	High
Causal beliefs	Consensual	Disputed or absent
Knowledge base	Shared	Not necessarily shared
Means of changing the world	Persuasion by facts and arguments	Persuasion and pressure by action and framing

Another neglected aspect in the study of transnational communities is, as pointed out by Mayntz (in this volume), the question of the different characteristics of both types of community in terms of how they relate to formal organizational structures. In Haas's (1992) conception of epistemic communities, individual actors span different organizational boundaries, but Haas does not expand on the role of formal structures in community development and efficacy. In social movement research, the influence of formal organization is acknowledged (Boli and Thomas 1999), but its consequences for the movement have long been in dispute: both an antithetical as well as a facilitating effect on (resource) mobilization can be found in the literature (Clemens and Minkoff 2004). The recent dialogue between scholars of social movement research and scholars of organization studies (for example, Davis *et al.* 2005) breaks with this antagonism and declares the relations of formal organizations and social movements to be an empirical question. Thus, classical concepts on the (dys)functionality of formal structures (Merton 1968) and bureaucracy (Blau 1963) may generate new insights when applied in the context of analyzing epistemic communities and social movement dynamics at their overlap with formal organizational structures.

The Creative Commons project presented in this chapter provides an interesting case study of how epistemic communities and social movements evolved in a specific field of transnational governance (Djelic and Sahlin-Andersson 2006) and in their further development became dynamically interlinked with a formal non-profit organization. Before discussing the case study in detail, we will first provide a short methodological section and some background information about the technological and political context in the field of copyright regulation.

Method and data

Tracking the development of transnational communities with geographically and temporally spread actors requires a longitudinal approach (Van de Ven and Poole 2005) that can cope with the complexity of both the case and the multifaceted data sources. The rationale for selecting Creative Commons for a case study is its identification as a "critical" case (Yin 1994) by means of theoretical sampling (Eisenhardt 1989).

The core of Creative Commons is a set of alternative copyright licenses developed by an international network of copyright lawyers – an epistemic community – that emerged out of, and still overlaps with, a social movement for the proliferation of open source software and free access to knowledge. Its rapid international dissemination – within five years the licenses were "ported" into forty-two different jurisdictions by local "affiliates" – makes it an interesting case for studying the (trans)formation of and interaction within transnational communities. Furthermore, the interplay between locally diverse and relatively independent actors, on the one hand, and transnational norms, procedures, and (organizational) structures, on the other, promise insights into the genealogy and governance of transnational communities in general.

For data collection, as well as for theorizing, it is important to differentiate (analytically) between communities of actors and focal and/or supportive organizations. For epistemic communities, Haas (1992) emphasizes the importance of organizational structures for the diffusion of consensual knowledge, and most of the empirical work to date has analyzed their impact on international organizations and supranational institutions. As far as social movements are concerned, Tilly (2004: 3, 5) warns about treating "'the movement' as a single unitary actor." He identifies, however, "the emergence of well-financed professional staffs and organizations specializing in the pursuit of social movement programs" as an integral characteristic of contemporary social movements.

As in the case of Creative Commons, there is a focal, eponymous organization whose history and formal members served as the starting point for gathering data on (the development of) the transnational communities that led to the organization's foundation and/or evolved and grew around it.

For triangulation reasons as well as "to deal with a full variety of evidence" (Yin 1994: 8) concerning the case, data have been collected from several different sources and consolidated into a case study database (see also Table 10.2):

Table 10.2 Case study database

	International level	National level	Σ
Interviews[a]	2	15	17
Mailing-list archives	48	38	10
Blogs	3	–[b]	3
Miscellaneous archival documents	23	14	37

Notes: [a] All but one interview has been recorded and transcribed; two interviews were conducted via telephone.
[b] Some national blogs have been used to cross-check mailing-list and interview data but have not been investigated systematically and/or entered into the case study database.

- Semi-structured, issue-centered (Witzel 2000) interviews with actors of so-called "affiliate organizations" in charge of local Creative Commons projects in fourteen different countries, as well as with the CEO of Creative Commons and the leader of the internationalization project. The interviews lasted from thirty minutes to two hours and were entered into the case study database as verbatim transcripts.
- Most of the communication and also substantial decisions between Creative Commons and its respective national project leaders, as well as within national Creative Commons communities, take place through mailing lists. Additionally, different subunits of Creative Commons communicate to the public via specific mailing lists. The archives of these mailings lists are accessible online and provide real-time data that enable the discussion and decision processes to be traced without the danger of post-hoc rationalization by the actors. The density and amount of mailing-list discussion, however, varies from country to country and from subunit to subunit.
- Other data sources include various blogs of actors and organizational subunits, and archival data such as license drafts, guidelines, slides, and handouts.

Whereas mailing lists, blogs, and archival data cover the whole period of investigation from 2001 to 2008 by means of real-time information, the interview data were collected during 2006 and 2007, addressing prior issues only in retrospect.

The chronological reconstruction of internationalization and reorganization processes in the form of a thick description was undertaken by reference to all the available data, using mailing lists and blogs mainly for cross-checking interview and archival data, as well as for determining the right temporal order.

Political and technological context: the Internet challenge to the traditional regulation of copyright

To understand the rise of Creative Commons and its struggle with defenders of a strong proprietary version of copyright, it is necessary to take into account the political and technical developments that have shaped the contemporary copyright regime. In this section we therefore undertake a short historical excursion, starting once more with Victor Hugo's inaugural address of 1878.

Behind the concerns which Victor Hugo expressed about a lack of international protection of authors' rights lay the increasing interconnectedness and interdependencies forming within Europe and across the Atlantic at the end of the nineteenth century. Eva Hemmungs Wirtén (2004) depicts nicely how increasing travel, international cooperation, and pan-European and transatlantic networks, together with technological advances in printing, international mail and telegraph services, created markets for literary and artistic production that reached out to an international constituency of consumers, transcending the borders of the still nascent nation-state. Translation of literary work became another forceful stimulant of the international diffusion of printed cultural goods.

While legal copyright statutes existed in some European countries (such as the Statute of Anne from 1710 in Great Britain and the 1793 Chénier Act in France), and bilateral treaties were becoming increasingly common (such as the British–Prussian agreement in 1846), the leading view in Europe was that an international agreement on copyright would be more effective. In 1887, the Berne Convention for the Protection of Literary and Artistic Works, an inter-governmental treaty that guarantees mutual recognition of copyrights between sovereign states, was agreed. According to this convention, states guarantee citizens of other contracting states the same protection of copyrights as they do their own citizens.

The rules laid down in the Berne Convention did not pass uncontested, however. Scandinavian and Southern European countries, and – ironically from today's viewpoint – the United States saw their nascent printing and publishing industries disadvantaged by a copyright regime that privileged the economic interests of France and Britain as the leading culture-exporting countries of the period (Hemmungs Wirtén 2004: 137). US copyright policy, in particular, remained protectionist for a long time. It was only in 1988 that the so-called manufacturing clause which required manufacturing of cultural goods in the United States or Canada in order to qualify for copyright was removed at the advent of the accession of the USA to the Bern Convention.

More than 120 years after Victor Hugo's speech, the dividing lines of interest and conflicts regarding international copyright have changed drastically. Cultural diffusion is now driven by world-spanning media companies, mostly located in the United States, which developed out of an increasing concentration of the publishing, music, and artistic industries, and a multiplication of cross-border mergers between leading firms from these branches (Hemmungs Wirtén 2008). French supremacy in literary markets has been replaced by English-language dominance in a variety of cultural goods markets ranging from literature, music, and film to software and scientific research. The export of cultural goods now addresses a potential audience that in theory spans to the poorest and least developed areas of the world.

For the global media conglomerates, trade policy and international property right regulation have become a playing field in which they strive to widen the realm of intellectual property, including copyright, to safeguard revenues from the works that they own for the maximum time period. This expansion affects the scope of what is considered as intellectual property, its geopolitical reach, and above all the length of time for which protection is granted before works enter the public domain. The so-called Revised Berne Convention recommends a minimum duration of protection for all works, except photographic or cinematographic, of fifty years after the death of the author. Contracting states can extend this period. In 1993, the European Union extended this period to 70 years. The United States subsequently adopted the same period in the so-called Sonny Bono Copyright Term Extension Act of 1998. Struggles about copyright issues are now increasingly fought out in global policy arenas outside the Bern Convention, particularly within and between the World Intellectual Property Organization (WIPO) and the TRIPS (Trade-Related Aspects of Intellectual Property Rights) negotiations in the World Trade Organization (WTO).

The TRIPS Agreement from 1994 turned the content of the Berne Convention (duration of copyright of 50 years after the death of the author) into a minimum protection standard and thereby extended its geographic reach to all WTO member countries. TRIPS has been blamed for maximizing the rights of publishers and distributors over the public interest in free access to knowledge (Helfer 2004). Even more importantly, it has been criticized for not taking into account the radical changes in the use of immaterial goods that have resulted from the introduction and spread of digital technology and the Internet since the 1970s.

The advent of the digital triad of the personal computer as an all-purpose device, the Internet as a digital all-media distributor, and web space as an all-data storage device has generated many new ways for the worldwide availability, reproducibility, and circulation of immaterial goods. By reducing both production and (worldwide) distribution costs of diverse kinds of goods to nearly zero, this technological triad has given rise to new ways of using, reusing, and mixing texts, music, and other artifacts (Lessig 2004). Widespread and low-cost access to these technologies has further contributed to an enormous growth of peer-to-peer file-sharing technologies such as the music file-sharing program Napster (Green 2002).

As a consequence, Internet-related technologies have challenged the position of the multinational media conglomerates and their business strategies built on restrictive copyright in at least three ways. First, digitalization allows the disentanglement of content and medium. This removes a link lying at the heart of traditional-content businesses that sell not music, films, or novels, but CDs, DVDs, and books. Second, the Internet facilitates lossless and immediate copying of all kinds of digital content, which is the technical basis for file sharing and undermines existing regulations on unprohibited private copying. Third, as the costs of both production and distribution of cultural goods continue to fall, authors are beginning to bypass their intermediaries and publish works on their own.

The substantial (economic) potentials paralleling the threats of the new digital era were first demonstrated in the software industry, where free and open source software development began to compete successfully with proprietary forms of software production (Wayner 2002; Metiu in this volume). The challenge to traditional copyright doctrines, arising from the advent of the digital and Internet technology and the licenses drafted and used by free and open source communities, has been aggravated by the actions of social movement organizations. The Free Software Foundation (FSF) and the Open Source Initiative (OSI) have run campaigns either against software patents or in favor of free data formats.[2] Events such as the annual O'Reilly Open Source Convention (OSCON) bring together members of user and practice groups, as well as social movement activists, and countless online petitions, mailing lists, and banner exchange programs display the Worthiness, Unity, Numbers, and Commitment ("WUNC" – see Tilly 2004) of the open source movement.

The practices and campaigns of the open source software community have spilled over to other users of the Internet (Benkler 2006). As a result, an increasing number of people around the globe have discussed or even tried out various possibilities of the open source approach beyond software development in areas such as audio, video, and text. They, too, have been confronted with the need to protect their content with private licenses. The most prominent example is, without doubt, the free online encyclopedia "Wikipedia." It was founded in 2001 and also needed license protection for its collaboratively generated content. Lacking other alternatives, the founders of Wikipedia chose the GNU Free Documentation License (GFDL), a sister license of the GPL that was originally developed for software manuals. At this time, initiatives for open content other than software and for open content licenses were still in their infancy.

Licensing along these lines operated largely through private contracting and was therefore potentially open to challenge in the courts, particularly when people from different countries contracted with each other. The great number and complexity of license contracts available on the Internet also made it difficult for users to decide which one would be the most appropriate for their purpose (Möller 2006). With the increasing number of so-called "copyleft" licensed works, the problem of license compatibility emerged: due to slight differences in the freedoms granted, even works licensed under very similar terms could only seldom be recombined ("mashed up") and integrated into new works. Together, these difficulties with free and open licensing were some of the reasons that led a group of mainly US copyright lawyers to attempt to establish private licensing standards. Therefore, the free/open source software movement not only highlighted the demand for *non-* software licenses, but also functioned as a "breeding ground" for the foundation of "Creative Commons."

Creative Commons: epistemic community concurring with a social movement

Birth of an epistemic community and formation of a non-profit organization in the USA

In the beginning of Creative Commons, there was theft and failure. Failure, as the (expected) defeat in the Supreme Court trial "Eldred vs. Ashcroft" had been the occasion for founding an organization called Creative Commons. Eric Eldred, an Internet publisher of public domain texts and derivative works, challenged the constitutionality of the United States Congress's Copyright Term Extension Act (CTEA) that prevented a number of works, beginning with those published in 1923, from entering the public domain in 1998 and subsequent years due to the expiration of their copyright protection term. One of Eldred's legal advisors in this trial was the Stanford law professor Lawrence Lessig. He became the first president of the newly founded charitable corporation and admits that the idea to give away free copyright licenses was not completely new: "We stole the basic idea from the Free Software Foundation." Hence there was also theft. Lessig explains the core concept of Creative Commons in more detail, as follows:

The idea ... was to produce copyright licenses that artists, authors, educators, and researchers could use to announce to the world the freedoms that they want their creative work to carry. If the default rule of copyright is "all rights reserved," the express meaning of a Creative Commons license is that only "some rights [are] reserved." (Lessig 2005)

In founding Creative Commons as a US charitable corporation in 2001 Lessig was the central node of a network of mostly academic lawyers[3] and financially supported by Stanford University and the Center for the Study of the Public Domain. These lawyers shared an episteme in terms of which there was a perceived need for an "environmentalist movement for culture" (interview with Lawrence Lessig). They had worked together on agenda-setting before, for example in their attempt to convince policy-makers of the advantages of tax deductions for donors of intellectual property. By naming the organization "Creative Commons," its founders tied into an ongoing discussion on digital commons (for example, Lawrence 1996) and emphasized the applicability of its activities to all kinds of creative works. Creative Commons was founded with the purpose of fund raising and administrating tasks necessary to realize their vision of a "digital commons" for cultural goods of all sorts, that is, a growing body of redistributable and reusable digital works.

    Thus, lawyers and legal experts involved in the founding of Creative Commons were "a network of professionals with recognized expertise and competence in a particular domain and an authoritative claim to policy-relevant knowledge within that domain or issue-area," to quote Haas's (1992: 3) definition of an epistemic community. They had more or less all the characteristics identified by Haas as constitutive of this type of community: as a network of US lawyers with a similar professional background they shared a *set of normative and causal beliefs* that led to social action on the part of community members. In point of fact, engagement in a Supreme Court trial to challenge "unfair" legislation is the standard form of social activism for lawyers in a common law system. For Lessig, it is not only in the context of intellectual property rights that this kind of motivation is typical for many

American lawyers: "[A] significant portion goes to American law school, imagining they are going to change the world." The Copyright Term Extension Act and its perceived negative consequences for common (intellectual) goods induced a "common policy enterprise . . . with a set of problems to which their professional competence is directed . . . out of the conviction that human welfare will be enhanced as a consequence" (Haas 1992: 3). Finally, as a community of lawyers mainly residing at university law schools, they enjoyed *shared notions of validity* – at least as far as the legal domain was concerned. Before founding Creative Commons, they did what lawyers at universities in all fields of interest do: theorize, write books and articles, and participate in legal arguments at and outside of court.

During the founding phase, the composition of the community behind Creative Commons did not change much, as the main task – developing a system of copyright license modules – was still mainly a legal enterprise. Consequently, the first outcome of establishing an organization called "Creative Commons" was a legal service: a toolbox of machine-readable license modules and corresponding iconographic markers that could be combined to form different standardized copyright licenses:

- Attribution: others are authorized to copy, distribute, display, and perform the copyrighted work – and derivative works based on it – but only if they give credit the way the creator requests.
- Non-commercial: others are authorized to copy, distribute, display, and perform the work – and derivative works based on it – but for non-commercial purposes only.
- No derivative works: others are authorized to copy, distribute, display, and perform only verbatim copies of the work, not derivative works based on it.
- Share alike: others are authorized to distribute derivative works only under a license identical to the one that performs the work.

Transnationalization of epistemic community and organization

The first versions of Creative Commons licenses were issued more than one year after the organization was founded in December 2002. While at this time the epistemic community behind Creative Commons was still directed toward the USA, it soon shifted toward other legal systems abroad, as did the activities of Creative Commons as an organization. Because of the existing latent demand from interested parties from around the world for licenses for open content, Creative Commons "never had to intentionally look for local partners," as a staff member put it. Foreign lawyers and experts inspired by the free/open source software movement contacted Creative Commons in the USA to obtain the right to transpose the licenses to different national legal systems. Only four months after the official US launch, Creative Commons opened a new "iCommons" office in Berlin "to coordinate with volunteers from around the world to develop versions of [its] licenses that were tuned to the law of local jurisdictions."[4] This localization of licenses was completely new in the field of standardized open content licensing. No free or open source software license, even now, offers different localized versions.

Started more or less accidentally, the process of license porting soon emerged as Creative Commons's most powerful "growth strategy." License porting "creates" the need for local affiliate organizations that administer the initial porting and the future license development and, at the same time, provides a task for interested parties in countries all over the world. Besides, Lessig argues, license porting "make[s] clear that it is not an American thing." By porting the license Creative Commons is effectively (trans)porting its ideas and concepts, as well as building an international community of (legal) experts. It allows different legal traditions to be addressed, such as issues of moral rights. These are obviously more important when dealing with cultural works compared to mere software source code, and their regulation differs significantly between countries in the common law tradition and countries in the European tradition. So, after Japan was the first country to port the licenses in spring 2004, the number of local branches of Creative Commons grew rapidly to total forty-two different jurisdictions by the end of 2007 (see Figure 10.1).

In order to port the licenses, a so-called "project lead" is appointed which might function as an affiliate organization in the country and provide legal expertise – either itself or via local partners. These affiliates have to bring in their own funding and are very autonomous in their work. Restrictions on their role as an affiliate relate exclusively to the use of Creative Commons as a trademark and the formal license porting processes, both of which are set forth in a short memorandum of understanding (MOU).

A close look at the individuals and affiliate organizations involved in license porting shows that transnationalization during the early period (2003–05) was fueled predominantly by the absorption of critical open source and Internet lawyers from outside the USA into the epistemic community. This highlights the importance of a pre-existing free/open source software movement for the speed of license porting during the first years of Creative Commons's existence. In seven of the first ten countries that "ported" the license into their

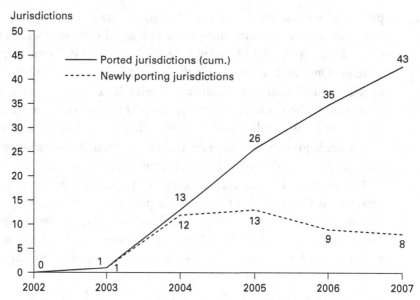

Figure 10.1   Number of jurisdictions that completed the license porting process per annum and over time

local jurisdiction, at least one of Creative Commons's affiliate organizations had a strong technological background and experience with free/open source software licensing.[5]

Many of the early project leads had previously participated in seminars or workshops held by the founding members of Creative Commons at Harvard or Stanford and subsequently developed personal contacts with them. The legal project leads of the first two porting countries, Japan and Finland, for example, both attended the same seminar of Lawrence Lessig at Stanford. Ronaldo Lemos, the Brazilian legal project lead, first came into contact with Creative Commons at Harvard's Berkman Center. At the same time as there was a strong socialization effect of the Harvard and Stanford groups on the early project leads, there were also other affiliation partners who joined independently but were inspired by a similar, at least partially political, interest in adopting copyright licenses for new digital media and open source technologies. For example, the project lead of the Netherlands – the sixth country to port the licenses – mentioned pre-existing plans "for a project on open source software and open content" even before he got to know Creative Commons.

In some early adopting countries, support for the community's episteme was more important than expertise in the field of copyright law per se. In Brazil, for example, the third country to port the licenses, the project lead reports approval from other camps of lawyers, but resistance among the

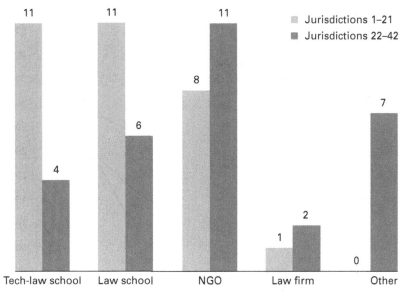

Figure 10.2 Types of affiliate organizations, grouped into early and late adopting jurisdictions
Note: Jurisdictions 1–21 adopted early; jurisdictions 22–42 adopted later.

"traditional" copyright lawyers. So, even though not all of the lawyers were copyright experts, legal professionals dominated the transnationalizing epistemic community during the early expansion phase of Creative Commons. Twenty-three out of 31 affiliates (about 74 percent) located in the early (first 21) adopting jurisdictions were lawyers originating from legal institutions (see Figure 10.2). During this phase, a strong professional focus helped to maintain the homogeneity of the epistemic community in the face of its transnational expansion, as Lawrence Lessig observes:

> Today, when I am in Bulgaria, the people I meet are the same compared to the people in Stanford, they know the same things, we are talking about the same issues. . . . That is completely different compared to the situation 25 years ago, a change due to the Internet. (Interview with Lessig, May 2007)

Unexpected effects of success: social movement organizations joining in

The rapid transnational diffusion of Creative Commons licenses made them a success. By 2005, twenty-six jurisdictions had translated the Creative Commons licenses and users from a broad range of applications fields started

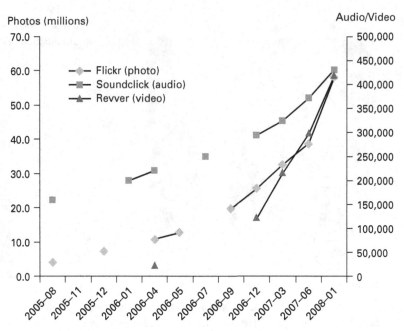

Figure 10.3   Usage of Creative Commons licenses in different fields of application by number of works available in content-hosting services
Note: Revver is an overestimate, probably the total number of uploads, some of which may have been removed or never published; data obtained from http://wiki.creativecommons.org/License_statistics. Accessed June 26, 2008.

to use them. In August 2005, 4.1 million photos hosted on Flickr and 159,000 audio files hosted on Soundclick already used a Creative Commons license. Over the next three years, the aggregate number of Creative Commons-licensed photo, audio, and video files in three popular online archives increased exponentially. In January 2008, Flickr listed 57.9 million photos, Soundclick 430,000 audio files, and Revver 417,000 video files under different Creative Commons licenses (see Figure 10.3).

During the same period, the number of Creative Commons jurisdiction projects rose further, from 25 in 2005 to 43 in 2007. The success of the Creative Commons licenses, however, attracted a new sort of project lead. As opposed to the early (first 21) adopting jurisdictions, where 23 out of 31 affiliates (about 74 percent) were legal institutions, in the late (last 21) adopting jurisdictions only 12 out of 30 affiliates (40 percent) were such. In contrast, the proportion of NGOs and other organizations concerned with the educational, cultural, and social issues of digital environmentalism was much higher among the late adopting jurisdictions. Whereas NGOs and other organizations accounted for not more than 8 out of 31 affiliates (about 26 percent) in the early adopting jurisdictions, they represented 18 out of 30 (60 percent) in the late adopting jurisdictions (see Figure 10.2).

The bandwidth of application fields among the affiliate organizations joining in the second half of the period is quite large. For example, the Austrian affiliate mainly focuses on projects in the education sector in order to collaboratively develop and freely provide course materials,[6] whereas one of the affiliates in Taiwan is cooperating with the governmental National Digital Archives Program (NDAP) to build a national commons archive. Other local branches focus in their work (at least for the moment) on particular artistic areas such as video and film (Poland) or music (Spain and Catalunya). In Switzerland the newly founded political non-profit association "Digitale Allmend" claims to work "for public access to and the further development of digital goods," having taken over the affiliate role from a group of open source lawyers ("Openlaw") in 2008. Similarly, the German "newthinking communication" was only recently accepted as an official affiliate and is engaged in what may be called "digital environmentalism."

In the later adopting Balkan States – where Croatia was the fourteenth adopter, with Slovenia (adopter 23), Macedonia (37) and Serbia (42) following – or other Central or Eastern European countries, such as Hungary (22) and Bulgaria (27), hardly any legal institutions act as official affiliates. Instead, it is mainly civil society organizations with stronger links to producers of cultural content that have become partners of Creative Commons. Their focus is on the cultural, educational, and political aspects of open access to knowledge and cultural artifacts, while they rely on external legal advice in license porting and adaptation. For example, a member of the Croatian affiliate "Multimedia Institute" describes his organization as "dealing mostly with culture, social theory, political activism, and culture policy."

One obvious reason for national differences in types of affiliate organizations is rather mundane: smaller countries such as the Balkan States, Hungary, or Austria have very small legal communities with very few copyright experts, and copyright enforcement is not a major priority either.[7] But the strong representation of civil society organizations among the second half of adopters cannot be fully explained by such geographical patterns of accession as we also find NGOs as national affiliation partners in Argentina, Switzerland, and New Zealand.

Behind these country patterns, therefore, lies a broader trend away from legal institutions toward NGOs and grassroots organizations. This reflects the nascent social movements which have been emerging over the last years, targeting the protection of civil rights to freedom of information on the

Internet. Out of the many existing initiatives, the Open Rights Group, established in 2005 in the UK, and the Electronic Frontier Foundation, launched 1990 in San Francisco, are two of the most well-established examples. Umbrella groups, such as Access to Knowledge (A2K), based at Yale University, or the Digital Future Coalition represent loose collections of civil society groups, governments, and individuals. Last but not least, this emerging social movement has already given birth to the establishment of political parties striving for reforms to the existing copyright regime. Starting with the establishment of a Pirate Party in Sweden in 2006, the idea has spread under the same name with similar goals in over twenty countries worldwide.[8]

The rise of a social movement for "digital environmentalism" has fueled part of the recent expansion of Creative Commons, as increasing numbers of NGOs from this camp have joined as new national lead partners, or replaced existing affiliates. Seven years after its founding and five years after going international, Creative Commons contracts with more than sixty-five affiliate organizations, but the types, organizational structures, and aims of the member organizations have become more heterogeneous. The rapid success of Creative Commons has challenged (as discussed in the next section) basic characteristics of the former, more exclusive and homogenous, epistemic lawyer community.

Organizational decoupling: a split-up for unity

Whereas license porting helped the transnational Creative Commons community to prosper, it complicated the management structures and tasks of the still very young Creative Commons organization: having started to port the licenses into local jurisdictions, an increasing number of local outposts of various national and professional backgrounds demanded coordination and involvement in further license development. What is more, after having released their license, different groups of previously non-organized but latently existing (collective) actors (Dahrendorf 1959; Dolata 2003) gravitated toward these newly founded outposts of Creative Commons. The German public project lead explains Creative Commons's appeal to pre-existing, politically motivated, but often dispersed copyright activists in terms of the "possibility to legally underpin your own views." This fact was soon recognized by the leaders of the focal organization themselves, who state that they "were surprised about how much of that activist component Creative Commons would inspire."

This dichotomy between a homogenous, still rather epistemic lawyer's community and a very diverse community – or even communities – of license users represented by the local affiliates led to debates over Creative Commons's structure, strategy, and license policies. Independent affiliates helpful for spreading Creative Commons urged participation in decision-making and turning a unilateral relationship of license translation into a bidirectional one of recursive interaction on organizational and licensing issues. This may be illustrated by two rather antithetical comments from mailing-list debates:

A shame that "open" and "democratic" are traveling in different directions. iCommons, the world is watching ... and you are creating a corporate machine rather than a democratic one ... is that what all the iCommoners, free culture and assorted supporters want?
We ... must overcome the problem that many activists try to exploit the ideas behind CC for some random political anti something agenda.

Cory Doctorow, a university professor and science-fiction author involved in Creative Commons from the beginning, referred explicitly in his response to the latter comment to the issue of Creative Commons as both an organization and a social movement:

The difference between a movement and an organization is that an organization is a group of people who want the same thing for the same reason. A movement is a collection of groups of people who want the same thing for different reasons. Movements are infinitely more powerful than organizations.

Unwilling and unable to control these "free spirits" in the social movement, focal actors still tried to protect the "core business" of providing copyright licenses that the organization Creative Commons was originally founded for. Consequently, Lawrence Lessig emphasizes that "CC has a real brand and product that it needs to guarantee and that requires a component of expertise more than democratic motivation."

The growing success in terms of both internationalization and usage in various areas of application raised debates within Creative Commons beyond the mere legal licensing of content. The same bureaucratic structures that led to professionalism in terms of license development and porting[9] appear rather dysfunctional (Merton 1968: 251) in terms of balancing the conflicting demands and interests of the growing and increasingly diverse non-legal sections of the community. In the terminology of Brunsson (2003), Creative Commons' organizational structures were designed for producing "action" in

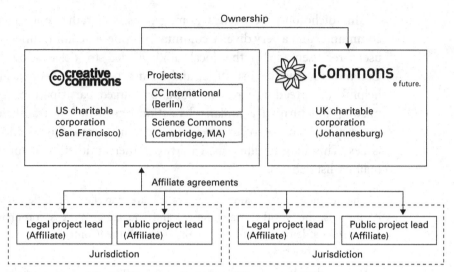

Figure 10.4 Formal structure of Creative Commons after hiving off iCommons in 2005

the form of standardized licenses, not (political) "talk," which would be able to cope with conflicting demands.

The response of the Creative Commons board to rising internal tensions was a radical organizational restructuring on both the international and the national level. On the international level, Creative Commons actually split into two parts when it hived off "iCommons" as a separate legal entity and organization situated in London in November 2005 (see Figure 10.4). At the same time, the internationalization project in Berlin was renamed Creative Commons International (CCi) and remained "just an office" of the US charitable corporation. On the national level, Creative Commons differentiates between legal and public project leads. Whereas the former must provide legal expertise and work in close cooperation with the CCi office in Berlin on license porting and development, the task of the public project lead is to do all the "community work," above all organizing events, marketing the licenses, and networking among different groups of license users.

While for Lawrence Lessig this organizational decoupling between the legal and the activist part of Creative Commons made clear "that there were two things going on ... the building of an infrastructure ... and activism around changing copyright laws," it remains to be seen whether the *organizational* split will generate a sustainable and productive interaction between the epistemic and the activist components of the transnational Creative

Commons community. More than three years after the split, the affiliates responsible for the public project leads still contract with Creative Commons and not with iCommons. And the paradoxical procedure of establishing top-down an organization explicitly designed as a platform for bottom-up processes is not without risks, as it provoked critique particularly from public project leads – iCommons's prime "target group."

Conclusions

The empirical evidence provided in this chapter shows how an epistemic community and a social movement came to interact around the non-profit organization "Creative Commons" in ways which provided unforeseen momentum for their common project of promoting a digital commons. The success of the Creative Commons project can easily be seen in the rise in the number of license porting jurisdictions (forty-three countries in 2007) and the exponential growth of license usage for various types of content on the Internet. Diffusion of Creative Commons's licenses has initiated new uses of open content in various fields and countries. Supported by public campaigns organized by the activist component of the community, this has attracted and activated previously non-organized "quasi-actors" (Dahrendorf 1959; Dolata 2003), but has also generated an increasing awareness of digital rights in civil society. While the intensity and focus of debate certainly varies, the question of how to balance the economic interest of the producers of immaterial goods in protection, on the one hand, with the interest of society in open access to ideas and knowledge, on the other, has made its way onto the agenda of policy-makers, academics, and regulators in many countries.

Three factors are important to understand the momentum which the Creative Commons project gained over the relatively short period from 2002 to 2007. The first factor is the foundation of a non-profit organization. Originally intended as a goal-oriented infrastructure for the development of standardized licenses, it eventually served as a discursive space in which members of the epistemic community, social movement activists, and participants of user and practice groups exchanged views and fought over the goals and directions of the overall community. The second factor which was crucial for the rapid expansion of Creative Commons is the transnationalization of the community and the organization. A large number of independent local outposts in different jurisdictions helped to spread Creative Commons's ideas and tools within an impressively short period of time. Last but not least, the success of Creative Commons is also a story of the intercohesion (Vedres and Stark 2008) of overlapping communities reinforcing each other's efforts toward a common goal. Epistemic reasoning and professional expertise have made licenses available, NGOs have promoted the idea of a digital commons to new application fields, users have applied licenses to new objects, new demands for licensing have emerged.

As beneficial as the intercohesion between the groups has been in terms of expansion, it has also generated internal tensions and conflicts over future directions and the modes of decision-making to be used. The growing number and more diverse nature of the national affiliation partners of Creative Commons had furthered these retroactive effects. Creative Commons's officials responded to these tensions via formal organizational decoupling. While critical reactions of various constituencies point to the limitations for actors to actively shape the features of a community, it also shows some benefits of transnational communities' emergent properties. As far as the Creative Commons community wishes to draw continued benefits from the diversity of its members' professional and political backgrounds in the future, it cannot even aim at resolving the ambiguities of the existing hetero-geneity completely.

We have shown that the hybrid constellation of two overlapping transna-tional communities and a non-profit organization has been able to produce and disseminate standardized open content licenses and thus qualifies as a private rule-setter in global governance. More research is required about the reactions of other players in the field to this initiative and to evaluate the effects it may have in the longer term on the existing copyright regime. Notwithstanding these caveats, the evidence presented in this chapter suggests that transnational communities can play an important role as rule-setting actors in transnational governance fields and that their involvement in rule-setting can go far beyond agenda-setting and issue-framing.

Acknowledgments

We would like to thank Marie-Laure Djelic, Ulrich Dolata, Thomas R. Eimer, Jürgen Feick, and Renate Mayntz for their valuable comments, as well as the participants of the subtheme on "Transnational Communities" at the EGOS Colloquium 2007 in Vienna and the participants of the Workshop on the same issue at the Max Planck Institute for the Study of Societies in April 2008 for insightful und helpful discussions.

NOTES

1. For example, the Budapest Open Access Initiative, www.soros.org/openaccess/.
2. www.germany.fsfeurope.org/projects/swpat/ and www.fsf.org/news/playogg.html.
3. For example, James Boyle (professor of law at Duke Law School), Michael Carroll (assistant professor of law at the Villanova University School of Law), but also Hal Abelson (MIT computer science professor) and Eric Saltzman ("lawyer-turned-documentary filmmaker-turned-cyberlaw expert"). A list of all twenty-nine participants – twenty-four of whom had been lawyers – at the "Inaugural Meeting" is available online (see http://cyber.law.harvard.edu/creativecommons/partic-pants.html).
4. Lawrence Lessig, http://creativecommons.org/weblog/entry/5689.
5. In Finland, the second country to port the licenses, lawyers with longstanding experience in free/open source software licensing at the Helsinki Institute of Technology became project lead. In Germany, the fourth jurisdiction, Creative Commons cooperated with the Institute for Legal Issues on Free and Open Source Software (iFROSS), and in Austria – country number seven – the Open Source Platform of the Austrian Computer Society (ÖCG) took the lead, while the legal tasks were commissioned to a German law firm.
6. One of the greatest users of Creative Commons licenses in the USA is also in the education sector, namely MIT and its Open Courseware project; cf. http://ocw.mit.edu.
7. Civil society organizations, however, have not acted everywhere as an alternative to law school affiliates. In Mexico the only affiliate is a privately owned law firm, and in countries such as Malta and Malaysia Creative Commons's partners are publicly founded governmental organizations.
8. www.pp-international.net/.
9. See, for example, the "CCi guidelines," which now formally standardize the license porting process for new jurisdictional branches: http://wiki.creativecommons.org/images/e/e6/CCi_Guidelines.pdf.

REFERENCES

Benkler, Y. 2006. *The wealth of networks: How social production transforms markets and freedom*. New Haven, CT: Yale University Press.

Blau, P. M. 1963. *The dynamics of bureaucracy: A study of interpersonal relations in two government agencies*. Revised edition. University of Chicago Press.

Boli, J. and Thomas, G. M. 1999. *Constructing world culture: International nongovernmental organizations since 1875*. Stanford University Press.

Brunsson, N. 2003. *The organization of hypocrisy: Talk, decisions and action in organizations*. Copenhagen Business School Press.

Clemens, E. S. and Minkoff, D. C. 2004. "Beyond the iron law: Rethinking the place of organizations in social movement research," in Snow, D. A., Soule S. A. and Kriesi, H. (eds.), *The Blackwell companion to social movements*. Malden, MA: Blackwell Publishing, pp. 155–70.

Cohen, R. and Kennedy, P. 2000. *Global sociology*. Basingstoke: Macmillan.

Dahrendorf, R. 1959. *Class and class conflict in industrial society*. Stanford University Press.

Davis, G. F., McAdam, D., Scott, R. W. and Zald, M. N. (eds.) 2005. *Social movements and organization theory*. Cambridge University Press.

Della Porta, D. and Tarrow, S. 2005. *Transnational protest and global activism*. New York: Rowman and Littlefield.

Djelic, M.-L., and Quack, S. (eds.) 2003. *Globalization and institutions. Redefining the rules of the economic game*. Cheltenham: Edward Elgar.

Djelic, M.-L., and Quack, S. 2008. "Institutions and transnationalization," in Greenwood, R., Oliver, C., Suddaby, R. and Sahlin-Andersson, K. (eds.), *Handbook of organizational institutionalism*. Thousand Oaks, CA: Sage, pp. 299–323.

Djelic, M.-L., and Sahlin-Andersson, K. (eds.) 2006. *Transnational governance. Institutional dynamics of regulation*. Cambridge University Press.

Dolata, U. 2003. *Unternehmen Technik. Akteure, Interaktionsmuster und strukturelle Kontexte der Technikentwicklung: Ein Theorierahmen*. Berlin: edition sigma.

Eisenhardt, K. M. 1989. "Building theories from case study research," *Academy of Management Review* **14** (4): 532–50.

Green, M. 2002. "Napster opens Pandora's Box: Examining how file-sharing services threaten the enforcement of copyright on the Internet," *Ohio Law Journal* **63**: 799–818.

Haas, P. M. 1992. "Introduction: Epistemic communities and international policy coordination," *International Organization* **46** (1): 1–35.

Haas, P. M. 2007. "Epistemic communities," in Bodansky, D., Brunnée, J. and Hey, E. (eds.), *The Oxford handbook of international environmental law*. Oxford University Press, pp. 791–806.

Helfer, L. 2004. "Regime shifting: The TRIPs agreement and new dynamics of international intellectual property lawmaking," *Yale Journal of International Law* **29**: 1–81.

Hemmungs Wirtén, E. 2004. *No trespassing*. University of Toronto Press.

Hemmungs Wirtén, E. 2008. *Terms of use*. University of Toronto Press.

Keck, M. E. and Sikkink, K. 1998. *Activists beyond borders: Advocacy networks in international politics*. Ithaca, NY: Cornell University Press.

Lawrence, J. 1996. "Intellectual property futures: The Paper club and the digital commons," in Ess, C. (ed.), *Philosophical perspectives on computer-mediated communication*. State University of New York Press, pp. 95–114.

Lessig, L. 2003. www.lessig.org/blog/2003/08/sigh_mp3com_we_hardly_knew_you.html, blog entry from August 7.

Lessig, L. 2004. *Free culture: How big media uses technology and the law to lock down culture and control creativity*. New York: Penguin Press.

Lessig, L. 2005. http://creativecommons.org/weblog/entry/5661, blog entry from October 6.

Merton, R. K. 1968. *Social theory and social structure*. Enlarged edition. New York: Macmillan.

Miller, D. and Slater, D. 2000. *The Internet: An ethnographic approach*. Oxford: Berg.

Möller, E. 2006. "The case for free use: Reasons not to use a Creative Commons-NC license," www.opensourcejahrbuch.de/download/jb2006/chapter_06/osjb2006-06-02-en-moeller.pdf.

Morgan, G. 2001. "Transnational communities and business systems, global networks," *A Journal of Transnational Affairs* **1** (2): 113–30.

Ren, Y., Kraut, R., and Kiesler, S. 2007. "Applying common identity and bond theory to design of online communities," *Organization Studies* **28** (3): 379–410.

Tarrow, S. 1998. *Power in movement: Social movements and contentious politics*. Cambridge University Press.

Tarrow, S. 2000. "Transnational contention," Working Paper RSC No. 2000/44. Florence: European University Institute.

Tilly, C. 2004. *Social movements, 1768–2004*. Boulder, CO: Paradigm Publishers.

Van de Ven, A. H. and Poole, S. M. 2005. "Alternative approaches for studying organizational change," *Organization Studies* **26** (9): 1377–404.

Vedres, B. and Stark, D. 2008. "Opening closure: Intercohesion and entrepreneurial dynamics in business groups." Manuscript. Budapest: Central European University. www.personal. ceu.hu/staff/Balazs_Vedres/papers/vedres.stark.intercohesion2.pdf.

Vertovec, S. 2001. *"Transnational social formations: Towards conceptual cross-fertilization."* Transnational Communities Programme WPTC Working Paper 01–16. University of Oxford.

Wayner, P. 2002. *Free for all. How Linux and the free software movement undercut the high-tech titans*. New York: HarperCollins.

Witzel, A. 2000. "Das problemzentrierte Interview," *Forum Qualitative Sozialforschung/ Forum: Qualitative Social Research* **1** (1): www.qualitative-research.net/fqs-texte/1–00/ 1–00witzel-d.htm.

Yin, R. K. 1994. *Case study research: Design and methods*. Thousand Oaks, CA: Sage Publications.

Part V

Transnational interest- or issue-based communities

11 The transnational temperance community

Mark Lawrence Schrad

The catholicity of the Temperance movement is remarkable. It links together in a fraternal bond of union, people of every nation, irrespective of colour, education, politics or religion, and through the agency of these bodies, the peoples of the earth are being linked together not only to drive the means of intoxication from the commerce of the world, but to secure peace and goodwill among nations.

Guy Hayler, International Prohibition Confederation (1914: 11)

The world of international relations is no longer the sole dominion of state actors. From assessing the threat of transnational terrorism to the promise of transnational human rights and environmental advocacy networks, scholars have attempted to come to terms with the sudden and widespread expansion of transnational activism since the 1960s and 1970s (Kahler 2009). For one, Sidney Tarrow explains this development in terms of fundamental sociocultural changes, including "the growth of a stratum of individuals who travel regularly, read foreign books and journals, and become involved in networks of transnational activism abroad" (Tarrow 2005: 35). While the explosion in the quantity of such transnational communities – in which activists share particular values, identities, and policy goals – is of recent vintage, the transnational community itself is not. As far back as the nineteenth century, extensive webs of interaction and information exchange linked individuals, advocacy organizations, and policy-makers of different nationalities, simultaneously reflecting and sustaining shared values, beliefs, and projects (Keck and Sikkink 1998). While the number of such communities may have increased dramatically since then, the basic structure and foundations for that transnational activism have not.

Study of early transnational communities has a great deal to contribute to contemporary debates. First, the fact that nineteenth-century activists established shared transnational identities based upon a common interest

This chapter draws on Chapter 2 of my book *The Political Power of Bad Ideas: Networks, Institutions, and the Global Prohibition Wave* (New York: Oxford University Press, 2010).

in abolishing the slave trade, furthering the rights of women, or (here) championing the cause of temperance is remarkable given early hurdles to international interaction (see: Keck and Sikkink 2000; Klotz 2002; Tilly 2004). "Modern" transnationalism relies greatly on modern technologies: instant messaging, emails, international phone services, and the ease of international air travel have all accelerated the pace of interaction. Absent such modern amenities, I argue, early transnational activists relied even more on shared identity, trust, and sense of inclusion in an international community to facilitate their activities and promote their aims both at home and abroad. Second, early impediments to transnational communication essentially allow us to consider the development of the transnational temperance community in slow motion compared to its more modern counterparts, enabling us to better understand how the community developed, how meanings were transmitted, and ultimately how it declined. Third, a historical perspective allows us to better see the forest for the trees: studying the evolution of transnational communities over ten, twenty, or thirty years (in the case of modern human rights or environmental networks) yields a significantly different perspective than consideration of one or two hundred years. Given the enormity of their goals, modern transnationalists would be hard pressed to envision a future without their movements. Yet a longer-term perspective demonstrates that, just as transnational communities are born and grow, they can also stagnate and die – perhaps due to the ultimate achievement of their aims (abolitionists, suffragists) or failure in that respect (temperance/prohibition).

The purpose of this chapter, then, is twofold. First, I examine the development, structuration, and temporal evolution of the transnational temperance movement in terms that are generalizable to movements of more recent vintage. Second, this allows me to present the credentials of the temperance cause in stimulating one of the first truly transnational communities. To that end, this chapter examines the transnational temperance movement and its evolution in terms of a four-stage lifecycle. I explore in turn the incipient, ascendant, mature, and declining stages, highlighting both the specifics of this particular story and broader, more generalizable features and trends. The four stages are separated analytically with respect to the depth, breadth, and regularity of interaction of like-minded temperance advocates hailing from different corners of the globe.[1] The chapter concludes by addressing some of the most vexing issues surrounding transnational temperance, including explications of why the network developed when and how it did, and whether it was a manifestation of an alleged American cultural-imperialist impulse to spread American morality, before addressing implications of the network and community lifecycle concept for the study of transnational communities more generally.

Incipient stage (1820s–1845): early steps in the construction of a transnational network

Temperance admonishments date practically from the discovery of the inebriating qualities of fermented beverages, and can be found in ancient Egypt, India, Persia, and China. From Shakespeare to Linnaeus, the promotion of sobriety in Europe began within the scientific and artistic communities, while European temperance organizations date from the "Order of Temperance," which was established by Maurice, Landgrave of Hesse in 1600 with the signatures of over two hundred German nobles dedicated to personal abstinence (Winskill 1892). In the United States, the temperance movement is routinely dated from the publication of Dr. Benjamin Rush's *Inquiry into the Effects of Ardent Spirits upon the Human Body and Mind* in 1784. By 1836, civic temperance organizations, including the American Temperance Society (ATS), claimed over 1.5 million members in over 8,000 auxiliaries – or about one out of every five free adults (Blocker 1989: 11–14).

The development of a transnational advocacy movement begins with small and often mundane linkages. In the incipient stage of network construction, activists first make contact with like-minded individuals abroad to exchange ideas and information. At this early stage, interaction is spontaneous and sporadic. Today, establishing international contact may be easily accomplished through email, telephone, or even a weekend trip abroad. In the early nineteenth century, the key actors were those most involved in international travel: traders, wealthy elites, ambassadors, and missionaries.

It may be impossible to identify the very first transcontinental temperance linkage, but as early as the 1730s a young Benjamin Franklin was reprinting English articles against the scourge of liquor (Rorabaugh 1979). By 1829, Massachusetts ship captains were winning applause from the ATS for introducing the temperance pledge to Liverpool, England (Harrison 1971). This Anglo-American axis, which would develop into one of the strongest bilateral temperance linkages, drew on the networks of transatlantic commercial, information, and religious ties that sustained American colonial subservience, and endured even following American independence (Baird 1851; de Tocqueville 1956: 199). These transatlantic ties directly facilitated the founding of the first British temperance society – the Glasgow and West of Scotland Temperance

Society – in 1829. In the previous year, John Dunlop, the "father of the temperance societies of Great Britain," had cobbled together information on American temperance through the testimonials of British emissaries and naval doctors stationed in North America. His resulting lecture, "On the Extent and Remedy of National Intemperance" (1829) became the first transnational temperance study, selling more than 140,000 copies in its first year. As copies of Dunlop's study multiplied, so too did the British temperance societies (Couling 1862).

Protestant missionaries provided another early conduit of transnational temperance communication. The American Board of Commissioners for Foreign Missionaries (ABCFM), established in 1811, supported generations of American evangelicals. The moralistic temperance message resonated within the missionary community: fourteen of the sixteen men who founded the ATS were ABCFM members, and each believed that "'the word of the Lord' would 'run swiftly' in a sober world and would usher in the fruits of 'millennial glory'" (Tyrrell 1991a: 12). These missionaries were charged to spread the perfectionist spirit associated with the Second Great Awakening within American Protestantism (1800–35), which held that individual piety and improving earthly society was a means of accelerating the coming of the millennium – a message that resonated with European Christian communities, such as the British Unitarians, who invoked similar justification in their transnational crusade against slavery (Strange 1984).

Not all early temperance organizations had such close relations with the Church: the Washingtonian movement of the early 1840s created secular institutions to forestall religious recruitment that would distract adherents from their personal struggles with alcohol, fostering mutual assistance and testimonials of reformed drunkards not unlike modern self-help groups such as Alcoholics Anonymous (Krout 1925). Instead of a central, hierarchical organization, the Washingtonian movement comprised a loose network of independent societies that booked lecturers and speaking tours, and published literature (Blocker 1989). Washingtonian societies, though, proved fragile: by either withering away or being co-opted by religious organizations, they failed to integrate within the growing transnational temperance community. Clearly, while temperance was not always equated with religion, the spiritual, financial, and network resources associated with Protestantism and its missionaries greatly facilitated the development of the temperance message beyond national borders.

Permanent organizational bodies such as temperance lodges first developed during this incipient stage of network development. In 1831, when Alexis de Tocqueville was undertaking his famous study of American democracy and civic associations – notably including temperance organizations – Nathaniel Hewett of the ATS was visiting France and Great Britain, assisting in the formation of the British and Foreign Temperance Society, charging followers there with the task of extending the movement's blessings "throughout the kingdom and throughout the world" (Tyrrell 1991a: 16). This exchange was hardly unidirectional: as American temperance organizations established international chapters, Irish and English immigrants brought their Father Mathew and Rechabite temperance societies to the United States in the 1830s and 1840s. A shared commitment to temperance even bridged divisions between Protestants and Catholics, as Protestants hailed Father Mathew during his extensive tours of Canada and the USA in the late 1840s (Quinn 2002).

Undoubtedly the most influential early transnational temperance trailblazer was the American Reverend Robert Baird, who sermonized throughout Europe as an emissary of the American Sunday School Union, the ATS, and the French Evangelical Association through the 1830s and 1840s (Sokolsky 1980). Blessed with a comprehensive command of Christian theology, temperance history, and a knack for persuasive oratory, Baird inspired a wave of temperance activity throughout northern Europe. Upon his arrival in France, Baird was approached by members of the French aristocracy and the American ambassador to the French court to prepare a brief historical sketch of American temperance activity. Over two thousand copies of the resulting *Histoire des sociétés de tempérance des États Unis d'Amérique* were quickly distributed amongst the most influential men of the continent. As Baird's son and biographer noted:

The wide diffusion of information respecting one of the most remarkable moral enterprises which the world has ever witnessed, by means of a language which is read by almost every well-educated man in Europe, was the motive which suggested the publication of this work. A minor, but still important consideration, was the hope that such a work might be the means of awakening France to the evils of the increasing use of brandy and other intoxicating liquors in all the . . . cities and villages of the kingdom. (Baird 1866: 106–7)

Baird's work spread quickly throughout Europe, as did his fame. In 1836, he was granted an audience with French King Louis Philippe, Danish King Frederick VI, Prussian King Friedrich Wilhelm III, Swedish King Karl XIV Johan, and innumerable queens, crown princes, princesses, barons, ministers, archbishops, gentlemen, professors, and ambassadors (Baird 1866). In 1837, Baird assisted in the formation of the Swedish Temperance Society – which claimed over 50,000 members when he returned to Sweden three years later. By his third visit in 1846, the society boasted 332 lodges with nearly 100,000 adherents (Baird 1841). In Prussia, Baird convinced the crown prince to join a total abstinence society, while Friedrich Wilhelm III ordered the establishment of temperance societies in every Prussian province.

News of Baird's arrival in Europe coincided with numerous reports throughout the continent that reflected favorably on the American example. Following the publication of an 1836 article concerning the ATS in a Riga journal, temperance missionaries sought the blessing of the Russian imperial government for a Baltic temperance society, but were quickly rebuked, "lest they should be mistaken for separate religious sects" (Burns 1889: 120; Johnson 1915). When Baird visited St. Petersburg in 1840, Tsar Nicholas I promised to translate his *History* into Russian and Finnish, and to distribute 15,000 copies throughout the empire.[2] Following his meeting, Baird wrote: "Never was I more convinced of *the importance of going directly to the source of power* than in this case. It will not be possible to form temperance societies here for years; but much may be done at once by diffusing information" (emphasis in original, Baird 1866: 195). By the time he returned to the United States, Baird's *History* was available not only in Russian and Finnish, but also in French, Dutch, German, Swedish, and Hungarian (Krout 1925).

At this early stage, it is difficult to speak in terms of the construction of a unified policy agenda or the establishment of a sense of common destiny reflective of a true transnational community. Instead of *coercive* government regulation in response to the "alcohol question," early temperance activists encouraged partial or total abstinence of the individual through moral *persuasion:* "They were confident that, since sin was due to ignorance, knowledge would turn men from vice to virtue" (Krout 1925: 125). Beyond traditional temperance admonishments, however, these new activists were now able to transmit a remedy based upon the experiences and effectiveness of the American temperance organizations. With the European press and temperance adherents hailing every progressive development in America, it should hardly be surprising to find a diffusion of American-inspired organizational arrangements such as local temperance lodges with close church ties to diverse national settings throughout Europe.

Given this brief description of the incipient stage of the transnational temperance advocacy network, a number of points are worth mentioning that are generalizable to the initiation of transnational communities broadly speaking. First, the establishment of transnational linkages was primarily an elite phenomenon. The foremost transnational temperance crusaders of the time, such as Nathaniel Hewett, Robert Baird, and Father Mathew, were not only men of faith, but also men of high educational and social standing. This elite status assisted in the formation of transnational linkages with national elites in other countries: certainly, not just *anyone* could routinely find sympathetic audience with the most influential royal families of Europe. This may also mark the first time that governments received ambassadors on behalf of social causes, rather than states.

Second, overcoming language barriers is important in facilitating the early spread of the cause. Since temperance missionaries such as Robert Baird could easily interact in French – the language of European high society – temperance sentiments could diffuse quickly through the salons of European capitals. While the *lingua franca* of transnational organization has shifted from French to English in the intervening centuries, the ability for activists to engage one another in a common language remains crucial to the formation of transnational networks.

Third, the presence of a transnational community of faith can greatly aid the development of a transnational issue community. Here, connections with the Protestant Church were crucial for transnational temperance activism; the temperance message resonated with broad public religious sentiments through foreign missionaries, while the links between churches internationally, as well as the links between parishes nationally, provided mobilizational resources and interpersonal networks to support the temperance movement (Bernard 1991).

Fourth, in the incipient stage, the transfer of ideas, information, and tactics inspires the emulation of the local organizational structures of the originating country. In-person encounters with transnational advocates were not necessary – information concerning foreign temperance developments was frequently enough to prompt the development of temperance adherents and organizations at home, often based upon emulation of American temperance institutions and practices: local lodges and the teetotal pledges of the ATS. This underscores the importance of early newspapers and journals and shows the critical significance of the translation and publication of temperance tracts.

The incipient stage of development of a transnational advocacy network depends upon sporadic, irregular efforts by a small number of devoted transnational actors. What differentiates this initial stage from later stages is the infrequent, irregular, and highly contingent nature of exchanges of information between the nascent national temperance organizations.

Ascendancy stage (1846–1885): structuring and organizing for transnational interaction

Beginning in the mid-1840s, a growing number of temperance organizations integrated into a transnational web of communication and interaction, highlighted by international temperance conferences, publications, and organizations with an explicitly transnational focus. Such increasingly broad and dense interactions were the seeds of a truly international temperance movement and a full-fledged transnational temperance community. This ascendancy stage of the transnational temperance movement lasted until the creation of the biennial International Congresses on Alcoholism in 1885.

While the Civil War devastated American temperance organization, the cause continued unencumbered in Europe. The Independent Order of Good Templars (IOGT) became the first organization to promote coercive measures such as prohibition, and to extend those ideas through the development of an extensive international organizational network. The first IOGT lodge was formed in 1851 in Utica, New York, claiming lodges throughout the Northeast, upper Midwest, and Southern Canada, before the Civil War. Rather than focusing on moral suasion and rehabilitation, the IOGT platform instead demanded a lifetime pledge of total abstinence by its members, while also promoting legislative palliatives, including the revocation of licenses to produce, distribute, or sell alcohol.

The IOGT experienced exceptional growth in the United States after the Civil War – though even more exceptional was its expansion internationally. Within five years of the establishment of the first English IOGT lodge in 1868, European IOGT flourished to the point that the annual Templar convention – the Right Worthy Grand Lodge – was first held outside of the United States in London in 1873. By the end of the decade, the IOGT boasted a worldwide membership of 721,000, earning it the title of the "leading temperance organization in the world" (IOGT 1890).[3] The first Scandinavian IOGT lodge was established by Swedish-American Olof Bergström, upon his return to Gothenburg in 1879 (Petersson 1903). While divisions over questions of race and integration within the American IOGT lodges led to schism and decline in the United States, the Templars' foreign expansion continued unabated, claiming activities in roughly eighty countries, American states, and colonial territories by 1887 (Fahey 1996). The metamorphosis of the formal IOGT institutions highlights this internationalization of the movement. From the 1850s through the early 1870s, the organization was governed by the "Right Worthy Grand Lodge of North America," which subsequently gave way to the "International Supreme Lodge," with representation from virtually all nations boasting Templar lodges. Annual conferences, initially held exclusively in the United States, gave way to biennial sessions on both sides of the Atlantic, and eventually to triennial conferences rotating between North America, the British Isles, and the European continent. The organization's executive, the

Right Worthy Grand Templar, was originally filled from the ranks of American or Canadian Templar leadership, though by the end of the nineteenth century, the office had been occupied by Englishmen, Swedes, and Norwegians. At the same time, members of the International Executive Committee speaking Scandinavian languages outnumbered those speaking English.

Similarly remarkable was the extent of the Templars' influence on subsequent temperance organization. In the United States, the Prohibition Party was organized at the behest of the IOGT, while the Woman's Christian Temperance Union (WCTU), the Anti-Saloon League of America (ASLA), and the International Prohibition Confederation were founded by individuals with significant experience and leadership in Templar work. Moreover, when these organizations created international bureaus, such as the World's WCTU and the World League against Alcoholism (WLAA), they again built upon the organizational structure of the IOGT (Brook 1972). Much of the IOGT's success can be credited to its open membership policies: the IOGT opened the door to women's involvement in the movement and advanced cooperation with non-secular temperance contemporaries, such as the Sons of Temperance and the Independent Order of Rechabites.

The most visible manifestation of the organizational web that would ultimately become the transnational temperance community was the international temperance conferences, at which like-minded individuals openly exchanged temperance-related ideas, information, and innovations. The increased frequency of interaction facilitated a fundamental shift from a handful of cosmopolitan activists with simple interests in foreign events to a genuinely transnational temperance community based upon a shared moral opposition to alcohol, and a common identity as members of a truly global movement. Following the tactics pioneered by the abolitionist movement, temperance advocates brought increased attention to the international dimension of their cause by labeling their meetings a "World Temperance Convention" and inviting delegates from other countries (Tyrrell 1991a). Initially, such conferences included only token international representation, but as the transnational advocacy network developed, the number of countries represented in such meetings grew in step.

When international temperance trailblazer Robert Baird returned to Europe in 1846, he did so as a delegate to two of the first international conventions on the temperance question: a first conference in Stockholm under the patronage of King Oscar of Sweden (Baird 1866), followed by a larger "World's Temperance Convention," held in London at the behest of the

National Temperance Society (NTS) of Great Britain. The plan for such an international temperance gathering in London was interwoven with another transnational crusade: the international abolition of slavery (Strange 1984; Kaufmann and Pape 1999). An international temperance conference was first proposed during the 1843 Anti-Slavery and Peace Conventions, subsequently spreading to temperance-minded individuals throughout the abolitionist networks, which included noteworthy abolitionists Lyman Beecher and William Lloyd Garrison (*Proceedings of the World's Temperance Convention* 1846).

Whereas the 1846 London convention drew upon the ideational foundations of equality of the abolitionist movement, the Whole World's Temperance Convention that coincided with the New York World's Fair of 1853 linked the abolitionist, temperance, and nascent suffragist movements, making it the most well-attended and influential international temperance convention during the ascendancy stage. The unanimous selection of woman's suffrage pioneer Susan B. Anthony as secretary of the convention and the unprecedented inclusion of women highlighted the universality of the temperance cause, which led conference attendees to proclaim that the convention was "world-wide in spirit," despite the fact that delegates were drawn solely from the United States, Canada, and the United Kingdom (*Whole World's Temperance Convention* 1853:13). While conference resolutions continued to encourage individual abstinence and spiritual growth, most of the proceedings constituted a debate over the appropriateness and enforceability of the recently enacted prohibition law in Maine in 1851–52. Lauding such developments, the conference resolved that the official position of the state vis-à-vis liquor traffic should be one of "declared and uncompromising hostility" (*Whole World's Temperance Convention* 1853: 20), thus marking the beginning of the transition of temperance ideas from tactics of mere moral suasion toward harnessing the coercive capacity of the state.

The summer of 1876 was a time of great excitement throughout the United States, with the centennial celebration of American nationhood. In addition to the festivities associated with the Centennial Exposition, *two* international temperance conferences were held that summer in Philadelphia, the mother-city of American democracy. President of the WCTU Annie Wittenmyer called to order the Woman's International Temperance Convention on June 10 – the "first ... international convention ... for women the world has ever known" – with delegates from Canada, England, Scotland, Japan, and twenty-one of the thirty-eight American States (Tyrrell 1991a: 20). This meeting included the first attempt to study the feasibility of a permanent women's international temperance union, or what would later become the

World's WCTU. A larger international Temperance Conference was held two days later, with over 420 delegates from Canada, England, Scotland, Sweden, and New Zealand. The conference not only addressed issues from licensing, liquor revenue interests, and the feasibility of prohibition, but also delivered histories of temperance developments in foreign lands, from European and Caribbean countries to Australia, New Zealand, China, British India, and colonial Madagascar (*Centennial Temperance Volume* 1877).

In 1885, the "Centennial Temperance Conference" was held to commemorate a hundred years of American temperance activity dating from the publication of Benjamin Rush's *Inquiry*. Accordingly, the conference was geared more toward historical sketches of various temperance and church organizations in addressing insobriety in the American context, with only token presentations given to developments in the British Isles and the Dominion of Canada (*One Hundred Years of Temperance* 1886). The same year, international meetings were held in London focusing on the development of temperance activities solely within the British Empire, with only token consideration of American developments (*British and Colonial Temperance Congress* 1886).

Beyond grand lodges and world conferences, temperance societies developed in-house presses to publish books, temperance tracts, sermons, and periodicals for members and subscribers. *The Nation*, the *National Temperance Advocate*, the WCTU's *Union Signal*, and the IOGT's *International Good Templar* all date from the 1880s. Of special note is the development of the National Temperance Society and Publication House, associated with the IOGT, which produced a number of the first comprehensive histories of the liquor question in different countries, as well as tracts addressing the ways in which different governments and leaders had addressed it (for example, Pitman 1878; Dorchester 1884; Burns 1889).

The expansion of the transnational temperance community was not everywhere greeted with the same acclaim as in northern Europe. Differences in culture and governance structures go far towards explaining why the temperance cause met with limited enthusiasm elsewhere. For instance, in the primarily wine-drinking regions of Southern Europe, including France, Italy, Spain, and the Balkans, the acceptance of consistent, yet moderate use of light alcoholic beverages limited the temperance message to a narrow stratum of temperate absolutists. In Russia, tsarist recalcitrance greatly inhibited the spread of the temperance cause through indigenous organizations. Again highlighting the importance of religious affiliations and resources in promoting temperance, the only grassroots temperance organizations were found initially in the non-Russian provinces of Finland, Poland, and the Baltics, which maintained international religious linkages based on Lutheranism (and Catholicism in the case of Poland), that transmitted the temperance cause despite government opposition (Schrad 2004).

In terms of generalizable analytical distinctions, we can delimit the ascendant stage of development with respect to the creation of an increasingly dense network of physical and informational connections and the broadening of the base of a transnational movement beyond the small network of elites evident in the incipient stage. First, we note the exponential growth of local temperance lodges in an increasingly diverse range of countries during the forty years between 1845 and 1885, as well as the proliferation of connections between them. This emerging transnational network provided new channels for the transmission of information to temperance activists and interested policymakers in diverse countries.

A second characteristic of the ascendancy stage was the creation of organizations with an expressly transnational focus. In particular, the development of the IOGT into a full-fledged international temperance organization with extensive transnational administrative linkages similar to modern international non-governmental organizations (NGOs), would be crucial to the subsequent development of a truly transnational temperance community.

A third development of the ascendancy stage pertains to international conferences as a means of transmitting ideas, information, and tactics, and reporting on the progress of the shared cause in foreign lands. Given the time and resources necessary for international travel, such early conferences were scheduled to "piggyback" on events of international significance: World's Fairs, centenary celebrations, and other international conferences. Drawing on tactics of the abolitionist cause, attaching an "international," or "world" label to such conferences, even though the actual amount of international content was frequently trivial, legitimized temperance activity as a worldwide moral battle. This "global framing" process can "dignify and generalize claims that might otherwise remain narrow and parochial" (Tarrow 2005: 76). International conferences bolster advocates' perceptions of the rightness of their cause based on shared understandings that the evil they were confronting was part of a universal struggle necessitating an international response. Yet for all their efforts, these early international temperance conferences were infrequent, highly contingent, and relatively light on genuine international participation in comparison with the more frequent and regularized meetings that would follow.

Also worthy of note in this stage is the transformation of the message of the temperance movement, from the persuasion and moral reflection of the incipient temperance movement toward coercive ends, including prohibition. This development is related to the evolution of the community itself: rather than simply transmitting appeals to public sentiments, the ascendancy stage witnessed the beginning of the transmission of different policies and the frames to justify them.

In sum, the ascendancy stage was marked by a rapid spread of temperance lodges and organizations, and a proliferation of contacts between temperance organizations in different countries, as well as between member-lodges. While these intra-organizational contacts were more frequent, inter-organizational, inter-governmental contacts were not. The development of a mature transnational community would include not only stable and enduring inter-organizational linkages through the holding of regular temperance conferences, but also increasing interaction of the network with the various policy-making and administrative bodies of national governance.

Maturity stage (1885–1925): towards social movement and transnational community

With the opening of the first biennial *Meeting International d'Anvers contre l'Abus des Boissons Alcooliques* in Antwerp, Belgium in 1885, the transnational temperance movement truly came into its own, both shaping and being shaped by national-level political developments. After 1885, transnational temperance meetings would be regularized, routinized, and professionalized, with conventions held every second year rotating throughout the various states of Europe – only once visiting the United States. As the transnational advocacy network grew broader and deeper, both the number of delegates to the congress and the number of countries represented would keep step (Figures 11.1–11.2). This transnational temperance movement, now poised to shape national political agendas with the tools for regulation (including outright prohibition), was aided by the emergence of a real transnational "community" of temperance that allowed like-minded advocates to interact easily based on shared values and goals.

The 1885 Antwerp Meeting sat 560 representatives from across the globe, including official delegations from temperance societies in the United States, the United Kingdom, Belgium, the Netherlands, France, Sweden, and Switzerland (Thomann 1886). The subsequent framework of regular

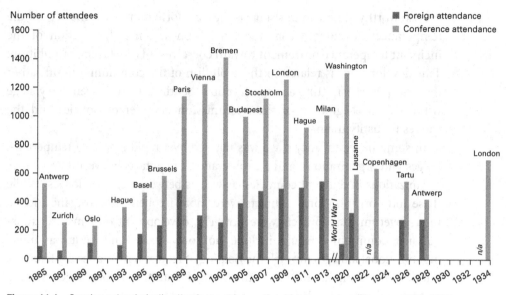

Figure 11.1 Gauging network depth: attendance at international temperance conferences, 1885–1934

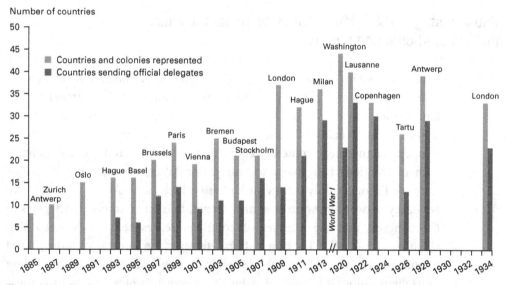

Figure 11.2 Gauging network breadth: number of countries represented at international temperance conferences, 1885–1934

conferences provided ample opportunity for temperance and prohibition advocates to network with like-minded individuals from distant lands. Following an opening address in the language of the host country; the conference proceedings, papers, and discussions were routinely conducted in

French, German, and occasionally English, with participants responding in whichever language most suited the conversation. Given the high educational level of the attendees, the polyglot character of the proceedings did not appear to hinder the temperance discussion (Thomann 1889: 7).

As the transnational network expanded, it also became more professional. The dominant role of religious figures was gradually overtaken by leaders of national and international temperance organizations, representatives from local temperance lodges, government regulatory bureaucrats, and delegates from legislative and executive bodies. Government representatives often arrived at these conferences with official communiqués from their presidents, kings, and prime ministers, charged with both conveying positive temperance developments in the country and learning of progress in other countries to be transmitted to legislators back home.

Another defining feature of network maturation is the formation of organizations with an explicitly transnational or global agenda. For one, the World's Woman's Christian Temperance Union (World's WCTU) had its organizational roots in the WCTU of the United States and aimed to promote temperance education and female suffrage. By 1885, the WCTU claimed "fraternal delegates" in Canada and the UK, while its charismatic president, Frances Willard, professed that the newly formed international branch of the WCTU would export temperance reform to every continent of the globe through missionary work.[4] Professional World's WCTU missionaries, such as Mary Clement Leavitt, enlisted over a half-million members worldwide; from North America, Scandinavia, and the British Empire to evangelical outposts in China, Japan, India, and the Pacific – in the process modifying the WCTU slogan from "for God and home and native land" to "for God and home and every land" (Tyrrell 1991b: 217–18). Once established, these interpersonal, inter-continental relationships proved quite robust, and were sustained through routine correspondence, publications, and meetings at international conventions that helped transmit ideas and tactics to promote the temperance cause, including holding prayer vigils outside of liquor stores and the stationing of matrons to oversee the operation of police stations – practices pioneered in the United States, and subsequently spread to Great Britain and even to India and Australia within a matter of years (Tyrrell 1991a). The World's WCTU enabled women to specialize in various branches of temperance, religious, social, and political work through specific organizational bureaucracies linked to a world-wide network of specialized agents, each of whom would report to local, state, and national conventions, which in turn sent delegates to international WCTU conferences and International Temperance Congresses.

Much of the success of the World's WCTU and other transnational temperance organizations was built upon the foundations of existing temperance community connections. Pioneers though they were, temperance missionaries such as Mary Leavitt were not simply thrown into the wilderness: "everywhere the WCTU missionaries went, they built upon the work already done by the Templars" (Tyrrell 1991a: 18). Further evidence of a shift toward the establishment of a genuinely shared transnational temperance community during this stage, the IOGT itself changed its name, from "Independent Order of Good Templars" to the "*International* Order of Good Templars" (Fahey 1996).

Former Templars also expanded the number and function of international temperance organizations, such as the International Prohibition Confederation, later known as the World Prohibition Federation (IPC/WPF) of the transnational temperance professional and long-time Templar Guy Hayler. Unsurprisingly, the principles of the IPC/WPF mirrored those of the IOGT with a more explicit international focus, namely: "to amalgamate the forces in various countries working ... toward the one common aim of the total suppression of the traffic in intoxicants," and "to obtain notes of progress, information, and news from all parts of the world, and to send such information to all organizations joining the Federation."[5] The IPC/WPF promoted these ideals primarily through direct solicitation of influential legislators and mass propaganda addressing the evils of alcohol. In less than two decades, copies of IPC/WPF publications in English, French, and German were in excess of five million. The IPC/WLF differed from other transnational temperance NGOs due primarily to its function as a clearing house of information provided by, and distributed to, affiliated organizations and individuals. This federative structure ultimately facilitated the co-opting of the IPC/WLF by the larger and better-funded World League against Alcoholism (WLAA) in the 1920s.

The WLAA was a latecomer to the transnational temperance community. Like the World's WCTU, the WLAA attempted to export the American understanding of prohibition as the solution to the "liquor question" to the rest of the civilized world. As the international branch of the Anti-Saloon League of America (ASLA) – the pressure group most frequently credited with securing prohibition in the American context – the WLAA comprised those same influential prohibition advocates, such as Ernest Cherrington, "Pussyfoot" Johnson, and James Cannon (Kerr 1985). At its peak in the mid-1920s, the WLAA boasted 59 member organizations, mailings to over 500 temperance organizations, 200 temperance publications, support for prohibition campaigns in Scotland, Sweden, New Zealand, Mexico, and

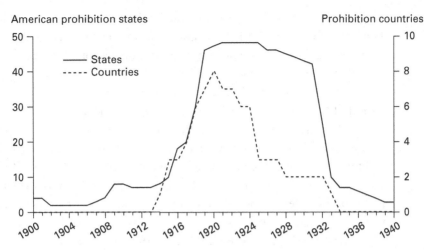

Figure 11.3 Number of countries and American states under prohibition, 1900–40

South Africa, two World League Conventions, and cordial relations with members of the League of Nations (Brook 1972).

A mature temperance advocacy network characterized by a growing number of regular and routine interactions, the development of transnational professionals, and the proliferation of NGOs with an expressly international agenda naturally built upon the foundation of earlier network relations (Hayler 1914). A mature transnational temperance community facilitated the international wave of anti-liquor legislation and prohibition that coincided with World War I by disseminating temperance frames for understanding significant international political developments through a shared community of temperance values. Transnational temperance organizations such as the IOGT, WLAA, World's WCTU, and IPC/WPF artfully framed the positive attributes of particular policies, such as prohibition, over less restrictive alternatives. In this way, the common language and common references of the transnational temperance community did not simply act as a conveyor of information as raw data, but rather promoted certain policy options that reflected the shared values of the community.

The "wave" of alcohol prohibitions associated with World War I (see Figure 11.3) was catalyzed by the transnational temperance community. News of the victory of prohibition in one land often bolstered the efforts of those in another. That the community served as a reliable conduit for ideas and information, organizational tactics, and normative frames suggests the importance of the community itself as a defining element in the mature stage of network development. Other distinguishing features of the mature stage go beyond the sheer quantity of transnational linkages and information exchange, to highlight the facilitation of these exchanges by the increasing depth, breadth, and professionalization of transnational linkages.

Transnational cooperation and interaction are deepest when organizations are most developed and interaction is most routine. To that end, the mature period of transnational temperance community development is marked not only by the rise of international temperance NGOs with an explicit worldwide perspective, but also by an expansion of press and periodicals, transnational meetings and conferences, that facilitated the rapid circulation of temperance literature and information. Finally, deeper cooperation is evident by the inclusion of different members within the temperance network: whereas the primary actors in earlier stages were disproportionately missionaries and high-minded elites, between 1885 and 1925 more and more government representatives were included in the network.

In terms of network breadth, it is easy to see that during this period the number of active participants in the transnational temperance community grew substantially. Rather than token representation, by the twentieth century international temperance congresses routinely included representatives from 30–40 countries – an overwhelming proportion of the countries of the day. Moreover, with the deepening of transnational information ties, developments in any given country were seen as integral to the international movement as a whole.

Finally, the mature stage of community development saw the rise of professional transnational advocates dedicated to the cause of temperance, with extensive careers in temperance organizations with the explicit function of temperance agitation. The proliferation of international temperance NGOs expanded the career opportunities for temperance-minded individuals seeking to promote the cause beyond the domestic context.

Declining stage (1925–35): when the collective energy recedes

The fate of the transnational temperance network was ultimately linked to the destiny of prohibition worldwide. When the prohibition inroads made in countries throughout North America and Europe were gradually repealed following World War I, support for the temperance cause eroded correspondingly, leading to the demise of the network. Thus, the final stage in the network lifecycle is a decline in the collective energy of the movement: the dissipation of the motivating temperance impetus, marked by the gradual curtailing of interactions and the bankruptcy, dissolution, or retooling of movement organizations.

The Anglo-American axis had long served as the keystone of the transnational temperance movement, and the community was disproportionately impacted by political developments in those countries. The emergency of war brought about strict alcohol restrictions – but not outright prohibition – in the United Kingdom, tying the temperance movement to the fate of prohibition in the States. The American temperance movement ultimately became the victim of its own success: the belief that the war on liquor had been won with the adoption of the prohibition amendment translated into fewer resources for the transnational temperance movement. Fewer dues-paying members meant that American temperance organizations such as the WCTU and the Anti-Saloon League were unable to support their vast international institutional structures, the World's WCTU and the WLAA.

By the late 1920s and early 1930s, the cause of transnational temperance seemed trivial in the context of the Great Depression, while even the staunchest outposts of prohibition faced immanent repeal. The WLAA had long since curtailed its European activities, concentrating instead on the enforcement of prohibition at home. As the Twenty-First (repeal) Amendment was ratified, the WLAA and ASLA finally and reluctantly succumbed to chronic budgetary arrears and non-existent public support (Brook 1972). Similar problems vexed the World's WCTU and the IPC/WPF, though in both cases the quixotic personal temperance crusade of some of the most dedicated members would continue until their death in the 1940s and 1950s.

Not all temperance organizations met with such an ignominious end. Some even thrived following the demise of the prohibition generation by expanding their focus to include other lifestyle issues. The IOGT, since rebranded as the "IOGT International," today boasts 115 affiliates in 53 countries, and has expanded beyond alcohol and drug-addiction issues to the provision of support for refugees, war victims, and street children, as well as spearheading sustainable development projects in the developing world.[6] The International Bureau Against Alcoholism, which provided the institutional support for the regular International Temperance Conferences, is now known as the International Council on Alcohol and Addictions (ICAA), which held its fifty-second conference on dependencies in Estoril, Portugal in late 2009.

As most studies of transnational advocacy networks focus on active movements, little consideration is given to the possibility of decline. We might thus learn quite a bit about sustaining transnational activism by studying network decline in historical perspective. Network decline should not be equated with failure: other early transnational communities, including the anti-slavery and suffragist movements, ultimately declined due to the victory of their aims in ending the slave trade and extending the vote to women. The displacement of community goals and the interplay between internal movement dysfunctions with exogenous shocks and crises suggest themselves for greater scrutiny as factors that facilitate the decline of a transnational community.

The decline of transnational temperance holds two practical insights for the study of social movement organizations. First, transnational advocates need to remain vigilant and active. After all, temperance activity both domestically and internationally waned most precipitously due to complacency about the perceived achievement of the movement's aims. Second, it appears that expansion and diversification are keys to longevity in a transnational NGO. Whereas organizations that were strictly bound to the development of one domestic parent-organization or founder (World's WCTU, WLAA, IPC/WPF) all went down with the sinking ship, organizations that had a more diverse foundation of support (IOGT, ICAA) proved more resilient to the reverse wave of anti-prohibitionism that doomed their more rigid institutional counterparts.

Discussion: transnational community in process – the exemplar of temperance

While this investigation tells us a great deal about how the transnational temperance community developed, the implicit questions of why it developed when it did have yet to be resolved. Perhaps the most logical reason to expect the development of such an international community against alcohol consumption was that the societal consumption of alcohol was on the rise everywhere, prompting popular opposition to facilitate a "return to sobriety." But even according to nineteenth-century comparative accounts, the amount of alcohol consumed per capita in Europe and North America did not increase. In fact, it declined markedly during the latter half of the century (Bureau fédéral de statistique 1884: 672). Hence, the rise of the international temperance movement was not premised on an objective increase in drunkenness, corroborating the historical lack of correlation between alcohol-related harms and degree of societal regulation (Blomqvist 1998: 287).

Temperance as "imagined community": intersubjective understandings

It appears, then, that the temperance movement had its foundations more in subjective assessments concerning the inappropriateness of drunkenness, coupled with the belief in social organization as an effective remedy. But this does little to explain the timing of the rise of the movement. Addressing the birth of modern forms of collective action, Sidney Tarrow notes a blossoming of eighteenth-century social movement activity embedded within larger social, political, and economic developments. The rise of capitalistic, mass-market publishing enabled reporting on both distant news developments (and attitudes about them) through "communities of print," that helped shape popular attitudes and perceptions beyond parochial social associations (Anderson 1991; Tarrow 1998). Additionally, while alcohol consumption may not have been on the rise, it was highly visible in the "degenerate" urban slums emerging as a consequence of industrialization – especially to Protestants intent on improving their earthly society as part of the Second Great Awakening. The perceived need to control drunkenness and rowdiness among the lower classes was part of the rationalization of industrial economic life (see Gusfield 1991). Thus, social changes associated with urbanization and industrialization, combined with the perfectionist spirit of the Second Great Awakening, highlighted drunkenness as a target for social activism. This subjective "pull" of perceptions of societal inebriety and degeneracy, combined with the "push" of a mass media linking local associations, goes far in explaining the rise of the temperance movement.

Advances in transportation and communication technologies accelerated the speed, quantity, and regularity of international interaction. Importantly, the development of transnational ties through the evangelical Protestant and abolitionist movements further spread temperance ideas and organizations beyond isolated localities: networks of evangelical churches and missionaries facilitated communication and interaction during the incipient stage of transnational development, while the movement also drew upon the individuals, resources, and organizational forms engaged in the transnational struggle to eliminate slavery. The abolitionist movement provided templates and repertoires for the development of a transnational advocacy network, including the use of conferences, organizations, and normative frames grounded in religious and liberal principles in mobilizing domestic and foreign public opinion to the cause. In the absence of such pre-existing transnational linkages, it is difficult to imagine that the temperance movement would have spread as widely as it ultimately did during the early stages of development.

Some historians have suggested that the transnational temperance movement was some manifestation of an inherently Anglo-American missionary impulse, leading to accusations of cultural imperialism, either overt or Gramscian (Tyrrell 1994; Dupré 2004; Marquis 2004). My analysis suggests that such indictments may be premature, especially given that previous historical analyses have limited their consideration both to English-language sources and American transnational temperance NGOs such as the WLAA and World's WCTU, which appear only late in the mature stage of the network lifecycle.

While early temperance organizations were often inspired by the American temperance trailblazers and policies, emulation does not necessitate control, as the onus of activism and implementation remains with domestic activists. An early example can be found in a speech of the Swedish Count Hamilton admonishing American temperance pioneer Robert Baird at the first international temperance conference in 1846:

Ever since Temperance Societies were first instituted in this country, and commenced their career among us, they have had their eyes constantly fixed upon your country, and they have followed your exertions in the common cause with the liveliest interest. You have been to us not only *models* by your zeal, but also *encouraging examples* by your success. (Emphasis in original. Baird 1866: 219)

In short, serving as an example worthy of emulation should not be conflated with the relations of hierarchy and control associated with imperial and hegemonic relationships.

Moreover, such imperial accusations must account for a number of historical inconsistencies: first, neither the USA nor the UK were the first to adopt prohibition – that dubious honor falls to Russia, while Britain never actually adopted prohibition at all. Second, the fact that organizations such as the IOGT blossomed throughout the states of northern Europe while they withered in the United States runs counter to the imperialism thesis. Third, such historical works do not consider international temperance conferences that seem inconsistent with imperialistic or hegemonistic interpretations. For instance, of the first international temperance conference in Stockholm in 1846, of the 244 delegates, only 4 were American, and none were British (Baird 1866). Moreover, it is surprising that both the United States and the United Kingdom were latecomers to international temperance conferences: it is telling that the primary languages of interaction at such conferences were German and French, and only rarely English – even when held in London or Washington – and that it took twenty-four years for the conference to be held in an English-speaking country (London in 1909), and thirty-five years for it to be held in the United States (Washington in 1920). In sum, having a strong Anglo-American element within the vast transnational temperance movement cannot be equated with Gramscian domination and subordination.

Implications for contemporary transnational communities

Questions of both the rise and the demise of the transnational temperance community have been addressed based on the extent, depth, and regularity of transnational linkages. The lifecycle heuristic has important implications for the study of transnational communities. This chapter suggests that the political influence of transnational communities is in part a function of the depth and breadth of transnational linkages. A nascent community in the incipient or declining stages would be expected to have dramatically less influence on the adoption of national policies than a mature community with extensive linkages with governments and societies around the world.

In the incipient stage, development of the community is contingent upon sporadic, irregular efforts by a small number of devoted, elite transnational activists. During the ascendancy stage, the quantity of transnational linkages expands with the advent of occasional international conferences and early issue-organizations engaged in multiple national settings. The community reaches maturity with the development of frequent and routine transnational linkages through regular international conferences and international NGOs with an explicitly transnational agenda. According to this analysis, the temperance community had matured for over thirty years before the actual adoption of prohibition throughout Europe and North America. This mature stage lasted approximately forty years (1885–1925) before the network began to experience decline and decay, evidenced by the diminishing quantity and regularity of international interaction, and the eventual demise or retooling of the major temperance NGOs.

Transnational communities are communicative structures, which use the power of information, ideas, and strategies to alter the ideational contexts in which states make policies through the dissemination and framing of information. Yet while the network function of these communities has garnered the lion's share of scholarly attention, relatively little consideration has been given to the ways in which such organizations begin, grow, and ultimately decline. Implicit in this discussion is the fact that the potential policy influence is greatest when the community is most mature: in other words, when community linkages are the most robust, transnational communities are most effective at drawing attention to particular issues (agenda-setting), and subsequently influencing actual policy decisions. While transnational communities can influence public sentiments about the appropriateness of government action, they are more effective when they directly incorporate national legislative and executive decision-making elites. In terms of the transnational temperance community, this is most evident in the increasing visibility of official government delegates to international temperance conferences – an outcome of the mature stage of transnational community development.

Contemporary accounts of modern transnational communities, including human rights, women's rights, and environmental protection movements, give little consideration to temporal issues, since these communities are typically still within the ascendant or mature stages of development. These different networks are thought to have begun between the 1950s and 1980s – a brief timeframe in comparison with over a century of temperance network activity. Consequently, consideration must be given to the trajectory of these modern transnational communities: will they continue to mature, or have some already begun to decline? How can activists help ensure that their communities remain healthy, robust, and influential, with a decline in network activity coming only with the ultimate attainment of the movement's goals? Consideration of the historical precursors to modern transnational communities helps to bring such issues into focus.

NOTES

1. This categorization, based upon the extent of transnational informational ties, is similar to the typology used by Jackie Smith, who uses such distinctions to compare different social movement organizations rather than to chart the evolution of a single transnational network over time (Smith 2005).
2. Baird correspondence to ASSU from St. Petersburg, October 20, 1840: *Presbyterian Historical Society, American Sunday School Union Papers, 1817–1915*; Reel 45 Series I, C:1840B, no. 200–202.
3. By 1876, the IOGT had established lodges in the USA, Canada, England, Scotland, Wales, Ireland, France, Belgium, Portugal, Malta, New Zealand, South Africa, Bermuda, East India, Ceylon, British Honduras, British Guiana, Jamaica, Malacca, China, Japan, Natal, Sierra Leone, St. Helena, the Argentine Republic, Trinidad, Grenada and the Bahamas (IOGT 1890).
4. Woman's Christian Temperance Union Series, WCTU National Headquarters, Evanston, IL, Roll 2 (Annual Meeting Minutes): October 30, 1885, Philadelphia, pp. 12, 62–67. See also: WCTU Roll 34, Scrapbook 20 (World's WCTU).
5. Correspondence: Guy Hayler to Francis Smith, February 11, 1896. Guy Hayler Temperance Tracts, Vol. XIV, no. 23.
6. www.iogt.org/index.asp (accessed September 11, 2006).

REFERENCES

Anderson, B. 1991. *Imagined communities*. Second edition. London: Verso.

Baird, R. 1841. *Visit to Northern Europe*, 2 vols., Vol. 2. New York: John S. Taylor & Co.

1851. *The progress and prospects of Christianity in the United States of America with remarks on the subject of slavery in America, and on the intercourse between British and American churches*. London: Partridge and Oakey.

Baird, H. 1866. *The life of the Rev. Robert Baird, D.D.* New York: A. D. F. Randolph.

Bernard, J. 1991. "From fasting to abstinence: The origins of the American temperance movement," in Barrows, S. and Room, R. (eds.), *Drinking: Behavior belief in modern history*. Berkeley: University of California Press, pp. 337–53.

Blocker, J., Jr. 1989. *American temperance movements: Cycles of reform*. Boston: Twayne Publishers.

Blomqvist, J. 1998. "The 'Swedish model' of dealing with alcohol problems: Historical trends and future challenges," *Contemporary Drug Problems* **25** (2): 253–320.

British and Colonial Temperance Congress, London, July 1886. 1886. London: National Temperance Publication Depot.

Brook, S. M. 1972. "The World League against Alcoholism: The attempt to export an American experience." MA thesis, University of Western Ontario.

Bureau fédéral de statistique, Switzerland. 1884. *Question de l'alcoolisme. Exposé comparatif des lois et des expériences de quelques états étrangers, par le bureau fédéral de statistique*. Berne: Imprimerie K.-J. Wyss.

Burns, D. 1889. *Temperance history*, 2 vols. London: National Temperance Publication Depot.

Centennial Temperance Volume: A Memorial of the International Temperance Conference, Held in Philadelphia, June 1876. 1877. New York: National Temperance Society and Publication House.

Couling, S. 1862. *History of the temperance movement in Great Britain and Ireland: From the earliest date to the present time*. London: William Tweedie.

Dorchester, D. 1884. *The liquor problem in all ages*. New York: Phillips & Hunt.

Dunlop, J. 1829. *On the extent and remedy of national intemperance*. Glasgow: William Collins.

Dupré, R. 2004. "The prohibition of alcohol revisited: The U.S. case in international perspective," *Cahier de recherche* **4** (11): 1–28.

Fahey, D. M. 1996. *Temperance and racism: John Bull, Johnny Reb, and the Good Templars*. Lexington: University Press of Kentucky.

Gusfield, J. 1991. "Benevolent repression: Popular culture, social structure and the control of drinking," in Barrows, S., and Room, R. (eds.), *Drinking: Behavior and belief in modern history*. Berkeley: University of California Press, pp. 399–424.

Harrison, B. 1971. *Drink and the Victorians: The temperance question in England, 1815–1872*. London: Faber and Faber.

Hayler, G. 1914. *Prohibition advance in all lands: A study of the world-wide character of the drink question*. Second edition. London: International Prohibition Confederation.

IOGT. 1890. *The leading temperance organisation in the world*. Birmingham: IOGT Grand Lodge of England.

Johnson, W. 1915. *The liquor problem in Russia*. Westerville, OH: American Issue Publishing House.

Kahler, M. 2009. "Networked politics: Agency, power, and governance." in Kahler, M. (ed.), *Networked politics: Agency, power, and governance*. Ithaca, NY: Cornell University Press, pp. 1–20.

Kaufmann, C. D., and Pape, R. A. 1999. "Explaining costly international moral action: Britain's sixty-year campaign against the Atlantic slave trade," *International Organization* **53** (4): 631–68.

Keck, M. and Sikkink, K. 1998. *Activists beyond borders: Advocacy networks in international politics*. Ithaca, NY: Cornell University Press.

Keck, M. and Sikkink, K. 2000. "Historical precursors to modern transnational social movements and networks," in Guidry, J., Kennedy, M. and Zald, M. (eds.), *Globalization and social movements: Culture, power, and the transnational public sphere*. Ann Arbor: University of Michigan Press, pp. 35–53.

Kerr, K. A. 1985. *Organized for prohibition: A new history of the anti-saloon league*. New Haven, CT: Yale University Press.

Klotz, A. 2002. "Transnational activism and global transformations: The anti-apartheid and abolitionist experiences," *European Journal of International Relations* **8** (1): 49–76.

Krout, J. A. 1925. *Origins of prohibition*. New York: Alfred A. Knopf.

Marquis, G. 2004. "'Brewers and distillers paradise': American views of Canadian alcohol policies, 1919 to 1935," *Canadian Review of American Studies* **34** (2): 135–66.

One Hundred Years of Temperance: A Memorial Volume of the Centennial Temperance Conference Held in Philadelphia, PA, September 1885. 1886. New York: National Temperance Society and Publication House.

Petersson, O. 1903. *Goodtemplarordens i Sverige Historia*. Stockholm: Svenska Nykterhetsförlaget.

Pitman, R. 1878. *Alcohol and the state: A discussion of the problem of law as applied to the liquor traffic*. New York: National Temperance Society and Publishing House.

Proceedings of the World's Temperance Convention, Held in London, August 4th and Four Following Days. 1846. London: Charles Gilpin.

Quinn, J. F. 2002. *Father Mathew's crusade*. Amherst, MA: University of Massachusetts Press.

Rorabaugh, W. J. 1979. *The alcoholic republic: An American tradition*. New York: Oxford University Press.

Schrad, M. L. 2004. "Religion, drunkenness, popular mobilization and the state: The rise and record of temperance societies in nineteenth century Russia and Sweden." Unpublished manuscript.

Schrad, M. L. 2010. *The political power of bad ideas: Networks, institutions, and the global prohibition wave*. New York: Oxford University Press.

Smith, J. 2005. "Globalization and transnational social movement organizations," in Davis, G. F., McAdam 'D., Scott, W. R. and Zald M. N. (eds.), *Social movements and organization theory*. New York: Cambridge University Press, pp. 226–48.

Sokolsky, B. A. 1980. *American Sunday School Union papers, 1817–1915: A guide to the microfilm edition*. Sanford, NC: Microfilming Corporation of America.

Strange, D. C. 1984. *British Unitarians against American slavery 1833–65*. Rutherford, NJ: Fairleigh Dickinson University Press.

Tarrow, S. 1998. *Power in movement: Social movements and contentious politics.* Second edition. New York: Cambridge University Press.

Tarrow, S. 2005. *The new transnational activism.* New York: Cambridge University Press.

Thomann, G. 1886. *Some thoughts on the International Temperance Meeting, held at Antwerp in September, 1885.* New York: United States Brewers' Association.

Thomann, G. 1889. *The Second International Temperance Congress, held at Zürich, Switzerland, in the year 1887.* New York: United States Brewers' Association.

Tilly, C. 2004. *Social movements, 1768–2004.* Boulder, CO: Paradigm Publishers.

Tocqueville, A. de. 1956 [1835/1840]. *Democracy in America.* Edited by Richard D. Heffner. Abridged. New York: Mentor Books.

Tyrrell, I. 1991a. *Woman's world, woman's empire: The Woman's Christian Temperance Union in international perspective, 1880–1930.* Chapel Hill, NC: University of North Carolina Press.

Tyrrell, I. 1991b. "Women and temperance in international perspective: The World's WCTU, 1880s–1920s," in Barrows, S. and Room, R. (eds.), *Drinking: Behavior and belief in modern history.* Berkeley, CA: University of California Press, pp. 217–40.

Tyrrell, I. 1994. "Prohibition, American cultural expansion, and the new hegemony in the 1920s: An interpretation," *Histoire sociale/Social History* **27** (54): 413–45.

Whole World's Temperance Convention Held at Metropolitan Hall in the City of New York on Thursday and Friday, Sept. 1st and 2nd, 1853. 1853. New York: Fowlers and Wells.

Winskill, P. T. 1892. *The temperance movement and its workers: A record of social, moral, religious, and political progress,* 3 vols., Vol. 1. London: Blackie & Son, Limited.

12 Industrial democracy in the European Community: trade unions as a defensive transnational community, 1968–1988

Thomas Fetzer

In recent years social scientists and historians alike have emphasized increasingly that national political systems, economies, and societies cannot be understood in isolation from their international environment (Osterhammel 2001; Djelic and Quack 2003). The growing prominence of such concepts as transnational governance (Djelic and Sahlin-Andersson 2006) or the network society (Castells 2000) is indicative of this trend. In the field of European Union studies – the more particular context of this chapter – a similar tendency has led scholars to focus on the "informal politics" (Middlemas 1995) of the EU's multi-level governance system, which is characterized by constant communication and negotiation between supranational, national, and regional policy-makers and non-governmental groups. Studies of transnational networks ranging from the Christian Democrats (Kaiser 2007) to competition lawyers (van Waarden and Drahos 2002) have demonstrated the innovative potential of this approach. However, as emphasized by Mayntz in this volume, most contributions in these literatures concentrate on relational processes of exchange and negotiation, and pay less attention to the "community" aspect of transnational governance, that is, the bonds of shared values, knowledge or skills that underlie processes of transnational group formation.

In this chapter I explore this community aspect in relation to trade unions in the European Community between the late 1960s and late 1980s, and more specifically, their involvement in European debates about industrial democracy. So far, trade unions have not been prominently represented in transnational networks and governance scholarship, which can easily be accounted for by their relative reluctance to approach supranational organizations such as the European Community/Union (EC/EU) as a political space beyond the nation-state (Pasture 2005). In turn, this is usually explained by the fact that

The author gratefully acknowledges funding assistance for this research by the Marie Curie Intra-European Fellowship program (project number 42032).

EC/EU encroachments on national regulatory power with regard to social welfare and industrial relations, the two key areas of trade union interest, have been more tentative than in many other realms of public policy (Streeck 1998).

These assessments are valid but they tell only half of the story. First, a predominantly national orientation in policy approach does not preclude involvement in transnational exchange and networking; indeed, recent evidence from social movement research suggests that the domestic strategies of NGOs are themselves partly informed by encounters with foreign practices (see, for example, Nehring 2005; see also Schrad, and Bartley and Smith in this volume). In this sense the EC/EU can be regarded as one of many transnational arenas for the exchange of ideas and experiences, which feed back into national settings. Second, with regard to supranational EC/EU regulation, the relative under-development of European industrial relations policy does not mean that attempts have been lacking in this direction. In the field of industrial democracy such attempts reach back to the late 1960s (see below), and it is precisely for this reason that the analysis takes the year 1968 as its starting point.

In this chapter I shall argue that trade union responses to these EC initiatives were premised on only one shared objective until the late 1980s, namely that European regulation should not negatively affect the achievements of industrial democracy at the national level. Trade unions were a defensive transnational community – the values and notions of solidarity that are crucial for communities (see Mayntz, and Djelic and Quack in this volume) were not related to European models but to mutual support for the protection of national patterns. In part, this reflected the broader attitude of most national trade unions to European integration, which emphasized subsidiarity in social policy and industrial relations matters. The protection of national rights was given preference to the potential achievement of new rights at the supranational level (Fetzer 2005). At the same time, the defensiveness was also the result of internal ideological disagreements, which made it difficult to agree on guidelines for European action; in this sense the defense of national rights was the "default" option that national delegates could accept. Moreover, given that European regulation affected national systems very differently, outcomes strongly reflected the positions of delegates who felt most threatened by European initiatives, namely German trade union representatives. It was only towards the end of the period under review that the defensive pattern began to be modified. Rather than using European action only to avert EC regulation that could restrict national policy the trade unions now made greater efforts to give workers' participation a European dimension. Defensive postures continued to be important but trade unions shifted from a protection to a protection plus European reregulation approach.

The chapter is divided into three parts. In the first part I explore the transnational dimension of industrial democracy debates since the nineteenth century and provide a brief account of the regulatory agenda of the EC/EU in the industrial democracy field since the late 1960s. The second and main part is dedicated to the analysis of European trade union debates about industrial democracy, and the concomitant emergence of a defensive transnational community since the late 1960s. The third part considers the interaction between European and national developments, focusing on the key case, the Federal Republic of Germany. I conclude with some brief reflections on developments in the period since the late 1980s and about the broader significance of defensive transnational communities.

Industrial democracy as a transnational issue field

In a broad and uncontroversial sense industrial democracy can be defined as the participation of workers and their representatives in the decision-making processes that govern their working lives (Schuller 1985: 4). The debates about the concept's more specific meanings and applications are of course much older than the EU, and the industrial democracy discourse community has always included actors other than trade unions, most importantly "enlightened" employers, social reformers, government officials, and academic experts from various disciplines.

Debates about industrial democracy have had a transnational dimension ever since Robert Owen's first initiatives towards a cooperative movement in the early nineteenth century because they responded to a problem – how to deal with the "labor question" created by industrial capitalism – that was shared across borders (Deutsch 2005). Clearly, industrial democracy meant different things to different actors. For conservatives and most employers, a limited degree of consultation with worker representatives appeared to constitute an instrument for containing social unrest, and for enhancing employee motivation and loyalty to the firm. Trade unions and socialists, by contrast, approached the issue predominantly in terms of how industrial democracy could be used to further employee interests not only in labor market terms, but also with regard to the emancipatory benefits arising from the acquisition of influence over decision-making processes in the economy. But contrasting opinions about how best to achieve these goals also soon led to distinct concepts of industrial democracy promoted by rival currents within the labor movement (socialism, anarchism, syndicalism, and so on).

The emergence of different national institutions of industrial democracy from the late nineteenth century had ambiguous effects. On the one hand, this process reduced the incentive to seek international solutions in the individual field. On the other hand, national institutionalization encouraged exchange through transnational networks, since looking abroad could serve as an inspiration for national institution-building, or, subsequently, as a comparative "check" for the appropriateness of domestic practices (see also Schrad in this volume). The pioneers of *Mitbestimmung* in Germany in the early nineteenth century, for example, were inspired by the model of the *conseil des prud'hommes* in France (Teuteberg 1981: 9–11). Clearly, foreign models had to be adapted to local conditions, and such "acculturation" processes were often very controversial; indeed, one important function of transnational exchange for national actors was that it provided "discursive ammunition," which could be used against domestic opponents in debates about the reform of national institutions (for a UK example see Fox 1985: 265–66).

Against this backdrop, industrial democracy continued to be debated in numerous transnational arenas. The cooperative movement retained a prominent place in these debates (Watkins 1970), as did syndicalist currents within the labor movement (Cole 1923). Following the Vatican's increasing interest in social and labor problems from the late nineteenth century there also emerged a debate about "Christian industrial democracy" (MacLean 1927).

In the post-1945 period the transnational industrial democracy discourse further intensified not least because, next to the "labor question," other considerations became associated with industrial democracy. In the immediate post-War period there was, for example, a lively debate on whether more industrial democracy was needed to prevent another collapse of parliamentary democracy, as witnessed in many European countries during the 1920s and 1930s. Soon, this concern was supplanted by the onset of the Cold War, which turned industrial democracy into a component of the ideological competition between capitalism and communism. Tito's Yugoslavia promoted its concept of worker self-management as a "third way" – again fueling debates at the transnational level (Deutsch 2005: 646–48). Within the Western world the trend towards larger firms, and the associated divorce of ownership and management functions, gave additional importance to the issue (Dartmann 1996: 210ff.). The debate reached its height in the 1960s and 1970s against the backdrop of full employment, growing worker confidence, and the generational change that culminated in "1968." Industrial democracy became a key concern for those on the Left who wished to accelerate change (Coates 1968), as much as for those who promoted modest forms of industrial democracy to contain strikes and social unrest. The growing importance of multinational firms accentuated the transnational character of debates (Piehl 1973).

In response to these developments, and facilitated by the increasing density of cross-border communication and organization in the post-1945 period, the transnational debate on issues of industrial democracy expanded. The issue featured prominently in the work of the OEEC/OECD and of the ILO's International Institute for Labour Studies; growing academic interest found expression in industrial democracy as a permanent topic on the agenda of organizations such as the Industrial Relations Research Association and the International Association of Labour Law. In many countries specialized research institutes were created, which promoted transnational debate through journals and conferences. Alongside academic experts, employers, and government officials, trade union representatives played an important role in such debates (Deutsch 2005: 648f.).

Next to these global or transcontinental arenas, industrial democracy also became associated with the development of regional political integration in post-War Europe. On the one hand, the establishment of the supranational institutions of the European Community (later European Union) simply added another platform for the transnational exchange of ideas and experiences about industrial democracy. This was clearly expressed in the work of specialized agencies such as the European Foundation for the Improvement of Living and Working Conditions, which has played an active role in the debate on industrial democracy since the mid-1970s, with the purpose of disseminating comparative data about the development of industrial democracy models in different European countries, and the promotion of cross-border encounters and mutual learning among actors (Deutsch 2005: 653).

On the other hand, EC/EU involvement in the industrial democracy debate went beyond being just another transnational arena of exchange to facilitate policy transfers across borders. Supranational European regulation itself touched on industrial democracy issues, and therefore the transnational debate became also a debate about a possibly harmonized European industrial democracy "model" that could form the basis for EC/EU legislation.

Reviewing developments since the 1960s this link has become manifest in three key regulatory initiatives whose origins stemmed, on the one hand, from the EC/EU's internal market agenda, which from early on included ideas for a European company law framework with provisions for employee participation, and, on the other hand, from the slowly emerging social policy agenda (see

Höland 2000). First, there was the long debate about the Statute for a European Company (or SE – Societas Europaea), which would allow firms to register under European law as an alternative to the law of individual member states. Following two expert studies on the provisions for worker involvement in such a European Company (Sanders 1967; Lyon-Caen 1970) the Commission presented a first draft Statute (ECS) in 1970, which was transmitted to the Council of Ministers in an amended form in 1975. The draft was fashioned after the German model of industrial democracy, providing for the establishment of a European works council and employee participation in the supervisory board in the form of one-third parity between shareholders, worker representatives, and "neutral" co-opted members (Gold and Schwimbersky 2008: 48–50). However, the proposal never passed the Council, and by the mid-1980s the debate was deadlocked. As part of the Single Market agenda the Commission launched a new attempt in 1988/89, this time adopting a more flexible approach by allowing member states to choose between different models of industrial democracy for European Companies (SEs) registered on their territory. After further debate, and a special report by a group of experts chaired by Lord Davignon in 1997, the flexibility principle was given yet more weight. A new draft directive gave preference to direct negotiations between company and employees to determine industrial democracy arrangements, supplemented by minimum fallback provisions for information, consultation, and board participation in case of failure to reach agreement. In this form the directive passed the Council of Ministers in 2001 (see Gold and Schwimbersky 2008: 52–58).

In a second field – the harmonization of company law in the member states – the Commission's efforts have yet to bear fruit. In contrast to the European Company Statute, which was to create an *additional* and non-obligatory European framework, the regulatory objective was more far-reaching here, since harmonization necessarily affects all already existing firms. Initially, along the lines of the first ECS draft, the Commission proposed a standard model designed largely along the lines of the German system in 1972. As in the case of the ECS, however, this approach triggered resistance in the Council. Notwithstanding subsequent modifications in the direction of greater flexibility (in parallel to the ECS) the directive has never been adopted (Höland 2000: 44–50).

The third area concerns regulation with regard to the information and consultation of employees. There has been a certain overlap here with the ECS proposals – the first Commission initiative in this field was related to the establishment of European works councils as part of the ECS draft in the early 1970s. However, regulatory objectives widened beyond companies adopting the ECS since the mid-1970s, nurtured by the widespread public debates about the growth of multinational firms. The unsuccessful Vredeling directive from 1980 attempted to introduce minimum information and consultation rights for employees in any firm with operations in more than one member state; in the early 1990s the discussion resumed and culminated in the adoption of the European works council directive in 1994. Subsequently, the information and consultation directive from 2001 again widened the regulatory scope to include any firm registered in a member state of the EU (Höland 2000: 55–61).

This was the regulatory framework against whose backdrop trade union debates unfolded from the late 1960s onwards

European trade unions as a defensive transnational community

The trade union movement has a long tradition of international activity, going back to the early nineteenth century and leading to the participation of unionists from many countries in the short-lived First International between 1864 and 1876. The first stable international organizations emerged in the 1880s in a number of industries. In 1903 the first international confederation of national union centers was created (van der Linden 2000). While internal ideological disputes had been strong already during the nineteenth century the movement formally split after World War I with the emergence of the separate Socialist, Communist, and Christian Internationals, a division that was reinforced as a result of the Cold War after 1945. Only recently, the merger of the former Socialist and Christian Internationals into the International Federation of Trade Unions (IFTU), and the affiliation of most former Communist unions with the IFTU, strongly reduced divisions within the international movement (van der Linden 2000: 155–71). In the post-1945 period there was also a process of regionalization as separate trade union bodies were set up to deal with the specific situations in different continents. In Europe this process was further accentuated by the onset of European integration. Already in 1958, prompted by the Treaty of Rome, the autonomous European Trade Union Secretariat (ETUS) was set up, comprising the national confederations of the six founding countries. In 1969, the ETUS was renamed the European Confederation of Free Trade Unions (ECFTU), before being transformed into the European Trade Union Confederation (ETUC) in 1973, which included not only the organizations of the new EC members Denmark, Ireland, and Britain, but also the trade unions of the EFTA countries. Further enlargements occurred in line with the accession of new members to the EC/EU (see Gobin 1996).

As already emphasized, trade unions have been active participants in the transnational debates about industrial democracy since the nineteenth century. In the post-1945 period this involvement further intensified as trade union delegates promoted worker participation in international organizations such as the ILO and the OECD. At the regional European level, too, industrial democracy became an important issue, perhaps most clearly demonstrated by the fact that a special working group entitled "democratization of the economy" was formed soon after the creation of the ETUS, and became a standing committee by the mid-1960s. Initially, the committee's three to four annual meetings focused on reports on industrial democracy developments in different European countries, and their discussion, at times also in the form of special seminars or conferences. Indeed, this exchange of ideas and experiences remained an important function throughout the committee's history. In the 1970s, for example, there were vivid debates on the new German codetermination legislation, the plans for company law reforms in France and the UK proposed by the "Sudreau" and "Bullock" committees, or Italian trade unions' initiatives to promote industrial democracy by extending the scope of collective bargaining. In this respect, the ETUS/ECFTU/ETUC deliberations simply continued the much older tradition of transnational exchange of ideas and experiences.

Industrial democracy and supranational legislation

From 1968, however, the agendas of meetings became dominated by debates about developments in industrial democracy at the European level – in response to the first EC initiatives with regard to the harmonization of company law. This transformed the character of gatherings from the previous informal exchanges of ideas to the discussion of common positions vis-à-vis the European institutions.

Finding common positions, however, soon turned out to be extraordinarily difficult. Partly, this was the result of the different emphases given to particular aspects of industrial democracy in different countries – be it with regard to the normative basis (law or voluntary bargaining), the level (workplace, enterprise, and/or macroeconomic), or the degree (consultation, joint regulation with employers, unilateral "workers' control") of industrial democracy arrangements.[1]

Even more importantly, different industrial democracy arrangements were linked to contrasting notions of trade union purpose and identity, which were brought out in sharp relief as EC legislation held out the prospect of harmonization across borders. Two issues were of particular importance. First, there was the question of whether the representation of employees should be the exclusive privilege of trade unions, or whether a "second channel" of interest representation through works councils established by law was acceptable or even desirable. This question loomed large in the deliberations on the European Company provisions for European works councils in the early 1970s, and again during the debate about the Vredeling directive in the early 1980s.[2] For the proponents of a dual channel system – first and foremost the German DGB – this was simply the extension of a successful domestic model of how to use the statutory rights of works councils for the benefit of trade unions in terms of labor market interests and organizational stability (see Streeck 1981). Those defending the "single channel" principle, not least the British TUC, associated works councils with employer attempts to dilute collective bargaining, and hence saw them as devices that could weaken trade union power.

Second, European Community regulation of company law raised the issue of the participation of worker representatives in company boards. This was a still more contentious matter, and it dominated in particular the early discussions within the ETUS/ECFTU about the European Company Statute in the late 1960s and early 1970s.[3] The issue resurfaced in the debates on the directive for national company law harmonization in the late 1970s, and on the revised ECS in the late 1980s. Usually led by representatives of the Belgian FTGB one group of delegates (also comprising French and Italian trade unionists) argued that a codetermination system was unacceptable because it would make trade unions coresponsible for company decisions, which would unduly restrict their freedom and violate their identity as a countervailing power in the economy and society. Based on a conflictual outlook on industrial relations they advocated the alternative concept of "workers' control" (see Coates 1968), with an emphasis on comprehensive information disclosure requirements, which would make it possible to control the operations of the firm from "outside." By contrast, the German and Dutch delegates – after 1973 assisted by their Scandinavian colleagues – promoted board codetermination, which they saw as a means of enhancing trade union influence in the economy without compromising their identity as representing workers' interests. As Hyman has demonstrated with regard to Germany, this position reflected a much less class-focused approach, which sought to combine the representation of member interests with the acceptance of coresponsibility for economic decision-making (Hyman 2001: Ch. 6).

Given these fundamental disagreements the most likely outcome of delib-erations would have been a failure to agree on a common position. In other words, it is surprising that agreements were made, even though it often took a very long time to reach them. What is even more surprising is that these common positions differed remarkably in their substance. For instance, the committee spoke in favor of a unitary German-style codetermination system as part of the European Company Statute throughout the first half of the 1970s, while the parallel debates about the Fifth directive on company law harmonization resulted in a document advocating a flexible "menu" of differ-ent forms of employee participation.[4]

To account for the fact that such common positions could be reached despite fundamental controversies I propose that trade unions be conceptua-lized as a defensive transnational community. What united them was not so much the urge to find political compromises that could enhance trade union power at the European level as the determination to prevent negative reper-cussions of European developments on national achievements as regards industrial democracy – repercussions that could result either from the direct legal impact of EC directives and/or from the more indirect impact of European initiatives on domestic *debates* in the industrial democracy field. To understand the dynamics of this defensive community it is instructive to look at two key debates in 1968/70 and 1973/77 related to the problem of employee participation in company boards.

The first of the two debates was triggered by the publication of the draft European Company Statute by law professor Pieter Sanders in 1967. Sanders's study, while refraining from concrete recommendations, pointed to the dilemma that, given the different national regulations of employee participa-tion in company boards, the ECS risked either imposing a codetermination system on all countries, or creating "islands" free of participation in a country such as Germany (Sanders 1967: 76–89). Against this backdrop the clashing trade union visions were brought out in sharp relief during the first half of 1968. Several heated exchanges between DGB and FTGB delegates revolved around what kind and degree of responsibility trade unions could or should accept in contemporary industrial societies.[5] Various compromise formulae were tabled.

However, no progress was made until, in late 1968, the German represen-tatives declared that they could not accept a formula that diverged too far from the domestic DGB position. IG Metall Chairman Brenner asked for the solidarity of non-German delegates to avoid a situation in which European developments weakened the position of trade unions in the Federal Republic in the debates about the reform of codetermination (see below).[6] This brought about a decisive shift, as documents of the ETUS/ECFTU secretariat, under strong DGB influence, now advocated a German-style system, including supervisory board representation in the form of one-third parity between shareholders, worker representatives, and "neutral" co-opted members.[7] DGB pressure was crucial in this process, but the outcome was not a German "diktat." The Dutch and Luxembourg delegates were largely sympathetic to the German position in any case, while the Belgian FTGB maintained its oppositional stance until the very end. Decisive were the attitudes of the French and Italian representatives who, while doctrinally rather on the FTGB side, were prepared to go along because they accepted the German solidarity pledge. One Italian CISL representative remarked that European decisions should not endanger the struggle of "our German friends" for enhanced codetermination.[8] At the same time, this defensive notion of solidarity also reflected a belief that the domestic impact of the European Company Statute in France and Italy was likely to be minimal – in contrast to the situation in the Federal Republic.

The second key debate started in 1973 after the Commission had presented a draft for the Fifth directive for the harmonization of company law, which again included provisions for employee participation in supervisory boards after the German model of the 1952 Works Constitution Act (Höland 2000: 44–50). The debate revealed a similar split of opinions as in the case of the ECS, yet it soon became clear that the outcome would be rather different. The skeptics of codetermination stressed that they could not accept a position along ECS lines since this time the stakes were much higher: rather than offering an additional legal form to multinational firms the new legislation would directly affect *all existing companies* throughout the EC.[9] The associated claim about the need to respect and protect the different national customs and regulations received further support from the new ETUC members from Scandinavia and the British Isles. Against this backdrop, the compromise formula reached by the ETUC in 1977 asked for a revision of the directive to provide for worker participation in one-tier as well as two-tier board structures, and, moreover, to leave it to employees and their representatives whether they wished to be represented in boards, or set up an alternative external "trade union control committee."[10]

Conceptualizing the trade unions as a defensive community allows us to understand why the outcome of this debate was so different from the one related to the European Company Statute. The crucial difference was that

European regulation was likely to affect national systems of industrial democracy and reform debates in a much more far-reaching way in the case of the Fifth Directive, and it was also likely to affect countries more evenly than in the case of the ECS. As a consequence, German delegates in particular, despite their clearly discernible misgivings about the move towards more flexibility, could not expect the same degree of solidarity from their European colleagues as in the ECS debate. What the German delegates could achieve was that the ETUC commitment to flexibility was qualified with the principle of "equivalence" between the different models of participation. The criteria for "equivalence," in turn, had a clear German yardstick, basically transposing the rights of supervisory board members to the "trade union control committee": the latter should hold its meetings in parallel with the board and should have the right to appoint board members, as well as to consent with regard to strategic company decisions, for example, plant relocation or closure.[11]

Thus, a focus on the defense of established national patterns of industrial democracy became the principal shared objective, allowing trade union delegates to overcome fundamental ideological cleavages. This, however, raises the question of why unions preferred defensive aims to that of enhancing their power at the European level itself. One answer, of course, leads back to the ideological clashes between different models of industrial democracy. Put simply, there was no realistic option for powerful European campaigns because opinions about the appropriate strategies diverged far too widely. In this sense, the defense of national rights was, so to speak, the "default" option, which all national delegates could accept.

But there is another, perhaps more important element that needs to be considered. Defensive trade union postures not only reflected the sheer impossibility of bringing about a united European trade union front but also the broader attitude of most national trade unions to European integration, which emphasized subsidiarity in social policy and industrial relations matters. Europe was primarily seen as an economic space with important implications for national economic growth, employment, and welfare – but not so much as a political arena in which trade unions needed to act (Fetzer 2005).

The importance of this broader framework for industrial democracy debates becomes clear if we look at the more general pattern of trade union involvement in these debates. What is striking here is the almost complete absence of autonomous trade union initiatives to advance industrial democracy at the European level between the late 1960s and the late 1980s – at a time when organized labor pushed for innovation in the industrial democracy field across the continent. Regulation of industrial democracy was perceived to be the competence of nation-states – unless it concerned issues with a cross-border dimension.

Of course there were a number of such issues already in the 1970s, notably related to the regulation of multinational companies. But here too, initiatives at the European level were slow to develop. The ECFTU/ETUC organized a number of conferences in the early 1970s but already these activities triggered skeptical reactions among some national affiliates, who preferred to deal with multinational firms within the framework of international union bodies. In 1975 the ETUC executive committee adopted a resolution urging EFTA and the European Community to provide a legal framework for the information and consultation of workers in multinational companies, but little was done to follow up the decision.[12] Still at the time of the struggle over the Vredeling directive in the early 1980s Socialist members of the European Parliament complained about a lack of trade union support in the face of the concerted efforts of European and American business interests to obstruct the legislation.[13]

Trade union impact on EC/EU decision-making

Against this backdrop, it should not come as a surprise that the trade union impact on European institutions in the field of industrial democracy was very limited until the late 1980s. Positions adopted on the basis of a defensive logic could have a certain influence at times, particularly in the early 1970s when the strong German imprint on European trade union positions reso-nated with widespread admiration for the German codetermination system across the Continent. It is clear, for example, that the trade unions' endorse-ment of parity participation on boards had a direct influence on the draft European Company Statute in 1975. After all, the Commission needed some legitimate grounds to justify its recommendation of codetermination against the outright opposition of European employers and despite the skeptical conclusions reached in the studies by Sanders (1967) and Lyon-Caen (1970). In fact, Sanders's study had itself pointed to the importance of the European trade unions' stance; while cautioning against any unitary solutions for the ECS he suggested that such a solution might perhaps be achieved if the trade unions were to favor a specific model of participation at the European level (Sanders 1967: 77). The Commission's 1975 draft even proposed exactly the same one-third parity formula that had been endorsed by the ECFTU earlier.

However, the failure of the 1975 Statute to pass the Council of Ministers indicates that occasional trade union influence on the Commission did not translate into legislative outcomes. There are even indications that the lack of a political rather than a symbolic compromise among the unions at European level left dissenting affiliates free to use their national lobby channels against ETUS/ECFTU/ETUC positions.[14] In any case, given the predominant focus on the protection of national achievements, the failure of legislation was not a major problem; from this perspective no regulation was better than regulation that had negative repercussions for union strength at the national level.

It was not before the campaign for European works councils in the late 1980s that the trade unions developed a serious autonomous industrial democracy initiative at the European level, helped by the conclusion of a number of voluntary agreements in French and German multinational firms since the mid-1980s, and the adoption of the EC Social Charter in 1989. A strong trade union lobby contributed to the passage of the directive in 1994, and it was followed by further initiatives, which indicate a new phase of trade union policies on industrial democracy. Rather than using European action to avert unfavorable EC regulation that could restrict national policy greater efforts were made to give workers' participation a European dimension (see Knudsen *et al.* 2007). Before offering some final reflections on the extent to which this marks a fundamental break with the past the analysis will briefly turn to examine in more detail the specific role the German DGB played in the emergence of a defensive transnational trade union community in the 1960s and 1970s. This will also illustrate the mechanisms of interaction between national and transnational communities in the field of industrial democracy.

The interaction between transnational and national communities: the case of the German DGB

As we have seen, the defense of national achievements in industrial democracy against potential negative effects arising from EC regulation became the core shared objective of European trade unionists from the late 1960s onwards. European solidarity did not stem from a joint commitment to a European model of industrial democracy but from the shared commitment to protect national patterns. We have also seen that German trade unionists played a crucial role in the emergence of this defensive transnational community. The question of why German DGB delegates felt particularly affected by EC developments, and how the interaction between German and European debates played out – that is, how German concerns shaped European debates, and how the latter fed back into the German domestic scene – remains open.

As for the causes the answer is simple: among EC countries German codetermination was the most advanced system of industrial democracy in terms of employees' participation rights in corporate decision-making. Regardless of the fact that these rights were heavily qualified by obligations it is clear that German trade unions had most to lose from European regulation in the 1960s and 1970s, all the more so since by the mid-1960s, having by and large abandoned ideas of socialist planning and public ownership with the 1963 Dusseldorf program, the DGB had adopted *Mitbestimmung* as its central political objective (Schneider 2000: Ch. 12). The cornerstone of trade union ambitions was to spread the advanced codetermination pattern of the coal and steel industry (parity in supervisory boards, labor director on the management board), which had been introduced as a result of contingencies in the Allied occupation policy (Dartmann 1996), to the entire economy (outside the coal and steel sectors only one-third of supervisory board members were employee representatives). Between the late 1960s and mid-1970s, importantly, the domestic debate on these issues reached a critical stage after the government, in 1967, appointed a commission under Kurt Biedenkopf to review codetermination experiences and make suggestions for the future. The Commission's 1970 report intensified controversies between unions and employers, and within the SPD–FDP coalition, and it was only in 1976 that a compromise was eventually reached (see Schneider 2000: 347–48).[15]

Against this backdrop the dynamic between national and European debates unfolded as company law harmonization at EC level became a major concern for the DGB's domestic agenda. Already in February 1967, shortly after the release of the Sanders study for a European Company Statute, several members of the DGB board pointed to European harmonization aspirations as a "deadly threat" to *Mitbestimmung*. IG Metall Chairman Brenner, for example, warned against German employers' aspirations to using European developments to reduce codetermination in the Federal Republic.[16] Subsequently the issue was discussed by the DGB board on several occasions, and it was also put on the agenda of the special committee, which had been created to promote the idea of *Mitbestimmung* during the proceedings of the Biedenkopf commission. The body elaborated a set of proposals for the ECS, and also for the more general task of popularizing codetermination internationally.[17]

From the DGB's point of view the potential danger of EC regulation was twofold: first, and directly, there was the danger that the European Company Statute, and/or a general harmonization of company law, would encourage

Mitbestimmungsflucht ("flight from codetermination"), whether because companies could be legally registered in Germany without the imposition of codetermination rules under national law, or, in the case of a flexible solution, because the possibility for such a registration in other EC countries would lead German firms to relocate their head office in order to circumvent *Mitbestimmung*. More indirectly, the DGB saw its position endangered by the repercussions of European developments for the *domestic debate* on the reform of codetermination launched by the Biedenkopf commission. Here, debates at the European level could entail a weakening of the unions' case for the extension of codetermination in Germany – for example, if European regulations were based on the old German model of codetermination outside the coal and steel industry. Though perhaps exaggerated these fears were not completely unfounded; at times leading employers' representatives such as Hanns Martin Schleyer attacked the DGB's domestic push for parity codetermination as "anti-European" because it would continue to obstruct harmonization of European company law.[18] German employers, as demonstrated by the later BDA/BDI action to challenge the 1976 codetermination law in the Constitutional Court, were determined to "freeze" board participation in the form of the one-third formula of the 1952 Works Constitution Act; "Europe" provided one more strategic element with which to achieve that objective.

Among the DGB's strategic objectives in countering this threat strong emphasis was put on the "popularization" of *Mitbestimmung* within the European trade union movement. DGB president Rosenberg argued as early as 1967 that this was particularly important because employer attacks drew their legitimacy partly from the argument that the harmonization of European regulation based on the German model would not be acceptable in other countries – not only for employers but equally for many trade unions.[19] One aspect of this was to emphasize the merits of codetermination in European trade union circles, and also through bilateral contacts, with a view to encouraging foreign labor movements to implement codetermination in their own countries.[20] The other major objective was to influence European trade union deliberations about the Europeanization of company law in a way that eliminated potential risks to the domestic codetermination campaign. In February 1969, for example, the DGB board adopted a list of "essentials" with regard to the European Company Statute (parity representation in supervisory boards, minimum codecision functions for supervisory board members), for which the German delegates subsequently invoked the solidarity of their European colleagues.[21]

The DGB thus considered it essential to create a shared vision among European trade unionists with regard to this agenda. As we have seen, the German confederation was successful with this solidarity pledge because it resonated with the shared broader defensive objectives of the European trade union community. This support was crucial for the subsequent lobbying of the EC to come up with proposals that took account of the aspirations of German trade unions for extended supervisory board codetermination. Incidentally, that lobbying found a sympathetic ear in the Commission given that the DGB had an erstwhile ally in Wilhelm Haferkamp, until 1967 head of the DGB's economic department, and from 1970 European Commissioner for Internal Market affairs – the DG in charge of European company law harmonization projects. Between 1970 and 1975, in the crucial phase of the ECS redrafting process, DGB leaders kept close contacts with Haferkamp and also, after 1974, with his Danish successor Finn Olav Gundelach.[22]

The example of the European Company Statute from 1975 also demonstrates that German unions, once they had achieved a favorable outcome at the European level, set out to use the results in the domestic debate. In 1975, for example, the DGB argued that special provisions for the representation of "executive employees," as foreseen in the domestic codetermination reform, were "out of touch" with broader trends at the European level, where no such ideas had ever been discussed. More broadly it was emphasized that the Commission proposal, taken together with the introduction of codetermination in a number of countries, represented a European trend, which confirmed the legitimacy of German union demands for an extension of *Mitbestimmung* in the Federal Republic.[23]

These examples also confirm once again that the German unions' European engagement arose predominantly from domestic concerns. The aim was not so much to widen its scope of action at the European level as to ensure that potential or actual European regulation had a positive rather than a negative impact on domestic DGB campaigns. As a matter of fact, little changed in this logic until the late 1980s when, as outlined above, the problem of information and consultation in multinational firms led unions to take a more active interest in European regulation as an end in itself. Indeed, German unions played a leading role in this reorientation, as evidenced by the fact that German firms were among the first to set up European works councils. The main driver of change was the Europeanization of many large German companies in response to the Single European Market since the mid-1980s. Given that this Europeanization could lead to a slow erosion of the effectiveness of domestic arrangements in industrial democracy the exclusive focus on the defense of the latter was considered to be no longer sufficient.[24] After a controversial internal debate between 1988 and 1990 the DGB shifted its position towards using European action not only as a means to avert unfavorable EC regulation that could restrict national policy, but also to intensify efforts to give workers' participation a European dimension. The European policy program adopted by the DGB board, and later confirmed by the 1990 union convention, emphasized that effective protection of national codetermination achievements now required at least a minimum degree of reregulation at the European level.

Conclusions

European trade unions have been part of a transnational debate on industrial democracy since the mid-nineteenth century. What has distinguished them from other groups (employers, social reformers, academic experts) is that they have approached the issue predominantly from the perspective of how to use industrial democracy to further employee interests, not only in labor market terms, but also with regard to the emancipatory benefits arising from obtaining influence over decision-making processes in the economy. From early on it became clear, however, that the cohesion stemming from this common purpose could be seriously compromised by contrasting opinions on how to achieve these goals (for a parallel threat in the early period of the community of liberal intellectuals see Plehwe in this volume).

This chapter has demonstrated that European trade union debates between the late 1960s and the late 1980s continued this pattern yet also brought a decisive transformation. As issues of industrial democracy became part of the supranational regulatory agenda of the European Community from the late 1960s, trade union delegates turned into a community of interests whose core objective was to ensure that EC legislation in the field of industrial democracy satisfied the aims and ambitions of the organized labor movement. It soon became clear, however, that this community had a predominantly defensive character, focusing on the protection of national achievements rather than aspirations to new rights at the European level. Partly this was the result of fundamental ideological disagreements, which made it difficult to agree on guidelines for common European action. On the other hand, this pattern also reflected the broader attitude of most national trade unions to European integration with its emphasis on subsidiarity in social policy and industrial relations matters.

In the late 1980s the situation changed. The campaign for a European works council directive signaled for the first time that European trade unions were no longer merely reacting defensively to European Community proposals but were starting to develop autonomous initiatives to give employee participation a European dimension. A great deal of debate has ensued about the extent to which this change represents a radical break with the past (see Streeck 1997; Lecher *et al.* 1999). There is enough evidence to suggest that a focus on the defense of national achievements continues to be a crucial motivation of trade unions (Streeck 1998). In the field of industrial democracy this is most clearly expressed in the strong ETUC focus on ensuring that renewed attempts for the creation of a European Company Statute during the 1990s were designed to minimize risks for domestic arrangements – again with a particular focus on the situation in Germany. As a matter of fact, as long as social citizenship rights continue to be vested predominantly at the level of the member states, trade unions will have a strong incentive to adopt such an approach. At the same time, there is also clear evidence that the accelerating processes of economic internationalization, which put pressure on these social citizenship regimes, have pushed trade unions towards reregulation at the European level. This is all the more plausible as the main development in industrial democracy in this respect – European works councils – is part of a broader reorientation of trade union strategies towards the EU, which perceives Europe increasingly also as a potential "savior" for national institutions threatened by globalization (Fetzer 2008).

What are the broader implications of this case study for the emergence of defensive transnational communities? At the most basic level, the evidence suggests that such defensive communities are likely to emerge when actors face the prospect of transnational regulatory interference with national practices – it was the onset of EC regulation that led trade unions to adopt their defensive stance. Support for this conclusion can be found in the growing literature about Eurosceptic movements, many of which have emerged in opposition to supranational European legislation (Taggart and Szczerbiak 2008). Likewise, anti-globalization groups direct their protests against regulatory institutions such as the IMF and the WTO, though it is important to distinguish between those who oppose these institutions in principle and those who push for their reform. Clearly, the latter stance corresponds to the attitude of the European trade unions with regard to EU regulation since the early 1990s.

A second set of implications can be derived from the factors that prevented trade unions from adopting a more proactive European strategy during the 1960s and 1970s. In this perspective, the emergence of a defensive transnational community depends on the degree to which the constituent national members have vested domestic rights in a given field, and, moreover, on the degree to which these different national systems are compatible with each other. Strong divergence will entail ideological conflicts and will make common action at the transnational level unlikely, in turn fostering the prospects of a defensive community. On the other hand, groups with weakly entrenched rights at the national level will lack the incentive for defensiveness. It would be interesting in this regard to compare the trade union case systematically with other communities with strongly entrenched domestic positions – for example, institutions of higher education or local/regional self-government bodies – which have displayed a tendency towards defensiveness vis-à-vis European institutions in the past (Smets 1998; du Réau 2000).

Finally, the transformation of trade union attitudes from the late 1980s onwards raises the question of historical change: are defensive communities a thing of the past, bound to slowly disappear as communities adapt to a new globalizing world? Judging from the case study evidence little points to such a radical conclusion (see also Harvey and Maclean in this volume). As we have seen, change has been partial in the case of the unions and, still more importantly, their "European turn" appears itself partly underpinned by a defensive logic that envisions EU regulation as a new protective buffer against the effects of economic globalization. Indeed, this is a logic that seems to have gained ground in many other areas of regulation – witness, for example, the European dimension of the new "economic patriotism" discourse in France. Rather than sounding the death knell of defensive communities globalization may encourage the reconfiguration of such communities at a different level.

NOTES

1. See, for example, Minutes of the meeting of the Committee on the Democratisation of the Economy, March 16, 1978, in: Archive International Institute for Social History Amsterdam (IISH), Collection ETUC, part II, file 2189.
2. See, for example, Minutes of the meeting of the Committee on the Democratisation of the Economy, April 5, 1973, in: IISH, ETUC, part I, file 2171.
3. See, for example, Protokoll der Sitzung des Exekutivausschusses des Europäischen Gewerkschaftssekretariats, January 29, April 25, 1968, in: IISH, ETUC, part I, files 471, 473.
4. Europäischer Bund Freier Gewerkschaften, Forderungen des EBFG zur Mitwirkung der Arbeitnehmer in der EAG, March 17, 1970, in: Archiv der sozialen Demokratie Bonn (AdsD), Bestand DGB, 24/704; Bemerkungen des EGB zum Grünbuch der EG-Kommission über die Mitbestimmung der Arbeitnehmer und die Struktur der Gesellschaften, January 19, 1977, in: IISH, ETUC, part II, file 2190.

5. See, for example, Protokoll der Sitzung des Exekutivausschusses des Europäischen Gewerkschaftssekretariats, April 25, 1968, in: IISH, ETUC, part I, file 473.

6. Procés-Verbal de la réunion du comité executif, December 5, 1968, in: IISH, ETUC, part I, file 476.

7. Europäischer Bund Freier Gewerkschaften, Forderungen des EBFG zur Mitwirkung der Arbeitnehmer in der EAG, March 17, 1970, in: AdsD, DGB, 24/704.

8. Procés-Verbal de la réunion du comité executif, December 5, 1968, in: IISH, ETUC, part I, file 476.

9. See, for example, Minutes of the meeting of the Committee on the Democratisation of the Economy, April 5, 1973, in: IISH, ETUC, part I, file 2171.

10. Bemerkungen des EGB zum Grünbuch der EG-Kommission über die Mitbestimmung der Arbeitnehmer und die Struktur der Gesellschaften, January 19, 1977, in: IISH, ETUC, part II, file 2190.

11. Bemerkungen des EGB zum Grünbuch der EG-Kommission über die Mitbestimmung der Arbeitnehmer und die Struktur der Gesellschaften, January 19, 1977, in: IISH, ETUC, part II, file 2190.

12. "Stand der Beratungen im Ausschuß 'Demokratisierung der Wirtschaft' zu der Frage einer Arbeitnehmervertretung in herrschenden Konzernunternehmen" (insbesondere in multinationalen Konzernen), October 24, 1975, in: AdsD, DGB, 24/1310.

13. Die Vredeling-Richtlinie: Eine Fallstudie zur demokratischen Kontrolle auf europäischer Ebene, undated, in: IISH, ETUC, part II, file 2202.

14. Mitteilung der Abteilung Europäischen Integration an die Mitglieder des Geschäftsführenden Bundesvorstands, May 8, 1973, in: AdsD, DGB, 24/2099.

15. The compromise formula underpinning the 1976 *Mitbestimmungsgesetz* provided for numerical parity in supervisory boards in firms with more than 2,000 employees, but reserving one seat on the workers' side for "executive employees," and, moreover, giving the employers' side the casting vote in cases of stalemate.

16. Protokoll der Sitzung des Bundesvorstandes des Deutschen Gewerkschaftsbundes, February 7, 1967, in: AdSD, DGB, 5/DGAI, 535.

17. See Protokoll der Sitzung des Bundesvorstandes des Deutschen Gewerkschaftsbundes, September 5, 1967, February 4, 1969, in: AdSD, DGB, 5/DGAI, 535, 536.

18. See letter from Walter Braun (ETUC) to Detlev Hensche, DGB Abteilung Gesellschaftspolitik, November 30, 1973, in: AdsD, DGB, 24/1518.

19. See letter from Walter Braun (ETUC) to Detlev Hensche, DGB Abteilung Gesellschaftspolitik, November 30, 1973, in: AdsD, DGB, 24/1518.

20. Little is known about these activities so far, and it is beyond the scope of this chapter to analyse them in detail.

21. Protokoll der Sitzung des Bundesvorstands des DGB, February 4, 1969, in: AdsD, DGB, 5/DGAI 461.

22. Aktenvermerk der Abteilung Gesellschaftspotlik, April 10, 1975, in: AdsD, DGB, 24/2077.

23. Deutscher Gewerkschaftsbund, Protokoll 10. Ordentlicher Bundeskongreß, May 25–30, 1975, p. 125.

24. See Protokoll der Sitzung des Bundesvorstandes des DGB, December 5, 1989, in: AdsD, DGB, 5/DGAI, 553.

REFERENCES

Castells, M. 2000. *The rise of the network society*, Second edition. Oxford: Basil Blackwell.

Coates, K. 1968. *Can the workers run industry?* London: Sphere.

Cole, G. D. H. 1923. *Workshop organization*. Oxford: Clarendon Press.

Dartmann, C. 1996. *Re-distribution of power, joint consultation or productivity coalitions? Labour and postwar reconstruction in Germany and Britain, 1945–1953*. Bochum: Brockmeyer.

Deutsch, S. 2005. "A researcher's guide to worker participation, labor and economic and industrial democracy," *Economic and Industrial Democracy* **26** (4): 645–56.

Djelic, M.-L., and Quack, S. 2003. *Globalization and institutions: Redefining the rules of the economic game*. Cheltenham: Edward Elgar.

Djelic, M.-L., and Sahlin-Andersson, K. 2006. *Transnational governance. Institutional dynamics of regulation*. Cambridge University Press.

du Réau, E. 2000. "La Conférence des recteurs des Universitées européennes : une expérience pionnière de coopération universitaire," in Bachoud, A. (ed.), *Les Intellectuels et l'Europe de 1945 à nos jours*. Paris: Publications Universitaires Denis Diderot, pp. 243–54.

Fetzer, T. 2005. "Europäische Strategien deutscher Gewerkschaften in historischer Perspektive," in Knodt, M. and Finke, B. (eds.), pp. 299–318.

Fetzer, T. 2008. "European Works Councils as risk communities: The case of General Motors," *European Journal of Industrial Relations* **14** (3): 289–308.

Fox, A. 1985. *History and heritage: The social origins of the British industrial relations systems*. London: Allen & Unwin.

Gobin, C. 1996. *Consultation et concertation sociales à l'échelle de la Communauté économique européenne. Etude des positions et stratégies de la Confédération européenne des syndicats (1958–1991)*. Dissertation, Université Libre de Bruxelles.

Gold, M. and Schwimbersky, S. 2008. "The European Company Statute: Implications for industrial relations in the European Union," *European Journal of Industrial Relations* **14** (1): 46–64.

Höland, A. 2000. *Mitbestimmung in Europa: Rechtliche und politische Regelungen*. Frankfurt a.M.: Campus.

Hyman, R. 2001. *Understanding European trade unionism: Between class, market and society*. London: Sage.

Kaiser, W. 2007. *Christian democracy and the origins of European union*. Cambridge University Press.

Knudsen, H., Whittall, M. and Huijgen, F. 2007. "European works councils and the problem of identity," in Whittall, M., Knudsen, H. and Huijgen, F. (eds.), *Towards a European labour identity. The case of the European works council*. London: Routledge.

Lecher, W. *et al.* 1999, *The establishment of European Works Councils: From information committee to social actor*. Aldershot: Ashgate.

Lyon-Caen, G. 1970. *Contribution a l'étude des modes de représentation des intérets des travailleurs dans le cadre des sociétés anonymes européennes*. Brussels: European Commission.

MacLean, D. A. 1927. "Christian industrial democracy: Its moral basis," *International Journal of Ethics* **37** (4): 377–89.

Middlemas, K. 1995. *Orchestrating Europe: The informal politics of the European Union, 1973–95*. London: Harper Collins.

Nehring, H. 2005. "National internationalists: British and West German protests against nuclear weapons: The politics of transnational communication and the social history of the Cold War, 1957–1964," *Contemporary European History*, **14**: 559–82.

Osterhammel, J. 2001. "Transnationale Gesellschaftsgeschichte: Erweiterung oder Alternative?," *Geschichte und Gesellschaft* **27**: 464–79.

Pasture, P. 2005. "Trade unions as a transnational movement in the European space 1955–65," in Kaiser, W. and Starie, P. (eds.), *Transnational European Union: Towards a common political space*. London: Routledge, pp. 109–30.

Piehl, E. 1973. *Multinationale Konzerne und internationale Gewerkschaftsbewegung. Ein Beitrag zur Analyse und zur Strategie der Arbeiterbewegung im international organisierten Kapitalismus insbesondere in Westeuropa*. Frankfurt a.M.: Europäische Verlagsanstalt.

Sanders, P. 1967. *Projet d'un statut des sociétés anonymes européennes*. Brussels: European Commission.

Schneider, M. 2000. *Kleine Geschichte der Gewerkschaften: Ihre Entwicklung in Deutschland von den Anfängen bis heute*, Second edition. Bonn: Dietz.

Schuller, T. 1985. *Democracy at work*. Oxford University Press.

Smets, I. 1998. "Les régions se mobilisent–quel lobby regional à Bruxelles?," in Claeys, P. (ed.), *Lobbyisme, pluralisme et intégration européenne*. Brussels: Presses Interuniversitaires Européennes, pp. 303–27.

Streeck, W. 1981. *Gewerkschaftliche Organisationsprobleme in der sozialstaatlichen Demokratie*. Königstein/Taunus.

Streeck, W. 1997. "Neither European nor works councils: A reply to Paul Knutsen," *Economic and Industrial Democracy* **18** (2): 325–37.

Streeck, W. 1998. "Gewerkschaften zwischen Nationalstaat und Europäischer Union," *WSI-Mitteilungen* **51** (1): 1–14.

Taggart, P. and Szczerbiak, A. (eds.) 2008. *Opposing Europe? The Comparative Party Politics of Euroscepticism*. Oxford University Press.

Teuteberg, H.-J. 1981. "Ursprünge und Entwicklung der Mitbestimmung in Deutschland," in *Mitbestimmung. Ursprünge und Entwicklung. Referate und Diskussionsbeiträge der 5. öffentlichen Vortragsveranstaltung der Gesellschaft für Unternehmengeschichte e.V. am 7. Mai 1980*. Wiesbaden: Steiner, pp. 7–73.

van der Linden, M. (ed.) 2000. *The International Confederation of Free Trade Unions*. Bern: Peter Lang.

van Waarden, F. and Drahos, M. 2002. "Courts and (epistemic) communities in the convergence of competition policies," *Journal of European Public Policy* **9** (6): 913–34.

Watkins, W. P. 1970. *The International Co-operative Alliance*. London: International Co-operative Alliance.

13 The making of a comprehensive transnational discourse community

Dieter Plehwe

Introduction

The critique of state-centered approaches to international relations and international political economy has resulted in a rapidly growing literature focusing on a variety of "private authorities" in international relations (Cutler *et al.* 1999). In this literature, arrays of transnational communities are prominent subjects of analysis. Epistemic communities promoting new environmental standards, discourse communities pushing for new public management across borders, and advocacy coalitions shaming the perpetrators of human rights abuses, for example, have been observed and conceptualized in order to shed light on the extent to which dispersed actors from diverse locations can build and maintain crucial links, and develop social identities across borders. In turn, these have been found important for setting political agendas, acquiring a voice in policy implementation processes, policing compliance, and spreading ideologies more generally (Haas 1992a; Keck and Sikkink 1998; Bislev *et al.* 2002; Djelic 2006). At the same time, it is becoming clear that many of these transnational communities recruit their members among private as well as public constituencies. A study of these communities thus also needs specifically to address the linkages between civil society, business, and the public sphere.

Transnational community research has also contributed to the rise of social constructivist approaches in international relations (Risse 2007). However, given the increasing attention paid to knowledge, ideas, and discourse, it is surprising how little international relations scholarship in general, and transnational community research in particular, have had to say so far about the global rise of neoliberal discourse. Even the neo-Gramscian international political economy literature has focused so far mostly on corporate planning groups and the rise of neoliberalism. Only recently has more attention been paid to the wider role of intellectuals and knowledge production (Plehwe *et al.* 2006; Horn 2009). Popular accounts of neoliberal hegemony once again privilege structural features of the remaining superpower, the USA, in combination with the power of global financial institutions or the financialization of big business, and pay scant attention to the role of intellectuals and the formation of actor preferences (Harvey 2005). The earlier rise of Keynesianism, by contrast, has been subjected to comparative analysis with one eye on the role of ideas and intellectuals at the national level (Hall 1989), and the authors were rightly scolded for ignoring the transnational dimension (Hirschman 1989). Given the present global financial and economic crisis, a better understanding of how neoliberalism became a key ideology for explaining the world is central to assessing how likely it is that alternative interpretations will become authoritative and politically relevant, both in leading global policy circles and among the general public.

In order to grasp how interests come to be understood and actor preferences formed in transnational communities which influence global policy-making, it becomes necessary – and particularly interesting – to attain a better understanding of intellectual efforts to develop, shape, prioritize, and possibly generalize preferences and perspectives. It certainly is not accidental that much research on private authority focuses on transnational communities specializing in matters of knowledge and expertise – sometimes, unfortunately, even at the expense of addressing the links between knowledge, interpretation, and interest. Specific and particularistic interests can attain the status of general interests only if they are well understood, expressed, and advocated, as well as effectively legitimized. Efforts to obtain authority and legitimacy for knowledge involve substantive, strategic, and tactical knowledge processing and, more often than not, claims about the scientific accuracy and truth of the generated results. In order to effectively organize the chain of knowledge required in this process, what was originally only an intuitive understanding of the intellectual division of labor has been developed more consciously since World War II in response to the important nexus of knowledge and power, the increasing importance of national and international media, and the ubiquity of information at the current stage of the knowledge society (Walpen 2004; Plehwe and Walpen 2006). At the same time, the relevance of ideology in the politics of knowledge has been effectively disguised by ubiquitous claims to scientific status (Fischer and Forrester 1993).

The argument in the present chapter is twofold. First, it is necessary to consider – both separately and together – the generation of philosophical or upstream knowledge, the production of disciplinary academic knowledge, and, further downstream, applied knowledge such as policy advice and journalistic information in order better to grasp the ways in which transnational communities rise and function. Second, a sufficiently detailed analysis of the organization of knowledge chains along the policy cycle and during specific stages (of alerting, agenda-setting, policy proposals, implementation, and so on) can yield important insights with regard to the influence of private authorities in international relations and the evolution of global knowledge fields.

In what follows, I will briefly discuss epistemic community, advocacy coalition, and discourse community research to establish why yet another category of transnational community is needed to understand the role and impact of transnational communities that are capable of knowledge production and processing well beyond the types that have been conceptualized and studied so far. The main body of the chapter investigates the historical roots and evolution of the comprehensive community of neoliberal intellectuals. The potential theoretical and empirical advances arising from a more systematic analysis of comprehensive transnational discourse communities are discussed in the conclusion.

Types of transnational community: commonalities, differences, and open questions

International relations scholars have observed and conceptualized various types of transnational communities in respect of their distinctive capacities for international policy-making. However, little is known about the emergence of the basic values and principled beliefs on which the working and regulatory impact of such communities are based. Typically, these values and beliefs are taken for granted, with no effort to analyze their origin. This can be argued, for instance, for three types of transnational community – epistemic communities, advocacy networks, and discourse communities – that are at the core of debates among international relations and international political economy scholars.[1]

Transnational epistemic communities

Epistemic communities have been conceptualized in an effort to explain preference formation in the face of new and challenging issues confronted by traditional players without prior experience and sufficient expertise. Foreign affairs officials, for example, operate in conditions of relative or substantial uncertainty. Haas (1992b: 1) emphasized the "growing technical uncertainties and complexities of problems of global concern," requiring improvements in international policy coordination. He challenged realist assumptions about easily identified state interests directly determining state preferences in international relations. Decision-makers are considered ill-prepared, if not incapable of identifying and pursuing interests if they are not sufficiently familiar with the technical aspects of specific problems.

In this context, epistemic communities of scientists and experts are seen as influential groups able to shape policy agendas. An epistemic community, according to Haas (1992b: 3), is "a network of professionals with recognized expertise and competence in a particular domain and authoritative claim to policy-relevant knowledge within that domain or issue area." Characteristic are shared normative and causal beliefs, shared notions of validity, and a common policy enterprise. An incipient epistemic community can be turned into a collective force when such individuals discover each other, and forge an alliance with social agency capabilities beyond a mere combination of individual capacities.

Various case studies (for example, free trade in services [see Drake and Nicolaïdis 1992] and the ban on chlorofluorocarbons [see Haas 1992a]) evidence the power of epistemic communities to set new agendas in international policy deliberations. A networked community's power can be seen to be waning, however, once the policy process moves downstream into formal arenas allegedly dominated by state interests, and thus into the realm in which traditional international relations approaches focusing on the explanatory power of national interests and relative positions of power are considered adequate.

While rightly praised for bringing into focus important transnational actor constellations in specific and important knowledge production areas relevant to agenda-setting processes, Haas focuses too strongly on the expert status of epistemic community members. In terms of the groups studied, however, such communities may be better understood as power elites in C. Wright Mills's sense due to their weight as corporate research directors or heads of public research institutions, for example. And their influence may not always be as positive as in the case of banning chlorofluorocarbons. The epistemic community approach has also been criticized as limiting the attention paid to such unofficial influence on agenda-setting, as well as to basic knowledge aspects within transnational epistemic communities (Bislev et al. 2002: 208; Adler 2005). Others have challenged the approach's elite focus, proposing consideration also of more stratified transnational advocacy networks.

Transnational advocacy networks

These can be considered transnational communities even if the authors settled for a different name. According to Keck and Sikkink (1998: 2), members of transnational advocacy networks are "bound together by shared values, a common discourse, dense exchanges of information and services." In issue areas such as human rights, ecology, gender, development, and peace such networks have built "new links among actors in civil societies, states, and international organizations" and thereby "multiply channels of access to the international system" (Keck and Sikkink 1998: 1).

Advocacy networks do not differ from epistemic communities because of the absence of shared values, as Keck and Sikkink (1998: 1) claim, but in terms of social composition and resources. While the latter are communities of scientists and experts primarily mobilizing their scientific knowledge, the former comprise a broader range of social strata and relatively weak – in terms of ready resources – non-governmental organizations that obtain influence due to their ability to gather and report reliable information (information politics), to dramatize facts (symbolic politics), to effectively exert material pressure by linking the issues to money, trade, or prestige (leverage politics), and to exert moral pressure by publicly scrutinizing the extent to which organizations adhere to principles they have endorsed (accountability politics). Another distinguishing feature is the degree of immediacy inherent in the two types. Members of epistemic communities are likely to know each other, while transnational advocacy networks are likely to operate frequently as distant, largely imagined communities many of whose members know *of* each other at best (see Djelic and Quack in this volume).

Finally, transnational advocacy networks have been shown to influence policy-making beyond the agenda-setting stage of the policy process. Keck and Sikkink (1998) observed a wide range of campaign influences. Such networks are found to be capable of correcting agendas, enforcing agenda elements, and punishing their neglect. These may be regarded as modification, maintenance, or reproduction functions in addition to the initiation and innovation functions attributed to epistemic communities. While focusing on a single issue such as tropical deforestation, the authors also account for the way in which a single environmental issue is linked to other environmental issues, and pay attention to interlocking epistemic communities, for example, linking environmental and social issue areas.

Curiously, all the examples studied are progressive transnational advocacy networks, which seems to reflect a normative bias and/or limits with regard to an analytical understanding of civil society in this framework – despite the conceptual understanding of civil society as a sphere of struggle between competing forces. By drawing too sharp a distinction between business and business-related actor groups and civil society actors, which are effectively identified with non-profit or third sector groups, Keck and Sikkink (1998) do not examine the extent to which a broader range of "private" knowledge actors – and neoliberal and neoconservative forces in particular – are likewise involved in the highly uneven formation of transnational civil society, for example, in the field of legal services. This contrasts with the work of Dezalay and Garth (2002) who strongly emphasize "top-down participatory development" in the field of human rights, designed to secure legitimacy for neoliberal capitalism rather than advance a genuine agenda for bottom-up networks.

Transnational discourse communities

Transnational discourse communities, in contrast, have been observed predominantly at the conservative end of the political spectrum. Bislev *et al.* (2002: 208) go beyond analysis of the production of basic knowledge in transnational epistemic and advocacy communities, and highlight the transmission of prescriptive knowledge. This implies a critical view of knowledge as part of the social power structure, which differs from the perception of knowledge as a "neutral" resource that prevails in much of epistemic community and advocacy coalition research (Fischer 2003). The analysis of discourse communities, therefore, avoids the normative and problem-solving bias that characterizes much of the transnational community research previously discussed.[2] But transnational discourse communities are found to influence knowledge transfer far beyond the agenda-setting stage. The promotion of public–private partnerships in local government and commercialization in higher education are illustrations.

According to Bislev *et al.* (2002), activities supported by the German Bertelsmann Foundation were crucial in developing and maintaining a transnational network of civil society actors and local public officials, and ultimately in transforming local government practices. Schöller's and Groh's (2006) work on a Bertelsmann-related discourse community in the field of higher education shows how Foundation officials have managed to concert an unlikely group of fellow travelers, including neoliberal think tanks such as Germany's Ludwig Erhard Foundation, as well as traditional constituencies of social liberalism such as Germany's Social Democrats, trade unionists, and Greens. They all embraced the Foundation's vision of marketizing higher education. Alas, neither study shows how the Foundation's neoliberal fundamental values and principled beliefs, evidenced in its promotion of new public management and the commercialization of culture, emerged in the first place.

Open questions: the origins of basic values and principled beliefs

While the international relations and international political economy literature, as summarized above, discusses the practices and effects of various types
of transnational communities, the origins of their underlying values and
principled beliefs remain obscure. In order to clarify them we must leave
behind specific transnational epistemic, advocacy, or discourse communities
and take a more comprehensive approach. Adler's (2005: 22) notion of
transnational communities of practice[3] attempts to provide a more generalized account of the ideational dimension of cross-border social formations.
"Most of the transnational communities described in the IR literature are in
fact species of communities of practice," according to Adler (2005: 16).

From this perspective, transmission of meaning rather than the provision of
"objective" information is considered the most important contribution of
transnational communities to policy-making. The most far-reaching effect
of epistemic communities, according to Adler (2005: 16), "is cognitive evolution, i.e., the constitution of new practices that may be used by both present
and future generations of practitioners and may constitute the basis of
transformation of the identities and interests of an increasing number of
people." However, Adler's effort to address the yawning gap in the literature
with regard to the explanation of shared values and principled beliefs unwit-
tingly turns into an effort to stress the fundamental importance of social
communication and constructivism in general. At least, he fails to explain
the origins and political nature of the social construction of fundamental
values and principled beliefs like the other transnational community scholars
who unequivocally emphasize their fundamental importance.

Considering different levels of abstraction, more concrete and competing
meanings are crucial in solving the puzzle of value origins. "Values emerge in
experiences of self formation and self transcendence," writes Joas (1999: 255)
in his summary of classical contributions by Nietzsche, Durkheim, Dewey,
and others. But unlike Adler he proceeds to clarify possible misunderstandings arising at such a general level of anthropological abstraction. For our
purposes it is interesting to look at his reflections on the polysemy of the word
"origin."

First, "origin" can refer to the historically first announcement of a value.
Second, it can refer to the efforts of a small, eventually growing group of
disciples championing this value – an original community. Third, it can mean
the rise of new ties between individuals and values (for example, conversion
from Catholicism to Protestantism), which are not historically new – the

joining of an imagined community. And fourth, it can refer to the revival of weak, almost forgotten values (Joas 1999: 257).

In the case of transnational epistemic communities, advocacy coalitions, and discourse communities we are probably dealing with origin in the third and fourth senses of Joas's enumeration – joining an existing imagined community and reviving a community – since it is unlikely that the values and principled beliefs uniting fairly recent and specific transnational communities are historically new. In order to understand the historical origins and evolution of fundamental meanings and values in the first and second senses, a certain amount of *longue durée* historical efforts to account for the birth of new philosophical systems (religious or secular, for example, Enlightenment, social democracy, and so on) are indispensable for understanding when and why intellectuals first announced and started to champion historically new values and principled beliefs, which in turn makes it possible for others eventually to convert to or revive them.

In order to explain the origins of neoliberal values and principled beliefs, and the evolution of knowledge based on neoliberal philosophical foundations, I suggest, one has to go back to a transnational community of neoliberal intellectuals (Walpen 2004; Plehwe and Walpen 2006; Mirowski and Plehwe 2009), which is best understood as a comprehensive discourse community. This is an organized network of intellectuals who originally conceive of or recombine, recognize, maintain, and further develop a distinct set of fundamental values and principled beliefs that constitute their social identity or an important part thereof. They forge a normative and transdisciplinary basis or worldview informing the development of knowledge and expertise, scientific and otherwise, as well as other professional competencies in multiple domains. Claims to authoritative policy-relevant knowledge within multiple domains or issue areas can be made within the community and in discourse coalitions. A comprehensive discourse community can be conceived as or turn into a transnational comprehensive discourse community depending on the circumstances of the making of the community.

Transnational roots and evolutions: the comprehensive community of neoliberal intellectuals

The term "neoliberalism" has a prehistory in early twentieth-century political and economic thought (Walpen 2000). But the post-World War II concept of neoliberalism developed and shared by the members of the neoliberal transnational discourse community first came into view in the 1930s.

Contemporary neoliberalism emerged as a result of intellectual confrontations triggered by the Great Depression. Mass unemployment and social unrest challenged the very existence of the capitalist order. This led the early associates of the emerging neoliberal community to face the shortcomings of traditional liberal values and principled beliefs, in addition to confronting the perceived threat of socialism and planning.

Uprooted cosmopolitans: neoliberalism in exile

Many of the participants in the initial neoliberal deliberations of the 1930s had already interacted across borders in numerous ways for at least a decade. Quite a few had passed through Vienna and Ludwig von Mises's *Privatseminar* during the 1920s, for example. In Vienna, the efforts of Austrian economists such as von Mises and von Hayek were dedicated to disputing the socialist claims to knowledge authority in the famous socialist calculation debate. By the mid-1930s, however, the participants in a by then more closely knit neoliberal community had experienced the collapse of traditional liberalism in country after country, and many had become uprooted cosmopolitans. Unlike Tarrow's rooted cosmopolitans (see the introduction to this volume), prominent Austrian, German, and Italian academics had become conservative refugees from the countries ruled by Nazis and fascists, and needed to develop flexibility with regard to their home bases. Swiss members of the incipient neoliberal community, such as William E. Rappard, provided a safe haven for the likes of Wilhelm Röpke, Ludwig von Mises, and Luigi Einaudi. Other Austrians and Germans found refuge in far away New Zealand (Karl Popper), the UK (Friedrich von Hayek), the USA (Gottfried Haberler, Fritz Machlup), and Turkey (Alexander Rüstow) (Feichtinger 2001).

If the Vienna of the 1920s displayed a very lively "science between cultures" (Feichtinger 2001), the exiled members of the transnational community were forced to cross cultures and to find a pedigree in a transnational community they themselves were nurturing jointly with like-minded colleagues from the UK and the USA, in addition to Switzerland, France, and a few other scattered places in Scandinavia, Mexico, and South Africa (Walpen 2004). Later characteristics of the comprehensive transnational community of neoliberals – internationalism, interdisciplinary work, and the mobilization of private business and corporate foundation resources for the advancement of academic and other projects – can be discerned in the formative life experiences of leading neoliberals. Many neoliberal intellectuals were not welcome at the universities of their home countries, but quite a few were unable to secure jobs at universities in their host countries either and so had to look elsewhere for ways of making a living. Entrepreneurship and cosmopolitanism thus were not just key aspects of economic theorizing; they had a distinct existential and emotional appeal apart from providing the material basis needed to procure economic – and intellectual – independence (Plehwe 2009a).

Partly due to emigration and parallel experiences the term "neoliberalism" started to appear in multiple contexts in the 1930s (in France, Switzerland, Germany, and the UK, for example), eventually to become established as the main designation of a new intellectual/political movement (Walpen 2000). An important discussion took place in France from 1935 onwards. A loose group of economists, philosophers, and sociologists[4] located in Paris would later be involved in organizing the Colloque Walter Lippmann (CWL 1939).

Walter Lippmann's book *An Inquiry into the Principles of the Good Society* published in 1937 (Lippmann 1937) contained a principled statement of the superiority of the market economy over an economy planned by the state. He restated many traditional liberal values and principled beliefs in terms of individual freedom, private property, and so on, but the book also featured a clear understanding of the fundamental and far-reaching positive role of the state in providing protection from interest group politics. Such a strong and impartial state was regarded as necessary for tasks that went far beyond the liberal night-watchman state, albeit in ways different from the planning state of the social liberals. This state was to be enabled to guide the population by learning what they want, namely a free capitalist economic and social order, as advocated by neoliberal intellectuals, and not socialist planning. Lippmann thus wanted individuals to be free to choose only what he and other neoliberals perceived as the best social order, and the state was regarded as quintessential to securing such an order. Traditional liberal political values such as the right to form coalitions and voting rights had at the same time become fundamentally suspicious due to the rise of socialist trade unions, and social democratic, communist, and fascist political parties. Significantly, "totalitarianism" was discussed by Lippmann primarily with regard to the absence of private property rather than the more commonplace reference to a lack of democracy or countervailing political power.

The French philosopher Louis Rougier invited over thirty intellectuals to Paris to discuss Lippmann's book at the Colloque Walter Lippmann: a total of twenty-six participated, and fifteen of those (among others Raymond Aron, Louis Baudin, Friedrich von Hayek, Ludwig von Mises, Michael Polanyi, Wilhelm Röpke, and Alexander Rüstow) would participate in the founding of the Mont Pèlerin Society nine years later. The participants discussed the need for a new liberal program in science and society, which was eventually labeled "neoliberal." The term won out over alternatives such as positive liberalism. The group launched a project agenda, a journal (*Cahiers du Libéralisme*), and a think tank with several locations (Denord 2001). The concept of "neoliberalism" was defined in 1938 as including:

- the priority of the price mechanism;
- free enterprise;
- competition; and
- a strong and impartial state (Walpen 2004: 60–61).

While opposing social liberalism and socialism, the participating intellectuals had to stop thinking of the state in mostly (if not purely) negative terms after the Great Depression, and formed the nucleus of the transnational neoliberal discourse community. The German contingent of economists, such as Walter Eucken, Alexander Rüstow, and Wilhelm Röpke, at this point had already gone further than the London-based scholars around Lionel Robbins and F. A. von Hayek in distancing themselves from classical liberalism. They were already discussing the tasks of a "new liberalism" on the eve of the Nazis' rise to power. Significantly for later developments, Rüstow explicitly called for a "liberal interventionism" (Ptak 2004).

The outbreak of World War II put an abrupt stop to this nascent attempt to consolidate the transnational community and to organize (neo)liberal forces. At the Paris conference it was also not yet time to further clarify the set of neoliberal values and principled beliefs. Twelve years later at the first meeting of the Mont Pèlerin Society (MPS) considerable work would be invested to this end by way of drafting this group's statement of aims. However, the clear recognition of a two-pronged effort – against socialism and naturalistic liberalism (compare Foucault 2004) – guided the work of the carefully selected intellectuals who were invited to join the subsequent discussion, deliberately excluding representatives of the other new liberalism, mainstream social liberalism.[5]

Consolidating the transnational discourse community

With the conclusion of the fighting in 1945, several members of the neoliberal community were eager to resume the tasks neglected during the war. A number of well-known intellectuals in Europe and the United States eventually assembled for more than a week over Easter in Mont Pèlerin, a village close to Lake Geneva. A Swiss businessman, Albert Hunold, and Hayek were the main organizers. The internationalist outlook and organizational effort were made possible by some timely corporate/institutional support. The Foundation for Economic Education in Irvington-on-Hudson, New York, which dated from 1946 and employed Ludwig von Mises, and the William Volker Fund based in Kansas City provided subsidies, as did European and US universities that employed community members (LSE, Chicago, and so on). The Volker Fund was led by future MPS member Harold Luhnow and provided travel funds for the US participants. Of the total conference costs of 18,000 Swiss francs, the Schweizerische Kreditanstalt (today Credit Suisse) paid 15,000 (Steiner 2007). US historian George H. Nash (1998 [1976]: 26) described the mood of the post-War community of neoliberals:

[T]he participants, high in the Swiss Alps, were only too conscious that they were outnumbered and without apparent influence on policy-makers in the Western world. All across Europe, planning and socialism seemed ascendant.

But the failure of classical liberalism continued to be high on the agenda as well. Traditional liberalism was doomed, according to Hayek, because of crippling conceptual flaws, and the only way to diagnose and rectify them was a withdrawal into a small and tightly controlled group – a comprehensive transnational discourse community. As Hayek said in his opening address at the first meeting:

[E]ffective endeavors to elaborate the general principles of a liberal order are practicable only among a group of people who are in agreement on fundamentals, and among whom basic conceptions are not questioned at every step . . . What we need are people who have faced the arguments from the other side, who have struggled with them and fought themselves through to a position from which they can both critically meet the objections against it and justify their own views . . . this should be regarded as a private meeting and all that is said here in discussion as "off the record" . . . it must remain a closed society, not open to all and sundry. (Hayek 1967: 149, 151, 153, 158)

Longstanding ties across borders had been important with regard to the early recruiting efforts of the MPS: Hayek, Mises, Polanyi, Robbins, and Röpke were MPS founding members who had already participated in the 1938 Colloquium, and other CWL participants (including Raymond Aron, Louis Baudin, and Alexander Rüstow) were involved in the efforts to launch the MPS (Walpen 2004: 84f., 388, 391). Despite the precautions taken over original membership and participation, it was by no means easy for the early MPS members to specify precisely what held them together, and even more what they wanted to achieve. But the forging of a purposeful transnational community required at least some clarification of the common understanding and objectives. To this end, the participating members engaged in a prolonged discussion of what eventually became the official statement of the aims of the Mont Pèlerin Society. Lionel Robbins was charged with drafting the statement:

The central values of civilization are in danger ... The group holds that these developments have been fostered by the growth of a view of history which denies all absolute moral standards and by the growth of theories which question the desirability of the rule of law. It holds further that they have been fostered by a decline of belief in private property and the competitive market; for without the diffused power and initiative associated with these institutions it is difficult to imagine a society in which freedom may be effectively preserved. Believing that what is essentially an ideological movement must be met by intellectual argument and the reassertion of valid ideas ...[6]

[...]

The group does not aspire to conduct propaganda. It seeks to establish no meticulous and hampering orthodoxy. It aligns itself with no particular party. Its object is solely, by facilitating the exchange of views among minds inspired by certain ideals and broad conceptions held in common, to contribute to the preservation and improvement of the free society. (Hartwell 1995: 41–42)

The statement of aims thus expressly refers to views inspired by certain ideals and broad conceptions. Among the key principled beliefs was a very clear understanding of the political character of the social order, and the state. To "preserve and improve" conditions for a "free society," individual "initiative," and a "liberal order," key neoliberal values, some of the sacred cows of traditional liberalism had to be slaughtered. Henceforth the debate was not about whether or not to intervene and regulate, but how and to what extent. Due to the recognition of social, political, and economic dynamics, a belief in immutable and universal liberal values, with the notable absence of democracy and timeless economic truths such as market competition and initiative, was combined with full recognition of the need to safeguard and protect such an order. The members of the comprehensive transnational community anticipated a wide range of battles to be fought – ranging from explaining the present crisis over redefining state functions and minimal standards to rewriting history. The tasks neoliberals felt in need of tackling indicate that not only Antonio Gramsci understood the preconditions of hegemony, the importance of civil society, and a long-term "war of position" necessary to exert influence. The neoliberal comprehensive discourse community in fact took a right-wing neo-Gramscian perspective at the transnational level.

At subsequent MPS meetings the transnational community made strong efforts to clarify the general understanding of neoliberalism in respect of more specific questions and issue areas. Discussion was dedicated to the question of the relationship between liberalism and Socialism, Christianity, or European integration, among other things. The Swiss MPS member and *Neue Zürcher Zeitung* journalist Carlo Mötteli reported on the debate on liberalism and underdeveloped countries in Beauvallon, France (1951) as follows: "But while the old system of laisser faire, laisser aller is as much out of the question in underdeveloped areas as elsewhere, hope exists that the principles and policies of neoliberalism will find a promising field of activity and development there" (Plehwe 2009b).

By means of the Mont Pèlerin foundation we can more easily observe the composition of a major part of the comprehensive transnational community of neoliberal intellectuals, which managed to consolidate during the 1950s and 1960s. At Mont Pèlerin and subsequent meetings university professors mingled with journalists, foundation/think tank executives, business executives, and publishing houses. By 1951 several leading political figures (including Ludwig Erhard and Luigi Einaudi) were accepted into the ranks. Throughout the history of the neoliberal discourse community members have been recruited with an eye to combining the academic and professional qualifications necessary to last the distance in public debates and battles of opinion. Alongside academics come more than a hundred members employed in partisan (advocacy) think tanks founded or run by MPS members, for example, and journalists of major (business) newspapers such as the *Wall Street Journal*, the *Neue Zürcher Zeitung*, and the *Frankfurter Allgemeine Zeitung* have regularly been recruited (compare Plehwe and Walpen 2006; Plehwe 2008 for further analysis of membership composition).

The neoliberal transnational community demonstrated comprehensiveness and considerable capacity with regard to both the conception of values and principled beliefs, and the pursuit of a wide range of knowledge projects. Only once so far, and relatively early, has the community experienced a serious crisis. In the late 1950s/early 1960s a group of community members led by Wilhelm Röpke and Albert Hunold wanted the Mont Pèlerin Society to go public directly with straightforward political, anti-communist messages. Other members, led by Hayek, objected, and the community almost disintegrated (cf. Walpen 2004: 145f. on the Hunold–Hayek affair). The crisis was solved by adhering to the original ideas about communal seclusion, combined with intermediate and decentralized public intervention relying on partisan think tanks. While the group lost a few of its prominent members as a result of the crisis, politicizing the community would surely have led to greater fatalities, and more likely than not discontinued the comprehensive neoliberal discourse community. Further and full consolidation of the original identity and purpose of the community instead provided the basis for future extension.

Expanding the community

The MPS community rapidly adjusted to the US post-War rise to economic hegemony in terms of membership,[7] though Europe arguably remained of equal if not greater importance as an epicenter of the neoliberal discourse community. When membership reached 500, the leaders of the MPS decided against further growth in an effort to preserve at least some of the immediacy and intimacy of the original community effort. By the end of the 1970s certainly many more community members existed than card carrying members of the MPS, and the immediate community of directly connected neoliberals had succeeded in creating an imagined community of intermediately connected neoliberals around the world. Partly responsible for this were dedicated efforts to establish partisan think tanks. By the late 1970s, more than thirty had been founded, even before the neoliberal think tank boom of the 1980s and 1990s (Walpen 2004). To accommodate more active community members, local groups were formed akin to the Mont Pèlerin Society in several countries, for example, the Philadelphia Society in the USA. By the time Reagan and Thatcher rose to power in the United States and the United Kingdom respectively, the comprehensive transnational community of neoliberal intellectuals was a well-established if barely visible para-political force around the globe.

Even if operating with 500 members already precludes the close acquaintance of most community members, the MPS can be considered an extremely important social context for the ongoing reproduction of an immediate neoliberal community. A quantitative analysis of participation in MPS general meetings from 1947 until 1986 proves that quite a number of members frequently and jointly participate in the general meetings.

Key community members attended 75 percent of the meetings held during particular periods or more (Plehwe 2008). Unsurprisingly, such frequent fliers include most of the key officials who formally served the MPS as presidents or general secretaries, but also includes a group of journalists and publishers, corporate leaders, think tank officials, and a politician. Marie-Thérèse Genin, a French publisher who helped to get major books by neoliberal authors translated and published, is the only woman among the regulars. She is among the few frequent attendants who never chaired a panel or gave a paper, a fate shared by the few other women who were among the earlier community members (Plehwe 2008). Only more recently have women moved higher up the ranks of the MPS; Professor Victoria Curzon-Price from Switzerland was elected president in 2004. Many MPS members met not only at conferences organized by the MPS, but also in other professional venues, and privately. Commenting on an early draft of Hartwell's (1995) MPS history, Christian Gandil (1986) named several friends he had made among US-based MPS members, and whom he visited privately when he travelled to the United States. Gandil explains that "the basis for a friendship is to be in agreement concerning outlook on life."

Beyond forging community ties among members, arguably the most important practical activity of the comprehensive neoliberal discourse community has been the founding and running of think tanks. More than a hundred think tanks can be identified with MPS members as founders or leaders (Plehwe and Walpen 2006). Think tanks such as the Heritage Foundation, the American Enterprise Institute, and the Cato Institute in the USA, the Institute of Economic Affairs and the Adam Smith Institute in the UK, and the Stiftung Marktwirtschaft in Germany have grown into major research, consulting, and lobby organizations. In both Guatemala and Argentina, efforts originally restricted to think tanks eventually led to the founding of major universities (Goodman and Marotz-Baden 1990). A few members of the comprehensive neoliberal discourse community have been instrumental in replicating think tank methodologies across the world. Antony Fisher, founder of the Institute of Economic Affairs, has been the key person behind neoliberal think tank entrepreneurship, founding the Atlas Economic Research Foundation in the early 1980s to assist and coordinate global think tank activities. Key neoliberal policy projects such as privatization, deregulation, or flat tax proposals were propagated first in neoliberal think tank circuits, and then conquered regulatory politics (Cockett 1994; Yergin and Stanislaw 1998; Frost 2002; Plehwe and Walpen 2006). It is impossible to explain the rise of regulatory capitalism (Levi-Faur 2005) without acknowledging the multiple role and singular agenda-setting power of the comprehensive neoliberal discourse coalition.

New frontiers: comprehensive transnational community and coalition research

The transnational community of neoliberal intellectuals introduced in this chapter differs in important ways from the transnational communities that have been studied so far, although it shares and combines important characteristics of epistemic communities, advocacy networks, and discourse communities. The comprehensive neoliberal discourse community comprises a knowledge elite membership similar to the one described in epistemic community research. But a careful look at the organizational background reveals the *partisan* political character of a knowledge power elite rather than conforming to the image of the international academy proposed by Hayek. The comprehensive transnational community of neoliberal intellectuals was capable alone or in discourse coalitions (Hajer 1993) of setting agendas and influencing agenda-setting, for example with regard to deregulation and privatization of regulated industries and public service monopolies. The community was subsequently active in correcting agenda-setting in these and many other issue areas, for example, suggesting stronger oversight regulation in cases where overdoses of unsupervised competition yielded disastrous results. The comprehensive discourse community was also able to orchestrate transnational publicity and lobby campaigns, against state aid in development for example. The community made it possible to monitor compliance with international treaty obligations protecting property rights, and even to develop a property rights approach allegedly to fight poverty. But members of the same community also opposed economic approaches to environmental policy-making and continue to attack the growing consensus on global warming (Stone 1996; Plehwe 2000; Plehwe and Walpen 2006; Weller and Singleton 2006; Mitchell 2009; Union of Concerned Scientists 2007; Plehwe 2008).

The academic members of the MPS have also been crucial in establishing and promoting internationally academic (sub)disciplines such as public choice and law and economics, disciplinary schools of thought (such as monetarism in economics), and transdisciplinary research perspectives such as rational choice-based neo-institutionalism. When looking at the comprehensive neoliberal discourse community within and around the MPS we can thus also observe a transnational community of academic intellectuals with diverse disciplinary backgrounds, which differs from the pluralist transnational communities of scientists and scholars who are more or less united by a common professional understanding of scientific inquiry and disciplinary boundaries and norms (compare Mayntz in this volume). Neoliberal scholars certainly take part and sometimes play major roles in scientific communities, but they can and indeed have established strong communities within such communities, even if such invisible colleges are rarely and fully visible. To establish more precisely if and to what extent the collaboration of intellectuals within the comprehensive neoliberal discourse community helped in shaping and transforming academic disciplines and academic communities of scientists is one of the important research topics for the future study of the Mont Pèlerin Society (most importantly but certainly not restricted to economics).

While all the different knowledge/power functions – initiating, innovating, monitoring, agenda correcting, enforcing, and so on – evidenced by the multiple involvements of neoliberal intellectuals deserve further attention, arguably the most important function has been the social construction of fundamental neoliberal values and principled beliefs, of a specific meaning that has been attached to many different bits and pieces of knowledge. The values and principled beliefs shared (in relative distance to socialism, conservatism, and traditional liberalism) enabled the members both collectively and individually to develop new interpretations of economic, political, social, and even cultural matters. While there is no such thing as a timeless and essential neoliberal truth shared by each and every member of the neoliberal discourse community, the range of interpretations emanating from this community is not openly pluralist either. The key strength of this comprehensive transnational community of neoliberal intellectuals has been a conscious nurturing of a pluralism within neoliberal confines that is still poorly understood by many observers (compare Feulner 2000 on the recruitment of different neoliberal wings of "academic" staff at the Heritage Foundation).

The neoliberal discourse community in any case can be considered comprehensive both in terms of linking upstream (philosophical) and downstream (academic and policy) knowledge spheres, and in developing a wide range of social technologies (and organizational bases) dedicated to the advance of neoliberal agendas in many countries, discourse fields, and issue areas. The community as a whole has mastered the art of consecutive and parallel processing of knowledge and expertise. The establishment of partisan think tanks such as the Foundation of Economic Education or the Institute of Economic Affairs in London (Cockett 1994; Frost 2002) was crucial with regard to the latter aspect, and presently several hundred neoliberal think tanks, of which at least 150 are linked to MPS members, are globally coordinated to a certain extent by the US-based Atlas Economic Research Foundation (www.atlasusa.org) (see Plehwe and Walpen 2006).

The story of the comprehensive transnational community of neoliberal intellectuals has long been one of a transnational community of intellectuals *and organizations*. The partisan think tanks founded and run by community members in the meantime provide for much of the longevity, stability, and resilience of the community, which has had to weather severe storms over the past two decades, and most recently has been declared a huge failure on various occasions (various financial crises due to Washington Consensus politics, Enron/Arthur Anderson, hedge fund collapses, and so on). The current global financial and economic crisis has also rightly been blamed on radical market recipes of neoliberal provenance. But many observers underestimate the staying power of the neoliberal community, which mostly remains ill understood. Recent critiques point to a takeover of the neoliberal community within the Mont Pèlerin Society by think tank professionals, and use the present MPS president Depaak Lal as a case in point. Lal is presented as someone from the Cato Institute and a radical anti-environmentalist (*Süddeutsche Zeitung* 11/24/08). Alas, Depaak Lal is a regular professor at UCLA. Although he considers eco-fundamentalists and Marxists as radical enemies of capitalist growth, he is a highly respected academic. A think tank professional – Ed Feulner of the Heritage Foundation – did indeed play a major role as president of the MPS, but this was arguably during its most successful period, the neoliberal heyday of the 1980s. Whether the influence of the neoliberal community withers or not remains to be seen. Among the solutions to the present global financial crisis advocated by important experts and politicians the social market economy figures prominently. Unfortunately for all who declare the neoliberal community dead, the origins of the idea of a social market economy can be traced back to Ludwig Erhard, Alfred Müller Armack, Wilhelm Röpke, and other German members of the Mont Pèlerin Society (Ptak 2009). If a number of neoliberal policy projects are presently endangered, the fundamental values and principled beliefs of the comprehensive neoliberal discourse community are certainly alive and kicking.

But the current challenge to neoliberal ideas, and the recognition and scrutiny of the "neoliberal international," will hopefully lead to the identification of other comprehensive transnational discourse communities, for example, based on ecological, communitarian, or Islamic values and principled beliefs, and possibly help to advance a comparative research agenda with an eye to common and idiosyncratic features of comprehensive discourse communities and coalitions in the present age of globalization.

NOTES

1. Critical communities represent another subtype, small groups of critical thinkers credited with creating new ideas (Rochon 1998).
2. See the issue of *Critical Sociology* guest edited by Joan Roelofs, Robert Arnove, and Daniel Faber (2007) for a number of articles that critically examine the impact of foundations on left-wing media, think tanks, and mass movements, for example.

3. Security communities, as a specialized type of community of practice, were first observed by Karl Deutsch (1957; see also Adler and Barnett 1998).
4. Raymond Aron, Marcel Bourgeois, Étienne Mantoux, Louis Marlio, Louis Rougier, and Jacques Rueff all belonged to the French group (see Denord 2001).
5. Hayek remained unconvinced by Popper's advocacy of a wider pluralism (Nordmann 2005: 218). He also disregarded interventions by von Mises who objected to "interventionists" such as Röpke and Rüstow (Walpen 2004: 100).
6. Six points were listed as worthy of further study, for example, the redefinition of the role of the state and social minimum standards.
7. Total US membership was 437, amounting to almost half of MPS numbers (Walpen 2004: 395).

REFERENCES

Adler, E. 2005. *Communitarian international relations*. London: Routledge.

Adler, E. and Barnett, M. (eds.) 1998. *Security communities*. Cambridge University Press.

Bislev, S., Salskov-Iversen, D. and Krause Hansen, H. 2002. "The global diffusion of managerialism: Transnational discourse communities at work," Global Society **16** (2): 199–212.

Cockett, R. 1994. *Thinking the unthinkable: Think-tanks and the economic counter-revolution 1931–1983*. London: Harper Collins.

Cutler, A. C., Haufler, V. and Porter, T. (eds.) 1999. *Private authority and international affairs*. Albany, NY: State University of New York Press.

CWL (Colloque Walter Lippmann) 1939. Compte-rendu des séances du Colloque Walter Lippmann. 26–30 aout, Paris (=Travaux du Centre International d'Études pour la Rénovation du Libéralisme. Cahier 1).

Denord, F. 2001. "Aux origines du neo-liberalism en France," *Le Mouvement Social* **195**: 9–34.

Deutsch, K. 1957. *Political community and the North Atlantic area*. Princeton University Press.

Dezalay, Y. and Garth, B. G. 2002. *The internationalization of palace wars*. University of Chicago Press.

Djelic, M.-L. 2006. "Marketization: From intellectual agenda to global policy making," in Djelic, M.-L. and Sahlin-Andersson, K. (eds.), *Transnational governance*. Cambridge University Press, pp. 53–73.

Drake, W. J. and Nicolaïdis, K. 1992. "Ideas, interests, and institutionalization: Trade in services and the Uruguay Round," *International Organization* **46** (1): 37–100.

Feichtinger, J. 2001. *Wissenschaft zwischen den Kulturen*. Frankfurt a.M.: Campus.

Feulner, E. 2000. "The Heritage Foundation," in McGann, J. G. and Weaver, R. K. (eds.), *Think tanks and civil societies. Catalysts for ideas and action*. London: Transaction, pp. 67–85.

Fischer, F. 2003. *Reframing public policy: Discursive politics and deliberative practices*. Oxford University Press.

Fischer, F. and Forrester, J. (eds.) 1993. *The argumentative turn in policy analysis and planning*. Durham, NC: Duke University Press.

Foucault, M. 2004. *Geschichte der Gouvernementalität II*. Frankfurt/Main: Suhrkamp Verlag.

Frost, G. 2002. *Antony Fisher: Champion of liberty*. London: Profile Books.

Gandil, C. 1986. *Comment on R. M. Hartwell: The history of the Mont Pèlerin Society.* Ghent: Liberaal Archief.

Goodman, J. C., and Marotz-Baden, R. (eds.) 1990. *Fighting the war of ideas in Latin America.* Dallas: National Center for Policy Analysis.

Haas, P. M. 1992a. "Banning chlorofluorocarbons: Epistemic community efforts to protect stratospheric ozone," *International Organization* **46** (1): 187–224.

Haas, P. M. 1992b. "Introduction: epistemic communities and international policy coordination," *International Organization,* **46** (1): 1–36.

Hajer, M. A. 1993. "Discourse coalitions and the institutionalization of practice: The case of acid rain in Britain," in Fischer and Forrester (eds.), *The argumentative turn in policy analysis and planning.* Durham, NC: Duke University Press, pp. 43–76.

Hall, P. (ed.) 1989. *The political power of economic ideas: Keynesianism across nations.* Princeton University Press.

Hartwell, R. M. 1995. *A history of the Mont Pèlerin Society.* Indianapolis: Liberty Fund.

Harvey, D. 2005. *A brief history of neoliberalism.* New York: Oxford University Press.

Hayek, F. 1967. *Studies in philosophy, politics and economics.* New York: Simon & Schuster.

Hirschman, A. O. 1989. "How the Keynesian Revolution was exported from the United States, and other comments," in Hall, P. A. (ed.), pp. 347–59.

Horn, L. 2009. "Organic intellectuals at work? The high level group of company law experts in European corporate governance regulation," in Apeldoorn, B. v., Drahokoupil, J. and Horn, L. (eds.), *Contradictions and limits of neoliberal European governance.* Basingstoke: Palgrave Macmillan, pp. 125–42.

Joas, H. 1999. *Die Entstehung der Werte.* Frankfurt a.M.: Suhrkamp.

Keck, M. and Sikkink, K. 1998. *Activists beyond borders.* Ithaca, NY: Cornell University Press.

Levi-Faur, D. 2005. "The global diffusion of regulatory capitalism," *The Annals of the American Academy of Political and Social Science,* **598** (1): 12–32.

Lippmann, W. 1937. *An inquiry into the principles of the good society.* Boston: Little, Brown.

Mirowski, P. and Plehwe, D. (eds.) 2009. *The road from Mont Pèlerin. The making of the neoliberal thought collective.* Cambridge, MA: Harvard University Press.

Mitchell, T. 2009. "The work of economics: How neoliberalism makes its world," in Mirowski, P. and Plehwe, D. (eds.).

Nash, G. 1998 [1976]. *The conservative intellectual movement in America since 1945.* Wilmington, DE: ISI.

Nordmann, J. 2005. *Der lange Marsch zum Neoliberalismus.* Hamburg: VSA.

Plehwe, D. 2000. *Deregulierung und transnationale Integration der Transportwirtschaft in Nordamerika.* Münster: Westfälisches Dampfboot.

Plehwe, D. 2008. "Im Schatten von Hayek und Friedman: Die Vielflieger im Kreise der Mont Pèlerin Society," in Unfried, B., Mittag, J. and Linden, M. v. d. (eds.), *Transnationale Netzwerke im 20. Jahrhundert.* Leipzig: Akademische Verlagsanstalt, pp. 235–64.

Plehwe, D. 2009a. "Introduction," in Mirowski, P. and Plehwe, D. (eds.).

Plehwe, D. 2009b. "Origins of the neoliberal development discourse," in Mirowski, P. and Plehwe, D. (eds.).

Plehwe, D. and Walpen, B. 2006. "Between network and complex organization: The making of neoliberal knowledge and hegemony," in Plehwe, D., Walpen, B. and Neunhöffer, G. (eds.), pp. 27–50.

Plehwe, D., Walpen, B. and Neunhöffer, G. (eds.) 2006. *Neoliberal hegemony: A global critique*. London: Routledge.

Ptak, R. 2004. *Vom Ordoliberalismus zur Sozialen Marktwirtschaft*. Opladen: Leske und Budrich.

Ptak, R. 2009. "Ordoliberal origins and stages of Neoliberalism in Germany: Revisiting the 'Social Market Economy'," in Mirowski, P. and Plehwe, D. (eds.).

Risse, T. 2007. "Social constructivism meets globalization," in Held, D. and McGrew, A. (eds.), *Globalization theory*. Cambridge: Polity Press, pp. 126–47.

Rochon, T. R. 1998. *Culture moves: Ideas, activism, and changing values*. Princeton University Press.

Schöller, O. and Groh, O. 2006. "The education of neoliberalism," in Plehwe, D., Walpen, B. and Neunhöffer, G. (eds.), pp. 171–87.

Steiner, Y. 2007. "Les riches amis suisses du néolibéralisme. De la débâcle de la revue Occident à la Conférence du Mont Pèlerin d'avril 1947," *Traverse: Zeitschrift für Geschichte/Revue d'histoire* **1**: 114–26.

Stone, D. 1996. *Capturing the political imagination*. London: Frank Cass.

Süddeutsche Zeitung. 2008. 'Kapitalismus in der Krise, Erinnerungen an alten Glanz' by Gerd Zitzelsberger, 24 November.

Union of Concerned Scientists. 2007. *Smoke, mirrors and hot air: How ExxonMobil uses Big Tobacco's tactics to manufacture uncertainty on climate science*. Cambridge, MA: Union of Concerned Scientists.

Walpen, B. 2000. "Von Hasen und Igeln oder: Ein Blick auf den Neoliberalismus," *Utopie kreativ* **121**/122: 1066–79.

Walpen, B. 2004. *Die offenen Feinde und ihre Gesellschaft*. Hamburg: VSA.

Weller, C. and Singleton, L. 2006, "Peddling reform: The role of think tanks in shaping the neoliberal policy agenda for the World Bank and International Monetary Fund," in Plehwe, D., Walpen, B. and Neunhöffer, G. (eds.), pp. 70–86.

Yergin, D. and Stanislaw, J. 1998. *The commanding heights*. New York City: Touchstone.

14 Global warming, transnational communities, and economic entrepreneurship: the case of carbon capture and storage (CCS)

Åge Mariussen

Introduction

The oil crises in the 1970s made national governments in countries such as the USA, Japan, Germany, Israel, Denmark, Sweden, and many others aware of their oil dependence and the threat to national security it created. At the same time, there was greater public awareness of the environmental problems created by carbon-based energy systems. National policies were put in place to promote new "clean" energy systems, such as solar, wind, wave, and bio-energy.

Policy instruments varied between subsidies – such as "feed-in tariffs" or subsidized prices to owners of wind or solar energy production infrastructure when they sell electricity to the public grid in countries such as Japan or Germany – tax relief (as in the USA), and government funding for R&D investments. During the 1970s and 1980s, these national R&D efforts were supported by NGOs and reinforced by industrial entrepreneurs and suppliers of technology. These national technological systems of innovation developed green technologies and made the new energy systems more efficient and hence more competitive with carbon-based energies (Jakobsson *et al.* 2002). Such developments were endorsed and encouraged by a number of transnational institutions. In the course of the 1970s, there was a rift between the "green" movement, promoting "clean and green" technology solutions that at the time were inefficient and seemed to be of little economic significance, and "industrial interests," promoting economic growth while generating pollution. At the time, only a minority saw the possibility of a compromise between these positions. The Brundtland Commission, convened in 1983 by the United

Nations (UN 1983, 1987) to explore concerns about the environment and resources, argued for "sustainable development."

Seen in retrospect, from the position of the current debate on CO_2 regulation, the concept of "sustainable development" is not easily expressed in terms of scientific indicators as policy guides (Halsnæs *et al.* 2007). Nevertheless, as a policy-making tool the concept of "sustainable development" provided a framework for regulations supporting industrial entrepreneurs in developing regional (Cooke 2008) and national technological systems of innovation promoting the new technologies, as their industrial strategies were recognized as contributing to economic development. The idea of sustainable development, one might say, is a hypothesis that "green" technologies will contribute to economic growth. These green technologies and associated support policies have characteristics that lend themselves to small-scale, bottom-up, technology development trajectories, starting with local experiments and regional innovation systems and evolving into larger industries (Cooke 2008; Jeroen and Bruisma 2008; Klitkou *et al.* 2008). Such systems are still at an early stage of development, however, and they are not likely to replace carbon-based energy production any time soon.

Unlike these national and regional systems of innovation in new green technologies, discussion of the relationship between the atmosphere, energy, and climate goes back to the sixteenth century (see "Communities and governance" section below). The major issue in the evolution of the transnational scientific community of weather research was to set up institutions able to produce and share standardized transnational weather data. As explained below, this global scientific community was the point of departure for institutions such as the Intergovernmental Panel on Climate Change (IPCC), a scientific inter-governmental body created in 1988 to provide decision-makers with information on climate change.

Recent reports are alarming. Based on new models of the global climate system, they indicate that what may look like small changes in the global average temperature could have a dramatic regional impact in certain parts of the world. These alarming reports underscore the importance of another kind of industrial strategy and development. They appear to justify the development of technologies that capture CO_2 from the chimneys of carbon-based energy producers and store it under the surface of the earth. This is referred to as "carbon capture and storage" or CCS (CO2GeoNet 2002; ADEME, IFP and BRGM 2005; Jakobsen *et al.* 2005; Stephens and Zwaan 2005; Kristiansen, B. 2007; Stangeland 2007; Bjerkestrand 2009; Blaker 2009; Røkke 2009; van der Beken 2009). The argument behind the development of CCS technologies is that we cannot wait until green technologies become mature and competitive.

We have to live with carbon-based energy systems by making them clean – that is, by removing their CO_2 emissions. This is a controversial approach that is actively supported by the EU but not yet by the IPCC. Some key NGOs, such as Greenpeace International, even oppose it outright.

Nevertheless a new global market for CCS is emerging progressively. This chapter explores this process, in particular by focusing on the construction of a transnational community. This community is characterized by (i) a common understanding of the need for this kind of solution to the problem of global warming, (ii) the fact that it shares the knowledge of its application, (iii) its support for and active participation in research and large industrial experiments, and (iv) its strong involvement in ongoing negotiations aimed at international institutionalization and regulation of CCS technologies.

This chapter shows that this transnational community has evolved through three main phases, in which the emphasis on what should be seen as shared knowledge has shifted. In the first phase, from 1996 to 2000, the technology existed essentially in the form of fairly isolated local industrial experiments, initiated by oil companies in different parts of the world, with no common framework for cooperation. In the second phase, between 2000 and late 2008, we witnessed the creation and stabilization of CO2NET, a network organization that defines itself as "a Carbon Dioxide Knowledge Transfer Network." The annual seminar of that organization has become a "flagship event for CCS networking in Europe" and in parallel there has been rapid growth in EU-supported research. Work to develop the technology through experiments and strategies of institutionalization and regulation has started. In the third phase, a new global market is to emerge in 2009 by means of the first commercial tenders for the construction of large-scale test plants in Norway, Canada, and the EU. We shall then see a shift of emphasis in the direction of advocacy, promoting public awareness but also building "people capability" through education. In this context, this chapter is a contribution to the discussion on the relations between the process of transnational community formation and the complex and fragmented dynamics of transnational governance.

Setting the stage

The *Gemeinschaft* vs. *Gesellschaft* dichotomy outlined by Tönnies is a useful point of departure for understanding communities as characterized by spatially bounded or localized interaction, combined with similarities creating ascriptive bonds. However, following the approach of Djelic and Quack (in this volume), communities should not necessarily be seen as static, localized structures. Instead, "they are fluid relational constructs, constantly on the move and in process ... being actively constructed and shaped over time by members or individuals involved in one way or another." This active construction sometimes includes the setting up of networks of activist organizations, possibly facilitated by transnational institutions, as described by Keck and Sikkink (1998). This modern form of connection between transnational institutions and transnational activism can arguably be traced back to the United Nations Conference on the Human Environment in 1972 in Stockholm (also known as the Stockholm Conference). As the conference was highly politicized from the outset, a parallel NGO conference was facilitated (Keck and Sikkink 1998).

A similar pattern emerged later with the Brundtland Commission. On December 19, 1983, the United Nations General Assembly passed Resolution 38/161 and established a special commission to work on "environment and development." The so-called Brundtland report, *Our Common Future*, was published in 1987 (UN 1983, 1987). One of the Commission's regional conferences was held in the Norwegian city of Bergen in 1990. In parallel with the conference, a dinner was organized and hosted by the International Chamber of Commerce. It took place in an old sailing ship, anchored in the port of Bergen. The guests were 140 business leaders and diplomats, who "dined in the ship's belly to discuss how business might join the global conversation around spearheading economic progress while safeguarding the environment" (Timberlake 2005). At this dinner table, and later in the Captain's Log, the World Business Council for Sustainable Development (WBCSD) was initiated. The individual motivation for the initiators and funders was that "up to that point, business had played no role to speak of, other than that of bystander" in the discussions on the environment (Timberlake 2005). The challenge, furthermore, was how to "get beyond the entrenched fighting" that tended to occur at the national level. Stephan Schmidheiny, the Chair of WBCSD, expressed it clearly:

Everywhere I looked, the issue of the environment was being caught in a political, partisan in-fight, in almost all countries. (Quoted in Timberlake 2005)

Schmidheiny was the owner of a Swiss company, the Eternit Group, that faced urgent problems with the emergence of government regulations on asbestos. According to Timberlake, recruitment into WBCSD was based on "an act of faith," a personal commitment to the cause of finding a solution to the problem of how to reconcile the interests of business and the environment.

This personal commitment was, in those early years, often at odds with what was ordinarily regarded as the core task of a business leader. The WBCSD community tended to mimic strategies of other environmental NGO networks. It attempted to influence UN conferences from an activist perspective, by being there, staging parallel events, and conferences.

One of the first achievements of WBCSD was the book *Changing Course*, which was presented at the 1992 Earth Summit, with a substantial WBCSD presence. This was followed up at the Kyoto Conference in 1997, where WBCSD brought together 800 business leaders in a parallel conference. In the following years, the WBCSD arranged seminars and hosted conferences at which business leaders discussed issues relating to "eco-efficiency," the question of combining business interests and concern for the environment, and discussed possible standards and indicators benchmarking the contributions of corporations in terms of environmental sustainability. The WBCSD did that through breaking what was, in 1990, a barrier between business, on the one hand, and on the other environmentalists, politicians, and civil servants working on the promotion of sustainable development through the regulation of business activity. WBCSD was later on also organized regionally, with one branch in China. In 2009, as we shall see, WBCSD is one of the partners in the EU-funded STRACO2 project (STRACO2 2007), within the framework of which the first steps are being taken towards creating new global standards and regulations for CCS technology, through negotiations between the EU and China within the framework of the EU–China Partnership on Climate Change (Fu 2007).

Another core contributor to these recent negotiations is CO2NET, which is a network organization that was established in 2001 within the framework of an EU project. It continues as a membership-funded organization (CO2NET 2008). CO2NET is dedicated to development of the collective knowledge required to capture carbon dioxide at the point of emission in the carbon-based energy-producing industries, and to store it permanently and safely under the earth's surface as part of the solution to the problem of global warming. In this way, the community sharing this knowledge is contributing to the formation of an emerging global market of carbon capture and storage technologies. As a collective, CO2NET has an opinion on the problem of climate change and its solution that clearly differs from the IPCC "mainstream" focus on "green technologies." This solution may be seen as competing with green energy systems such as wind, sun, and bio-energy. Some of its opponents may also simply see it as an attempt to "preserve" carbon-based energy technologies, by cleaning them up rather than developing new energy systems. Storage safety is controversial. Accordingly it has met with resistance from some of the core green-tech activist networks, such as Greenpeace International, and it has not yet been endorsed by IPCC. In this way, as pointed out by Djelic and Quack (in this volume), transnational communities become "devices for ongoing struggles and interactions about 'collective sense-making' in transnational governance."

What are the functions or contributions of such transnational communities in relation to transnational institutions and indeed in relation to the wider issue of global governance? At this point, Djelic and Quack turn to Norbert Elias and his discussion of the relationship between institutional differentiation and community. "Communities exist," Elias tells us, "in less or more differentiated societies alike but their features and structures differ markedly depending upon the degree of differentiation of the society. More specifically, communities tend to become less differentiated as societies become more differentiated" (cited by Djelic and Quack in this volume). The notion of differentiation within a national system is often associated with a hierarchically coordinated division of labor, likely to lead to knowledge compartmentalization, preventing cross-sectoral and cross-disciplinary problem-solving. Transnational institutions are located outside the realm of coordination and strategic decision-making characteristic of a national system with a state and a government. Here, as we shall argue below, differentiation is likely to lead to fragmentation (DiMaggio and Powell 1983; Scharpf 1988; Mariussen 2002). At this level, Elias's point may be reformulated. The significance of integrated, transnational communities in global governance must be seen as a result of the fragmentation of transnational institutions, and of the resulting perceived failure of these institutions in handling complex but, according to some, urgent global challenges, such as global warming. Table 14.1 identifies two

Table 14.1 Transnational communities, institutions, and global markets

Level	Institutional fragmentation	Communities	Transnational governance
Global–national	National closed shops	Discursive coordination	EU–China climate change partnership
	Tragedy of the global commons	Activism	Decisions on CO_2 and CCS regulations
Transnational	Overlapping and inconsistent institutions	Crossing institutional divides	Bridging institutional controversies
	Lack of value chain and supporting institutions	Cognitive framework for industrial self-organization	Emerging global market for CCS technology

different levels of coordination – global–national and transnational – in the context of which this relationship between institutions, communities, and governance may be taking place. In the following sections, we shall discuss this further.

Institutional fragmentation

When it comes to institutional fragmentation in the context of the interplay between the national and the global, there are two main problems, one conceptual and the other game-theoretical. The conceptual problem is straightforward. From the perspective of an actor in a transnational institution, national policy-making systems will likely be seen, at least during the initial phase of contact, as so many different "closed shops" with unique system configurations and institutional complementarities varying from country to country (Böhme 2006). This creates a gap between the policy message of the transnational institution and the national system. The solution can be provided by micro-level interpersonal communities evolving within networks between the transnational institution and its national-level contact points. People on both sides of the divide get involved in the development of a transnational framework of shared understandings, taking national system peculiarities into consideration. This may be seen as a new operational version of the original mission statement of the transnational institution. Once established, the hegemonic transnational framework enables discursive reinterpretations of national systems as subsystems or varieties of general transnational shared understandings. [0]The case in point in this chapter is the aforementioned negotiations of transnational standards for CCS technology, within the framework of the EU–China partnership (EU Commission 2005; Innovation Norway and Gassnova 2008).

Fragmentation, however, has another implication: the lack of a strategic and unique decision-making power, or "global government." Instead of global-level decisions taking the interests of humanity as a point of departure, issues involving resource allocation have to be negotiated between national governments and, in a sense, upwards.[1] This level of decision-making opens itself up for the game-theoretical tragedy of the global commons. If successful, investments aimed at saving the world from global warming are likely to produce a collective good. According to the activists arguing for CO_2 reductions, this common good is a matter of humanity avoiding disasters caused by new and dynamic forms of flooding, drought, desertification, forced climate migration, and starvation, to mention only a few. The game-theoretical problem is that the result of these investments cannot be privatized by the investor. The issue, accordingly, is all about not getting into a position in which your country or your business must pay the bill.

This absence of a strategic global decision-making power was anticipated within the policy paradigm of Brundtland-style sustainable development, which was to be achieved through local actions ("think global – act local"), sustained through positive local feedback loops (development). In some countries – such as the USA, Germany, and Japan – domestic industries supported by markets for "clean" energy technologies (Jakobsson *et al.* 2002) became locally profitable with the assistance of national support policies. In the late 1970s, the UN's endorsement of sustainable development policies contributed to boosting the development of these "clean-tech" industries, many of them based on local and regional clusters, embedded in localized communities where physical proximity is crucial to innovation (Cooke 2008). The hope is that the market and local forms of self-organizing green business dynamics will be able to support the evolution of clean energy technologies that sometime in the future will become mature and economically competitive with carbon-based systems. In this way, bio-business might be able to solve the problem of global warming, and create environmentally sustainable economic development.

However, the idea that environmental sustainability is possible through economic self-organization driven by positive feedback loops is an intuition – a weak hypothesis that remains to be tested by hard evidence. On the other side of the table, there is the *geophysical* approach to climate change and global warming seen as caused by CO_2 emissions created by human energy systems, technologies, and patterns of consumption. The message from geophysics is not necessarily congruent with the idea of sustainable development. On the contrary, restricting CO_2 emissions is likely to hurt growth in several developing countries, where coal and other carbon-based sources of energy are the obvious choice to promote further growth. This brings back the game-theoretical problem. Should rich countries that already consume a lot of energy and emit lots of CO_2 pay by reducing their emissions, or should developing countries, such as China and India, pick up the bill and restrict their economic development? So far, transnational institutions have failed to provide an answer. In the face of this problem, as this case study documents, the EU–China partnership agrees that a common understanding of the problem of CO_2 regulation is impossible, but at the same time there is a continued effort to transfer technology and develop shared standards through the STRACO2 project (see below).

This global-level institutional failure has had a remarkable outcome. There is a widening tension between, on the one hand, the development of a shared understanding of the problem through sense-making communities of global warming, and on the other hand the inability of transnational institutions to solve the problem. But this very institutional weakness is energizing communities. Transnational activists typically take a long-term position in favor of the planet rather than the narrower short-term interests of any particular national economy. These forms of activism may evolve within, and indeed draw upon, generalized frameworks for cooperation provided by the aforementioned multiple layers of transnational institutions and networks. We may add that transnational institutions themselves may deliberately enable this form of diverse community-building as complementary to their own more narrowly defined "iron cage." In the case of CO_2 and global warming, this is illustrated by the role played by research and business communities such as CO2NET, and others such as the World Business Council for Sustainable Development, in the current negotiations between the EU and China on global warming (see below).

At the level of transnational coordination there are two related problems. The first has to do with the existence of conceptually inconsistent and overlapping institutions (Mariussen 2002; Mariussen and Uhlin 2006). Secondly, with a new technology such as CCS, there is no transnational institutional framework in place to give the technology legitimacy. There are no shared and institutionalized standards for technological performance and safety. In terms of CCS, the establishment of these standards early on was recognized as a core precondition for the creation of a global market for this technology. As transnational institutions more often than not are set up on an ad hoc basis by joint decisions made by national governments, their own power to coordinate, whether hierarchically or through formalized negotiations, is often limited. Once transnational institutions are established, inertia at the level of inter-governmental or inter-ministerial cooperation tends to protect them and prevent major top-down reforms. Transnational institutions are often invented and referred to through fairly generalized and unrelated concepts, such as "sustainable development" or "global warming." The need for CO_2 regulation as expressed by the global warming community and institutions is based on earth science, with no initial concern for economic development. The concept of "sustainable development" is often seen as assuming, in an unsubstantiated way, that a compromise between environmental protection and economic development is possible. These concepts continue to coexist, despite much effort to reconcile them (Halsnæs *et al.* 2007). Again, this tension at the institutional level is fertile ground for activist strategies and communities promoting new forms of understanding across institutional divides. The lack of authoritative transnational institutional guidance opens the way for competing strategies emerging from different epistemic communities.

Communities and governance

In terms of geophysics, the debate on the relationship between the atmosphere, energy, and climate goes back to the sixteenth century (Le Treut *et al.* 2007). The major issue in the evolution of the transnational scientific community of weather research was to set up institutions able to produce and share standardized transnational weather data. The first suggestion for such a globally standardized system for monitoring weather was made by the Royal Netherlands Meteorological Institute in Utrecht in 1874. The International Meteorological Organization (IMO) was set up in 1873. The objective for IMO – as well as the heir of IMO, the World Meteorological Organization (WMO) – was to produce and exchange standardized meteorological observations. The World Weather Records were set up, a monthly statistical publication, based on a standard defined at the 1923 IMO conference. Based on these statistics, it became possible to observe global temperatures.

The first articles on the relationship between global temperature and CO_2 emissions were published by Callendar in 1938, based on 200 station records. Systematic data collection on human CO_2 emissions into the atmosphere was initiated by Charles David Keeling, who in 1958 started to measure CO_2 concentrations in the atmosphere in Mauna Loa in Hawaii (Le Treut *et al.* 2007). In the 1950s, scientific publications on those issues started to grow exponentially, with a doubling time of eleven years. A crucial link between climate research and global governance was provided by models of global climate change. Earth science has serious methodological problems. First, earth scientists have only one "earth" on which to compile reliable data. Second, controlled experiments on global climate are not possible. This turns models into an important scientific instrument, since they can be tested against historical climate data. Consensus on model-building was a new step in the evolution of the scientific community.

The first models were fairly simplistic, with a few overall geophysical variables. However, it was clear that the relationship between CO_2 in the atmosphere and changes in global average temperature depended upon processes in complex natural and societal subsystems. In this way, different scientific disciplines were involved, and the field became increasingly trans-disciplinary. A core challenge in the evolution of these more complex models was to include geographical factors. In this way, models could also be used to produce scenarios for specific regions. This led to a higher and higher "spatial resolution" in the models (Le Treut *et al.* 2007). Better models provided more detailed, cross-disciplinary analysis, and also new understanding of important factors that were left out of the early meteorological models. Examples are a new understanding of the relationship between temperature, melting of glaciers, rivers, and desertification, which are crucial in the current understanding of carbon capture and storage. As mentioned in the introduction, the difference in problem definition between IPCC and CO2NET is due to a new perception of the problem of global warming. This new understanding is due to the evolution of new climate change models, which, through higher resolution, are able to produce more and more sophisticated regional-level climate change scenarios. At the regional level, what may look like small changes in global temperature, such as 2 degrees Celsius, may have wide-ranging implications. In the IPCC approach the thawing of glaciers and permafrost is important because it contributes to a rise in global sea level. Still, this threat is fairly remote in time. In the CO2NET regional perspective, on the other hand, glaciers resting on permafrost are seen as part of regional systems that also include rivers and deserts. In that way, the network has discovered a regional threat. If the global average temperature rise exceeds 2 degrees by 2050, there is a real possibility that the glaciers of the Himalayas and the Alps will thaw, and the great glacier-based rivers of China, India, Italy, and France will dry up. The result is likely to be widespread desertification of Southern Europe, China, and India by 2050. Desertification, so the story goes, is likely to lead to destruction of agriculture, starvation, and mass migration, as well as other related, and particularly nasty, problems, such as plagues and wars. That is, unless humanity manages to cut CO_2 emissions by 20 percent from the current level (Stangeland 2007).

In terms of this new understanding, if humanity is to be able to survive, we need to act now. This new understanding defines an agenda more urgent than the one supported by IPCC. The market will not be able to deliver clean technologies quickly enough. We have to clean up carbon-based energy production. This new understanding has led to a rather surprising alliance – demonstrated by the membership of CO2NET – between the oil industry, environmental activists, and research communities. Due to this urgency, the CO2NET community is now growing a new global market for

CCS technology. We have to adapt carbon-based energy production to the requirements of a future global regime of CO_2 taxation. By applying CCS technology, carbon-based energy can be produced with no CO_2 emissions. You just remove carbon dioxide from the chimney of the coal- or oil-based energy producer, and store it in the ground. In doing so, however, you need a fairly robust set of global rules on CO_2 emissions, the efficiency of the CCS technology has to be improved substantially, and proper standards for safe storage have to be agreed.

Like all new inventions, the CCS technology has a long way to go. First, there is the problem of cost and inefficiency. Within the framework of CCS, when energy producers build large-scale factories they are obliged to ensure that their emissions are clean. These factories also use energy to remove CO_2. So far, costs are fairly high, at roughly 50 US dollars for one tonne of CO_2 removed from the atmosphere, as well as a fairly substantial reduction in energy efficiency. These have been seen as major obstacles to further development of this technology. Another major objection is storage. The captured CO_2 that results from the process is liquid and stored under high pressure. It must be transported through pipelines into safe deposits, in appropriate geological formations, under the sea or in safe, subterranean areas. However, once inside these formations, the CO_2 is likely to start seeking ways of escaping to the surface. Leaks may create a range of problems, such as uncontrolled rises in atmospheric CO_2, which in large concentrations may cause considerable damage, and even be toxic. The gas has to be stored in geological formations that may provide closed lids preventing leaks for several thousand years, before carbon is finally separated from the oxygen and solidifies. It has long been understood that in order to become a credible alternative as a technology for reducing CO_2 emissions into the atmosphere, CCS technology needs to be developed, not just through research, but also through large-scale industrial experimentation. This barrier has long blocked further development.

Before 2000, most industrial projects involving carbon capture and storage were motivated by the need to reinject gas into the geological formation to extract more resources. This was the case in the Statoil project in the In Salah gas field in Algeria. Similar experiments are being carried out by other oil companies, in Weyburn in Saskatchewan, Canada; in Australia, and in the Netherlands. However, in the largest industrial storage project, in the Sleipner gas field in Norway, operated by Statoil, the motive was to prevent CO_2 emissions from gas-based energy production from reaching the atmosphere. This was caused by a dilemma which had haunted the Norwegian government for a long time. Since Norwegian energy production is based on hydroelectric power, there is a national ban on all CO_2 emissions in energy production. This became a problem when Norway discovered large domestic resources of natural gas. The solution was to export the gas, and to apply a strict rule of carbon capture and storage on domestic gas-based energy production. The Statoil strategy was supported by both national authorities and local environmental NGOs, such as Bellona and the national branch of Greenpeace. Norwegian research institutes were also involved. Those participating in the national-level network became aware of the limitations of this industrial strategy.

At the same time, they realized that the development of this technology could not be undertaken by a single small country, such as Norway, with a small domestic oil company. It was necessary to mobilize an international alliance to develop CCS as a global solution to the problem of global warming. In that way, the technological barriers could be overcome through transnational cooperation between several oil companies and research efforts. In this way, importantly, it was anticipated that it would also be possible to implement international regulation and a system of taxation of CO_2 polluters, which would render CCS technology profitable. In order to do so, it was necessary to mobilize a global shared knowledge within the framework of which several oil companies and research institutions would share the technology and promote it jointly. This strategy was made possible by the European Commission, which started to fund research to support these experiments under the Fifth Framework Programme for Research, which started in 2001.

CO2NET was set up through one of these projects, as a Carbon Dioxide Thematic Network. CO2NET continues to see the development of CCS as a safe, technically feasible, socially acceptable option to help reduce the effects of human-influenced climate change and to meet the CO_2 emissions reduction target set by the Kyoto Agreement with a view to even greater emissions reductions across Europe and beyond (CO2NET 2008). The lead partner in the network organization was the Norwegian oil company Statoil. From the start – in 2000 – the core objective was to promote and share carbon capture and storage knowledge. This knowledge-sharing established a foundation for continuing the network as an industry-led, participant-funded activity, and for organizing CCS networking opportunities, including the Annual Seminar. According to the organization's homepage (www.clubco2.net), the latter is a core component of CO2NET operations. The CO2NET Annual Seminar has established itself as the flagship event for CCS networking in Europe,

Table 14.2 CO2NET members, 2000–09

	Members 2000		Members 2009	
Country	Total	Large	Total	Large
UK	9	2	6	4
France	5	0	4	2
Netherlands	4	0	4	0
Italy	1	0	3	1
Norway	5	1	3	1
Sweden	1	1	3	1
Other countries	3	0	17	2
Total countries	9	3	24	7
Total members	28	4	40	11

Source: CO2NET homepage: www.co2net.eu.

providing an arena for sharing the latest CCS knowledge and enabling the newest CCS recruits to become acquainted with colleagues. Many projects and partnerships have been brokered at this event to fill gaps in R&D and commercial deployment, and it has helped move CO_2 technology towards a commercial reality and a safe, technically feasible, socially acceptable mitigation option, providing a safe, secure, climate-friendly energy supply for the EU.

Members are obliged to share knowledge. With a view to building the optimum Seminar agenda, each member undertakes to keep the Secretariat informed of CCS developments, projects, or studies in which the member company is involved, subject to protection of the member's reasonable business interests, and/or undertakings of confidentiality. There are different types of membership status. Full members are oil companies, other energy companies, and large-scale petroleum technology suppliers. Standard members are medium-sized companies and large universities or research institutes. Basic members are small firms, research institutes, and NGOs. CO2NET East brings together members from Eastern Europe. From the outset, a core mission was to recruit new members. In 2000, companies and research institutions from nine countries were members (see Table 14.2). As of 2009, the number has increased to twenty-four European countries and Australia. The four leading countries in terms of membership in 2000 were the UK, France, Norway, and the Netherlands. In 2009, Italy and Sweden each have substantial participation, with three member organizations each. Concerning full members – that is, oil companies, major energy companies, and petroleum technology suppliers – we find the same basic pattern, with the UK, France, Italy, Norway, and Sweden having large-scale industries, large and small research institutes, and NGOs as members. Two countries, Finland and Belgium, have only full members. From its founding until the present, thirty-six EU Framework Programme Projects have participated in the network. This participation means, importantly, that findings from these projects were shared and disseminated through the network.

In addition to this transnational level, the CO2NET has national nodes, such as the French Club CO2. The Norwegian NGO Bellona has played a core role in the organization of CO2NET, not least because of the long-term collaboration between the NGO Bellona and the Norwegian oil industry. CO2NET also has other related scientific communities, such as GTNet-P, which is a cross-disciplinary, transnational scientific network based on transnational scientific communities. It cuts across scientific borders in order to enhance our understanding of the interaction between glaciers, permafrost, and permafrost thawing in different parts of the world. CO2NET is run by a small management board of fully paid up large company (major oil companies and other energy producers) and standard members (universities, NGOs, and research institutes), with a rotating chair. The board appoints a technical planning team of members to decide the content of the GTNet-P Annual Seminar, which takes place in parallel with the Annual General Meeting for members. These mechanisms are in place to ensure the open dissemination of information. The board meets once or twice a year, as required. Network members have collectively authored several technical publications, established a university course in CCS, and set standards for CCS research and development.

Transnational communities such as CO2NET cultivate a shared knowledge, which facilitates analysis of global problems – in this case the problem of global warming – as well as the generation of solutions, such as CCS, that can be diffused into different national policy-making systems. However, CO2NET is predominantly European. One of the major challenges in developing a global market for CCS technology is that it has to be accepted and applied in countries with high CO_2 emission rates, such as China. This is why the EU has put CCS technology on the agenda in its cooperation with China. This has led to cooperation between the EU and China on research, technology transfer, and the regulation of CCS technology. Through this connection, Chinese researchers and other partners are involved in the development of regulations on CCS and CCS technology in Europe. The institutional framework of regulation of this technology is being developed through a network of networks which includes WBCSD, GTNet-P, and CO2NET, organized as an EU Framework Programme project, STRACO2, set up to support the development of a regulatory framework for CCS in the EU. By supporting a CCS regulatory framework inside the EU, STRACO2 will also be instrumental in establishing best practice standards globally. This builds on networks established through a sequence of earlier FP5 and FP6 European projects, and it includes Chinese partners. In this way, STRACO2 is a part of the EU–China partnership on Climate Change (European Commission 2005; European Policy Centre 2007; STRACO2 2007). The ambition is that micro-level connections, involving transfer of technology and sharing of knowledge between researchers, experts, and other professionals in different countries, will in the long run form a platform for CO_2 regulation, enabling the application of CCS technologies to reduce Chinese CO_2 emissions.

At the time of writing, in 2009, CCS is due to enter a new phase, as several large-scale test industrial projects are being initiated. These are seen as the commencement of the new global market. This involves a shift from the mobilization phase to a situation in which oil companies will be competing. This new role for CO2NET is reflected in the plan for 2010–11 as follows:

The members recognize that a substantial knowledgeable skills base is required and that a prime concern is building the "people capability" in CCS. CO2NET has evolved as CCS has developed and now has a niche role in providing education to understand CCS in detail across all its disciplines, to enable sharing of crucial lessons learned and transfer skills to personnel incoming to CCS. Its key role is now assisting its members to build the much needed "people capability" in CCS. (CO2NET 2008)

Conclusions

Some of the problems humanity is facing today are too complex – and sometimes even impossible – to solve at the national level. They are, according to Rotmans and Loorbach (2008: 15), "persistent problems whose symptoms are becoming more and more apparent." In looking for forms of societal organization that could help humanity solve these types of problems, the notion of community should be approached carefully. Transnational epistemic communities battling with the problem of global warming are genuinely bottom-up phenomena that cannot be restricted to conceptualization in terms of transition management, which is a top-down process. Through knowledge-sharing and other interpersonal community-building processes, transnational communities contribute to overcoming the problems of global-level institutional fragmentation. At the same time, the evolution of these communities depends on institutionalized networks.

The case of CO2NET illustrates two somewhat surprising findings. First, there is active cooperation between environmental NGO activists such as Bellona and big oil companies in seeking new solutions to the problems of CO_2 emissions causing global warming. This is a step beyond the entrenched fighting and confrontation that characterized the years of the Stockholm Conference. Development of this common ground started through initiatives such as WBCSD, as well as, in the Norwegian context, micro-level contacts between NGO activists and people in the Norwegian oil industry working on environmental regulation. Second, there seems to be a mutual awareness, both in the funding institutions – such as the EU Framework Programme for Research – and in the oil companies and research institutions applying for funding that there is a synergy between the objectives of institutions such as the EU and the micro-level development of a shared knowledge. This understanding is crystallized in networks such as CO2NET that enable both long-term knowledge accumulation across several projects and knowledge diffusion across widely dispersed institutional barriers, both between otherwise competing oil companies, and between countries with widely different outlooks in terms of the regulation of CO_2 emissions, such as the EU countries and China.

Transnational institutions have limitations in terms of coordination. The development and diffusion of new energy technologies face tough competition from existing, well-documented solutions. Some of these limitations may be overcome by frameworks that enable the development of micro-level epistemic communities across institutional divides.

Between 2001 and 2009, CO2NET helped to mobilize supporters, both large energy companies and universities and research institutes, which collectively generated enough pressure to initiate the now ongoing large-scale industrial experiments. These experiments may turn CCS into a possible future path of industrial development, in which CO_2 is removed at the point of emission. After 2009, as the oil companies switch to competition mode, and the role of CO2NET is more restricted, the focus will again shift to promotion of public awareness and knowledge diffusion. In 2009, the goal in terms of globally accepted and implemented regulations and taxation of CO_2 polluters – which could make CCS technology into a profitable and self-sustaining global technological market – is far from having been achieved. This still seems to depend on the outcomes of the large-scale industrial experiments now being launched and funded by the EU, as well as the Canadian, US, and

Norwegian governments. We still do not know whether the strategy of the EU–China partnership of promoting a shared knowledge opening closed national systems by means of technological diffusion and integration of Chinese researchers and businesses in the development of European CCS regulations will overcome the aforementioned game-theoretical barrier.

Returning to the point made by Elias on the issue of institutional differentiation and community, additional comments can be offered. At the transnational level, the empirical material presented in this chapter seems to suggest that there is room for synergy between institutions and communities. This is partly due to the inability of institutions to deliver solutions to seemingly urgent problems, as well as their ability to enable community development and knowledge-sharing. The CCS solution is now being allowed, by means of these inconsistent institutional arrangements, to compete with other solutions – such as wind, solar, and bio-energy systems – through large-scale industrial experiments, combined with a sustained effort to develop transnational standards for risk assessment and control. In other words, the loosely coupled social system resulting from this mixture of fragmented institutions and competing transnational communities seems to be facilitating industrial experimentation in different directions. Within this shifting context, and at least in the case of CCS, as documented in this chapter, epistemic communities seem able to grow strong enough to maintain a long-term focus, and to push immature technologies towards commercialization and institutionalization. Until we know what the right answer to the problem of global warming is, this kind of experimental competition is far from being the worst option.

NOTE

1. This problem is overlooked in Rotmans and Loorbach's discussion of transition management as an answer to the persistent problem of anthropogenic climate change (Rotmans and Loorbach 2008), where transition management is possible because the complex problem may be contextualized by a national system.

REFERENCES

ADEME (Agence de l'Environnement et de la Maîtrise de l'Energie), IFP and BRGM. 2005. CO2 *capture and geological storage.* Geoscience Issues No. 5505. www2.ademe.fr.

Bjerkestrand, J. R. 2009. "Norsk teknologi I verdensklasase–hvordan? Aker Clean Carbon." Paper presented at the Norwegian Research Council Energy Week, Oslo.

Blaker, A. M. 2009. "Gassnova. Innovasjon og teknologiutvikling" [Innovation and technological development]. Paper presented at the Norwegian Research Council Energy Week, Oslo.

Böhme, K. 2006. "European integration in the field of spatial policies," in Mariussen, Å. and Uhlin, Å. (eds.), pp. 149–68.

CO2GeoNet. 2002. *What does CO2 geological storage really mean?* Report, CO2GeoNet: www. co2geonet.com.

CO2NET. 2008. *CO2NET 2009–2011 Proposal for continuation of the network.* Kent: Technology Initiatives Ltd.

Cooke, P. 2008. "New insights into socio-technical transitions: Green technology cluster emergence evolving viable market niches." Paper presented at NIFU STEP seminar, Oslo.

DiMaggio, P. and Powell, W. W. 1983. "The iron cage revisited: Institutional isomorphism and collective rationality in organizational fields," *American Sociological Review* **48**: 147–60.

EU Commission. 2005. "EU and China partnership on climate change." Memo/05/298. Brussels: European Commission.

European Policy Centre. 2007. "Europe and China: Interdependence on energy and climate security," Event report. Brussels.

Fu, P. 2007. "Status of and perspectives on CCS in China." Presentation at RITE Carbon Capture and Storage Workshop, February 15, Kyoto, Japan. China: Office of Global Environmental Affairs, Ministry of Science and Technology.

Halsnæs, K. *et al.* 2007. "Framing Issues," in Solomon, S. *et al.* (eds.), *Climate change 2007: Mitigation of climate change.* Contribution of Working Group III to the Fourth Assessment Report of the Intergovernmental Panel on Climate Change. Cambridge University Press, pp. 117–68.

Innovation Norway and Gassnova. 2008. "China: Governmental programs and strategies," *International CCS Technology Survey* 3/2008: 115–120.

Jakobsen, V. E., Hauge, F., Holm, M. and Kristiansen, B. 2005. *Environment and value creation: CO2 for EOR on the Norwegian Shelf.* Bellona Report. Oslo: Bellona Foundation.

Jakobsson, S., Andersson, B. A. and Bångenes, L. 2002. "Transforming the energy system. The evolution of the German technological system for solar cells." *SPRU Electronic Working Paper Series* 84. Brighton: University of Sussex.

Jeroen, C. and Bruisma, F. (eds). 2008. *Managing the transition to renewable energy: Theory and practice from local, regional and macro perspectives.* Cheltenham: Edward Elgar.

Keck, M. and Sikkink, K. 1998. *Activists beyond borders.* Ithaca, NY: Cornell University Press.

Klitkou, A., Pedersen, T. E., Scordato, L. and Mariussen, Å. 2008. *"Competitive policies in the Nordic Energy Research and Innovation Area eNERGIA."* NIFU STEP Report 24. Oslo: NIFU STEP.

Kristiansen, B. 2007. "Do we need CCS?" Bellona presentation at Green Week, Brussels, June 2007. Oslo: Bellona Foundation.

Le Treut, H. *et al.* 2007. "Historical overview of climate change science," in Solomon, S. *et al.* (eds.), *Climate change 2007: The physical science basis.* Contribution of Working Group I to the Fourth Assessment Report of the Intergovernmental Panel on Climate Change. Cambridge University Press, pp. 93–128.

Mariussen, Å. 2002. "Sustainable fragmentation: Regional organizations in the north," in Hedegaard, L. and Lindström, B. (eds.), *NEBI Yearbook 2001/2002: North European and Baltic Sea Integration*. Berlin: Springer Verlag.

Mariussen, Å. and Uhlin, Å. (eds.) 2006. *Transnational practices. System thinking in policy making*. Stockholm: Nordregio.

Røkke, N. 2009. "Framtidas fangstteknologi – hvor er vi på vei?" [*The capture technology of tomorrow – where are we heading?*]. SINTEF paper presented at the Norwegian Research Council Energy Week 2009, Oslo.

Rotmans, J. and Loorbach, D. 2008. "Transition management: Reflexive governance of societal complexity through searching, learning and experimenting," in van den Bergh, J. C. J. M. and Bruinsma, F. R. (eds.), *Managing the transition to renewable energy*. Cheltenham: Edward Elgar.

Scharpf, F. W. 1988. "The joint decision trap: Lessons from German federalism and European integration," *Public Administration* **66**: 239–78.

Stangeland, A. 2007. "CCS – A powerful catalyst for change: Power, industry, hydrogen." Biomass presentation at the Green Week, Brussels. Oslo: Bellona Foundation.

Stephens, J. C. and van der Zwaan, R. 2005. "The case for carbon capture and storage," *Issues in Science and Technology* Fall 2005. www.issues.org.

STRACO2. 2007. "Support to regulatory activities for CO_2 capture and storage." Cordis homepage: http://cordis.europa.eu.

Timberlake, L. 2005. *Catalyzing change: A short history of the WBCSD*. Geneva: World Business Council for Sustainable Development.

United Nations. 1983. "Process of preparation of the environmental perspective for the year 2000 and beyond." General Assembly Resolution 38/161, December 19, 1983. Accessed April 11, 2007.

United Nations. 1987. "Our common future." Report of the World Commission on Environment and Development. Published as Annex to General Assembly Document A/42/427, Development and International Co-operation: Environment.

van der Beken, A. 2009. "Addressing the remaining technical challenges in storage– Schlumberger approach." Paper presented at the Norwegian Research Council Energy Week, Oslo.

Communities of practice as cause and consequence of transnational governance: the evolution of social and environmental certification

Tim Bartley and Shawna N. Smith

When communities of organic farmers began certifying ecologically friendly agriculture, they could never have guessed how prominent the certification model would become. Nearly four decades later, consumers can buy products not just from certified farms, but also certified forests, fisheries, and factories – with standards pertaining not only to the environment, but also to "social" conditions of labor and community development. Firms interested in "corporate social responsibility" and "ethical sourcing" can now draw on a growing set of suppliers whose labor or environmental standards have been certified by an independent body. For their part, the certification associations that oversee this activity – the Fairtrade Labeling Organization, Forest Stewardship Council, Social Accountability International, and others – find themselves entwined in an increasingly elaborate web of transnational governance, layered with evolving rules about trade and standard-setting, competing initiatives, and a variety of questions about the legitimacy and effectiveness of their activities. Certification of *quality* and product safety has, of course, existed for many years (Cheit 1990), but the transformation of certification into a mode of social/ environmental regulation has occurred mainly since the 1990s.

Most observers of certification initiatives have focused on a single sector or issue domain. Thus, we have a range of studies of forest certification, organic agriculture, Fair Trade certification, labor standards monitoring, and the sustainable management of fisheries. More general theories of this form often portray it as a solution to several types of problems. For some, the growth of private sector certification reflects its potential to address vexing problems of ecological sustainability and social justice that governments have been unwilling or unable to resolve (Conroy 2007). Others emphasize how certification can solve reputation problems faced by firms that have been "named and shamed" by activists (Gereffi *et al.* 2001). Alternatively, some set aside the functional aspects of certification systems and treat them as symbols of rationalized virtue on the global stage (Boli 2006).

We agree with these scholars that social and environmental certification is more than a scattered set of initiatives and amounts rather to a distinctive model of transnational private regulation. We view the certification model as neither pure myth and ceremony nor fully functional solution, but rather as an evolving transnational institution-building project (Bartley 2007a, 2007b). Particular actors have seeded and cultivated the certification project, and some have even worked across different initiatives to structure a field of social/environmental certification (Bartley and Smith 2008; Dingwerth and Pattberg 2009). The expansion of the certification model is partly a function of spiraling questions of trust – that is, "who watches the watchdog?" – and partly a result of institutional entrepreneurs pushing this model of governance. But conflict is also prevalent in this project. Industry associations and NGOs have repeatedly fought for control of this form. Critics on the Left often portray certification associations as little more than greenwash/cleanwash, while "market fundamentalists" charge that certification is a disguised form of protectionism. Unlike the relatively consensual communities documented elsewhere in this volume, our chapter provides a case in which cooperation and growing coherence exist alongside conflict and debate.

Examining transnational communities sheds light on two aspects of this model and the institution-building projects that underlie it. First, the initial development of influential certification programs can be traced to relatively small communities of practice, organized around political, religious, and professional commitments. Fair Trade certified coffee, for instance, grew out of the transnational work of small groups of peace and religious activists. Second, the recent growth of linkages among previously distinct certification associations – and the many actors involved in their operation – provides an infrastructure for new transnational communities of practice to emerge. As certification associations have grown and become more interconnected across national and issue-based boundaries, their identities have shifted – from mechanisms for serving niche markets to systems of standard-setting for the global economy. Through this process, new transnational communities of practice appear to be emerging as individuals from different programs come together to legitimate their activity. Even representatives of competing certification initiatives have engaged in loose forms of cooperation.

At its core, the certification model is multivalent and rooted in a set of compromises. Certification inserts an alternative "order of worth" (Boltanski and Thévenot 2006) into markets even while it embraces the market as the means to do so – that is, with a label to inform consumer choice. It suggests an alternative to neoliberal globalization, yet it resonates with neoliberal prescriptions (that is, the power of markets to solve social problems) and proscriptions (that is, against government intervention). It faces a multi-level problem of legitimacy – in markets, where it needs firm support and credibility among consumers; vis-à-vis national governments; and in global governance arenas, where consistency with both NGO agendas and World Trade Organization (WTO) rules is important. In addition, certification associations face serious questions about their ability to transform conditions "on the ground," particularly as evidence mounts that private monitoring and product labeling are often ineffective (Mutersbaugh 2005; Locke *et al.* 2007; Seidman 2007). Table 15.1 lists the certification associations featured in this chapter,

Table 15.1 Dedicated social and environmental certification associations (founded before 2001)

Name	Year founded	Constituency	Industries/products
Environmental			
IFOAM: International Federation of Organic Agricultural Movements	1972 (1997 as cert. assn.)	Multi-stakeholder	Food and agriculture
FSC: Forest Stewardship Council[a]	1993	Multi-stakeholder	Forest products
SFI: Sustainable Forestry Initiative/ Board	1994 (1998 as cert. assn.)	Industry association	Forest products
PEFC: Programme for the Endorsement of Forest Certification	1999	Industry association	Forest products
MAC: Marine Aquarium Council	1998	Multi-stakeholder	Ornamental/exotic fish
MSC: Marine Stewardship Council	1999	Multi-stakeholder	Fishing and seafood
Social/labor			
FLO: Fairtrade Labeling Organization	1997	Multi-stakeholder	Food and agriculture
SAI: Social Accountability International	1997	Multi-stakeholder	Apparel, toys, food, etc.
FLA: Fair Labor Association	1996 (1999 as cert. assn.)	Multi-stakeholder[b]	Apparel and footwear
WRAP: Worldwide Responsible Apparel Production	1999	Industry association	Apparel and footwear

Note. Cert. assn. = certification association.

[a] Though the FSC also includes social standards, it has largely positioned itself as an eco-labeling initiative and is much more closely tied to environmental organizations than to labor groups.

[b] The FLA is considered multi-stakeholder but lacks support from organized labor.

which make up the set of dedicated social or environmental certification associations founded by 2001. Other organizations that are engaged in this activity but are not dedicated certification associations – such as stand-alone certifiers (for example, Rainforest alliance) or multi-purpose standard-setting bodies (for example, International Organization for Standardization [ISO]) – are included in our analysis to the (considerable) extent that they intersect with these certification associations.

We proceed by discussing conceptions of transnational communities and their application to our case. Next we show that the roots of certification lie in transnational communities forged in an earlier period. We then examine network data on infrastructure for new transnational communities, focusing on ties to intermediary organizations – the NGOs, governments, firms, and foundations engaged with multiple certification initiatives – and community formation within and across domains.

Conceptions of transnational communities

Mayntz (in this volume) argues that transnational communities consist of individuals bound across borders into a group with a strong collective identity. Though full consensus among community members is not necessary, this definition does require that they be "equals with respect to the shared characteristic" and share a "we" feeling that transcends their differences. However, examining contentious topics such as the governance of global industries uncovers groupings that resemble communities in some ways but which lack this strong sense of collective identity. To make sense of these groupings, more expansive definitions are useful. Morgan (2001) begins by identifying a transnational *space*, or a loosely bounded arena of cross-border connections that represent something more than the negotiation of distinct national interests. A transnational community is a set of actors held together through "structured interactions [that] are based not on contracts or markets but on the recognition of a shared set of interests within a specific transnational social space" (Morgan 2001: 117), which may or may not translate into strong cognitive or affective ties. As Waldinger and Fitzgerald (2004) argue, strong bonds to particularistic groups, even when practiced across borders ("transstate particularism"), may actually conflict with transnationalism in the sense of universalistic, cosmopolitan commitments.

Adler's (2005) conception of a "community of practice" helps specify the character of more loosely bounded communities. Extending research on epistemic communities, Adler focuses on sets of actors involved in a "joint enterprise that is constantly being renegotiated by its members" and held together through "relationships of mutual engagement" (Adler 2005: 15; see Plehwe in this volume). This conceptualization is useful for studying contentious forms of global governance because it allows that communities can be organized around practical activities, motivated by multiple normative rationales; and community members are not limited to recognized experts from scientific and governmental organizations, but may also include representatives of NGOs, firms, trade unions, industry associations, and so on. Our discussion of communities of practice, then, is mostly consistent with Djelic and Quack's (in this volume) argument that communities exist when there is "mutual orientation and dependence of members; articulated around a common identity and/or a common project; a form of active engagement and involvement from at least a minority of members; ... translating into and sustaining a sense of belonging." The extent to which the mutual orientations to a common project we are studying translate into a "sense of belonging" is not entirely clear, however. Indeed, many of the emergent community-like formations in transnational governance are conflicted, such that participants recognize mutual engagement, yet still view each other as "others." Environmentalists and executives engaged in a partnership, for instance, may develop a common language and sense of purpose yet retain a sense of serving different constituencies and reserving the right to bolster cooperation through threat of exit (see Bartley 2007a; Conley and Williams 2008). We believe that scholars of transnational regulation need new tools to understand these loose, conflicted communities of practice. At the risk of overestimating coherence, we use a permissive definition of community requiring only a weak sense of belonging.

Our analysis also raises questions about the relationship between organizations and individual members of communities. While some see organizations as parasitic on communities of individuals (Mayntz in this volume), it seems possible that this relationship could also be symbiotic. Communities of individuals may be important in the founding of new organizations, for instance. Furthermore, organizational networks and fields may serve as an infrastructure for new rounds of community formation at the individual level. Individuals representing organizations at a conference, for instance, may come to perceive themselves as part of a community of practice.[1] We find evidence that each of these dynamics is relevant to the case of social and environmental certification.

Especially important in generating new rounds of transnational community formation are organizations situated as intermediaries. Theoretically, they are the organizational analogues to the individual "rooted cosmopolitans" that bring the legacies of different national and industrial settings into a transnational space (Djelic and Quack in this volume). Empirically, in our case, these intermediaries create indirect linkages between different certification initiatives, as with an NGO or retailer that supports both Fair Trade and forest certification. As these linkages integrate different certification initiatives and structure an organizational field, they may also create new transnational communities of individuals. We find evidence of a growing set of practice-based ties and transnational, trans-issue communities of actors with *partially* shared understandings and projects. As our analysis shows, standard-setting in this arena is deeply imbued with conflict, especially between actors based in industry and NGOs. Here, community formation has entailed some combination of mutual attention, commensuration, and competition.

Communities of practice as sources of transnational governance

Pre-existing communities of practice may be important in generating new modes of governance for several reasons. First, since such communities transcend particular organizations, their members are better situated to develop and implement projects at the level of the field rather than only within organizations. The double-embeddedness of community members should enhance their interest and ability to strategize and experiment beyond their organization's parochial interests, increasing their chances of being effective institutional entrepreneurs. DiMaggio (1991) argues that this is why professions – and professionals – are so important for institutional change. But it may be unnecessary to limit this to professions, which are just one type of community of practice – albeit with legitimated monopolies over abstract areas of knowledge (Quack 2007; Ramirez in this volume). Other communities of practice, based on political, religious, or technical bodies of knowledge, ought to be similarly situated, even if their status is lower.

Second, to the extent that they are already transnational in scope, communities of practice are well positioned to meet the growing demand for rule-making in transnational arenas. Economic globalization, the diffusion of information technologies, and the expansion of rights-based claims all generate demand for rules – whether pertaining to intellectual property, technical coordination, human rights, or environmental sustainability. Pre-existing transnational communities that can demonstrate practical experience working across borders may have unique opportunities to shape transnational rule-making projects. Certainly, not all such communities will have an equal chance to enter arenas of rule-making, since power will partly determine who gets a seat at the table. But the combination of cross-border ties and some degree of collective identity should marginally increase the chances of actors becoming prominent players in transnational rule-making.

The rise of transnational governance at the turn of the twenty-first century can to some extent be described as a process of older transnational communities – forged in the context of twentieth-century Cold War geopolitical conflicts – being reconfigured, amplified, and integrated into new rule-making projects. In the remainder of this section, we describe how several communities of practice contributed to the initial development of social and environmental certification associations.

Much of the inspiration for the recent rise of certification comes from the development of organic agriculture. Organic farming originated as a movement and community of farmers stretching back to the 1930s. The first attempts to certify organic crops occurred in the early 1970s, with the founding of the California Certified Organic Farmers (CCOF) group (Guthman 2004), and the International Federation of Organic Agriculture Movements (IFOAM) in Europe, where organic farmers argued that "the food quality and ecology crisis is no longer a national problem, but an actual international concern" (Chevriot 1972). Initially, IFOAM only issued programmatic statements, but as the organic food market grew in the 1980s and 1990s it began issuing standards and coordinating an otherwise chaotic world of competing certifiers. In 1997, IFOAM introduced a system for accrediting certifiers, making it a full-fledged certification association (Bernstein and Cashore 2007). Though some organic certification functions have now been taken up by national governments, IFOAM continues to play an important role at the transnational level, bringing together hundreds of organizations from nearly a hundred countries, such as the UK-based Soil Association, the Swiss-based Institute for Marketecology (IMO), Ecocert Brazil Certificadora, and the pioneering CCOF.

The founding role of particular communities of practice is even clearer in several other cases. Fair Trade certification for coffee and other agricultural products, for instance, has grown from a few small experiments into a vast transnational project. Currently, the Bonn-based Fairtrade Labeling Organization (FLO) links a growing number of consumers and coffee roasters in Europe and North America with producer cooperatives in Mexico, Ethiopia, Colombia, Uganda, Guatemala, and elsewhere. Though often heralded as a testament to a new transnational civil society, the roots of this project can be traced to older transnational communities, forged in the context of the Cold War. A set of peace activists formed of one of the earliest fair trade coffee projects. In the mid-1980s, US-based peace activists began importing and selling coffee grown by Nicaraguan farmers (calling it "Café Nica"), in defiance of a US trade embargo of Nicaragua and its Sandinista government (Rice and McLean 1999; Auld 2007). The organization behind this action, Equal Exchange, soon became the main purveyor of fairly traded coffee in the USA. Its leaders also became a driving force behind TransFair USA, which linked up with initiatives in Europe to move toward a unified fair trade certification system (Conroy 2007). European efforts had similarly been pioneered by a community of activists, this time united by religious convictions. In the late 1980s, the Dutch Christian ecumenical NGO Solidaridad (Inter-Church Foundation for Action for Latin America) created the Max Havelaar label – the first label for certified fair trade coffee, named for the protagonist of an anti-colonial Dutch novel – in response to a call from a Dutch liberation theology priest who was working with a cooperative of coffee farmers in Oaxaca, Mexico (Mace 1998; Jaffee 2007). As coffee prices plummeted after the 1989 collapse of the International Coffee Agreement, farmers and activists increasingly turned to fair trade certification as a way to counteract poverty and build an alternative system of value (Linton et al. 2004). Max Havelaar and Equal Exchange were soon joined by national fair trade labels throughout Europe, and by the late 1990s, these initiatives came together under the umbrella of FLO. While many factors fueled Fair Trade certification, several initial sparks emerged from cross-border communities of activists navigating Cold War political and religious terrains.

Communities of practice also shaped the earliest experiments with forest certification, leading to the rise of the Forest Stewardship Council (FSC). Between 1989 and 1991, a group of environmentalists, foresters, and woodworkers began to formulate plans for an independent association to certify sound forest management practices. Central to this group were two small but ultimately influential communities of practice. One consisted of members of the Woodworkers alliance for Rainforest Protection (WARP), who first suggested establishing an "international forestry monitoring agency" (Ecological Trading Company 1990), which soon evolved into the FSC. These specialty woodworkers were bound together not only as a set of businesses facing questions from environmentally concerned customers, but also as individuals with a shared biography and sense of purpose. As described by one participant, "the community of woodworkers in the late '80s [was] represented by people who had essentially dropped out of more conventional career tracks in the '60s and

'70s. . . . That type of person was, I think, heavily represented among the early members of WARP" (interview with WARP member, 7/30/02).

The other influential group consisted of foresters who had built up expertise, trust, and networks that helped them become key architects of the FSC. Dubbed the "Peace Corps-Paraguay mafia" by their collaborators, this group "formed very strong ties when they were working in the Peace Corps" (interview with FSC organizer, 8/22/2002) and honed their theories of sustainable forestry while working on various community forestry projects in Peru, Ecuador, Haiti, and Paraguay in the 1980s. Among other projects, they had worked with the Yanesha Forestry Cooperative in Peru, an endeavor funded by the US Agency for International Development (USAID) just after Peru had emerged from a Soviet-allied military government (Morrow and Hull 1996). At the Yanesha Cooperative, these foresters had applied a promising set of forestry methods (Simeone *et al.* 1993) and had begun to think more about market linkages. As one participant later noted, the Yanesha managers:

showed me a letter from their trading partner in Europe [saying] . . . due to what the company perceived to be the market demand, only a small number of the many valuable hardwood species from the Peruvian forest would be marketable. This illustrated to me the fact that the forest is part of a market chain – you can't just support sustainable forest management on the ground without learning more about the supporting marketing system. (Michael Jenkins, quoted in Koenig and Headley 1995: 44)

It was this sort of project that early FSC developers referenced when they noted that growing green markets in Europe and the USA presented a "tremendous market opportunity for the 'wood producer projects' in the US and overseas" (Donovan 1990). Furthermore, the emphasis on community forestry helped foresters and environmentalists to find a balance between "telling people not to buy tropical timber but at the same time [asking] 'how do these communities fit in and how can we support them in the marketplace?'" (interview with environmental activist and FSC developer, 8/23/02), thus building a consensus that could sustain forest certification. The "Peace Corps Paraguay mafia" also proved powerful in their ability to mobilize funding streams for the nascent FSC. One member of this community headed up a small foundation (the Homeland Foundation) that funded much of the FSC's initial development, and another joined the MacArthur Foundation and made it the first of a series of large foundations to support the FSC (Bartley 2007a). In the case of forest certification, then, one can see several ways in which early founding communities left their mark on transnational governance.

The recent rise of labor standards monitoring and factory certification is also linked, albeit indirectly, to earlier transnational communities. The rise of anti-sweatshop activism and experiments with independent factory monitoring (by civil society organizations) in the mid-1990s indirectly fueled later initiatives such as the Fair Labor Association (FLA), Social Accountability International (SAI), and the Worker Rights Consortium (WRC). In the early 1980s, dissatisfied with the AFL-CIO's (American Federation of Labor and Congress of Industrial Organizations) anti-communist cooperation with the CIA in Central America and concerned about civil wars in El Salvador and Guatemala, some left-wing American labor activists split from the AFL-CIO to focus on cross-border solidarity. Among the new groups formed was the National Labor Committee in Support of Democracy and Human Rights in El Salvador. Created in 1981 and fearing that "El Salvador could turn into another Vietnam" (Krupat 1997: 64), this group "sponsored fact-finding delegations and released a series of reports ... condemning the AFL-CIO's policies" (Armbruster-Sandoval 2005: 19–20). With the end of the Salvadoran civil war, this group renamed itself the National Labor Committee and began drawing attention to labor exploitation in Central America. By the mid-1990s, this organization was the loudest and most active leader of the anti-sweatshop movement, "naming and shaming" the Gap, Wal-Mart, Disney, Kathie Lee Gifford, and others over subpar conditions in suppliers' factories. The ability to mount these campaigns hinged on both drumming up media interest and what the group's leader called "deep contacts on the ground in Central America" (Charles Kernaghan, quoted in Krupat 1997: 71).

Other actors in the labor rights community began building experiments with "independent monitoring" of factories, conducted by local NGOs. The Interfaith Center on Corporate Social Responsibility (ICCR) – itself formed during the Vietnam War and active in Central American peace movements of the early 1980s – forged an innovative partnership in 1995 to monitor the Gap's factories in El Salvador. As an ICCR leader explained, "Our participation created what [the] Gap couldn't create on their own–trust with the groups in El Salvador. We could provide expertise and a different perspective" (David Schilling, quoted in Zachary 2002: 3). Similar experiments were conducted in Honduras and Guatemala (Bonacich and Appelbaum 2000; Armbruster-Sandoval 2005). In Guatemala, the coherence of activist communities – also forged within the framework of the peace movements of the 1980s – strengthened independent monitoring. As described by Seidman (2007), "[T]ransnational contacts – specifically, personal visits by American unionists to the region and person contacts between individual activists across borders – altered the way American activists understood regional repression" (Seidman 2007: 109). Within Guatemala, the staff of the monitoring group consisted largely of "activists who had participated in civil society monitoring efforts of the 1980s and 1990s, and who viewed their work for COVERCO [the factory monitor] as a logical extension of earlier efforts to bring peace and democracy to their country" (Seidman 2007: 125). Though these monitors later supported the WRC and some even became accredited auditors for the FLA, factory monitoring has mostly been taken over by for-profit auditing firms with few ties to activist communities. Nevertheless, communities of practice, organized around political and religious resistance to American Cold War foreign policy, laid the groundwork for the expansion of transnational governance in the twenty-first century.

Communities of practice have been innovators, instigators, and collective institutional entrepreneurs for certification as a new form of transnational governance. All of these communities were rooted in participants' shared convictions and knowledge bases – whether religious, political, or professional – and were often intertwined with Cold War geopolitics. Most were forged through common experiences and interpersonal connections across borders. Some directly advocated the certification model (as in forestry and fair trade), while others worried that it would water down their efforts (as with labor activists). But in every case, when we trace the process by which these new forms of governance were developed, we find historically situated communities of practice, not isolated, calculating actors or structural imperatives. The next sections examine how these largely orthogonal communities became intertwined.

Inter-organizational linkages as infrastructures for communities of practice

Linkages between social and environmental certification associations have grown dramatically over a short time period. Certifiers have participated in joint projects, conferences, and umbrella organizations. Competition among industry- and NGO-sponsored programs has led to a series of formal comparisons and, in some instances, mutual adjustment (Overdevest 2005). As this world of standards has grown in size and complexity, a number of NGOs, auditors, retailers, and government agencies have become involved in multiple certification initiatives, with some becoming central intermediaries that pull different initiatives further into an increasingly structured field.

To trace these evolving linkages – and thus the lines upon which new transnational communities of practice may emerge – we developed a strategy for measuring the relationships between dedicated social or environmental certification associations and the variety of other organizations involved in their operation at two points in time, 2001 and 2006. Since certification associations have different structures and logics of participation, our strategy defines involvement broadly and looks for traces that an organization is in some way affiliated with (for example, on a board of directors, as accredited auditor, providing consultation) or referenced by (for example, as a basis for particular standards) a certification association. Data on these linkages come from certification association websites, with 2001 data collected using the Internet Archive (www.archive.org). Such websites provide valuable, if imperfect, information on the operation and self-presentation of certification associations.[2]

We examined the entire contents of each certification association's website and recorded all organizations mentioned. Given our interest in intermediaries, we excluded from analysis organizations tied only to a single association. The result is a two-mode matrix of ties from ten certification associations (eleven in 2006) to hundreds of intermediary organizations (firms, NGOs, government agencies, and so on). We used NetDraw in UCINET 6.16 to develop visualizations of these networks, using the spring-embedding algorithm, which arranges nodes based on cohesion. We combined these network data with more qualitative evidence to examine the integration of certification associations within and across issue domains and to identify settings in which individual-level community-building also appears to be occurring.

Elaboration and integration in the environmental arena

From pioneers such as IFOAM and the FSC to later entrants such as the Marine Stewardship Council (MSC) and the Programme for the Endorsement of Forest Certification (PEFC), a variety of environmental certification associations have emerged. We highlight two key mechanisms – competition and diffusion – behind this expansion.

Competition among multiple certifiers accounts for much of the expansion of forest certification, leading to a conflicted and divided community of certification advocates. Soon after the FSC's founding, industry associations in North America, Europe, and several timber-exporting countries began developing their own certification systems to counter the perceived NGO dominance of the FSC (Elliott 2000). In the USA, the American Forest and

Paper Association (AFPA) converted its code of conduct into a full-fledged certification program, the Sustainable Forestry Initiative (SFI). In Europe, a coalition of forestry firms created the Pan-European Forest Certification system (PEFC, later the Programme for the Endorsement of Forest Certification). Canadian firms enlisted the Canadian Standards Association (CSA) to draw up standards for sustainable forest management, though this initiative never became an organization in its own right. Even as arguments raged about whether these systems were credible, their emergence demonstrated the attraction of the certification model that the FSC had introduced to the industry.

The results of this competition have been mixed. On the one hand, as Cashore et al. (2004) show, supporters of different initiatives worked strategically to attract key companies, convert opposition into pockets of support, and gain market acceptance of their label. Competition also forged mutual attention and discussions among representatives of competing programs, and made some intermediaries into brokers. Independent studies were commissioned to "objectively" compare the different programs (Meridian Institute 2001), thus making them commensurable (Espeland 1998) and easier to perceive as different instantiations of the same basic form. As Meidinger (2003) describes, conflict bred a form of integration:

all of the forest certification programs self-consciously operate in a larger context best described as a sprawling, largely unmapped, highly changeable, loosely networked social field in which there are several centers of activity that closely monitor each other. It includes many environmental organizations, large and small production, wholesale, and retail firms, trade associations, professional certifiers, labor unions, human rights organizations, indigenous groups, government agencies, [and so on] . . . Relations among them involve a complex, shifting mix of mutual observation, direct communication, trust, distrust, mutual adjustment, cooperation, coordination, and competition. (Meidinger 2003: 276)

In the case of forest certification, a field of organizations and a community of individual actors coevolved with competition over what certification should entail and who should control it.

The FSC's founding also spurred the diffusion of the certification model to other industries that helped to forge a broader community of certification experts and advocates. Of course, the FSC itself had been constructed partly out of materials imported from other initiatives, especially organics, and organic certifiers such as the Soil Association and the Institute for Marketecology (IMO) soon became forest certifiers (interviews with FSC developers, 7/8/02, 7/22/02,

7/25/02). Several years after the FSC's founding, one of its key architects and supporters, WWF (World Wide Fund for Nature), began introducing the certification model into other sectors. In 1996 WWF paired with Unilever (a major purchaser of frozen fish) to develop the Marine Stewardship Council (MSC) as a response to problems of overfishing and damaging commercial fishing methods. As one observer put it, "WWF sort of took the FSC model and applied it to fisheries" (interview with FSC official, 7/22/02), mimicking the FSC's accreditation and certification system, discursive frame, and even its name and "check mark" logo, while seeking to avoid the "psychotic democracy" perceived to have resulted from the FSC's governance arrangements (Auld *et al.* 2007). WWF also played an important role in the formation of the Marine Aquarium Council (MAC), designed to guarantee that ornamental, exotic fish were harvested in a safe and sustainable way, rather than using cyanide and reef-destroying practices (Bunting 2001). WWF clearly invested in the certification model and became its most important "carrier" into new industries. WWF representatives also played key roles in creating more recent certification initiatives, such as the PAN Parks program for protected areas and the Gold Standard program for carbon credits (Auld *et al.* 2007).

Figure 15.1 provides a bird's-eye view of the expansion of organizations and networks in the area of environmental certification. It illustrates the increasing number of intermediaries and the evolution of indirect ties between certification associations. The shape of the nodes represents the type of organization (grouped according to capital, labor, states, and NGOs), while the shading represents the region of the organization's headquarters, thus providing a glimpse of the transnational character of this arena.

In 2001 (Figure 15.1a), a variety of different organizations occupied intermediary positions between environmental certification associations. Most were either NGOs (for example, WWF, World Resources Institute) or governments/inter-governmental organizations (for example, UK government, United Nations). Regionally, organizations based in Europe (black) or North America (light gray) predominated, indicating that intermediaries brought some degree of transnational, though not truly global, representation to this field. Reflecting their intertwined origins and early operation, FSC, MSC, and MAC share ties to NGOs such as WWF, auditors such as Société Générale de Surveillance (SGS), donors such as the MacArthur Foundation, and several governmental and inter-governmental organizations. Intermediaries also create close connections between these programs and the world of organic certification, including IMO and the Soil Association. Competing forest certification programs (FSC, PEFC, SFI) are linked through several

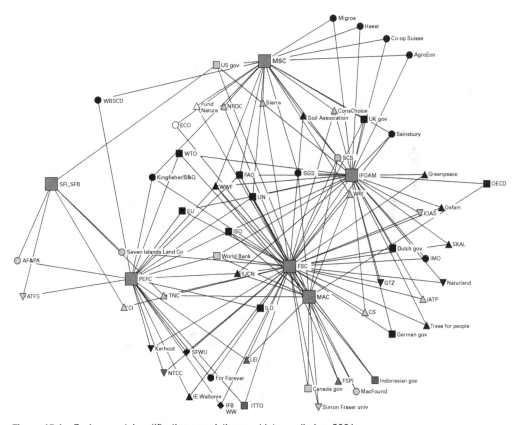

Figure 15.1a Environmental certification associations and intermediaries, 2001
Note. Shapes denote the type of organization: circle = capital (company, trade association, foundation); diamond = labor; square = governmental or inter-governmental; upward triangle = NGO; downward triangle = other. Shading denotes the region of an organization's headquarters: light gray = North America; black = Europe; white = Central and South America; dark gray = other.

common ties. To some degree, this reflects their competition for the support of particular firms, such as the British retailer Kingfisher, and American firm Seven Islands Land Company, which was certified under both FSC and SFI (Patrick 2000). It also reflects some limited success by industry-backed programs in garnering support from environmental NGOs such as Conservation International (CI) and The Nature Conservancy (TNC) (interviews with SFI representatives, 6/26/02, 7/29/02).

The number of intermediaries had increased by nearly 140 percent (from 109 to 260) by 2006 (Figure 15.1b), indicating a more integrated arena of transnational governance. The center of the diagram shows the most central intermediaries at this time. The most central intermediary was WWF, which was tied to all six environmental certification associations. Four others also

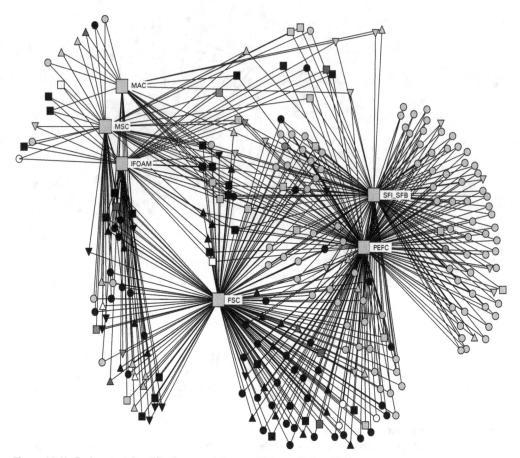

Figure 15.1b Environmental certification associations and intermediaries, 2006

had six ties: SGS, a widely accredited auditor; ISO, an increasingly important developer of rules for certification itself; the US government; and the UN – the latter two interfacing with certification associations through a variety of agencies. The European Union, the Canadian government, the Food and Agriculture Organization (FAO), and the German government's International Development Consultancy (GTZ) were connected to all but one environmental certification initiative.

In sum, these network diagrams show the growing interconnectedness of environmental certification and positions of various intermediaries. They also show traces of the mechanisms that we have argued are behind the elaboration of environmental certification – competition (for example, between FSC, SFI, and PEFC) and diffusion, primarily via WWF as a carrier. Many of the ties we have measured at the inter-organizational level are likely to play out at the interpersonal level, as individuals come together in conferences and joint projects, develop a common discourse, and share experiences.

Labor and social standards

Though not as interconnected as environmental certification initiatives, programs focused on labor and social standards have also grown over the past two decades. In terms of market penetration, Fair Trade is clearly the leader, with sales of its certified coffee growing more than fivefold by volume between 1999 and 2007 (www.fairtrade.net/coffee.html) and markets for Fair Trade chocolate, tea, bananas, flowers, cotton, and wine also expanding (Raynolds *et al.* 2007). Though a variety of other labels compete with Fair Trade – including those developed by the Rainforest alliance, Utz Kapeh, and many companies – no full-fledged alternative certification associations have emerged in this arena.

Competition has led to elaboration in labor standards certification/monitoring in manufacturing industries (especially apparel, footwear, and toys). "Naming and shaming" campaigns fueled the emergence of the FLA and SAI, developed by coalitions of firms and NGOs, with support from the US government, starting around 1996. Although neither developed a product label, these two initiatives represent innovative, though controversial attempts to certify labor conditions in global supply chains and provide information for consumers.[3]

Two initiatives emerged as alternatives to these innovators. On the one side, the American Apparel Manufacturers Association (AAMA) created the Worldwide Responsible Apparel Production (WRAP) program, which was somewhat weaker than the earlier programs. Nevertheless, some of WRAP's accredited auditors, such as Intertek Testing Services (ITS) and Bureau Veritas Quality International (BVQI), have also worked with the FLA and SAI, creating more ties among these initiatives than are initially apparent. On the other side, the FLA's monitoring system (and to a lesser extent SAI's) was harshly criticized by trade unions and labor rights activists, many of which dropped out of negotiations leading to the FLA, fearing that it would repair firms' images without altering the balance of power at the point of production. In Europe, the Clean Clothes Campaign's (CCC) network of activists developed pilot projects to raise the quality of factory monitoring. American activists developed the WRC, focused on collegiate-licensed apparel, which rejected the notion of credentialing companies' claims in favor of independent investigations to "credential workers" and their claims (interview with WRC developer, 7/8/02). A series of debates about the legitimacy of the FLA and WRC ensued, while SAI faced its own set of critics (Labor Rights in China

1999). Despite these early tensions, the WRC and FLA have engaged in some cooperative activities. They cooperated tacitly in some negotiations with companies (Rodríguez-Garavito 2005) and were tied together by some individual collegiate licensing officers, most notably Rut Tufts from the University of North Carolina, who served on the boards of both organizations. The FLA, WRC, SAI, CCC, and the Ethical Trading Initiative all participated in the Joint Initiative on Corporate Accountability and Workers Rights, funded in part by the EU and the US government. Cooperation in this arena has been tenuous, however. Debates about factory monitoring continue (Seidman 2007), and few labor rights activists have fully bought into the certification model (Maquila Solidarity Network 2006).

Figure 15.2 illustrates the fragmented yet evolving field of social certification. As of 2001, intermediaries were mainly American firms such as Liz Claiborne,

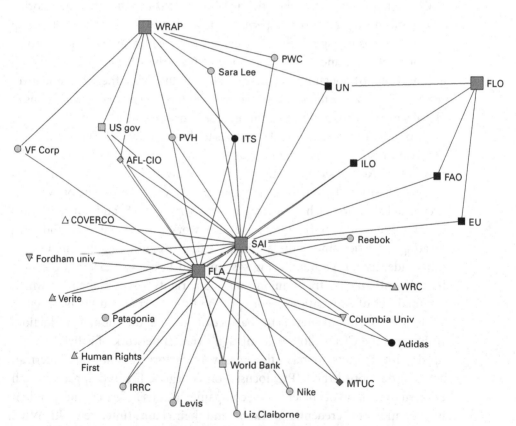

Figure 15.2a Social certification associations and intermediary organizations, 2001
Note. See Figure 15.1a for legend.

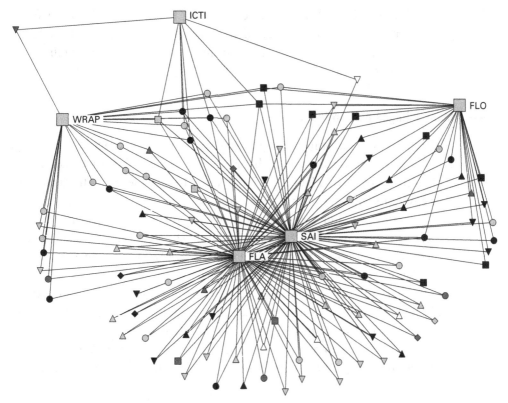

Figure 15.2b Social certification associations and intermediary organizations, 2006

Reebok, and PricewaterhouseCoopers, each of which was linked to two of the three programs for manufacturing sectors (FLA, SAI, and WRAP). Fair Trade certification (FLO) was connected to programs focused on manufacturing only through a few inter-governmental organizations. By 2006 (Figure 15.2b), the number of intermediaries nearly quadrupled (from 26 to 103) and Fair Trade and manufacturing-focused programs became more integrated. There was also greater national diversity by 2006, with more European organizations – especially NGOs – serving as intermediaries. A new entrant, the International Council of Toy Industries CARE program (ICTI), emerged by 2006 but was not closely connected to intermediaries. The most prominent intermediaries in 2006 were the ILO, the US government, and three corporate auditing/certification bodies, SGS, BVQI, ITS, and Cal Safety Compliance Corporation (CSCC). The centrality of for-profit auditors in this arena is especially striking, with these four auditing firms connected to *all* programs except FLO.

Although networks in this arena were certainly sparser than for environmental certifiers, we nevertheless find evidence of growing integration at the organizational level. Individuals representing these organizations have also come into contact with one another more routinely, through conferences sponsored by SAI, ETI, Intertek, Business for Social Responsibility, and several universities, for instance.

Cross-domain linkages and projects

The infrastructure for new transnational communities of practice may emerge not only *within* issue domains (that is, environmental and social certification) but also *across* them. Figure 15.3 looks at ties to intermediaries from all social or environmental certification associations.

In both 2001 and 2006, intermediary organizations were fairly diverse, though far from fully representative of all locations or stakeholders. Intermediaries most often represent capital, NGOs, or the state, rarely represent labor, and are headquartered primarily in North America and Europe. From 2001 to 2006, the number of intermediaries nearly quadrupled (from 109 to 401), reflecting, in part, greater bridging of traditionally distinct issue domains. In spite of this, there is still a rough clustering of certification initiatives by issue domain. In Figure 15.3a, labor/social certification programs cluster on the right side of the diagram, largely connected to domain-specific

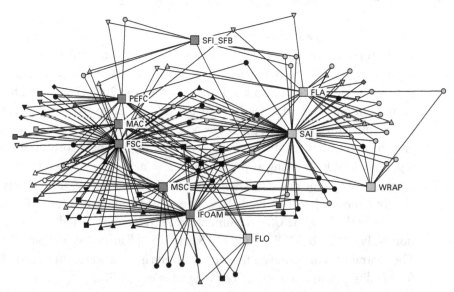

Figure 15.3a All social and environmental certification associations and intermediaries, 2001
Note. See Figure 15.1a for legend.

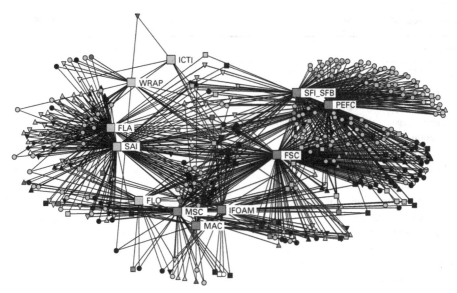

Figure 15.3b All social and environmental certification associations and intermediaries, 2006

intermediaries rather than to those also working in the field of environmental certification. The pattern remains similar in 2006 (Figure 15.3b), though the (arbitrary) sides of the diagram are reversed. Given this, the organizations that sit in the middle of the diagrams are the most interesting, and probably the most consequential for forging an organizational field and individual community of practice. In 2001, there were only a handful of these bridging ties, mostly governmental or inter-governmental organizations (for example, the UN, the US government and the EU) or companies (for example, SGS, Sainsbury's, IKEA), and a few NGOs (for example, Oxfam, Amnesty International). The number had expanded dramatically by 2006. Table 15.2 shows the most central intermediaries overall in that year, and their ties to environmental and social certification associations. Highly central boundary-spanners include NGOs (Oxfam and HIVOS), auditors (SGS and BVQI), retailers (Marks & Spencer), and a number of governmental and inter-governmental organizations.

This network analysis shows that a heterogeneous set of organizations has become increasingly engaged in a transnational, multi-issue standard-setting and certification project. There is also evidence that several actors in this arena have begun to strategize at the level of the field itself, in some cases working to construct both inter-organizational ties and an individual community of practice.

A number of American foundations (MacArthur, Ford, Rockefeller Brothers, and several others) have spread the certification model across

Table 15.2 Most-central intermediaries in the transnational space of social and environmental certification, 2006

Organization	No. of ties to cert. assns.	Environmental	Social
SGS (Société Générale de Surveillance)	10	6	4
US government	10	6	4
International Labor Organization (ILO)	9	4	5
International Organization for Standardization (ISO)	9	6	3
United Nations (UN)	9	6	3
Bureau Veritas Quality International (BVQI)	7	3	4
Deutsche Gesellschaft für Tech. Zus. (GTZ)	7	5	2
European Union (EU)	7	5	2
Food and Agricultural Organization (FAO)	7	5	2
World Trade Organization (WTO)	7	4	3
World Wide Fund for Nature (WWF)	7	6	1
ISEAL alliance (ISEAL)	6	4	2
Oxfam Intl	6	3	3
Canadian government	5	5	0
HIVOS	5	3	2
International Accreditation Forum (IAF)	5	4	1
Marks & Spencer	5	2	3
UK government	5	3	2

Note. Cert. assn. = certification association.

issue domains and have built communities around the social/environmental certification project. They first became enthusiastic about the certification model with the rise of the FSC. To support the FSC and its surrogates, they created a "Sustainable Forestry Funders" network, which granted over $33 million to forest certification projects between 1995 and 2001 (Bartley 2007a). In the late 1990s, several of these foundations began supporting an expanded certification project, first making grants to support the MSC and MAC, then Fair Trade systems, then newer pilot projects such as the Sustainable Tourism Stewardship Council and the Initiative for Responsible Mining Assurance. The Ford Foundation, for instance, provided massive support for forest certification and made sizeable grants for Fair Trade coffee and the certification of eco-tourism and responsible mining practices (Foundation Center database). One program officer in particular, Michael Conroy, became a strong advocate for the certification model, later becoming a board member of the FSC, TransFair USA, FLO-CERT (the certification wing of the FLO), and an NGO that championed the Initiative for Responsible Mining Assurance, as well as the author of a book entitled *Branded!: How the Certification Revolution is Transforming Global Corporations* (Conroy

2007). The MacArthur Foundation provided some support to certification projects for forestry, marine life, fair trade agriculture, and labor standards in manufacturing (Foundation Center database).

Community formation has also been facilitated by face-to-face interaction among individuals working in the transnational space of social/environmental certification. Since 2003, FLO, IFOAM, and the FSC have all had their head-quarters near each other in Bonn, which should increase the possibilities for interaction. A number of conferences on certification, CSR, and ethical sour-cing have also brought together individuals from different initiatives and issue domains. For instance, looking at recent conferences sponsored by GTZ, Intertek, and Business for Social Responsibility, one finds representatives of the Rainforest Alliance, Chiquita, and International Labor Organization at all three, and individuals from SAI, WRAP, FLA, Oxfam, WWF, Transparency International, Levi Strauss, Mattel, Starbucks, PricewaterhouseCoopers, and several other organizations at two of the three conferences.

Perhaps the most important factor in structuring a cross-domain community of practice has been the formation of the ISEAL alliance (International Social and Environmental Accreditation and Labeling). This umbrella organization was formed in 1999 by "mission-driven, NGO-based" certification associations – IFOAM, FLO, FSC, MSC, SAI, and MAC – to legitimate their activity and differentiate themselves from industry-based competitors. They "faced a number of similar challenges, and they felt that if they could work together, they could pool resources to reduce costs – and having a kind of a common voice they'd actually have a louder voice" (interview with ISEAL representative, 3/8/06).[4] ISEAL developed a "Code of Good Practice for Setting Social and Environmental Standards" and has worked to ensure that multi-stakeholder certification initia-tives are compatible with other forms of international governance, especially the WTO Technical Barriers to Trade agreement, which bans governmental stan-dards that restrict trade but is less clear on the legitimacy of private-sector standards (Bernstein and Hannah 2008). We see ISEAL as a nascent community of practice formed both to fend off challenges from industry and to build legitimacy in a transnational space of evolving rules about standard-setting. Of course, the community around ISEAL largely excludes actors from industry-sponsored certification associations. It remains to be seen whether these lines will continue to structure communities of practice in the transnational space of social and environmental certification, or whether broader settlements are possible. It is clear, however, that as this space has become more complex, opportunities and incentives for community-building among previously disconnected actors have increased.

Conclusion

With the expansion of transnational governance comes new, loosely organized, and hybridized social configurations. At the organizational level, these
can be described as fields. The related concept of communities of practice
allows one to consider configurations of individual actors. Our examination of
social and environmental certification shows how communities of practice
can be both cause and consequence of transnational governance. Older communities of practice, organized around some combination of religion, politics,
and expert knowledge, played an important but often overlooked role in the
emergence of certification systems. As certification expanded, however, new
lines of connection, far from the visions of the early founders, developed. It is
along these lines, sometimes crossing issues and constituencies, that new
communities of practice appear to be emerging. Intermediaries such as GTZ
and the Ford Foundation, and spaces for interaction such as ISEAL and
numerous conferences, play an especially important role in that process.

There are a number of reasons to think that these new communities will
shape the future of transnational governance. First, community formation
may give new actors a "seat at the table" in defining and negotiating rules for
the global economy. For instance, to the extent that communities form around
those certification initiatives that are not dominated by industry associations,
this may establish new actors as legitimate standard-setters for global industries. Such communities are unlikely to garner the credibility afforded to
professions or the resources available to industry associations, but they may
nevertheless be recognized as knowledgeable, authorized transnational actors.

Second, one would expect certification-oriented transnational communities
of practice to carry this model into even more settings. Such a community
might successfully frame a variety of global problems – climate change,
poverty, financial regulation, and others – as amenable to the certification
solution. To a growing extent, one might see a solution in search of problems.
Though this could indeed bring about some positive changes, it would also
represent an elaboration of neoliberalism – albeit a particular form of neoliberalism that seeks to build new markets to rectify market and government
failures. Some observers have begun to worry that principles of democratic
citizenship would be neglected in such a shift (Seidman 2007).

Finally, in considering the significance of certification communities, it is
important to remember that for all the language of multi-stakeholder engagement, there is still inequality in terms of representation and voice in this arena. On

the one hand, advocates of multi-stakeholder certification systems are forced to mobilize to establish their right to set international standards and gain a seat at tables that are typically closed to all but business and government elites. Even in the communities surrounding multi-stakeholder initiatives, however, some actors clearly have more power than others. Labor unions – especially those from developing countries – are, for a variety of reasons, under-represented in these arenas (Fetzer in this volume). Though some locally based NGOs representing indigenous communities, small farmers, and migrant workers are engaged with certification associations, they are certainly not central actors. Clearly, not all potential transnational communities are equally capable of organizing globally or equally powerful when they do so.

NOTES

1. One might even question the assumption that organizations cannot identify with one another sufficiently to constitute a community. While it is surely true that organizations cannot "feel" in the same way individuals can, neither can organizations make rational decisions or associate with others in quite the same way that individuals can. Nevertheless, this does not prevent us from considering them as actors in markets or networks. Organizations function in that way by developing routines for decision-making, raising the question of whether they might also utilize routines for identifying with other organizations. Indeed, this is what theorists of organizational fields imply in defining a field as "a community of organizations that partakes of a common meaning system and whose participants interact more frequently and fatefully with one another than with actors outside of the field" (Scott 1994: 206–07).
2. The disadvantage is that that the content of websites may be only loosely coupled with the concrete practices of the organization. Yet for organizations of this sort, websites are important tools for information-dissemination and self-presentation. Even if a certification association presents itself as *unlike* some other organization, this indicates one sort of attention that constitutes an organizational field and increases the probability of interpersonal contact, compared to those actors that "fly under the radar."
3. The FLA does not "certify" particular factories but does use factory audits to certify that the labor compliance activities of its participants meet basic standards.
4. Another umbrella project, the Ethical Certification and Labelling Authentication Project (www.eclspace.org) is led by individuals from Rockefeller Brothers, ISEAL, FSC, Imaflora, Unilever, and others, but appears to have done little since its creation in 2003.

REFERENCES

Adler, E. 2005. *Communitarian international relations: The epistemic foundations of international relations.* New York: Routledge.

Armbruster-Sandoval, R. 2005. *Globalization and cross-border labor solidarity in the Americas: The anti-sweatshop movement and the struggle for social justice.* New York: Routledge.

Auld, G. 2007. "The institutionalization of global private regulation: Lessons from social and environmental certification in the coffee, forestry, and fishery sectors." Paper presented at the conference of the American Political Science Association, Chicago, August.

Auld, G., Balboa, C., Bartley, T. Levin, K. and Cashore, B. 2007. "The spread of the certification model: Understanding the evolution of non-state market-driven governance." Paper presented at the annual conference of the International Studies Association, Chicago, February.

Bartley, T. 2007a. "How foundations shape social movements: The construction of an organizational field and the rise of forest certification," *Social Problems* **54**: 229–55.

Bartley, T. 2007b. "Institutional emergence in an era of globalization: The rise of transnational private regulation of labor and environmental conditions," *American Journal of Sociology* **113**: 297–351.

Bartley, T. and Smith, S. 2008. "Structuring transnational fields of governance: Network evolution and boundary-setting in the world of standards." Working paper, Department of Sociology, Indiana University.

Bernstein, S. and Cashore, B. 2007. "Can non-state global governance be legitimate? An analytical framework," *Regulation & Governance* **1**: 347–71.

Bernstein, S. and Hannah, E. 2008. "Non-state global standard setting and the WTO: Legitimacy and the need for regulatory space," *Journal of International Economic Law* **11**: 575–608.

Boli, J. 2006. "The rationalization of virtue and virtuosity in world society," in Djelic, M. -L. and Sahlin-Andersson, K. (eds.), *Transnational governance: Institutional dynamics of regulation.* New York: Cambridge University Press, pp. 95–118.

Boltanski, L. and Thévenot, L. 2006. *On justification: Economies of worth.* Princeton University Press.

Bonacich, E. and Appelbaum, R. P. 2000. *Behind the label: Inequality in the Los Angeles apparel industry.* Berkeley: University of California Press.

Bunting, B. 2001. "Buy a fish, buy a coral, save a reef." Presentation at the Marine Ornamentals 2001 conference, Lake Buena Vista, FL. www.aquariumcouncil.org/pdf/FINALStingspeech.pdf. Accessed February 11, 2007.

Cashore, B., Auld, G. and Newsom, D. 2004. *Governing through markets: Forest certification and the emergence of non-state authority.* New Haven, CT: Yale University Press.

Cheit, R. E. 1990. *Setting safety standards: Regulation in the public and private sectors.* Berkeley: University of California Press.

Chevriot, R. 1972. "Letter to organic agriculture groups: Subject: Creation of an international federation." IFOAM (International Federation of Organic Agriculture Movements), www.ifoam.org/about_ifoam/inside_ifoam/pdfs/Founding_Letter.pdf.

Conley, J. M. and Williams, C. A. 2008. "The corporate social responsibility movement as an ethnographic problem," UNC Legal Studies Research Paper 1285631. Accessed on SSRN, http://papers.ssrn.com/sol3/papers.cfm?abstract_id=1285631#.

Conroy, M. E. 2007. *Branded!: How the certification revolution is transforming global corporations.* Gabriola Island, BC, Canada: New Society Publishers.

DiMaggio, P. 1991. "Constructing an organizational field as a professional project: U.S. art museums, 1920–1940," in Powell, W. W. and DiMaggio, P. (eds.), *The new institutionalism in organizational analysis*. University of Chicago Press, pp. 267–92.

Dingwerth, K. and Pattberg, P. 2009. "World politics and organizational fields: The case of transnational sustainability governance," *European Journal of International Relations* **15** (forthcoming).

Donovan, R. 1990. Memo of 12/2/90. Personal archives of Forest Stewardship Council (FSC) organizer.

Ecological Trading Company. 1990. "Letter of July 1990." Personal archives of a member of the Certification Working Group.

Elliott, C. 2000. *Forest certification from a policy network perspective*. Jakarta: Center for International Forestry Research (CIFOR).

Espeland, W. N. 1998. *The struggle for water: Politics, rationality, and identity in the American Southwest*. University of Chicago Press.

Gereffi, G., Garcia-Johnson, R. and Sasser, E. 2001. "The NGO-industrial complex," *Foreign Policy Issue* **125**, July/Aug: 56–65.

Guthman, J. 2004. *Agrarian dreams: The paradox of organic farming in California*. Berkeley: University of California Press.

Jaffee, D. 2007. *Brewing justice: Fair trade coffee, sustainability, and survival*. Berkeley: University of California Press.

Koenig, K. M. and Headley, J. 1995. "Sustainable forest management: Where do you fit in?," *Wood and Wood Products* **100**: 44–48.

Krupat, K. 1997. "From war zone to free trade zone: A history of the National Labor Committee," in Ross, A. (ed.), *No sweat: Fashion, free trade and the rights of garment workers*. New York: Verso, pp. 51–77.

Labor Rights in China. 1999. *No illusions: Against the global cosmetic SA8000*. Hong Kong: Labor Rights in China.

Linton, A., Liou, C. and Shaw, K. A. 2004. "A taste of trade justice: Marketing global social responsibility via fair trade coffee," *Globalizations* **1**: 223–46.

Locke, R., Qin, F. and Brause, A. 2007. "Does monitoring improve labor standards? Lessons from Nike," *Industrial & Labor Relations Review* **61**: 3–31.

Mace, W. G. 1998. "Global commodity chains, alternative trade, and small-scale coffee production in Oaxaca, Mexico." MA thesis, Miami University, Department of Geography.

Maquila Solidarity Network. 2006. "Is fair trade a good fit for the garment industry?" MSN Discussion Paper 1. Toronto: Maquila Solidarity Network. http://en.maquilasolidarity.org/en/node/215.

Meidinger, E. 2003. "Forest certification as a global civil society regulatory institution," in Meidinger, E., Elliot, C., and Oesten, G. (eds.), *The social and political dimensions of forest certification*. Remagen-Oberwinter, Germany: Forstbuch.

Meridian Institute. 2001. "Comparative analysis of the Forest Stewardship Council and sustainable forestry initiative certification programs." Washington, DC: Meridian Institute. www.merid.org/comparison.

Morgan, G. 2001. "Transnational communities and business systems," *Global Networks* **1**: 113–30.

Morrow, C. E. and Hull, R. W. 1996. "Donor-initiated common pool resource institutions: The case of the Yanesha Forestry Cooperative," *World Development* **24**: 1641–57.

Mutersbaugh, T. 2005. "Fighting standards with standards: Harmonization, rents, and social accountability in certified agrofood networks," *Environment and Planning A* **37**: 2033–51.

Overdevest, C. 2005. "Treadmill politics, information politics, and public policy: Toward a political economy of information," *Organization & Environment* **18**: 72–90.

Patrick, K. 2000. "Seven Islands achieves world's first FSC and SFI forestland certification," Pulp and Paper Online article, October 12. Erie, PA. www.pulpandpaperonline.com.

Quack, S. 2007. "Legal professionals and transnational law-making: A case of distributed agency," *Organization* **14**: 643–66.

Raynolds, L. T., Murray, D. L. and Wilkinson, J. (eds.) 2007. *Fair trade: The challenges of transforming globalization*. New York: Routledge.

Rice, P. D. and McLean, J. 1999. "Sustainable coffee at the crossroads." Report for the Consumer's Choice Council, Washington, DC.

Rodríguez-Garavito, C. A. 2005. "Global governance and labor rights: Codes of conduct and anti-sweatshop struggles in global apparel factories in Mexico and Guatemala," *Politics and Society* **33**: 203–33.

Scott, W. R. 1994. "Conceptualizing organizational fields: Linking organizations and social systems," in Derlien, H. -U., Gerhardt, U. and Scharpf, F. W. (eds.), *Systemrationalität und Partialinteresse*. Baden-Baden: Nomos Verlagsgesellschaft, pp. 203–22.

Seidman, G. 2007. *Beyond the boycott: Labor rights, human rights and transnational activism*. New York: Russell Sage Foundation/ASA Rose Series.

Simeone, R., Pariona, M. and Lazaro, M. 1993. "A natural harvest," *Cultural Survival Quarterly* **17**: 48–50.

Waldinger, R. and Fitzgerald, D. 2004. "Transnationalism in question," *American Journal of Sociology* **109**: 1177–95.

Zachary, G. P. 2002. "Who monitors?," Business for Social Responsibility (document ID 929), www.bsr.org. Accessed September 17 2002.

Part VI

Conclusion

16 Transnational communities and their impact on the governance of business and economic activity

Marie-Laure Djelic and Sigrid Quack

The collective endeavor that has culminated in the production of this volume has allowed us to explore an interesting diversity of empirical settings in which transnational communities could be identified and seemed to play a role. In this concluding chapter, we take stock of what we can learn from a systematic comparison of transnational communities and of their role in those very different settings. Through such a comparison, we get a clear picture of the peculiar nature of communities with a transnational scale and scope. In the first section of the conclusion, we outline some key findings in that regard. In the second section, we then reflect more particularly on the impact that transnational communities have on the governance of business and economic activity.

The nature of transnational communities: outlining some key findings

In the introduction to this volume, we suggested five structuring and defining features of transnational communities. First, they represent, for their members, one among several community affiliations. Second, members are cosmopolitans but usually of a "rooted" kind. Third, transnational communities are imagined communities of a fluid and dynamic nature. Fourth, they exhibit a fair amount of within-community diversity. Fifth and finally, transnational communities are time-bound, non-essential and non-permanent collectives. After our journey through a multiplicity of diverse empirical settings, we should reflect a bit more on those five defining features – asking ourselves, in particular, how they might play out in the governance activities of transnational communities.

Five defining features

First, transnational communities represent, for their members, one amongst several community affiliations. Membership in a transnational community generally comes on top of that in other community circles; it does not have to displace involvement in and the sense of belonging to these other circles. In that respect our transnational world seems to confirm Georg Simmel's (1955 [1908]) insight that the progress of differentiation and individualization could lead to a multiplication of community circles and to more opportunity for social belonging. The different chapters document, in particular, a multi-level layering – where an individual can share in local, national, and transnational communities. Of great interest, naturally, is what takes place at the different points of interface. The dynamics bridging communities across different levels – and in particular across the national and the transnational levels – will be discussed more systematically below. The role that transnational communities play in governance cannot be understood without an exploration of those dynamics.

Second, and as a consequence of this multi-level community-belonging, we regularly find across the diverse empirical cases that members of transnational communities tend to be rooted cosmopolitans. However, the degree to which they are rooted (nationally) and/or the degree to which they have developed a cosmopolitan (transnational) identity vary quite markedly. In fact, transnational communities are themselves concentric circles, where the degree of activity and involvement can vary. Those members most actively involved in the characteristic project of a given transnational community will be more likely, on the whole, to develop a cosmopolitan identity. Comparing the different empirical cases, we can identify essentially three patterns. In a first pattern, local or national rootedness is so strong and powerful that it effectively creates obstacles and slows down significantly if not prevents altogether the construction and development of a cosmopolitan project and community (Fetzer or Harvey and Maclean in this volume). In a second pattern, we document an active and aggressive transnational community that often has a clear origin in a nation or a small group of nations and an expansive and imperialist project. Generally, in order to succeed, this project will require at least a partial weakening of the local or national rootedness of associated members in different countries but also some weakening of targeted institutions and arrangements in those same countries (see, for example, Morgan and Kubo or Ramirez in this volume). Those first two patterns tend to point to a zero-sum game between cosmopolitanism, on the one hand, and local or national rootedness, on the other. But most of the empirical cases that are explored in this volume suggest a third pattern, in which the intensification of a cosmopolitan identity does not mean a weakening of (national) rootedness (see, for example, Schrad, Metiu, Dobusch and Quack, Mariussen, Bartley and Smith in this volume). In fact, transnational cosmopolitanism and national rootedness seem to combine and articulate with each other along complementary and mutually reinforcing lines. As we will argue below, this coexistence and complementary articulation might, in fact, be a key factor explaining the impact of a transnational community in a particular governance domain.

Third, not unlike other kinds of communities, transnational communities are "imagined" (Anderson 2006 [1983]). Through time, a sense of reciprocal engagement around a common objective or project or around shared convictions, ideas, values, or practices progressively crystallizes into a sense of belonging and identity. As we know from the history of nation-states, the process of crystallization of an imagined community is a long and complex one. It calls for time, naturally, but also for powerful mechanisms of integration, socialization, and control. The different empirical settings explored in this volume show transnational community in process – being built and in the making but also maturing and declining (Schrad) or transforming (Dahles). A number of the chapters focus more particularly on temporal dynamics (Schrad, Plehwe, Eder and Öz, Dobusch and Quack). Other chapters adopt a transverse focus and provide a more static image of the community-building process at a particular stage (Metiu, Morgan and Kubo, Harvey and Maclean). In any case, the transnational communities explored in this volume are fluid and dynamic imagined communities, many of which are still very much in the making and some are even fragile and only weakly integrated (Fetzer, Harvey and Maclean, Eder and Öz). Considering the complexity of a community-building process but also the relative "youth" of most of the communities we explore – they are generally less than fifty years old and some are even much younger – the weakness and fragility of integration were to be expected. In fact, we were surprised in some cases by the speed and intensity of the community-building process (Dobusch and Quack, Morgan and Kubo, Mariussen). We will discuss below what the comparison of our different empirical settings tells us about the mechanisms of integration, socialization, and control in processes of transnational community-building.

Fourth, the transnational communities we have explored in this volume are bound to retain, over the long run, a fair amount of internal complexity and are likely to exhibit within-community heterogeneity and conflict (Bartley and

Smith, Mariussen, Dobusch and Quack, Ventresca and Hussain). In fact, one could probably argue that those communities will only be able to survive if they manage to strike a healthy balance between integration and differentiation. Because of the objective diversity and heterogeneity within those communities, a tight integration effort might actually endanger their very existence. The emergent common identity needs to be pluralist. It should be a container of diversities – keeping them within bounds while still accommodating them. The plurality of transnational communities does not have to be a source of fragility; but it could be, if the "inherent discordance subverts the apparent coherence which is expressed by the boundaries of the community" (Cohen 1985: 20). It could also be a source of strength and stability through the flexibility and adaptability that are associated with plurality and diversity. "The reed bends but does not break" (La Fontaine 2002 [1668]).[1] As we will argue below, this weaker form of integration could also be a factor explaining the impact of transnational communities on different governance domains.

Finally, transnational communities appear to be "communities of limited liability" to a greater extent than traditional communities of the ascriptive kind (Janowitz 1952). Members are free to come and go, and their degree of involvement will vary from member to member but also through time for the same members. Furthermore, the communities themselves can grow and expand but also wane and even disappear (Schrad and Dahles in this volume). Interestingly and in a somewhat non-intuitive way, this feature can be a source of strength for the community. Members choose to belong, and they are free to go if and when a gap emerges between the collective identity and their own or between the collective project and their own. When they are in and as long as they do not leave, they may, as a consequence, invest much more into the community and into the common identity and project than they would in communities in which they were "born." Even though there will be internal variability, as argued above, the members of those transnational communities are thus likely, as a whole and on average, to be quite involved, engaged, and active. This feature goes some way, we propose, in explaining both the presence of those communities in governance contexts and their impact and "efficacy" there. We use the term "efficacy" in the value-neutral sense proposed by Thrift (2006: 296), as the "capacity or power to produce an effect" or the "ability to produce the results" that the actors involved desire. We do not imply, through the use of this term, any form of necessarily progressive impact of transnational communities, far from it. Most cases show that transnational communities tend to mobilize for influence, power, and different kinds of associated resources. As such they are far from neutral and benign and the somewhat "romantic" undertones often associated with the term "community" should not lead us to forget that. The transnational communities we have been talking about are political actors like others. They have an agenda, ideologies, and interests and they mobilize resources and strategies to further those. In the process, they might serve certain groups, weaken or destroy others. They might solve certain problems but they might as well create new ones, possibly more disturbing.

The relevance and importance of transnational communities

At first sight, the picture we draw of transnational communities suggests that they are rather fluid and unstable social formations. When we look closer, though, some of the features that could be interpreted as sources of weakness can, in certain circumstances, turn out to be factors of strength. Diversity and heterogeneity mean flexibility and adaptability (see Dobusch and Quack, Hussain and Ventresca, Mayntz in this volume). Limited liability can translate into stronger forms of involvement at least during the period of involvement (see Schrad, Bartley and Smith, Mariussen in this volume). Chapter after chapter in this volume, we see documented evidence of the presence, role, and significance of transnational communities. Specific communities may weaken or even disappear altogether, but the phenomenon as such persists. From a comparison of our different empirical settings, we argue that transnational communities turn out to be of high relevance in many fields of governance with an impact on business and economic activity. What the chapters in this volume suggest is that transnational communities may be a permanent fixture of the transnational governance of business and economic activity, but also of far more than this.

This seems to be particularly clear in the case of contemporary transnational governance, as the contributions by Ramirez, Metiu, Dobusch and Quack, Plehwe, Mariussen, and Bartley and Smith all show. There would seem to be a constant "sparking up" of transnational communities in the making, fueled by policy issues that are defined or redefined as cutting across national borders or as having by nature a global dimension (environmental issues, for example, or the governance of financial activity today). Different issues give rise to a flurry of attempts at collective sense-making and mobilization. The progressive constitution of an imagined community would seem to be a necessary precondition to the deployment of a collective project and common goals and to their transformation into political action at a transnational level (Graz and Nölke 2008). This is reminiscent and compatible with the idea proposed by Nils Brunsson that organizational action requires the irrationality associated with a shared ideology. Irrationality in the form of ideology is not only unavoidable, it has also "a highly functional role and is fundamental to organization and organizational action." Irrationality as ideology is the "rationality of action" (Brunsson 2000: 3). This perspective certainly can help us understand why the community dimension – development of shared meanings, references, and identities – is essential to the possibility and to the effectiveness of political action in a transnational context.

The importance and relevance of transnational communities in contemporary transnational governance is difficult to miss. But transnational communities apparently also played a role in other periods of history. The contributions by Schrad or Fetzer in this volume suggest and document this. We propose that it could be extremely interesting and useful to have more historical empirical cases documenting and exploring the role of transnational communities in the context of governance with a transnational scale and scope.

In the nineteenth and early twentieth centuries, there were transnational communities involved behind the (transnational) fights for the abolition of slavery or for the rights of women. The Workingmen's Internationals also represent highly interesting historical precedents. We probably could learn a lot through a study of those movements from the perspective outlined in this volume. The First International was created in London in 1864, with the clear objective of becoming a transnational community united around the preoccupation for any and all governance issues having to do with the fate of the working classes.

This Association is established to afford a central medium of communication and cooperation between Working Men's Societies existing in different countries, and aiming at the same end, viz., the protection, advancement, and complete emancipation of the working classes. (IWA 1864)

At this early stage, the projected community was an attempt to bring together around a common project and vision a great diversity and multiplicity of views, nationalities, and traditions. Hence, the need for a balance between integration and differentiation was expressed from the start, and another founding rule was that

[w]hile united in a perpetual bond of fraternal co-operation, the workingmen's societies joining the International Association will preserve their existent organizations intact. (IWA 1864)

Partly in reaction to the fear of a Socialist and Communist threat, a movement mobilized across national borders in the nineteenth century in favor of social protection. There again, we could probably explore the process of emergence of transnational communities – in particular around various forms of social Christian identity – and their role in working towards reforms (Aerts *et al.* 1990; Kersbergen 1995; Kalyvas 1996). We could certainly learn a lot in the process. One could also turn to the transnational communities that emerged through international cartelization starting in the 1920s and contributed to the strengthening and tightening of the governance of transnational competition until World War II (Mezaki 1992; Maddox 2001). Going back further in time, there were unmistakably transnational communities involved in the formalization of the medieval merchant law (Trakman 1980; Michell 2008 [1904]). We could, along the same lines, explore transnational trading communities in the medieval Mediterranean (Quack forthcoming). The Hanseatic League, between the thirteenth and the sixteenth centuries, in all likelihood reflected, as an institutional and organizational construction, the importance and role of transnational communities. Once running and established as a structure, it also further nurtured, strengthened, and broadened those communities until it finally declined and disappeared in the seventeenth century (Wernicke 1983; Postel 1996).

Let us reiterate at this stage what emerges as a key common finding shared across this volume: transnational communities are important and relevant for the transnational governance of business and economic activity. Those communities are fluid and not rigid; they might be at various stages of integration and definitely allow for a fair amount of within-community diversity. They often develop as hybrid formations out of formal organizations and/or networks; in return, they can foster and sustain the development of organizations or networks. In any case, they play a role, quite often an important one, when it comes to transnational governance. In the process, they are likely to serve particular interests while marginalizing other actors and agendas. Transnational communities are potentially powerful arenas in governance processes but they are arenas that are themselves rife with conflict and power struggles. They are far from neutral and can even carry around certain forms of exclusion and violence. In the second section of this conclusion, we will articulate more systematically the *ways* in which those communities matter and are relevant for the transnational governance of business and economic activity.

Social networks, movements, communities – and the temporal dimension

A systematic comparison of the different contributions to this volume makes it plain that there is both a justification and an intellectual value added to use the term "transnational communities" – over and beyond a focus on "transnational networks" or "transnational social movements" (Powell 1990; Smith *et al.* 1997; Keck and Sikkink 1998; Tarrow 2005). Naturally, the three terms are sometimes used in partly interchangeable ways. There is an interesting analytic distinction, though, on which we propose to build.

On the one hand, the use of the term "community" allows us to point towards an important feature of those transnational aggregates – a common "culture," to use Mayntz's term in this volume. Mayntz suggests that, in contrast to "network,"

[t]he notion of "community" emphasizes a different aspect of social reality, an aspect subsumed under "culture" rather than "institution." (Mayntz, this volume)

This common "culture" connects and binds together the members of those transnational aggregates. There is more than the "network" – or, in other words, the node-to-node set of connections – to those transnational aggregates. A transnational community is a transnational network, while the reverse is not necessarily true. The emergence of a transnational community reflects a process where node-to-node connections get progressively embedded and set, as it were, in a background frame of common meanings, references, and identity markers. In the meantime, the network may densify and expand, but, more importantly, it comes to develop a "cultural flesh." In the different cases we explored in this volume, this progress of developing a common culture could be documented, although such development occurs with varying degrees of speed and intensity.

On the other hand, the notion of "transnational social movement" suggests, like that of "transnational community," a collective frame and culture and the possibility for collective action. Arguably, transnational social movements are often one form of transnational community (see Mayntz, Schrad, Dobusch and Quack in this volume). But we propose that the term and the way it is often used lack a pointillist perspective.[2] The notion of "transnational social movement" puts stronger emphasis on the overall common project, culture or action than on the individual nodes and connections that structure it in the background. However, the definition of community that we proposed in

Chapter 1 underscores the importance of the "mutual orientation and dependence of members." Hence, nodes and the ways in which they connect and interact are important dimensions of this definition of community. The notion of community, as we define it, is therefore an interesting one if we want to reconcile a focus on what Tarde calls "inter-cerebral connections" with the way in which a multiplicity of such connections makes up broader patterns, currents, social movements, and flows (Tarde 2000 [1899]: 18–20). In other words, it allows us to reconcile explicitly the central structuring role of elementary nodes with the idea of a broad emergent collective that, in turn, can come to play a defining role for both members and non-members. Community-building is akin, we suggest, to a pointillist painting. The collective logic, culture or pattern emerges from the aggregation and, more importantly, from the mutual orientation and dependence of nodes (dots). In a community (particularly in the transnational communities we have explored), the shared culture is activated by a multiplicity of individual dots or nodes, leading to a fair amount of complexity and discontinuity. In turn, though, the nodes (dots) progressively come to be set and framed by a broader logic, culture or pattern, as the painting evolves or the community-building process moves along. The transnational communities we have explored in this volume are like many pointillist paintings – at least, this is a good simile when our perspective is a static one. If we step back and focus only on the social movement dimension, we might lose sight of the complexity involved and forget about the importance of the structure of the nodes or dots and their connections. If we move in too closely and focus on the network, on the nodes or dots and how they connect, we might then miss the collective logic and movement that is visible from afar.

As soon as we move beyond a static perspective, though, and adopt a longitudinal focus, then things become even more complex. We have to think in terms not only of a pointillist painting, but of an ever-changing, never completed one – to which dots could be added and erased, where they could get closer together or move further apart (leading to a more or less integrated whole), where the colors could change ... The constitution of communities is a process that implies and requires time. The construction and progressive stabilization of a common culture, of an "imagined collective identity," call for an investment in time. They also imply, on the way there, multiple conflicts and struggles; the triumph of certain actors and interests and the marginalization of others. Many of the chapters in this volume point indeed to the step-by-step and processual nature of community constitution – and possibly of community decline. They document either the dynamics of that process or its particular features at different stages. Again and again, the chapters appear to suggest a relatively clear pattern.

First, relational connections are prompted by and structured around a broadly common project and/or some common frames and references – that seem all the more "common" the further we stand from them. In reality, the degree of heterogeneity and conflict can be extremely significant at this stage, and this becomes all the more obvious as we get closer to the different nodes in the picture. Second, these relational connections stabilize through time in the form of networks that can be more or less systematically relayed by organizational arrangements – whether ad hoc and seasonal (i.e. conferences or meetings) or permanent. Third, more often than not, the web of relational connections expands in the process and becomes denser. Fourth, through the increasing density and regularity of those interconnections, the common frame of meaning and references is also being worked upon and tightened. This transformation of networks into a more integrated collective is effectively stimulated in situations when those collectives define their common project in policy-making or political terms.

The development we describe here does not lead towards a monolithic culture. However, time and again, the chapters document a tightening of the common frames over time. The focus becomes clearer, and the dots get closer to each other, becoming more interdependent in the process. Once again, this does not happen through benign convergence but will imply, most of the time, conflicts, power struggles, violence or exclusion. The speed of the process varies enormously, and the existence of a project that can be formulated in policy or political terms at the transnational level is unmistakably an accelerator, as the contributions by Plehwe, Schrad, Mariussen, Bartley and Smith, Dobusch and Quack all illustrate. Therefore, a sense of common identity and belonging builds up, step by step. This process can probably work backwards, as it were, even though there is less evidence of this provided in the chapters here. One mechanism for such a reverse process could be that the common project runs its course and loses its mobilizing stamina. Another parallel and complementary mechanism could naturally be the weakening of the networks over time, as organizational devices lose steam and key nodes redefine the intensity of their involvement and reorient their personal sense of priorities (Dahles and Schrad in this volume) or as conflicts and power struggles generate powerful interference.

Mechanisms of integration, socialization, and control

The constitution through time of "imagined communities" with a transnational scale and scope reveals the existence of integration, socialization, and control mechanisms. Many of these mechanisms appear to be quite similar, in fact, to the mechanisms generally at work in the construction of national or even local imagined communities.

Chapter after chapter, we find evidence that direct contact, physical interaction, and face-to-face exchange are important mechanisms of integration, socialization, and control. They remain so, interestingly, in the world of transnational communities – even though the latter are not based upon physical proximity or direct and regular interactions within bounded territories. While physical and face-to-face encounters are rare in the world of transnational communities, they can have a degree of regularity (a yearly conference, quarterly meetings of working groups...). Precisely because they are so rare, but often eagerly anticipated if they are regular, these opportunities for face-to-face interaction can become highly symbolic. They can turn into real "totem" moments or events in which the community materializes (Durkheim 2001 [1912]). These types of encounters proved to be necessary and important even in transnational communities of the past, when they were complex and costly to organize (see Schrad in this volume). They are much easier to organize today but, in principle, should also be far less necessary, as multiple technologies allow for instant communication over great distances (Metiu and Dobusch and Quack in this volume). In spite of this, though, it is interesting that an opportunity for physical and face-to-face encounters retains its relevance and significance in contemporary transnational communities (see Plehwe, Mariussen, Bartley and Smith in this volume). These symbolic moments also enable people participating in them to go beyond a dry, formal exchange of information to more meaningful forms of expression and develop richer, denser, and more contextualized repertoires of interaction.

The regular exchange of documentation and information is also an important mechanism fostering integration. Historically, the density of information flows has increased with the sophistication of information technologies. The circulation of information is much more instantaneous today than it was in the times of the temperance movement (Schrad in this volume), but in both periods it played a key role in the process of bringing the different nodes of an emergent community closer together. The circulation of information and documentation will become all the more powerful as an integrator, if and when it is combined with the systematic standardization of patterns of information collection and presentation. Another powerful factor of integration, naturally, is the standardization of language. While in the context of historical transnational communities, the circulation of information required translation into multiple languages (see Schrad in this volume), in contemporary times this circulation often takes place in English. Today, the working language of many transnational communities has de facto been standardized – it is English. The circulation of information includes the broad diffusion, within the collective, of "best practices," which are packaged strategies or solutions that have been decontextualized and are proposed as having "universal" value and applicability across the emergent collective. If and when they effectively spread and are appropriated, they do indeed become key factors of integration, socialization, and control. They provide an ever-ready frame with which the members of the community can define problems and find solutions. They shape not only behaviors but also the conceptual reading of situations. In modern language, "best practices" can have a "performative" role (MacKenzie *et al.* 2007). They "change the world" and, in the process, become constitutive of the community that adopts and appropriates them.

While the circulation of information, documentation, ideas, or practices is important, integration, socialization, and control can also happen through more in-depth processes of acculturation. The time element, here again, is key. Let us think about imagined communities we know quite well, nations and nation-states. A powerful way for nations to construct and stabilize them-selves as coherent imagined communities is through a national education system. To inscribe common meaning and reference patterns early on in the heads of young (future) citizens is certainly the most potent way for a nation to invent itself. This process of national coherence-building is often con-comitant with exclusion or destruction of previously strong identities, whether subnational or even supranational ones. Following the break-up of Yugoslavia, for example, history books were rewritten in Croatia, Serbia, and Slovenia. The cultural and literary heritage was redefined. Curricula, from primary school to university, were reinvented. In each case, new heroes and new symbols were introduced and/or rediscovered. To some extent, transna-tional communities might be able to use similar kinds of mechanisms and can generate parallel patterns of exclusion and destruction. Transnational com-munities might be able to build upon the basis of a strong, pre-existing acculturation. A common educational credential, shared beyond nationality and national borders, can serve, for example, as an entry point into those communities (see, for example, Morgan and Kubo or Harvey and Maclean in this volume). Transnational communities in the making can also contribute, either directly or indirectly, to the progressive homogenization or standardi-zation of acculturation frames. They can create their own training programs or missions and their own educative modules that can be potentially connected to annual meetings and events. More interesting, even, is the indirect role transnational communities can come to play through their influence on education systems, transnationally. For example, the indirect role of the Mont Pèlerin Society (MPS) has been unmistakable in this respect over the past decades (see Plehwe in this volume, Djelic 2006). As it was building itself up as a community, the MPS was also powerfully extending its reach and leverage through an indirect impact on and involvement in the reforms of economics and business-school curricula in many parts of the world. In a similar way, the constitution through time of a transnational accounting community has had a progressive, sometimes indirect impact on accounting programs and curricula in many parts of the world (Ramirez this volume, Botzem and Quack 2006). These transformations in powerfully structuring acculturation and education patterns are bound, in turn, to reinforce further and strengthen the transnational communities with which they are associated.

At first sight, it would seem that transnational communities, in contrast to the more classical *Gemeinschaft*-type ones, would have to forego direct forms of control and would have to rely instead on the softer mechanisms of interaction, imitation, persuasion, or acculturation presented above. As argued in the first part of this chapter, membership in transnational communities tends to be chosen and voluntary. Members are free to come and go, and those communities do not seem essential, in a profound way, to the identity of individual members. In contrast to nation-states, furthermore, transnational communities do not have the legitimate power to prevent or punish deviant behavior – the type of behavior that questions or threatens the common identity. So, it would seem at first that transnational communities cannot use coercive mechanisms to control their members or to foster integration. In reality, things are not so simple. First, direct interaction and the different mechanisms of socialization, whether face-to-face or technologically mediated, create the conditions for a more or less strong type of peer pressure. Such peer pressure, particularly when it is strong, can feel quite coercive. Second, when transnational communities develop or embrace a governance project and are ultimately successful in imposing their preferred solution, they create the conditions for a more coercive influence. "Deviant" behavior and resistance then become much more costly. Hence, in spite of their voluntary nature in appearance, transnational communities have the capacity to generate and use coercive resources.

Those different, broad types of mechanisms will not always be present or used. In the early periods of their lives, transnational communities rely mostly on direct interface and indirect socialization mechanisms, mainly through the circulation of information, ideas, and templates. This is documented in most contributions to this volume. Mechanisms of acculturation will only emerge when transnational communities have reached a degree of maturity, stability, integration, and strength. They will also generally require a capacity to gain leverage well beyond the boundaries of the community itself. Finally, stronger forms of coercive mechanisms will tend to reflect what we could call an institutionalization of transnational communities, particularly in the form of an influential governance project with an identifiable impact. Such institutionalization reflects the "efficacy" of the community and its ability to turn a project into a legitimate framework for governance.

The dynamics bridging communities across levels

Transnational communities are an important fixture of transnational governance, but they are so to some paradoxical degree when they articulate with nationally rooted communities. Saskia Sassen suggests that the transformations we classify under the broad label of globalization take place inside national territories to a larger extent than we generally suspect (Sassen 2006). She calls this process globalization through "denationalization" – the hollowing out of particular components of the national through "structurations of the global inside the national" (Sassen 2003: 5). As a consequence, she argues that

[s]tudying the global ... entails not only a focus on that which is explicitly global in scale, but also a focus on locally scaled practices and conditions articulated with global dynamics, and a focus on the multiplication of cross-border connections among various localities fed by the recurrence of certain conditions across localities. (Sassen 2003: 3)

We prefer the concept of "transnationalization" to that of "denationalization" – as the former affirms more clearly the continued role and importance of the national. Still, this volume and the collection of empirical chapters it contains confirm in many ways the multi-level nature of globalization identified by Sassen (2003, 2006). Globalization – as captured in this volume through our preoccupation for transnational governance – is not, we find, a process taking place simply and neatly in a global arena, beyond and over local and national territories. Globalization is a complex, multi-level process, with a lot of fluidity and movement in different directions across levels (see also Djelic and Quack 2003; Djelic and Sahlin-Andersson 2006). The introduction of the notion of "communities" allows us to be somewhat more precise here. What needs to be understood are the mechanisms connecting and articulating "global dynamics" with "locally scaled practices and conditions" (Sassen 2003: 3). Those mechanisms, we propose, are to a significant extent about the dynamics bridging communities across levels – and particularly about the dynamics bridging transnational and national communities.

From the empirical contributions in this volume, we identify three main patterns. First, transnational communities can be progressively – and possibly quite slowly – built up, structured, and stabilized through the interplay and interaction between different, often local and national communities (Harvey and Maclean, Schrad, Eder and Öz, Mariussen). This interaction or interplay articulates around the awareness and realization of the existence of a common interest, project, activity or preoccupation that may either have a transnational scope and reach from the start (Mariussen) or else be progressively constituted as such (Schrad, Harvey and Maclean, Eder and Öz, Dobusch and Quack). In this case, heterogeneous groups – mostly with a local or national basis – realize in a step-by-step manner that they have compatible, either similar or complementary, interests, activities, and preoccupations. The dynamics, then, are both lateral and bottom up – at least during the initial period. Lateral interactions between different local or national communities come to suggest the existence of a broader, shared community and identity. This is a long and slow process that involves a lot of mutual learning, adaptation, transformation, conflict, power struggle, compromise, and hybridization but also the eventual acceptance of a fair degree of remaining heterogeneity (Bragd *et al.* 2008). The transnational community that emerges from these lateral and bottom-up dynamics can become more or less integrated and more or less organized. In time, it may be able to affirm its autonomy as an entity from its component parts, leading then to a stronger reverse pattern of influence – from the "top" (transnational community) "down" (national or local components). The contributions by Schrad, Eder and Öz or Mariussen in this volume all show such an evolution, which can happen, naturally, at different rates of speed. The chapter by Harvey and Maclean focuses on an earlier stage of the process and leaves the question of possible further integration open for now.

Looking through our cases, we identify a second pattern, which might be seen arguably as a variation on the first one. Interestingly, a transnational community can emerge out of a common defensive reaction against transnational pressure, transnational developments, or transnational projects that appear to endanger nationally based identities, rights, practices or prerogatives (see also Böhm *et al.* 2008). In the contribution by Fetzer in this volume, nationally based labor communities initially came together at the European level mostly around the "determination to prevent negative reper-cussions of European developments on national industrial democracy achievements." Interactions between locally or nationally rooted communities around such a defensive agenda might ironically contribute, in time, to the construction and stabilization of a sense of community that crosses national and local boundaries. Nationally rooted communities working together to protect their national rootedness might turn into a transnational community in the process. Lateral dynamics with a defensive goal might pave the way, in time, for the emergence of a transnational collective with community features. This emergent community might then come to redefine progressively its own agenda in a more constructive, and even offensive way.

The contribution by Fetzer in this volume shows indeed that the defensive nature of the transnational community of trade unions in Europe faded somewhat over time. Instead, the transnational community – which had grown more integrated through the years – came to define more offensive European-level challenges and agendas for itself and its national members. Another instructive example of such a transition from a defensive towards a more constructive and offensive community is the World Social Forum, which originally started in 2001 as a direct counter-reaction to the annual World Economic Forum in Davos and as a defensive campaign against neoliberal economic policy (Smith 2004). Since then, the experience of collective mobilization has brought a broad range of individuals and (mostly) civil society organizations closer together. This initial common, defensive experience gave rise progressively to a more proactive – though still rather loose and heterogeneous – community, which now appears to be geared towards the voluntary construction of an active transnational civil society (Della Porta 2004).

Third, some of the contributions in this volume point to a third pattern. The dynamics there are more top down. They start with the constitution of a small transnational group and its self-definition around a particular agenda. From this small transnational base, the next stage will then be the attempt to try to root this agenda in different local and especially national contexts (Plehwe, Morgan and Kubo, Ramirez). There are different ways in which this can be attempted. The transnational community can identify and connect with those local or national groups or individuals that are more likely to be interested and seduced by the pursued agenda. The articulation, in other words, between the transnational community and the local or national communities that are seen as potentially receptive is certainly one way to go (see Djelic 2004). The transnational community can deploy different strategies, using direct contacts, seduction and persuasion, advocacy tools and strategies, or the manipulation of various kinds of resources (material or symbolic) and hence more or less potent forms of coercion. Local or national communities can be receptive to these for different reasons. They may have their own agenda that would be helped and reinforced by the agenda of the transnational community. They may be attracted by the resources associated with the transnational community and by the potential local or national leverage such a connection could give them (Kleiner 2003; Morgan and Kubo in this volume). They may be seduced through co-optation into what can be seen as an exclusive elite club or worry instead about exclusion (see Plehwe in this volume). Another way in which transnational communities can go about rooting their agenda locally is by gaining more macro-influence on governance frames or education systems (Ramirez, Plehwe in this volume). Instead of co-opting local or national communities into a given agenda through seduction and peer pressure, the idea here is to shape national institutions in ways that will in turn have a transformative impact on local and national communities. The pressure is thus more indirect, but arguably also more coercive. We are closer here to the construction of hegemony than to the exercise of raw power.

Beyond the differences that set those patterns apart, what seems clear across the different contributions in this volume is that a certain form of articulation and fluid interplay between transnational and national or local communities is a necessary, albeit not sufficient condition of impact and "efficacy" when it comes to governance. The complementary articulation between a degree of transnational cosmopolitanism and a form of national rootedness is what we find across the different chapters time and again. This articulation certainly explains the coexistence of what Tarde calls "the repetition of phenomena" across multiple localities and the "adaptation of phenomena" in each locality (Tarde 2001 [1895]). Transnational communities, in their cosmopolitan dimension, can produce "imitation" or "repetition" (Tarde 2001 [1895]). However, in their rooted dimension and connections (often national), transnational communities are also powerful mechanisms of "adaptation" and "translation" (Czarniawska and Sevon 1996; Tarde 2001 [1895]), and also of appropriation and recombination (Quack and Djelic 2005). We propose that this capacity to articulate "repetition" and "adaptation" is an important explanation of the impact and "efficacy" of transnational communities when it comes to governance.

Exploring the impact of transnational communities on governance

After bringing together our common findings on the nature of transnational communities, we now turn to the question of impact. The contributions to this volume show that transnational communities play a role – sometimes a quite significant one – in the governance of business and cross-border economic activity. We outline below the characteristic features of this impact as we saw them emerge from a systematic comparison of our rich empirical cases. For our understanding of governance we build on recent scholarship. Our contemporary episode of economic globalization is one in which privatization and deregulation, fostered by neoliberalism, have combined with an explosion of rule-setting and rule-monitoring activities at the national and transnational level (Majone 1991; Vogel 1996; Levi-Faur and Jordana 2005; Djelic and Sahlin-Andersson 2006; Graz and Nölke 2008, Schneiberg and Bartley 2008).

Patchwork forms of governance

The governance of cross-border economic activity is much more complex, if we follow recent scholarship, than earlier perspectives opposing "states" to "markets" had envisioned (Boyer and Drache 1996). Transnational governance suggests "a complex compound of activities bridging the global and the local and taking place at the same time within, between and across national boundaries" (Djelic and Sahlin-Andersson 2006: 3). First of all, transnational governance is characterized by changes in the range of actors involved. We note, in fact, a proliferation of actors with a role in governance. Multiple private or non-state actors play a significant, albeit non-exclusive role. Nation-states, supranational authorities, and inter-governmental organizations remain actively involved. However, they no longer have an exclusive role and responsibility when it comes to governance (Rosenau and Czempiel 1992; Cerny 2006). The literature provides clear evidence of an unmistakable expansion of governance constellations that transcend the state/non-state, public/private divides (Levi-Faur and Jordana 2005; Djelic and Sahlin-Andersson 2006; Graz and Nölke 2008).

Transnational governance also implies a consequential redefinition of modes of coordination, rule-making, and rule-monitoring. The boundaries between rule-setters and rule-followers tend to blur – as the latter are often actively involved at different stages of the governance process. The governance "products" that emerge tend to be "soft" – norms, standards, and "soft law" (Brunsson and Jacobsson 2000; Mörth 2004). Hence, many transnational governance systems are hybrid in character. They involve both state and non-state actors and combine top-down with bottom-up efforts (Kersbergen and van Waarden 2004). Transnational governance arrangements exist in many global policy domains, such as trade or finance but also environment, health, and security. They have direct and indirect regulatory effects on business and cross-border economic activity in many different sectors (Djelic and Sahlin-Andersson 2006; Mayntz 2009).

In many of these policy domains, but also as a broad phenomenon in itself, transnational governance exhibits a patchwork character – with coexisting and often overlapping forms of self-coordination, public regulation, and complex linkages between them (Héritier 1996). In a number of transnational industries, we find attempts at self-regulation coordinated by multinational companies (Cutler *et al.* 1999; Cashore *et al.* 2004). Social movements and non-governmental organizations also exert significant pressure on business actors to address issues of public interest such as fair wages, acceptable working conditions, and the protection of natural resources. Private standard-setting (Brunsson and Jacobsson 2000; Tamm-Hallström 2004) and certification or labeling initiatives (Bartley 2007; Overdevest 2005) have crossed multiple boundaries. They have generated encompassing rule-systems and rating and ranking schemes (Hedmo *et al.* 2006) that apply across many different jurisdictions. Still, competition between different rule-systems or schemes, on the one hand, and enforcement, on the other, remain the two main Achilles' heels of transnational governance.

The situation is not very different in the emerging field of global administrative law (Kingsbury *et al.* 2005). Inter-governmental institutions like the United Nations or the World Trade Organisation, informal inter-governmental networks (Slaughter 2004), and hybrid public-private bodies (Quack 2007; Dilling *et al.* 2008) have all been involved. The result is a burgeoning of principles, practices, and legal mechanisms, but again of a patchy and fragmented nature. The European Union, arguably the most developed supranational political construction in the world today, also works through a variety of governance modes. It has "hard" law-making capacities (Stone Sweet *et al.* 2001; Plehwe with Vescovi 2003), but it also uses experimentalist governance schemes (Dorf and Sabel 1998; Sabel and Zeitlin 2008). In the end, "hard" and "soft" law combine and overlap in many different policy fields (Mörth 2004; Falkner *et al.*2005; Trubek and Trubek 2005).

Thus, while documenting a surprising proliferation of rule-setting and monitoring activities, current research also points to the weak points of transnational governance. Transnational "governance activism" (Djelic and Sahlin-Andersson 2006) is striking, but it is a giant with "feet of clay." The patchwork character of transnational governance is clearly visible in the competition that exists between different governance constellations. Such competition, as it crosses over multiple jurisdictions, regularly leads to governance contradictions or even loopholes (Fischer-Lescano and Teubner 2004; Picciotto 2008). This has raised doubts, naturally, on the capacity of transnational governance, as it exists today, to handle effectively complex challenges such as, for example, global warming, financial risk or corporate ethics.

There are different explanations for this observed fragmentation, its associated contradictions, and, in some cases, its incoherence. First, it needs to be related to the polycentric and multi-layered nature of transnational governance – where activities traverse the national and the transnational but also the different and partly overlapping policy domains and arenas (Braithwaite and Drahos 2000; Djelic and Sahlin-Andersson 2006; Bartley and Smith in this volume). Second, it reflects the absence, in the transnational governance world, of an ultimate seat of legitimacy. Problems of accountability abound and are compounded by the weakness of enforcement and sanctioning mechanisms (Power 2007; Black 2008, Dilling et al. 2008). This means, ultimately, that transnational governance can have the feel of what Nils Brunsson calls "organized hypocrisy" (Brunsson 1989). Sometimes, it might not be much more than a discourse. Naturally, this discursive character does not mean it is unimportant, far from it (Brunsson 1989; Grant et al. 1998; Bragd et al. 2008). Yet it does point to a major limitation of transnational governance, in a number of situations.

Another weakness of transnational governance is that while attempting to reduce existing uncertainty, it often generates new uncertainty. Transnational governance, as it functions today, produces rules that are open and flexible and therefore can be interpreted, adapted or translated according to need and circumstances (Djelic and Sahlin-Andersson 2006). As a result, while the overarching objective behind transnational governance is to reduce uncertainty in cross-border economic transactions, it also tends to generate new uncertainties and new accountability issues (Power 2007). Djelic and Sahlin-Andersson (2006: 380f.) attribute this effect to a "distrust spiral" that is fostered and reinforced by three broad forces operating in transnational governance fields: scientization, marketization, and deliberative democracy.

Others have pointed to the ambivalence of rule interpretation in general, and more particularly in the context of pluralistic, multinational, and multicultural environments (Quack 2007; Picciotto 2008).

Communities in transnational governance

As far as collective action in the transnational sphere is concerned, a lot of research has hitherto concentrated on the role of organizations and networks. This is true for world society theory (Drori *et al.* 2006) as well as for international relations approaches to world politics and the European Union (Kohler-Koch and Eising 1999; Barnett and Finnemore 2004). Social movement theory similarly has pointed to the importance of activist networks and non-governmental organizations (Keck and Sikkink 1998; Tarrow 2005). There is no doubt that these social formations play a significant role in transnational rule-setting and monitoring.

However, the contributions to this volume suggest that there is also a community dimension to transnational governance that so far has been largely neglected. The chapters point to various forms of transnational communities. The members of those communities share projects, interests, values, and normative orientations. Over time, after many struggles and possibly some destruction along the way, this interpersonal orientation, magnified by direct and indirect interactions, has a bonding effect and contributes to social integration. In the case of transnational communities, this integration takes place across national boundaries but also across formal organizations and/or networks or even across nationally or locally based communities. While many of the transnational communities analyzed in this volume are depicted as relatively fluid, unstable, and loosely integrated, they nevertheless seem to add a crucial dose of social structuring to the transnational sphere and, by reflection, to transnational governance. They produce "emergent effects by virtue of the fact that the expertise, skills or convictions which are their basis guide the autonomous behavior of the community members" (Mayntz in this volume). This is very much in line with Morgan's (2001) statement that the contribution of transnational communities to transnational governance seems to lie in "background processes."

In our view, the additional value of the community dimension for understanding transnational governance arrangements lies in their potential to align the cognitive and normative orientations of their members over time. Therefore, the inclusion of transnational communities will enrich accounts of cross-border governance, which so far have focused primarily on the role of formal organizations and networks (Kohler-Koch and Eising 1999; Drori *et al.* 2006). This inclusion shows how vital cognitive frames and, to some extent, cognitive alignment can be for the effectiveness of coordination and govern-ance activity on many levels. Transnational communities are able to generate these effects because they are able to integrate – through mutual interaction, socialization, learning, mutual adjustment but also social control, coercion or exclusion – the practices, beliefs, norms, and identities of many different individuals. Each of those individuals is personally involved in multiple spheres of commitment, be they organizations, networks, nations, or even other communities, particularly at the national or local level.

In this sense, transnational communities have an affinity to forms of coordination that involve many actors and levels and diverge from the command-and-control conceptions of governance. As Bartley and Smith (in this volume) put it, transnational communities are likely to be cause and consequence of non-bureaucratic types of governance, not least because of the blurring of boundaries between rule-setters and rule-followers (Schneiberg and Bartley 2008). This affinity, however, does not mean that communities are the only social formations contributing cohesion, integration, and cognitive alignment to the transnational sphere – in part through processes of hege-mony construction. But we have focused in this volume on transnational communities and their particular impact.

Understanding the role of transnational communities in the governance of business and economic activity implies a "study of process and emergent features" (Morgan in this volume; see also Mayntz in this volume). It requires following the interactions of individuals and groups and the sense of belong-ing that these interactions generate. It suggests an exploration, in turn, of how this sense of belonging enables coordinated action at a distance, or what Tarde (2001 [1895]) would have called "repetition of phenomena" across multiple types of organizations, networks, associations, cultures, and nations.

The exploration of "process and emergent features" should start with a consideration of multiple community affiliations (Simmel 1971; Djelic and Quack in Chapter 1 of this volume). Many contributions to this volume provide evidence of self-reinforcing processes. Certain individuals see their horizon of action extend progressively beyond national borders and national communities. As these actors become enmeshed in an emerging set of trans-national interactions, social networks, and organizational arrangements, their transnational horizon of action broadens in parallel (see, for example, Morgan and Kubo, Bartley and Smith, Dobusch and Quack, and Schrad in this volume). From the contributions to this volume, we see though that processes of transnational community-building did not always live up to this potential to the same degree. Several chapters in this volume refer to cases of transnational communities that at the time of observation were still at an embryonic stage. This is most evident in the account of board directors in transnational companies located in France and Britain (Harvey and Maclean in this volume). Fetzer's analysis of European trade unions shows here an interesting evolution (Fetzer in this volume). Nationally rooted trade unions started to work together initially in order precisely to protect and defend this strong national rootedness. Ironically, a sense of belonging was progressively constructed around this initial common defensive objective. In time, this emerging sense of belonging became the basis for a more proactive and even offensive collective mobilization at the European level!

Playing different roles

The contributions to this volume suggest that the governance impact of transnational communities has several dimensions. When it comes to the governance of business and economic activity, transnational communities can play different roles. The empirical cases we have explored show, furthermore, variable combinations of those different roles.

Defining and framing

At a basic level, transnational communities can play an instrumental role in the *definition of governance problems and issues*. This will be particularly the case in situations requiring cross-border coordination and revealing, initially, broad heterogeneity. The elaboration and expression of a common definition is an important first step to the *framing* of problems and issues as domains of public attention (Dewey 1938). The chapters in this volume document quite clearly that transnational communities also play a key role when it comes to *framing* and creating a transnational public "problem space" – where a multiplicity of actors actively search for solutions. Framing then also generates new opportunities for strategizing. A multiplicity of individuals, organizations, and associations meet each other in this transnational "problem space," with different goals and strategies. These encounters can be conflict-ridden, but they also tend to foster and encourage, in time, community-building and the emergence of an overarching identity – in spite of and beyond competitive strategizing.

As the diverse contributions to this volume show, it is by no means easy to predict which issues will be identified as such and framed as requiring

transnational attention and possibly governance. Defining and framing transnational "problem spaces" is, in other words, a historically and contextually
contingent process. As illustrated by Schrad's chapter in this volume, the rise
of temperance as a transnationally relevant policy issue was not rooted in any
statistical increase in drunkenness, but was rather based on subjective assessments concerning the inappropriateness of drunkenness in different countries
at a given point in time. Similarly, environmental protection (Bartley and
Smith in this volume), access to a digital commons (Dobusch and Quack, and
Metiu in this volume) or global warming (Mariussen in this volume) have all
been shaped and constructed as issue-fields calling for transnational governance. In all those cases, the role of emerging transnational communities has
been unmistakable.

At a broader or even a meta-level, it is important to underscore the pivotal
role of certain comprehensive discourse communities. In his description of the
Mont Pèlerin Society and emerging neoliberal movement, Plehwe (in this
volume) does not actually document the framing of an issue but, as it were, the
framing of a "framing scheme" with an hegemonic potential (see also Djelic
2006). Clearly, this was Friedrich Hayek's vision from the start in 1949, when
he called for the articulation of a "liberal utopia," a "truly liberal radicalism"
(Hayek 1949: 432). He saw a role for an avant-garde liberal group of original
thinkers:

We need intellectual leaders who are willing to work for an ideal, however small may
be the prospects of its early realization. They must be men who are willing to stick to
principles and to fight for their full realization, however remote. (Hayek 1949: 433)

This case shows how a transnational community has been instrumental in
shaping a broad ideological structure that has come, in time, to influence and
frame the principled beliefs, worldviews, and practices associated with many
transnational governance processes – irrespective of the nature of the issue
(see Hall 1993 for the parallel influence of the Keynesian paradigm until the
1970s and Hayek 1949 on the role and power of socialism).

Framing has also been identified as a constitutive activity in processes of
market formation (Callon 1998; MacKenzie and Millo 2003). Framing leads to
mutually shared expectations and norms that make it possible to deal with
coordination problems in markets (Beckert 2009). Chapters in this volume
make it plain that markets are not "born global," but that they are typically
(and often only progressively) framed as transnational markets (Morgan and
Kubo, Mariussen in this volume). Since the framing of transnational markets
involves actors originating from different countries, with distinct institutional

and cultural traditions, it generally demands intense and complex collaborative efforts. Those heterogeneous actors need to work together to elaborate shared justifications and definitions of value, compatible business models, and common rules of exchange and competition (Quack forthcoming 2009). Hence, the framing of markets – and particularly of transnational markets – is bound to coevolve and interplay with processes of community-building. Transnational communities can be either challenging or defending different "control conceptions" of markets (Fligstein 2001). Those transnational communities will be, in the process, constructing themselves as communities. Eder and Öz (in this volume) suggest, for example, that an emerging community of trading practice fed back into the operation of the informal shuttle trade in the Laleli market in Istanbul, generating trust and thereby reducing the risk involved in these informal market exchanges (see Dahles, in this volume, for a failed example of using ethnic ties to overcome market uncertainty). Morgan and Kubo (in this volume) show that the formation of a global market for private equity was supported by a community of private equity practitioners that was "transient yet powerful in impact" (see also Hussain and Ventresca for parallels in global financial markets, and Ramirez in global accounting markets). Finally, Mariussen (in this volume) documents the role of scientific and expert communities as they enter "narrative competition" with the aim to gain a first-mover advantage on the emerging market for carbon capture and storage. The latter account confirms ongoing research in other issue-fields – for example, what takes place around CO_2 emissions trading (Engels 2006) or around new medical treatments for breast cancer (Mützel 2009).

Mobilizing collective action

Transnational communities are platforms for the mobilization of collective action. This is indeed a second important role that they can play in governance processes. While transnational communities are often loose and transient in nature, they nevertheless are able to reach decisions, to jointly control resources, and to strategize for their goals, often to the detriment of other actors and interests. A number of chapters provide evidence that communities were able to mobilize diffuse agency and to direct it in a common direction – towards a jointly defined and framed issue, goal or interest (Eder and Öz, Dobusch and Quack, Schrad in this volume). Transnational communities also often gave birth to or co-opted other kinds of collective actors, such as formal organizations and associations (Schrad and Fetzer in this volume). In most cases, the relationship between communities and those other associated actors was synergetic and reinforcing (see Hussain and Ventresca in this volume on an archipelago of associations; see also Dobusch and Quack in this volume). In particular, the malleability of transnational communities gives, as Bartley and Smith (in this volume) suggest, new actors "a seat at the table." Amongst those "new actors" entering the definition and negotiation arenas, we find multiple kinds of non-governmental organizations (NGOs), civil society associations, think tanks, and various consulting or expert organizations (Dobusch and Quack, Bartley and Smith, Schrad, Metiu, Plehwe, and Mariussen in this volume). Particularly striking in that respect is the contribution by Metiu (in this volume). It shows the enabling effects of the open source software community on skill development among programming communities in developing countries (see the parallel openness in Dobusch and Quack in this volume).

Delineating public arenas

A third important role for transnational communities is to delineate – or serve as – public arenas, within which discussion, contention, and conflict are possible but contained. As Bradg et al. (2008) argue, discourse can be a means to create a community. Discourse and deliberation are essential features of transnational communities of practice, episteme, and interest. Many of the transnational communities discussed in this volume are not simply quiet arenas of compromise and agreement. They are also social spaces where opposition and conflict are voiced – but also contained – and where different views, norms, and interests confront each other. The community of practice of certification specialists depicted by Bartley and Smith (in this volume) is, for example, a community where different perspectives and even interests collide. Being a transnational space where contrasting and sometimes conflicting perspectives can be confronted and discussed and where compromise can be sought, this community contributes – like others around global warming (Mariussen in this volume) or open content (Dobusch and Quack in this volume) – to the alignment of preferences and to the generation of broadly and on average acceptable solutions to transnational public policy problems. Insofar as communities do actually nurture discussion, discourse, or even deliberation in a more organized sense, they become public arenas where compromise solutions to complex governance issues can emerge (Quack 2007).

Contributing to preference transformation

Over time, transnational communities can also come to play another important role. They can foster preference transformation in some or all of their members. This role is, in part, a direct consequence of the three previous ones. Preference transformation does not necessarily lead to preference alignment of all community members. As a community develops and matures, though, centripetal pressures will emerge, and preferences will move closer to each other. Consequently, the transformation of preferences will tend, in that phase, to facilitate coordination across different interest groups. The transformation of preferences can be a result of learning processes, but it can also be an expression of mutual adjustment under peer pressure or even of coercion through more or less formal sanctioning and the threat of exclusion. Furthermore, it can take place in such a way that actors from different backgrounds end up bringing their differences and heterogeneities under the umbrella of more encompassing principles, as in the advocacy networks discussed by Keck and Sikkink (1998). Examples for such processes are provided by the chapters in this volume that deal with alignments of informal practices and formal standards but also, ultimately, of underlying principled beliefs. The emergence of an informal market of shuttle traders studied by Eder and Öz (in this volume) shows nicely how shared routines and mutual expectations evolved over time out of rather instrumental exchanges between ethnically and socially distinct market actors. Ramirez (in this volume) shows how conceptions of professionalism in France were transformed by the integration of the French accounting elite into the transnational accounting community (see also Morgan and Kubo for transformations of the Japanese private equity community). Braithwaite and Drahos (2000) in their seminal book on "Global Business Regulation" argued that "webs of dialog" were often more effective in generating transnational coordination than the top-down implementation of rules. The findings of our studies support their conclusion while further elaborating the community dimension of what they referred to as "webs of dialog" in a rather loose way. Even though we do not have evidence of this in this volume, one might wonder, finally, whether the decline of certain transnational communities, as analyzed by Schrad in this volume, could not also be explained by a transformation of preferences. This time, though, pressures would be centrifugal. Transnational communities would tend to weaken or even decline when the preferences of their members began to diverge or when control mechanisms started to weaken.

Participating in rule-setting

When it comes to transnational governance, transnational communities are also instrumental because they stimulate and participate in rule-setting. We find them both in situations of private rule-setting and in cases where public

actors (national governments, supranational authorities, international organizations with a public stature, or inter-governmental bodies) are much more
central. As understood here, this role goes beyond that of framing and agenda-
setting, which Haas (1992) associates with epistemic communities. It also
differs from the preference-changing impact of political communities of
practice, as described by Adler (2005). Transnational communities are powerful instruments for generating rules that can help to overcome the institutional
fragmentation characteristically associated with transnational governance.
The defining features of those communities – in particular their ability to
traverse organizational membership and national citizenship, their limited
liability, and their internal heterogeneity – are all extremely important here.
They allow transnational communities to cut more pragmatically across
entrenched perceptions and interests than organizations, whether public or
private, can generally do. In other words, transnational communities are often
able to generate the type of cognitive and normative alignment that is necessary for the setting of rules in contexts where many different institutional
traditions overlap (Oberthür and Gehring 2006). In addition, transnational
communities can often draw on rather unique and up-to-date pools of knowledge and experiences relevant for rule-setting in specific policy domains.
Schrad (in this volume) shows how the transnational temperance movement
served as a powerful conveyor belt – framing policy initiatives, transforming
them into legislative rules, and carrying them across borders to multiple
national jurisdictions. Bartley and Smith (in this volume) show how a transnational community became innovative – turning certification into a new
form of private transnational governance. Adherence to a certification scheme
creates, as Glinski (2008: 63) argues, immediate legal obligations for the
certified company and may have a ripple-like impact on many companies
(including non-certified ones) by defining what constitutes fair business
conduct under tort law. Transnational professional communities also played
a significant role in the rule-making process and associated legislative lobbying that have led to the widespread adoption of the IFRS as a new set of global
accounting standards (Ramirez in this volume; Botzem and Quack 2006).

Sanctioning and exerting control

Finally, transnational communities can have a profound impact in governance
processes as they exert their capacity for informal sanctioning and social control.
This role proves to be particularly important in the later phases of governance,
when the time comes for rule implementation, compliance, and monitoring. This
capacity takes various forms. Benchmarking and peer pressure are undeniably a

conduit for social control. Systematic, "transparent" comparisons through labelization, certification, accreditation, or ranking are a strong and institutionalized form of social control. Those mechanisms can be "neutral" benchmarks and comparisons, but they can also be morally weighed. Moral suasion, particularly through naming and shaming, can be a powerful mechanism of social control indeed (Boli 2006). The recent elaboration and officialization by G20 members of a "black list" of tax-haven countries is an example (G20 2009). Ultimately, the strongest source of sanctioning power is the threat of exclusion from or refusal of admission into an existing community – particularly when this community is associated with significant resources and legitimacy.

The chapters in this volume suggest the importance of such informal sanctioning, although it is sometimes difficult to document it explicitly. Within the open software and open content communities, for example, those who violate the principle of sharing are likely to face informal mechanisms of naming and shaming but also run the risk of exclusion (Metiu, Dobusch and Quack in this volume). The loose certification community described by Bartley and Smith (in this volume) exerts pressures for public comparison and benchmarking between different programs and thereby threatens the reputation of those who do not conform or perform according to the standards defined by or through the community. When transnational communities are ultimately successful in imposing their preferred solution and the latter is indeed appropriated by various public authorities, they create the conditions for a more coercive impact. For example, once the European Union had decided to make international financial reporting standards (IFRS) legally binding, membership in the transnational accounting community became all the more unavoidable. From that moment, an accountant who chose not to make the effort to adapt to or comply with the cultural frame of the new transnational community found himself or herself marginalized in professional terms. Hence, the professional community of transnational accounting experts was able from then on to exert even stronger pressure on the French accounting profession (Ramirez in this volume) and naturally on other national accounting communities as well (Botzem forthcoming). Altogether, the voluntary nature of transnational communities should therefore not lead us to overlook the coercive resources they can muster and manipulate, both directly and indirectly!

Creating order and legitimacy in a complex world

Transnational communities generate and foster the development of practices, standards, and different kinds of "soft law" (Mörth 2004, 2006). In parallel, transnational communities also need to engage in justification and legitimacy-building – showing how these practices, standards, and rules are useful and implementable but also arguing that they are superior to existing or possible alternatives (Quack 2010). This is an important, necessary – albeit not sufficient – condition for the broad sharing of those blueprints within the community but also for their impact well beyond it. The chapters in this volume indicate that communities engage in the justification of competing "orders of worth" (Boltanski and Thévenot 2006). The open source and open content communities analyzed by Metiu, and Dobusch and Quack (in this volume) are clear and univocal when it comes to their justification strategy; they argue for the unmitigated superiority of sharing knowledge over traditional copyright regulation. Some of the other communities deploy more complex justification strategies and even find themselves standing simultaneously on different sides of the fence in certain cases. Environmental and labor certification, for example, reconciles awkwardly a justification of market principles in rule-setting and monitoring with a preoccupation for long-term economic and environmental sustainability (Bartley and Smith in this volume; Engels 2006). The community studied by Mariussen (in this volume) is searching for ways to limit the negative externalities of profit- (and market-) oriented business activity while, at the same time, being itself actively involved in the creation of a new market around carbon capture and storage.

In most chapters in this volume, transnational communities function also as "legitimacy communities" (Black 2008). They issue legitimacy claims just as much as they are the audience to which legitimacy claims are addressed. Their role might change over time. In their early stage of development, communities are more likely to act as challengers and to contest the legitimacy of existing rules. After a while, they might turn into stabilizers and protectors of specific governance rules and monitoring systems (see, for example, Morgan and Kubo, Ramirez, or Hussain and Ventresca in this volume). Ultimately, though, the current financial crisis indicates that the stabilizing function of communities and their legitimacy claims can always be contested and threatened irrespective of the strength of the position achieved.

An interesting feature of the cases analyzed in this volume is that transnational communities, in a number of cases, started off as relatively small, interpersonal networks or social groups. Typically, there was a small rather elite core group who then initiated a broader community or social movement (Schrad, Plehwe, Dobusch and Quack, and Mariussen in this volume). We also found interesting differences with regard to the social openness or closure of communities over time. Questions emerge, naturally, as to the performance and "efficacy" of these different types of communities with regard to leadership and governance. Smaller communities can lead and coordinate more easily. Still, it often takes a broader community to effectively mobilize and widely cultivate particular types of discourse, standards, and practices. Broader and more inclusive communities are also able to incorporate and take advantage of the diversity of experiences, knowledge, and practices of a large community membership, marshaling this vast experience in the service of the common project.

Exclusive communities, as illustrated by the neoliberal discourse community or the transnational community of accounting professionals, tend to maintain an elite character and tightly restrict the admission of new members. If they do not manage to link up with broader and more inclusive audiences, though, small and exclusive transnational communities run the risk of establishing expert governance regimes that operate in a rather top-down, bureaucratic fashion with, ultimately, limited support and impact. Reflecting in 1949 on the broad impact of socialism, Hayek showed how important it was for a small group of original thinkers to articulate their ideas and then connect with broader circles of what he called "second hand dealers in ideas" (Hayek 1949: 418). Such a combination, he believed, would also be key to the future ideological and political impact of liberalism. Inclusive communities, on the other hand, like the open source and open content movement in particular, have fluid boundaries. Not only are they interested in continuously attracting new members but they also try to orchestrate a balance between the core and the broader membership of the community that allows in principle for reciprocal exchange and collective learning (Bohman 2007). Inclusive communities may be more difficult to manage, but they ensure a broader reach. They also make it possible for a large diversity of experiences, knowledge, practices, and ideas to be brought into the common project of the community (see Metiu, Dobusch and Quack, Bartley and Smith and Schrad in this volume).

In conclusion, the chapters in this volume document the rather comprehensive impact of transnational communities on the governance of business and economic activity. This impact is comprehensive in at least a double sense. First, we find that the impact of transnational communities extends well beyond the early stages of the policy cycle – where earlier literature has often tended to confine it (Haas 1992; Plehwe in this volume). Second, we also find that the role of transnational communities does not stop with intergovernmental politics. This is not only true for the comprehensive discourse community analyzed by Plehwe (in this volume) but also applies to other types of transnational communities analyzed here, including those of practice, episteme, and interest operating in various fields of transnational governance. Returning to the key issues of the research agenda outlined by Adler and Haas (1992) more than fifteen years ago for the study of (epistemic) communities, this volume suggests that there is still a lot to be discovered by following a reflexive approach to world politics that includes various types of communities in which ideas, practices, and interests are intermediating between international structures and individual and collective agency.

This volume constitutes an attempt to assess systematically the role of communities in transnational governance. There is renewed interest, currently in sociology and business studies, for the concept of community. Most of this interest, though, tends to focus on a classical understanding of the notion of "community" – bringing us back to local communities of belonging with often an ascriptive character (Lounsbury and Marquis 2007; Marquis and Battilana 2009). This volume shows that a renewed interest in the notion of community is indeed important. However, we argue that it should come with at least a partial redefinition of the notion and with an enlarged focus to include transnational imagined communities, often of the limited liability kind (Janowitz 1952). All contributions to this volume indicate that the organization and governance of contemporary business and economic activity connect, to a significant degree, with the emergence and development of complex overlaps among geographically widespread transnational communities. The transient and hybrid nature of transnational communities means that their effects on transnational economic governance can be determined only by taking account of the full social context in which they operate. We have shown, in this volume, that transnational communities often evolve out of markets, networks or organizations and that they, in turn, can generate the structuration of those other types of social formations. In other words, transnational communities develop and evolve in tightly intertwined ways with many other kinds of social entities or aggregates. Therefore, it is both methodologically and substantively difficult to isolate precisely the impact of transnational communities per se in the complex ecology of contemporary transnational governance. Still, as this volume has demonstrated, this is far from meaning that transnational communities do not make a difference. We have argued and provided illustrative evidence that they do! This volume, though, is only the beginning of the journey. It is an invitation to explore further the complex aspects of community in global economic governance.

NOTES

1. "Le roseau plie et ne rompt pas."
2. Pointillism is a postimpressionist school of painting, with roots in France at the end of the nineteenth century. The work of painters like George Seurat, Paul Signac, or Camille Pissaro is representative of that school. The technique associated with this school is characterized by the application of paint in small dots and brush strokes. *Point* in French, from which the name *pointillisme* derives, means "dot."

REFERENCES

Adler, E. 2005. *Communitarian international relations*. London: Routledge.

Adler, E. and Haas, P. M. 1992. "Conclusion: Epistemic communities, world order, and the creation of a reflective research program," *International Organization* **46** (1): 367–90.

Aerts, E., Béaud, C. and Stengers, J. (eds.) 1990. *Liberalism and paternalism in the 19th century*. Leuven University Press.

Anderson, B. 2006 [1983]. *Imagined communities*. London and New York: Verso.

Barnett, M. N. and Finnemore, M. 2004. *Rules for the world: International organizations in global politics*. Ithaca, NY: Cornell University Press.

Bartley, T. 2007. "Institutional emergence in an era of globalization: The rise of transnational private regulation of labor and environmental conditions," *American Journal of Sociology* **113**: 297–351.

Beckert, J. 2009. "The social order of markets," *Theory and Society* **38**: 245–69.

Black, J. 2008. "Constructing and contesting legitimacy and accountability in polycentric regulatory regimes," *Regulation and Governance* **2**: 137–64.

Böhm, S., Spicer, A. and Fleming, P. 2008. "Infra-political dimensions of resistance to international business: A neo-Gramscian approach," *Scandinavian Journal of Management* **24** (3): 169–82.

Bohman, J. 2007. *Democracy across borders. From Dêmos to Dêmoi*. Cambridge, MA: MIT Press.

Boli, J. 2006. "The rationalization of virtue and virtuosity in world society," in Djelic, M.-L. and Sahlin-Andersson, K. (eds.), pp. 95–118.

Boltanski, L. and Thévenot, L. 2006. *On justification: Economies of worth*. Princeton University Press.

Botzem, S. forthcoming. *The politics of accounting regulation: Organizing transnational standard setting in financial reporting*.

Botzem, S. and Quack, S. 2006. "Contested rules and shifting boundaries: International standard-setting in accounting," in Djelic, M.-L. and Sahlin-Andersson, K. (eds.), pp. 266–86.

Boyer, R. and Drache, D. 1996. *States against markets: The limits of globalization*. London: Routledge.

Bragd, A., Christensen, D., Czarniawska, B. and Tullberg, M. 2008. "Discourse as the means of community creation," *Scandinavian Journal of Management* **24**: 199–208.

Braithwaite, J. and Drahos, P. 2000. *Global business regulation*. Cambridge University Press.

Brunsson, N. 1989. *The organization of hypocrisy*. Chichester: John Wiley & Sons.

Brunsson, N. 2000. *The irrational organization*. Stockholm: Fagbokforlaget.

Brunsson, N. and Jacobsson, B. (eds.) 2000. *A world of standards*. Oxford University Press.

Callon, M. (ed.) 1998. *The laws of the markets*. Oxford: Wiley Blackwell.

Cashore, B., Auld, G. and Newsom, D. 2004. *Governing through markets: Forest certification and the emergence of non-state authority*. New Haven, CT: Yale University Press.

Cerny, P. G. 2006. "Restructuring the state in a globalizing world: Capital accumulation, tangled hierarchies and the search for a new spatio-temporal fix," *Review of International Political Economy* **13** (4): 679–95.

Cohen, A. P. 1985. *The symbolic construction of community*. London and New York: Routledge.

Cutler, A. C. Haufler, V. and Porter, T. (eds.) 1999. *Private authority and international affairs*. State University of New York Press.

Czarniawska, B. and Sevon, G. (eds.) 1996. *Translating organizational change*. Berlin/New York: Walter de Gruyter.

Della Porta, D. 2004. "Multiple belongings, tolerant identities, and the construction of 'another politics': Between the European Social Forum and the local social forum," in Della Porta, D. and Tarrow, S. (eds.), *Transnational protest and global activism*. Lanham, MD: Rowman and Littlefield, pp. 175–202.

Dewey, J. 1938. *Logic: The theory of inquiry*. New York: Henry Holt.

Dilling, O., Herberg, M. and Winter, G. (eds.) 2008. *Responsible business*. Oxford: Hart.

Djelic, M.-L. 2004. "Social networks and country-to-country transfer: Dense and weak ties in the diffusion of knowledge," *Socio-Economic Review* **2**: 341–70.

Djelic, M.-L. 2006. "Marketization: From intellectual agenda to global policy making," in Djelic, M.-L. and Sahlin-Andersson, K. (eds.), pp. 53–73.

Djelic, M.-L., and Quack, S. (eds.) 2003. *Globalization and institutions: Redefining the rules of the economic game*. Cheltenham: Edward Elgar.

Djelic, M.-L. and Sahlin-Andersson, K. (eds.) 2006. *Transnational governance*. Cambridge University Press.

Dorf, M. C. and Sabel, C. F. 1998. "A constitution of democratic experimentalism," in *Columbia Law Review* **98** (2): 267–473.

Drori, G., Meyer, J. and Hwang, H. (eds.) 2006. *Globalization and organization: World society and organizational change*. Oxford University Press.

Durkheim, E. 2001 [1912]. *The elementary forms of religious life*. Oxford University Press.

Engels, A. 2006. "Market creation and transnational rule-making: The case of CO_2 emissions trading, in Djelic, M.-L. and Sahlin-Andersson, K. (eds.), pp. 329–48.

Falkner, G., Treib, O., Hartlapp, M. and Leiber, S. 2005. *Complying with Europe: EU harmonisation and soft law in the member states*. Cambridge University Press.

Fischer-Lescano, A. and Teubner, G. 2004. "Regime-collisions: The vain search for legal unity in the fragmentation of global law," *Michigan Journal of International Law* **25** (4): 999–1045.

Fligstein, N. 2001. *The architecture of markets*. Princeton University Press.

G20. 2009. "Leaders' statement: The global plan for recovery and reform," Communiqué of the G20 Meeting in London, April 2. www.g20.org/Documents/final-communique.pdf. Accessed April 8, 2009.

Glinski, C. 2008. "Bridging the gap: The legal potential of private regulation," in Dilling, O., Herberg, M. and Winter, G. (eds.), pp. 41–66.

Grant, D., Keenoy, T. and Oswick, C. (eds.) 1998. *Discourse and organization.* Thousand Oaks, CA: Sage.

Graz, J.-C., and Nölke, A. (eds.) 2008. *Transnational private governance and its limits.* London: Routledge.

Haas, P. 1992. "Introduction: Epistemic communities and international policy coordination," *International Organization* **46** (1): 1–35.

Hall, P. 1993. "Policy paradigms, social learning, and the state: The case of economic policy-making in Britain," *Comparative Politics* **25** (3): 275–96.

Hayek, F. 1949. "The intellectuals and socialism," *University of Chicago Law Review* **16**: 417–33.

Hedmo, T., Sahlin-Andersson, K. and Wedlin, L. 2006. "The emergence of a European regulatory field of management education," in Djelic, M.-L. and Sahlin-Andersson, K. (eds.), pp. 308–28.

Héritier, A. 1996. "The accommodation of diversity in European policy-making and its outcomes: Regulatory policy as a patchwork," *Journal of European Public Policy* **3** (2): 149–67.

IWA. 1864. "The International Workingmen's Association (IWA): General Rules," *The Bee-Hive Newspaper*, November 12, accessed April 8, 2009. www.connexions.org/CxLibrary/Docs/CX5581-GeneralRules.html.

Janowitz, M. 1952. *The community press in an urban setting.* Glencoe, IL: The Free Press.

Kalyvas, S. 1996. *The rise of Christian democracy in Europe.* Ithaca, NY: Cornell University Press.

Keck, M. and Sikkink, K. 1998. *Activists beyond borders: Advocacy networks in international politics.* Ithaca, NY: Cornell University Press.

Kersbergen, K. v. 1995. *Social capitalism: A study of Christian Democracy and the welfare state.* London: Routledge.

Kersbergen, K. v. and Waarden, F. van 2004. "'Governance' as a bridge between disciplines: Cross-disciplinary inspiration regarding shifts in governance and problems of governability, accountability and legitimacy," *European Journal of Political Research* **43**: 143–71.

Kingsbury, B., Krisch, N., Stewart, R. B. and Wiener, J. B. 2005. "Foreword: Global governance as administration–National and transnational approaches to global administrative law," *Law and Contemporary Problems* **68** (3 & 4): 1–13.

Kleiner, T. 2003."Building up an asset management industry: Forays of an Anglo-Saxon logic into the French business system," in Djelic, M.-L. and Quack, S. (eds.), pp. 57–82.

Kohler-Koch, B. and Eising, R. (eds.) 1999. *Transformation of governance in the European Union.* London: Routledge.

La Fontaine, J. 2002 [1668]. *Les Fables de la Fontaine.* Paris: Le Livre de Poche.

Levi-Faur, D. and Jordana, J. (eds.) 2005. The rise of regulatory capitalism: The global diffusion of a new regulatory order. *The Annals of the American Academy of Political and Social Science.* Vol. 598. London: Sage.

Lounsbury, M. and Marquis, C. 2007. "Vive la résistance: Competing logics in the consolidation of community banking," *Academy of Management Journal* **50**: 799–820.

MacKenzie, D. and Millo, Y. 2003. "Constructing a market, performing theory: The historical sociology of a financial derivatives exchange," *American Journal of Sociology* **109**: 107–45.

MacKenzie, D., Muniesa, F. and Siu, L. (eds.) 2007. *Do economists make markets*? Princeton University Press.

Maddox, R. 2001. *The war within World War II: The United States and international cartels*. New York: Praeger.

Majone, G. 1991. "Cross-national sources of regulatory policy making in Europe and the United States", *Journal of Public Policy* **11** (1): 79–106.

Marquis, C. and Battilana, J. 2009. "Acting globally but thinking locally? The enduring influence of local communities on organizations," *Research in Organizational Behavior* **29**: 283–302.

Mayntz, R. 2009. *Über Governance. Institutionen und Prozesse politischer Regelung*. Frankfurt a.M.: Campus.

Mezaki, I. 1992. *International cartels in business history*. Tokyo University Press.

Mitchell, W. 2008 [1904]. *An essay on the early history of the law merchant*. Whitefish, MT: Kessinger.

Morgan, G. 2001. "Transnational communities and business systems," *Global Networks: A Journal of Transnational Affairs* **1** (2): 113–30.

Mörth, U. (ed.) 2004. *Soft law in governance and regulation: An interdisciplinary analysis*. Cheltenham: Edward Elgar.

Mörth, U. 2006. "Soft regulation and global democracy," in Djelic, M.-L. and Sahlin-Andersson, K. (eds.), pp. 119–38.

Mützel, S. 2009. "Koordinierung von Märkten durch 'narrativen Wettbewerb,'" *Kölner Zeitschrift für Soziologie und Sozialpsychologie* **49**: 87–106.

Oberthür, S. and Gehring, T. 2006. "Institutional interaction in global environmental governance: The case of the Cartagena Protocol and the World Trade Organization," *Global Environmental Politics* **6** (2): 1–31.

Overdevest, C. 2005. "Treadmill politics, information politics, and public policy: Toward a political economy of information," *Organization & Environment* **18**: 72–90.

Peters, A., Koechlin, L., Fenner, G. and Forster, T. forthcoming. *Non-state actors as standard setters*. Cambridge University Press. In press.

Picciotto, S. 2008. "Regulatory networks and multi-level global governance," in Dilling, O., Herberg, M. and Winter, G. (eds.), pp. 315–41.

Plehwe, D. with Vescovi, S. 2003. "Europe's special case: The five corners of business-state interactions," in Djelic, M.-L. and Quack, S. (eds.), pp. 193–219.

Postel, R. 1996. "The Hanseatic League and its Decline," www.unibw-hamburg.de/PWEB/hisfrn/hanse.html. Accessed April 20, 2009.

Powell, W. 1990. "Neither market nor hierarchy: Network forms of organization," *Research in Organizational Behavior* **12**: 295–336.

Power, M. 2007. *Organized Uncertainty*. Oxford University Press.

Quack, S. 2007. "Legal professionals and transnational law-making: A case of distributed agency", *Organization* **14** (5): 643–66.

Quack, S. 2009. "'Global' markets in theory and history: Towards a comparative analysis," *Kölner Zeitschrift für Soziologie und Sozialpsychologie* **49**: 125–42.

Quack, S. 2010. "Law, expertise and legitimacy in transnational economic governance: An introduction", *Socio-Economic Review*, **8**: 3–16.

Quack, S. and Djelic, M.-L. 2005. "Adaptation, recombination, and reinforcement: The story of antitrust and competition law in Germany and Europe," in Streeck, W. and Thelen, K. (eds.), *Beyond continuity: Institutional change in advanced political economies.* Oxford University Press, pp. 253–81.

Rosenau, J. N. and Czempiel, E.-O. (eds.) 1992. *Governance without government: Order and change in world politics.* Cambridge University Press.

Sabel, C. F. and Zeitlin, J. 2008. "Learning from difference: The new architecture of experimentalist governance in the EU," *European Law Journal* **14** (3): 271–327.

Sassen, S. 2003. "Globalization or denationalization?," *Review of International Political Economy* **10** (1): 1–22.

Sassen, S. 2006. *Territory, authority and rights.* Princeton University Press.

Schneiberg, M. and Bartley, T. 2008. "Organizations, regulation, and economic behavior: Regulatory dynamics and forms from the nineteenth to twenty-first century," *Annual Review of Law and Social Sciences* **4**: 31–61.

Simmel, G. 1955 [1908]. "The web of group affiliations," in Simmel, G., *Conflict and the web of group affiliations.* New York: Free Press, pp. 125–95.

Simmel, G. 1971. *On individuality and social forms,* edited by D. Levine. University of Chicago Press.

Slaughter, A.-M. 2004. *A new world order.* Princeton University Press.

Smith, J. 2004. "The World Social Forum and the challenges of global democracy," *Global Networks* **4** (4): 413–21.

Smith, J., Chatfield, C. and Pagnucco, R. (eds.) 1997. *Transnational social movements and global politics.* Syracuse University Press.

Stone Sweet, A., Sandholtz, W. and Fligstein, N. 2001. *The institutionalization of Europe.* Oxford University Press.

Tamm-Hallström, K. 2004. *Organizing international standardisation.* Cheltenham: Edward Elgar.

Tarde, G. 2000 [1899]. *Social laws: An outline of sociology.* Kitchener, ON: Batoche Books.

Tarde, G. 2001 [1895]. *Les lois de l'imitation.* Paris: Les Empêcheurs de Penser en Rond.

Tarrow, S. 2005. *The new transnational activism.* Cambridge University Press.

Thrift, N. 2006. "Re-inventing invention: New tendencies in capitalist commodification," *Economy and Society* **35** (2): 279–306.

Trakman, L. 1980. "The evolution of the law merchant: Our common heritage. Part I: Ancient and medieval law merchant," *Journal of Maritime Law and Commerce* **12** (2): 153–82.

Trubek, D. M. and Trubek, L. G. 2005. "Hard and soft law in the construction of Social Europe: The role of the open method of co-ordination," *European Law Journal* **11** (3): 343–64.

Vogel, D. 1996. *The market for virtue.* Washington, DC: Brookings Institution Press.

Wernicke, H. 1983. *Die Städtehanse 1280–1418: Genesis – Strukturen – Funktionen.* Weimar: Hermann Böhlaus Nachfolger.

Index

Printed in the United States
By Bookmasters